NATIONAL INDEX OF PARISH REGISTERS

VOLUME 8

PART 3

SOMERSET

Compiled by
Cliff Webb, M.A., F.S.G.

SOCIETY OF GENEALOGISTS

Published by
Society of Genealogists
14 Charterhouse Buildings
Goswell Road,
London EC1M 7BA
1998

ISBN 1 85951 085 X

Volumes of the National Index of Parish Registers already published

Volume 1   General Sources of Births, Marriages and Deaths before 1837.
Parish Registers, Marriage Licences, Monumental Inscriptions, Newspapers,
Clandestine Marriages, Divorce, Mediaeval Sources, Other Records. General
Bibliography.

Volume 2   Sources for Nonconformist Genealogy and Family History.
The Three Denominations (Presbyterians, Independents and Baptists). Society
of Friends, Moravians, Methodists, Foreign Churches. Other Denominations.

Volume 3   Sources for Roman Catholic Genealogy and Family History.
With a short section on Jewish Records contributed by Edgar Samuel. Index to
Volumes 1, 2 and 3.

Volume 4   South East England. Kent, Surrey and Sussex (a revised edition of Surrey has
appeared as Volume 4 Part 1 of the series).

Volume 5   South Midlands and Welsh Border. Gloucestershire, Herefordshire,
Oxfordshire, Shropshire, Warwickshire, Worcestershire.

Volume 6   North and East Midlands.
Part 1: Staffordshire. Part 2: Nottinghamshire. Part 3: Leicestershire and
Rutland; Part 4: Lincolnshire. Part 5: Derbyshire.

Volume 7   East Anglia. Cambridgeshire, Norfolk, Suffolk.

Volume 8   The West of England. Part 1: Berkshire. Part 2: Wiltshire. Part 3: Somerset.

Volume 9   Home Counties (North of the Thames) and South East Midlands.
Part 1: Bedfordshire, Huntingdonshire. Part 2: Northamptonshire.
Part 3: Buckinghamshire. Part 4: Essex. Part 5: London and Middlesex.

Volume 10   North West England. Part 1: Cheshire.

Volume 11   North East England. Part 1: Durham, Northumberland.
Part 2: Yorkshire (East and North). Part 3: Yorkshire (West).

Volume 12   Sources for Scottish Genealogy and Family History.
Historical background. Parish Registers, Ancillary Sources. Nonconformists.
Bibliography.

[Volume 13] Parish Registers of Wales.

[Volume 14] Nonconformist Registers of Wales.

Volume 8

Part 3

SOMERSET

ABBREVIATIONS

()	After parish name enclose population in 1831
Add Ms	Additional Manuscripts: British Library
b	built
B	Burials
BL	Department of Manuscripts, The British Library, Great Russell St., London WC1B 3DG. A reader's ticket is necessary
Boyd	Marriage Index by P.Boyd. Copies at GL, SG and SLC. see NIPR Vol. 1
BT	Bishop's transcripts. For convenience this abbreviation is used for any annual register copy sent to an ecclesiastical superior
c	circa
C	Baptisms (also used for adult Baptisms of Baptists)
Ch Sec	Church or Chapel Secretary
cl	closed
C of A	College of Arms, Queen Victoria Street, London EC4V 4BT. The Library is not open to the public
Cop	Modern copies
CRS	Catholic Record Society publications
D	Deaths
DCI	Dr Campbell's Index, Somerset Record Office
Extr	Extracts
f	founded
fl	flourished
I	Indexed
Inc	Incumbent
K	Kelly's Directory
M	Marriages
Mf	Microfilm or microfiche
M Lic	Marriage Licences
Ms	Manuscript
NIPR	*National Index of Parish Registers*
NSMI	North Somerset Marriage Index
OR	Original Register
Phil Ms	Manuscript copies of parish registers in the possession of Phillimore and Co.Ltd, Shopwyke Manor Barn, Chichester, West Sussex PO20 6BG. A fee is normally charged
PRO	The Public Record Office, Ruskin Avenue, Kew, Richmond, Surrey TW9 4DK. A reader's ticket is necessary.
PRS	Parish Register Society
Ptd	Printed
reb	rebuilt
SBDB	Somerset Burials Database
SCDB	Somerset Baptisms Database
SG	Society of Genealogists, 14 Charterhouse Buildings, Goswell Road, London EC1M 7BA. The Library is open to non-members on payment of hourly, half-daily and daily fees
SLC	The Genealogical Society of Utah, 35 North West Temple Street, Salt Lake City, Utah 84150, U.S.A.
SMI	Somerset Marriage Index
SRO	Somerset Record Office, Obridge Road, Taunton TA2 7PU.
Ts	Typescript
Z	Births
+	Onwards. Invariably means 'until after 1837', and in the case of OR normally indicates that they continue to the present

RECORD REPOSITORIES AND LIBRARIES

Somerset Record Office, Obridge Road, Taunton TA2 7PU.
Tel: 01823 337600 (appointments only); 01823 278805 (enquiries)
Hours: Mon 2 pm to 5 p.m.; Tue to Thu 9 am to 4.50 pm; Fri 9 am to 4.20 pm

This record office is the county record office and the diocesan record office for its area. It holds the vast majority of the registers and bishop's transcripts of the ancient county, together with a very large collection of manuscript material concerning the county.

Bristol Record Office, B Bond Warehouse, Smeton Road, Bristol BS1 6XN.
Tel: 0117 922562
Hours: Mon to Thu 9.30 am to 4.45 pm; 9.30 am to 8 pm first Thu of the month (by appointment only). The office closes the last two weeks of January every year. Advance booking is always advisable and essential for the Thursday late opening.

This record office holds the registers and bishop's transcripts of Bedminster, the registers and most bishop's transcripts of Brislington and Abbots Leigh, and the registers of Whitchurch. It also holds the records of Bristol corporation and parishes in that city, and a large collection of nonconformist (especially Methodist) material from a wider area than its Anglican holdings.

Devon Record Office, Castle Street, Exeter EX4 3PU.
Tel: 01392 384253
Hours: Mon to Thu 9.30 am to 5 pm, Fri 9.30 am to 4.30 pm; first and third Sat of each month 9.30 am to 12 noon.

This office holds the bishop's transcripts of Churchstanton.

Dorset County Record Office, Bridport Road, Dorchester DT1 1RP
Tel: 01305 250550
Hours: Mon to Fri 9 am to 5 pm; Sat 9.30 am to 12.30 pm

This office holds the registers of Goathill, Poyntington, Sandford Orcas, Seaborough and Trent.

Wiltshire Record Office, County Hall, Bythesea Road, Trowbridge BA14 8JG
Tel: 01225 753641
Hours: Mon, Tue, Thu, Fri 9 am to 5 pm; Wed 9 am to 5 pm, but until 8.30 pm on second and fourth Wed

This record office holds the registers and bishop's transcripts of Maiden Bradley and Stourton, the registers only of Kilmington and the bishop's transcripts only of Wambrook.

THE COUNTY OF SOMERSET

Somerset is in the south west of England. The Bristol Channel lies to the north and north west, Gloucestershire to the north, Wiltshire to the east, Dorset to the south and Devon to the south and south west. The ancient administrative county, with associated county borough was 78 miles long, 36 miles wide and covered 1,636 square miles or 1,037,594 acres. The population of this area in 1801 was 273,577, which had risen to 403,795 by 1831, 443,916 by 1851 and 508,256 by 1901.

Somerset is a county of hills - the Mendips stretching for 25 miles across the north, the Polden Hills lie to the south of Glastonbury, the Quantock Hills run from Cothelstone north west, the Brendon Hills run west from Tolland right into Devon and the Blackdown Hills lie on the Devon border. There are many rivers, of which the principal are the Lower Avon, the Parret, the Yeo, the Tone, the Brue and the Axe. In Chard is the watershed of the county; a stream on one side of a street flows to the Bristol Channel, on the other side one flows to the English Channel.

Much of Somerset was, and is, concerned with agriculture. The county has always had a large population of cattle and sheep, and produces several varieties of cheese. Fishing, especially of salmon and herring was also a considerable activity until fairly recent times. Most of the early manufacturing industry comprised the processing of agricultural materials - woollen, worsted and silk goods, gloves, lace etc. Some agricultural implements were also made, and bricks at Bridgwater. The Avon boasted several iron, copper and weaving mills along its banks. Few English counties did not have large breweries, and Somerset had one at Shepton Mallet and another at Crewkerne.

There were a small number of coal mines, mainly near Compton Dando, but a large number of quarries of stone, slate and sand.

The great port of Bristol was divided between Somerset and Gloucestershire, and has been dealt with entirely in the Gloucestershire volume of the National Index. Other than its part of Bristol, the largest population centre in Somerset was the City and County Borough of Bath. The other large towns were Weston-super-Mare (which was, however, of late development), Taunton, Bridgwater and Yeovil.

ANCIENT PARISHES AND CHANGES IN COUNTY BOUNDARIES

The ancient county had 487 civil parishes, and was mainly co-extensive with the diocese of Bath and Wells, within the province of Canterbury, and was divided into the three archdeaconries of Bath, Taunton and Wells. Abbots Leigh and Bedminster were transferred to the diocese of Bristol in 1845, and Maiden Bradley and Stourton were within the diocese of Salisbury.

In 1896 the parishes of Goathill, Poyntington, Sandford Orcas, Seaborough and Trent were transferred to Dorset, Churchstanton from Devon, Wambrook from Dorset and Gasper, Kilmington and Yarnfield to Wiltshire. In 1974 86 ancient parishes were transferred to the new administrative county of Avon. Never popular, Avon was abolished in 1995 and all but a few of these parishes (which were incorporated in Bristol) reverted to Somerset. The existence of Avon has been ignored in the parish listings.

ORIGINAL PARISH REGISTERS

For some reason, Somerset registers have suffered losses more than those of many similar counties; not only is the average date at which they start later than in many comparable counties, but there seem to be many more parishes than usual with substantial gaps in coverage after the registers have started. There are 483 ancient parishes which are, or have been, within the county.

The earliest marriage in the register of Northover is dated 1531, but this is almost certainly an error for 1541. However the baptisms of Northover do start in 1534, and all three categories of registration start in that year at Charlton Musgrove, while the registers of Langford Budville and Rimpton both start in 1537. 23 more parishes (Baltonsborough; Buckland St Mary; Corton Denham; Dodington; Kelston; Kilve; Kingsdon; Milborne Port; Milverton; Newton St Loe; Orchard Portman; Pitcombe; Sandford Orcas; Shepton Montague; Stockland Bristol; Tellisford; Tickenham; Trull; Twerton on Avon; West Buckland; Weston All Saints; West Pennard; Wrington) begin in 1538 and four more (Combe Hay; Goathurst; Hemington; North Curry) in 1539. 29 more registers start before the beginning of the reign of Elizabeth I, 52 more start in 1558, 67 more in the first decade of her reign and thirty more before the end of the century. 47 parishes have records dating back to the first half of the seventeenth century, and no less than 145 start in the second half. 64 parishes have records starting in the first half of the eighteenth century. Seventeen parishes have no registers from 1750 or before (Stoke Trister 1751; St Catherine 1752; Bathampton 1754; Bratton Seymour 1754; Langridge 1756; Alford 1758; Priddy 1759; Hatch Beauchamp 1760; Thorne St Margaret 1761; Hornblotton 1763; Binegar 1769; Withypool 1771; Sutton Mallet 1781; East Cranmore 1783; Ston Easton 1813; Wheathill 1813; Woolverton 1813; Raddington 1814).

Lists produced in 1914 and the 1930s show that all too many of these losses occurred in this century. On the other hand, a number of early registers have been recovered since these lists were prepared.

The Somerset Record Office has been successful in attracting deposit from the vast majority of ancient Somerset parishes at least until 1812. Of parishes which have not deposited their registers, Somerset Record Office has full films of Baltonsborough, Cheddar, Chew Magna, Litton and Milborne Port. It has also a complete transcript of Wells Cathedral, a transcript of Frome to 1812, and complete bishop's transcripts from 1813 to 1846 and a complete copy of Kelston to 1812, with incomplete bishop's transcripts from then. Only for Dundry is there no film, and only the very patchy collection of bishop's transcripts (of which, however, there is a transcript at the Society of Genealogists).

However, many parish deposits of baptisms and burials end in 1812; 42 parishes have deposited no later baptism or burial registers, four more no post-1813 baptism register and another 43 no post-1813 burial register.

BISHOP'S TRANSCRIPTS

Somerset bishop's transcripts are a rather untidy collection. While, in general, they begin quite early, they peter out after the Restoration, and late seventeenth-century returns are patchy, as are transcripts for the whole of the eighteenth century, indeed in some parishes there are no, or virtually no bishop's transcripts for the whole of this period. Even in the early nineteenth century, surviving returns are very far from complete.

In addition to the main collection of returns, a number of peculiars have some additional returns. They have been especially listed in detail for this book by Sir Mervyn Medlycott.

The earliest bishop's transcripts listed is that for Aisholt (1558) however this may well be an error for 1598. Apart from an isolated couple of parishes, no other returns begin until the 1590s. 280 of the 476 parishes having early sequences begin in that decade, with 112 starting in 1598 alone. 172 more sequences start in the first decade of the seventeenth century. Seventeen more parishes have bishop's transcripts starting before the Civil War. Notably, Woolavington bishop's transcripts continue through the period 1643-62. Just four parishes have sequences starting after the Restoration (Abbots Leigh 1673; Seavington 1678; Wyke Champflower 1746; Upton Noble 1754) and the last two of these are chapelries, where earlier returns are conceivably contained within the mother parish's returns.

In all 525 entities (including late-starting chapelries) have bishop's transcripts in Somerset. One of these, Williton, ends as early as 1781. Twelve more parish's bishop's transcripts end in the second decade of the nineteenth century, 46 more in the next ten years and 178, 91, 98 and 56 in the subsequent four decades. 43 series of returns continue later than 1871, but 28 of these have ceased by 1880. Only three very isolated returns survive for the twentieth century (Whitestaunton for 1909 and North Barrow and South Barrow for 1917).

MODERN COPIES OF PARISH REGISTERS

Printed copies

There are three major series of printed Somerset parish registers: firstly, as in so many other counties, fifteen volumes of marriages were produced between 1898 and 1915 by Phillimore, secondly between 1913 and 1926 Edward Dwelly produced twelve volumes of Somerset bishop's transcripts (with a few transcripts of original registers) and, recently, the late T.L. Stoate has added to the enormous debt which West Country family historians owed him, by having published several volumes of parish register transcripts (Luccombe, Selworthy, Stoke Pero, Timberscombe and Wootton Courtenay). It is understood that Mr Stoate left material for several more volumes when he died.

The following were the volumes of Phillimore's marriage transcripts issued for Somerset:

I (1898): Aller 1560-1812; Charlton Adam 1707-1812; Charlton Mackrell 1575-1812;
High Ham 1569-1812; Huish Episcopi 1698-1812; Kingsdon 1540-1812; Long Sutton 1559-1812; Muchelney 1703-1812; Northover 1531-1812; Langport 1728-1812

II (1899): Pitney 1623-1812; Limington 1695-1812; Podimore Milton 1744-1811;
Somerton 1697-1812; Yeovilton 1655-1802; North Curry 1539-1812; Barrow Gurney 1593-1811

III (1901): West Hatch 1604-1812; Long Load 1749-1808; Martock 1559-1812; Drayton 1577-1812; Curry Rivel 1642-1812

IV (1902): Ashill 1558-1815; Isle Brewers 1705-1812; Beercrocombe 1542-1812;
Ilton 1642-1811; Whitestaunton 1606-1811; Stocklinch Magdalen 1712-1776; Stocklinch Ottersay 1558-1812; Barrington 1654-1812; Shepton Beauchamp 1558-1812; Buckland St Mary 1538-1812; Wraxall 1562-1812; Puckington 1695-1812; Swell 1559-1812

V (1904): Crewkerne 1559-1812; Swell 1713-54; Fivehead 1656-1812; Kingsbury Episcopi 1557-1812

VI (1905): Aisholt 1654-1812; Broomfield 1630-1812; Charlynch 1745-79; Dodington 1538-1805; Durleigh 1683-1807; Enmore 1653-1812; Otterhampton 1656-1749; Over Stowey 1558-1812; Stockland Gaunts 1538-1807; Cannington 1559-1812; Spaxton 1558-1812

VII (1906): Angersleigh 1693-1812; Pitminster 1542-1812; Corfe 1687-1812;
Orchard Portman 1538-1812; Stoke St Mary 1679-1812; Thurlbear 1700-1812; Trull 1671-1744; Creech St Michael 1665-1814; Bradford 1558-1812

VIII (1906): Hillfarance 1701-1812; Heathfield 1700-56; Thorn Falcon 1720-1812;
West Monkton 1710-1812; Ruishton 1679-1812; West Buckland 1538-1812; Cothelstone 1664-1715; Ash Priors 1700-1812; Norton Fitzwarren 1565-1812; Cheddon Fitzpaine 1559-1812; Langford Budville 1607-1812; Nynehead 1670-1812

IX (1907): Taunton St Mary Magdalen 1558-1728

X (1907): Taunton St Mary Magdalen 1728-1812; Bishops Hull 1562-1812;
Halse 1559-1812

XI (1908): Wellington 1683-1812; Ashbrittle 1563-1812; Runnington 1586-1812; Otterford
1568-1812; Sampford Arundel 1698-1812; Thorne St Margaret 1721-1812

XII (1910): Stogursey 1595-1812; Nether Stowey 1645-1812; East Quantoxhead 1654-1812;
Fiddington 1706-1812; Holford 1558-1812; Goathurst 1539-1812; Chedzoy
1558-1812; Kilve 1638-1812; Crowcombe 1641-1812; Thurloxton 1559-1812;
Stringston 1634-1812; Kilton 1683-1812; Lilstock 1661-1812

XIII (1910): Staple Fitzpaine and Bickenhall 1682-1812; Lopen 1723-1812; Whitelackington
1695-1837; Hinton St George 1632-1837; Ilminster 1662-1812; Milverton 1538-1812

XIV (1913): Combe St Nicholas 1678-1812; West Bagborough 1565-1812; Isle Abbots
1562-1837; Kittisford 1695-1812; Kilmington 1582-1837; East Pennard 1608-1812;
Midsomer Norton 1701-1837; Weston super Mare 1682-1837

XV (1915): Taunton St James 1610-1837

E. Dwelly published many volumes of parish registers and bishops' transcripts
between 1913 and 1922 listed below. Volume 3 concerned Kent records, volume 6 Devon.
He concentrated most of his efforts on the pre-Restoration bishop's transcripts. Because a
number of further transcripts were discovered in 1924, many parishes appear in more than
one Dwelly volume. Each volume in which a parish has records has been printed, but not a
detailed breakdown of each volume's coverage, which would have added substantially to the
length of this volume.

1 (1913) Early bishop's transcripts for parishes Abbas Combe to High Ham
(indexed edition at SG)

2 (1914) Early bishop's transcripts for parishes H to Y

4 (1915) Abbas Combe; Aisholt; Alford; Aller; Allerton; Almsford; Angersleigh;
Ashbrittle; Ashcott

5 (1917) Ash Priors; Ashington; Ashwick; Axbridge; Babcary; Babington; Backwell;
Badgworth; Barrow (South); Ansford (1807); Wrington (1806-07)

7 (1919) Othery; Bath

8 (1921) Chipstable; Kittisford; Pitcombe; Raddington

9 (1922) Bath; Durston; Chipstable; Raddington; Northover; Ilchester; Broadway

10-13 (1922-24) North Petherton

14 This volume was projected to contain the index to North Petherton, but never appeared

15 (1926) (a) North Petherton; (b) extra bishop's transcripts discovered 1924 for parishes:
Abbas Combe; Aisholt; Alford; Aller; Allerton; Almsford; Angersleigh; Ashbrittle;
Ashcott; Ashill; Ashington; Ashwick; Axbridge; Babcary; Babington; Backwell;
Barrow (South); Chipstable; Durston; Ilchester; Northover; Raddington; (c) new
bishop's transcript series: Broadway; Badgworth; Bagborough; Baltonsborough;
Barrington; Barrow Gurney; Barrow (North)

Various other publishing societies and journals have included Somerset material: early Street registers, transcribed by A.J. Jewers, appeared as a supplement to *The Genealogist* for 1898, the Parish Register Society printed Bruton (vols. 60, 78, 1908-11) and St Michaelchurch (vol. 72, 1914), the Harleian Society published Bath Abbey to 1800 in two volumes (1900-01), the Catholic Record Society published early Bath Roman Catholic registers in 1976, while Bath Synagogue marriage registers appeared in *Jewish Historical Studies* (1988)

In addition to these series, there have been various individual printed editions. What appears to be the first printed edition of a Suffolk parish register was Wedmore which was published, eccentrically, as Suffolk Green Books volume 22, edited by E. Jackson in 1886-90. Wilton edited by J.H. Spencer was printed in 1890, W.E. Daniel printed Horsington in 1907 and E.E. Britten and E.J. Holmyard edited Butcombe marriages (1913).

Typescript and manuscript copies

As elsewhere the Society of Genealogists has encouraged the transcription of registers, and the local family history societies have since their foundation actively encouraged such work. The result is that most Somerset parishes have at least some of their registers copied, though much remains to be done.

OTHER INDEXES

Boyd's Marriage Index, available at the Society of Genealogists, covers portions of 123 parishes, much of its coverage being from those registers printed by Phillimore. Full details are given in the text.

The Mormons have filmed registers from approximately 70% of Somerset parishes, and almost all Somerset bishop's transcripts. Full listings of Mormon film holdings are given, but it is an ongoing process, and further filming may take place at any time. Some baptisms and a few marriage entries from these films have been included in the International Genealogical Index, as elsewhere. Since, however, coverage is in many places uncertain, no attempt has been made to give detailed listing in this book.

Dr Campbell's Index is a huge card index at the Somerset Record Office. It contains (*inter alia*) entries for baptisms, marriages and burials, for various periods up to 1899, for approximately 30% of the county, mainly from the west of the county, encompassing Taunton Archdeaconry with its attendant peculiars. with a few parishes elsewhere.

Members of local family history societies are compiling a number of general indexes.

North Somerset Marriage Index 1754-1837. Compiled by Bristol and Avon Family History Society, it is on microfiche and open access at Somerset Record Office and Bristol Central Library. The index contains marriages 1754-1837 for the 110 or so parishes that were in the county of Avon 1974-1995, together with Quaker entries and some earlier material.

Somerset Marriage Index and Somerset Monumental Inscriptions Index with:

Michelle Merrick, 91 Pine Road, Bournemouth, Dorset BH9 1LU

Somerset Baptisms and Burials database with:

David Hall, The Old Vicarage, Elm Grove, Taunton TA1 1EH

Full details of coverage of these indexes as at February 1998 has been included in the parish listings, however these last two indexes are growing at a rapid pace, and any attempt to list them will be out of date by the time of publication. Searchers should check with the compilers for updated listings of coverage and current search fees.

NONCONFORMISTS

Old Dissent was relatively weak in Somerset, but the Methodist revival saw a very large number of Wesleyan chapels formed in the early nineteenth century.

All Nonconformist chapels for which archives are known are listed, as are all those appearing in either Lewis's Topographical Dictionary 1831 '(Lewis 1831)' or in Kelly's Directory of Somersetshire 1931 '(K 1931)'.

ROMAN CATHOLICS

As elsewhere, a few recusant families kept Roman Catholicism alive in Somerset through the penal period. The Poyntz family chapel was founded in the early seventeenth century, the Clifford family chapel in the late eighteenth century. Both have surviving registers. Bath had several early Roman Catholic churches, including one which was burnt, together with its registers, in 1780. A Roman Catholic cemetery was opened there in 1859. Other early churches were at Shepton Mallet (registers from 1765, church built 1804), Taunton 1790 and Hinton Blewitt 1806.

BAPTISTS

There were relatively few Baptist chapels in Somerset. The only chapels with seventeenth-century foundations were Chard, Frome, Horsington, Paulton, Stogumber, Wedmore and Yeovil. Early registers survive from Wellington 1714, Hatch Beauchamp 1742, Bath 1763, Isle Abbots 1777, Taunton 1782, Road 1783, Frome 1785, Paulton 1785, Beckington 1786, Chard 1786 and Keynsham 1787.

INDEPENDENTS

Many Somerset villages have Independent congregations. There are seventeenth-century foundations at Bishops Hull, Bishopsworth, North Cadbury, Churchill, Combe Abbas, Dulverton, Frome, Glastonbury, High Ham, Kenn, Kingsdon, Lydeard St Lawrence (two chapels), Milborne Port, Norton sub Hambdon, Shepton Montague, Taunton, Winsham, Wiveliscombe and Wrington. Further chapels were established at Bath, Bridgwater, Brislington, Broadway, Brompton Ralph, Buckland St Mary, Creech St Michael, Frome Selwood, Henstridge, Ilchester, Long Ashton, Maiden Bradley, Milverton, Moorlinch, North Petherton, Nunney, Pensford, Pill, Pitminster, Somerton, South Petherton, Stogursey, Stringston, Wells, Wincanton and Yatton.

Early registers, as elsewhere, are, however, few. The earliest register is that of Taunton, beginning in 1699. Other eighteenth-century starting registers are Pitminster 1705, Wiveliscombe 1709, Chelwood 1721, Bishops Hull 1734, Nunney 1760, South Petherton 1773, Broadway 1777, Milborne Port 1780, Milverton 1784, Bath 1785, Chard 1786, Frome Selwood 1786, Wells 1790, Frome 1793, Yeovil 1793 and Wincanton 1798.

COUNTESS OF HUNTINGDON'S CONNEXION

A chapel of this sect at Bath, founded in 1765 and with registers beginning in 1788 later became Presbyterian.

PRESBYTERIANS AND UNITARIANS

The Presbyterians (whose chapels frequently later became Unitarian) had only a modest presence in Somerset. Barrington, Bath, Crewkerne, Ilminster, Shepton Mallet, South Petherton, Taunton and Wellington, Yeovil had seventeenth-century Presbyterian chapels. Registers were surrendered from South Petherton 1694, Yeovil 1704, Ilminster 1718, Shepton Mallet 1757, Taunton 1762, Crewkerne 1785 and Wellington 1786.

METHODISTS

Almost every Somerset village had one or more Methodist chapels. Only Banwell, Pensford and Taunton have registers starting before 1800. The Wesleyans were very strong, there being very few Primitive Methodist chapels, the earliest register being Bath, starting in 1813.

Somerset Circuit was formed in 1777, it became Taunton and Wellington Circuit in 1840 and Taunton Circuit 1886. Banwell Circuit was formed from it in 1797 (and became Cheddar and Banwell Circuit in 1911, and Weston super Mare Circuit was formed from Banwell Circuit in 1851), South Petherton Circuit in 1807, Axminster Circuit in 1813, Wells Circuit from Taunton Circuit in 1833, to which it was reunited in 1840 and re-formed in 1886 and Bridgwater Circuit in 1840. Bath Circuit was formed from Bradford on Avon Circuit in 1791; from Bath Circuit, Frome Circuit was formed in 1812. Blandford and Sturminster Circuit was formed in 1794 (called Poole Circuit from 1797 to 1804) and Blandford Circuit was re-formed 1866. Shaftesbury Circuit was formed from Salisbury Circuit in 1809 (from 1891 it became Shaftesbury and Gillingham Circuit); from it Sherborne Circuit was formed in 1818 (and from it Yeovil Circuit was formed in 1862). Shepton Mallet Circuit was formed from Bradford on Avon Circuit in 1789.

SWEDENBORGIANS

The Swedenborgians established a church at Bath in 1829 which surrendered a register in 1837.

SOCIETY OF FRIENDS (QUAKER)

The Quakers were very active in Somerset. Meeting houses were established in the seventeenth century at Alford, Burrington, Bridgwater, Butcombe, Creech St Michael, Crewkerne, Misterton, Polden Hill, Portishead, Publow, Stanton Drew, Street, Wellington and Yatton. Most surrendered registers in 1837.

MORAVIANS

The Moravians established a chapel at Bath in 1765 which surrendered registers in 1837.

JEWS

There were Jews in Bristol (see Gloucestershire NIPR) but no synagogue in Somerset until the establishment of one at Bath in 1838.

MARRIAGE LICENCES, BONDS AND ALLEGATIONS

Marriage licences date from 1574, but there are few before 1645, and continue to 1899. All are deposited at the Somerset Record Office. There are various printed, typescript and manuscript indexes at the Somerset Record Office and the Society of Genealogists, but none are comprehensive. See also:

Marriage Allegation Bonds of the Bishop of Bath and Wells from their commencement [c1645] to the year 1955 (A.J. Jewers, 1909, reprinted from *The Genealogist* NS 15-26 (1898-1910)

REGIMENTS AND MILITARY HISTORY

Somerset men could of course join any regiment, but the two specifically Somerset regiments were the 13th and 40th regiments. Histories of the Somerset regiments, and Somerset volunteer forces have appeared, mainly with detailed lists of officers, etc.

Historical Record of the thirteenth, first Somersetshire, or Prince Albert's regiment of
    Light Infantry (W.O. Mitchell, 1867)
Historical Records of the 40th (2nd Somersetshire) regiment ... (A.H. Swiss, 1894)
A History of the Somerset yeomanry, voluntary and territorial units (W.G. Fisher, 1924)
History of Somerset Light Infantry (H. Everett, 1934)

BIBLIOGRAPHY

Somerset has a modern genealogical bibliography:

Somerset: a genealogical bibliography (S.A. Raymond, 1991)

and two which are much older but very comprehensive for early historical material:

Bibliotheca Somersetensis (E. Green, 3 vols., 1902)
Somersetshire Parishes (A.L. Humphreys, 2 vols., 1905)

Major county histories include:

History and Antiquities of the County of Somerset (J. Collinson, 1791)
History and Antiquities of Somersetshire (W. Phelps, 1836-39)
Victoria County History of England: Somerset (6 volumes, 1906 to date, in progress)

Somerset has not yet been dealt with by the English Place-Name Society. A general discussion is provided by:

The Place-Names of Somerset (J.S. Hill, 1914)

Two previous lists of parish registers are still useful as including lists of other material extant at the time they were compiled. They have been extensively used to annotate the parish lists in this book:

Ecclesiastical Records of the Diocese of Bath and Wells (T.S. Holmes, 1914)
Somerset Parochial Documents (J.E. King, 1938)

Major record and historical serial publications for Somerset include:

Somerset Archaeological and Natural History Society Proceedings 1849 to date
Somerset Record Society 1887 to date
Somerset and Dorset Notes and Queries 1890 to date

ACKNOWLEDGMENTS

I should like to acknowledge the help of the Somerset Record Office, especially in supplying lists of their holdings of bishops' transcripts and the coverage of Dr Campbell's index, to Tim Wilcock who electronically scanned the text of these lists and to Michelle Merrick and David Hall for supplying lists of the coverage of the indexes they hold. Above all, Mervyn Medlycott gave much encouragement and advice, and read the text eliminating some of the more egregious errors and omissions. Remaining errors and omissions, of course, remain entirely my responsibility.

ABBAS COMBE *see* **COMBE ABBAS**

ABBOTS LEIGH *see* **LEIGH, ABBOTS**

AISHOLT All Saints (228) (Cannington Hundred; Bridgwater Union)
(registers *c.*1640-65 destroyed by fire)
OR C 1652-1812, M 1654-1994, Banns 1654-58, 1744-1805, B 1653-1811 (CB 1798-1812
defective) (SRO); CB 1813+ (Inc)
BT 1598-99, 1606-11, 1613, 1615, 1617, 1621-24, 1640-41, 1666-68, 1670, 1672-73,
1679-80, one between 1672-99, 1704-05, 1709, 1719-20, 1735-36, 1748-51, 1756, 1772,
1774-75, 1777, 1779, 1781-84, 1786-87, 1789-93, 1795-96, 1800-38, CB 1840, C 1841,
CB 1842-44, CMB 1845, CB 1846-59 (SRO)
Cop M 1654-1812 (Ptd, Phillimore 6, 1905); 1598-1653 (Ptd, Dwelly 1, 4, 15, 1913-26);
M 1813-37 (Ts SLC); M 1654-1812 (Boyd); B 1679-1884 (SBDB); M 1598-1837 (SMI)
Cop (Mf) 1558-1859 (BT) (SLC, SRO); C 1652-1812, M 1654-1837, B 1653-1811 (SLC)

ALCOMBE (created 1953 from Dunster)
OR M 1938-55 (SRO)

ALCOMBE (Wesleyan) b 1846

ALFORD All Saints (137) (Catsash Hundred; Wincanton Union)
OR C 1766-1993, M 1758-1992, Banns 1759-1812, B 1765-1993 (SRO)
BT 1575, 1594-99, 1602-03, 1605-06, 1608-09, 1611, 1617, 1621-23, 1629, 1634-35, 1640-41,
1666-69, 1679, 1690, 1749-51, 1754-56, 1800-24, 1826-27, 1836, CB 1838, CMB 1843,
CB 1844-45, 1847-53 (SRO)
Cop 1594-1811 (Ptd, Dwelly 4, 15, 1915-26); B 1755-1859 (SBDB); M 1594-1679 (BT),
1754-1837 (SMI)
Cop (Mf) 1575-1853 (BT) (SLC, SRO); C 1764-1812, M 1754-1839, Banns 1759-1812,
B 1765-1811 (SLC)

ALFORD Meeting House (Society of Friends) (Monthly Meeting of Middle Division)
OR Z 1650-1837, M 1657-1748, 1778-1836, B 1651-1837 (PRO: RG 6/12, 40-41, 85-86,
168, 1439)

ALLER St Andrew (490) (Somerton Hundred; Langport Union)
OR C 1561-1867, M 1560-1966 (gap 1746-49), Banns 1754-1809, 1824-1900, B 1560-1909 (SRO)
BT 1598-1600, 1602-12, one between 1610-23, 1612-13, 1617-18, 1621-22, 1626-27, 1629-30,
1636, 1640-41, 1663-65, 1694-96, 1704-05, 1731-32, 1741-42, 1749-52, 1760-63, 1767-70,
1773-76, 1783-88, 1800-19, 1821, 1829-35 (SRO)
Cop M 1560-1812 (Ptd, Phillimore 1, 1898); CB 1598-1811 (Ptd, Dwelly 4, 15, 1915-26);
M 1560-1812 (Boyd); B 1813-1992 (SBDB); M 1560-1837 (SMI)
Cop (Mf) 1598-1835 (BT) (SLC, SRO); C 1561-1867, M 1560-1900, Banns 1754-1809, 1824-1900,
B 1560-1900 (SLC)

ALLER (Independent) b 1888 (K 1931)

ALLERTON, CHAPEL (dedication unknown) (313) (Bempstone Hundred; Axbridge Union)
OR C 1690-1908, M 1693-1749, 1754-1988 (gap 1721-29, 1731-32, 1837-39; 1720, 1730-49
defective), Banns 1754-96, 1826-86, B 1708-09, 1717-1812 (SRO); B 1813+ (Inc)
BT 1598, 1606-11, 1613-15, 1619-24, 1628, 1634-35, 1640-41, 1665-69, 1771-74, 1802-27 (SRO);
1750-51, 1753-55, 1761, 1774-75, 1777-1802 (SRO: D/D/Pd:26/1)
Cop 1598-1810 (Ptd, Dwelly 4, 15, 1915-26); 1690-1908 (I SRO); M 1563-1837 (SMI)
Cop (Mf) 1598-1827 (BT) (SLC, SRO); C 1693-1886, M 1693-1886, Banns 1754-96, 1826-86,
B 1708-1812 (SLC)

ALLERTON, CHAPEL (Baptist) b 1840

ALLERTON, CHAPEL (United Methodist) b 1874

ANGERSLEIGH St Michael (54) (Taunton and Taunton Dean Hundred; Taunton Union)
OR C 1693-1991, M 1693-1991, Banns 1755-1812, B 1678-1991 (SRO)
BT 1594-99, 1602-06, 1611-13, 1615-17, 1619-24, 1629-30, 1636, 1638, 1661-63, 1666-70,
    1679-80, 1707-08,1720-21, 1725-26, 1736, 1748-49, 1765-68,1779-83,1785-89, 1802-22 (SRO)
Cop M 1693-1812 (Ptd, Phillimore 7, 1906); 1595-1811 (Ptd, Dwelly 1, 4, 15, 1913-26);
    M 1693-1812 (Boyd); B 1678-1991 (SBDB); M 1594-1680 (BT), 1693-1837 (SMI);
    C 1693-1811, M 1814-30 (DCI)
Cop (Mf) 1594-1822 (BT) (SLC, SRO)

ANSFORD St Andrew (304) (Catsash Hundred; Wincanton Union)
OR C 1555-1903, M 1559-1978, Banns 1754-1887, B 1554-1957 (SRO)
BT 1598-99, 1601-03, 1605-09, 1611-14, 1622-23, 1629-31, 1634, 1636-38, 1640-41,
    1663-64, 1668-70, 1699, 1704-10, 1732-33, 1802-37 (SRO)
Cop 1807 (Ptd, Dwelly 5, 1917); C 1554-1837, M 1559-1837, B 1555-1837 (Ts SG, SLC, SRO);
    B 1813-86 (SBDB); M 1559-1837 (SMI)
Cop (Mf) 1598-1837 (BT) (SLC, SRO); C 1555-1886, M 1559-1885, Banns 1754-1887,
    B 1554-1886 (SLC)

ASH Holy Trinity (chapelry in Martock until 1845) (Yeovil Union)
OR C 1845-94, M 1846-1975, B 1845-1964 (SRO)
Cop C 1845-93, M 1846-94 (DCI)
Cop (Mf) C 1845-94, M 1846-1901, B 1845-1905 (SLC)

ASHBRITTLE St John the Baptist (625) (Milverton Hundred; Wellington Union)
OR C 1563-1650, 1689-1917, M 1569-1646, 1691-1981, B 1563-1650, 1691-1915 (SRO)
BT 1599-1602, one between 1568-1618, 1605-09, 1611-13, 1616-17, 1619-20, 1622-23, 1628-30,
    1636-373, 1640-41, 1662-64, 1672-73, 1682-83, 1713, 1735-38, 1741-42, 1747-55, ?1757,
    1759-60, 1762-65, 1769-73, 1777-87, 1789-1804, 1806-22, 1824-37 (SRO)
Cop M 1563-1812 (Ptd, Phillimore 11, 1908); CB 1599-1812 (Ptd, Dwelly 1, 4, 15, 1913-26);
    M 1563-1812 (Boyd); B 1765-1855 (SBDB); M 1563-1837 (SMI); C 1563-1899, M 1813-99
    (DCI)
Cop (Mf) 1599-1837 (BT) (SLC, SRO)

ASHCOTT All Saints (834) (chapelry in Shapwick) (Whitley Hundred; Bridgwater Union)
OR C 1744-1982, M 1754-1838, Banns 1824-85, B 1743-1982 (gap 1803-12) (SRO) (M from 1674
    and CB from 1678 survived in 1914)
BT one between 1586-1607, 1599-1600, 1603, 1606-08, one between 1609-31 (maybe Twerton),
    1611-12, 1621-22, 1629-30, 1640-41, 1662-65, 1709-11, 1724-25, 1731-33, 1749-53, 1756-58,
    1800-25, CB 1841-47 (SRO); CMB 1671-72, M 1706 (SRO: D/P/Can.23/8)
Cop 1599-1812 (Ptd, Dwelly 4, 15, 1915-26); B 1742-1874 (SBDB); M 1606-1837 (SMI)
Cop (Mf) 1599-1847 (BT) (SLC, SRO); C 1744-1886, M 1754-1887, B 1743-1886 (SLC)

ASHCOTT Higher Pedwell (Wesleyan) (Lewis 1831) b 1838 (K 1931)

ASHCOTT (Primitive Methodist) b 1857 (K 1931)

ASHILL St Mary (403) (peculiar of Preb. of Ashill) (Abdick and Bulstone Hundred; Chard Union)
OR C 1558-1921, M 1558-1985, Banns 1754-1885, B 1558-1899 (gap CMB 1629-52) (SRO)
BT 1598, 1605-08, 1611-13, 1615-16, 1621-24, 1628-29, 1662-64, 1667-68, 1755-57, 1776-77,
    1813-21, 1824-26, 1828-32 (1739-42, 1750-51, 1759-64 in peculiar series) (SRO)
Cop M 1558-1815 (Ptd, Phillimore 4, 1902); CB 1598-1757 (Ptd, Dwelly 1, 15, 1913-26);
    M 1558-1815 (Boyd); B 1747-1885 (SBDB); M 1558-1837 (SMI); C 1558-1899, M 1814-37
    (DCI)
Cop (Mf) 1598-1832 (BT) (SLC, SRO); CB 1558-1886, M 1558-1885, Banns 1754-1885 (SLC)

ASHINGTON St Vincent (74) (Stone Hundred; Yeovil Union)
OR C 1569-1813, M 1567-1836, Banns 1755-1813, B 1567-1813 (gap C 1730-63, M 1726-54,
   B 1730-83; defective 1672-89) (SRO); CB 1813+ (Inc)
BT 1571-73, one between 1571-74, 1602-03, 1605-08, 1611, 1615, 1617-18, 1620-21,
   1623, 1629-30, 1636, 1640-41, 1663-66, 1733-34, 1800-32, 1834-35, CB 1840-44 (SRO)
Cop 1572-1812 (Ptd, Dwelly 5, 15, 1917-26); B 1764-1813 (SBDB); M 1569-1725,
   1750-1837 (SMI)
Cop (Mf) 1571-1844 (BT) (SLC, SRO); C 1569-1812, M 1569-1836, B 1567-1810 (SLC)

ASH PRIORS Holy Trinity (210) (West Kingsbury Hundred; Taunton Union)
OR C 1700-1970, M 1700-1959 (gap 1727-31), Banns 1754-1812, B 1700-1812 (SRO)
   (earlier registers already mislaid, 1831); B 1813+ (Inc)
BT 1595-99, 1606-11, 1625-26, 1629-31, 1636-38, 1640-41, 1662-63, 1679, 1707-08, 1720-21,
   1725-26, 1728-29, 1746-52, 1759, 1762, 1765, 1767, 1769-70, 1775, 1778-79, 1786, 1789-92,
   1801-05, 1807-12, 1821-35 (SRO)
Cop M 1700-1812 (Ptd, Phillimore 8, 1906); 1595-1812 (Ptd, Dwelly 1, 5, 1913, 1917);
   M 1700-1812 (Boyd); B 1700-1812 (SBDB); M 1700-1837 (SMI); C 1700-1899, M 1813-99
   (DCI)
Cop (Mf) 1595-1835 (BT) (SLC, SRO); CM 1700-1902, B 1700-1812 (SLC)

ASHTON, LONG All Saints (1,423) (Hartcliffe with Bedminster Hundred; Bedminster Union
   1836-99, Long Ashton Union 1899-1930)
OR C 1558-1896, M 1558-1911, Banns 1754-1811, B 1558-1871 (SRO)
BT one between 1592-1617, 1599-1601, 1606-07, 1609-13, 1619-20, 1621-24, 1629-30,
   1636-41, one between 1640-79, 1662-65, 1667-72, 1679-80, 1800-23, 1825-37, CB 1838-59
   (1808-10, 1813-24 in peculiar series) (SRO)
Cop 1623-99 (SG); CMB 1558-1600 (Ms SLC); M 1754-1837 (NSMI); B 1691-1832 (SBDB);
   M 1662, 1668, 1671, 1679, 1691-1708, 1754-1837 (SMI)
Cop (Mf) C 1558-1896, M 1558-1901, Banns 1754-1811, B 1558-1871 (SG, SLC);
   1599-1859 (BT) (SLC, SRO)

ASHTON, LONG (Independent) b 1792 (K 1931)
OR C 1826-37 (PRO: RG 4/1557)
Cop (Mf) C 1826-37 (SLC, SRO)

ASHWICK St James (995) (chapelry in Kilmersdon until 1826) (Kilmersdon Hundred;
   Shepton Mallet Union)
OR C 1701-1982 (defective 1714-28), M 1701-1960 (defective 1705-34), Banns 1763-1812,
   1826-1900, B 1701-1930 (defective 1710-28) (SRO)
BT 1595-99, 1603-12, 1621-23, 1630-31, 1638-41, 1802-37, CB 1838-45, CMB 1846-47, CB 1848,
   CMB 1849-73 (SRO)
Cop 1595-1812 (Ptd, Dwelly 1, 5, 15, 1913-26); B 1783-1843 (SBDB); M 1595-1640, 1754-1837
   (SMI)
Cop (Mf) 1595-1873 (BT) (SLC, SRO); CB 1701-1901, M 1701-1900, Banns 1763-1900 (SLC)

ASHWICK (Presbyterian)
OR C 1761-1837, B 1796-1835 (PRO: RG 4/2052, 2345, 2346)
Cop (Mf) C 1761-81, B 1796-1835 (SRO)

ASHWICK (Independent) b 1817

ASHWICK (Wesleyan) (Lewis 1831) (K 1931)

ASHWICK Nettlebridge (Independent) b 1876

AXBRIDGE Board of Guardians
OR Z 1838-1903, D 1838-66 (SRO)

AXBRIDGE St John the Baptist (998) (Winterstoke Hundred; Axbridge Union)
OR C 1561-1905, M 1561-1971, Banns 1754-1812, B 1561-1899 (SRO)
BT 1597-99, 1602-03, 1605-06, 1611, 1621-22, 1629-30, 1635-36, 1640-41, 1663-65, 1669-70,
    1682-84, 1699-1705, 1707-11, 1719-21, 1726-27, 1731-32, 1741-42, 1747-52, 1754-57,
    1759-62, 1793-94, 1800-18, 1820, 1823-35, CB 1838-58 (SRO)
Cop 1597-1812 (Ptd, Dwelly 1, 5, 15, 1913-26); B 1718-1837 (SBDB); M 1562-1837 (SMI)
Cop (Mf) 1597-1858 (BT) (SLC, SRO)

AXBRIDGE (Baptist) (Lewis 1831)

AXBRIDGE High Street (Wesleyan) (Lewis 1831) (K 1931)

AXBRIDGE (Plymouth Brethren) 19th century

BABCARY Holy Cross (453) (Catsash Hundred; Langport Union)
OR C 1648-88, 1801-83, 1889, 1902, M 1754-1975, Banns 1754-1812, B 1801-1936 (SRO)
    (C from 1704 and MB from 1726 survived in 1914)
BT one between 1587-1629, 1598-99, 1606-09, 1611-12, 1617-18, 1629-30, c.1629, 1637-39,
    c.1660, 1663, 1667-69, 1751-52, 1800-12, 1815-37, CB 1838 (SRO)
Cop 1598-1812 (Ptd, Dwelly 1, 5, 15, 1913-26); C 1648-88 (SRO); B 1801-85 (SBDB);
    M 1598-1751 (BT), 1754-1837 (SMI)
Cop (Mf) 1598-1838 (BT) (SLC, SRO); C 1861-1902, M 1755-1886, B 1801-86 (SLC)

BABCARY (Wesleyan) b 1808 (K 1931)

BABINGTON St Margaret (206) (Kilmersdon Hundred; Shepton Mallet Union)
OR C 1726-1812, M 1725-1911, B 1725-1812 (SRO); CB 1813+ (Inc)
BT 1606-12, 1615-17, 1622-23, 1634, 1801-25, 1828 (SRO)
Cop 1607-1812 (Ptd, Dwelly 1, 5, 15, 1913-26); B 1804-12 (SBDB); M 1606-34 (BT),
    1725-1837 (SMI)
Cop (Mf) 1606-34, 1801-28 (BT) (SLC, SRO); C 1726-1812, M 1725-1886, B 1725-1812 (SLC)

BABINGTON (Wesleyan) (Lewis 1831)

BACKWELL St Andrew (1,038) (Hartcliffe with Bedminster Hundred; Bedminster Union 1836-99,
    Long Ashton Union 1899-1930)
OR C 1558-1900, M 1558-1968 (gap 1725-53), Banns 1754-1811, 1823-1946, 1959-68,
    B 1558-1954 (SRO)
BT 1598-99, 1603-09, 1611-12, one between 1614-34, 1617-20, one between 1626-71, 1629-30,
    1634-37, 1639-40, 1750, 1757, 1768, 1775, 1784, 1800-37, CB 1838-39, CMB 1840,
    CB 1841-42, CMB 1843-47, CB 1848, CMB 1849-67 (SRO)
Cop 1598-1813 (Ptd, Dwelly 1, 5, 15, 1913-26); M 1754-1837 (NSMI); B 1693-1850 (SBDB);
    M 1558-1837 (SMI)
Cop (Mf) 1598-1867 (BT) (SLC, SRO)

BACKWELL Downside (Wesleyan) f 1800, b 1830 (K 1931)
OR C 1833-37 (PRO: RG 4/1824)
Cop (Mf) C 1833-37 (SRO)

BACKWELL (Free Methodist) b 1853

BACKWELL (Plymouth Brethren) b 1872

BACKWELL (Baptist) (K 1931)

BADGWORTH St Congar (352) (Winterstoke Hundred; Axbridge Union)
OR C 1671-1933, M 1688-1985, Banns 1754-1812, B 1671-1985 (SRO)
BT 1598-1600, 1607-08, 1617-18, 1621-24, 1628-29, 1636-38, 1666-68, 1709-10, 1720-21,
    1748-51, 1754, 1756-57, 1759-60, 1766-67, 1769, 1771-72, 1776-84, 1786-87, 1789-1816,
    1818, 1822-37, CB 1838, 1840, 1842-47, CMB 1848, CB 1849-55 (SRO)
Cop 1598-1813 (Ptd, Dwelly 5, 15, 1917-26); B 1671-1883 (SBDB); M 1598-1668 (BT),
    1688-1837 (SMI)
Cop (Mf) 1598-1855 (BT) (SLC, SRO)

BAGBOROUGH, WEST St Pancras (453) (renamed Bagborough, 1972) (Taunton and Taunton Dean
    Hundred; Taunton Union)
OR C 1558-1870, M 1565-1837, Banns 1754-98, 1853-1952, B 1564-1933 (gap B 1682-1700)
    (SRO)
BT one between 1578-1601, 1598-1600, 1602-03, 1606-07, 1613, 1616, 1618-19, 1621, 1628-29,
    1633-34, 1636-38, 1640-41, 1662-63, 1666, 1668-69, 1678-80, 1687-88, 1690-91, 1707, 1725,
    1727-28, 1732, 1743, 1747-52, 1754-59, 1764-75, 1777-78, 1789-90, 1808-29 (SRO)
Cop 1598-1809 (Ptd, Dwelly 15, 1926; M 1565-1812 (Ptd, Phillimore 14, 1913);
    M 1565-1812 (Boyd); B 1813-59 (SBDB); M 1565-1837 (SMI); C 1558-1870, M 1813-37 (DCI)
Cop (Mf) 1598-1829 (BT) (SLC, SRO)

BALTONSBOROUGH St Dunstan (675) (chapelry in Butleigh until 1895) (Glastonbury Twelve
    Hides Hundred; Wells Union)
OR CMB 1538+ (gap M 1639-54, B 1644-53) (Inc)
BT 1599-1600, 1605-06, 1607-08, 1610-12, 1617-18, 1621-23, 1629-30, 1634-36, 1639-41,
    1662-64, 1668-69, 1672-73, 1682-83, 1720-21, 1731-33, 1739-40, 1749-53, 1755-58, 1765-72,
    1775, 1778-79, 1800-13, 1819-35, 1838, CB 1840 (SRO)
Cop 1599-1813 (Ptd, Dwelly 1, 15, 1913-26); M 1599-1663 (BT), 1754-1837 (SMI)
Cop (Mf) 1599-1840 (BT) (SLC, SRO); C 1538-1853, M 1539-1706, 1714-1987, Banns 1824-74,
    B 1539-1882 (SRO)

BALTONSBOROUGH Southwood (Wesleyan) b 1844 (K 1931)

BALTONSBOROUGH (Moravian) b 1852 (K 1931)

BANWELL St Andrew (1,623) (peculiar of Banwell at Wells) (Winterstoke Hundred;
    Axbridge Union)
OR C 1569-1960, M 1570-1977 (gaps 1635-52, 1668-94), Banns 1754-1810, 1824-61, B 1569-1937
    (SRO)
BT 1606-09, 1621-22, 1629-30, 1636-37, 1773-74, 1776-1813, 1815-18, 1820-36 (1765-67,
    1775-76 and 1807-08 in peculiar series) (SRO)
Cop C 1569-1723, M 1569-1754, B 1569-1797 (SRO); M 1754-1837 (NSMI); C 1673-1759
    (SCDB); B 1682-1838 (SBDB); M 1754-1837 (SMI)
Cop (Mf) C 1569-1901, M 1570-1899, Banns 1770-1810, 1824-61, B 1569-1900 (SG, SLC);
    1606-1836 (BT) (SLC, SRO)

BANWELL (Wesleyan) f 1792 b 1862 (K 1931)
OR ZC 1796-1837 (PRO: RG 4/7540); Circuit C 1838-97 (Bristol RO)
Cop (Mf) ZC 1796-1837 (SLC, SRO); C 1838-97 (Bristol RO, SLC)

BANWELL (Free Methodist) b 1872

BANWELL (Baptist) b 1880 (K 1931)

BARRINGTON St Mary (468) (South Petherton Hundred; Langport Union)
OR C 1653-1907, M 1654-1983, Banns 1754-1900, B 1654-1893 (SRO)
BT 1597, 1606-14, 1617-24, 1629-30, 1636-37, 1662-63, 1666-69, 1730-32, 1738-39, 1745-47,
    1749, 1755-56, 1760, 1764, 1768, 1774-75, 1789-90, 1801, 1804-05, 1807-37, CB 1839-47
    (CB 1840-41 in Drayton returns) (SRO)
Cop M 1654-1812 (Ptd, Phillimore 4, 1902); 1597-1812 (Ptd, Dwelly 15, 1926); M 1813-37
    (Ts I SG); C 1653-1913, MB 1654-1964 (SRO); M 1654-1812 (Boyd); B 1784-1878 (SBDB);
    M 1654-1837 (SMI); C 1653-1899, M 1813-37 (DCI)
Cop (Mf) 1597-1847 (BT) (SLC, SRO); C 1653-1901, M 1654-1900, Banns 1754-1900,
    B 1654-1893 (SLC)

BARRINGTON (Presbyterian later Independent) f 1672 *fl*.1851

BARRINGTON (Wesleyan) f 1808 b 1859 cl 1965

BARROW GURNEY St Mary the Virgin and St Edward, King & Martyr (279) (Hartcliffe with
    Bedminster Hundred; Bedminster Union 1836-99, Long Ashton Union 1899-1930)
OR C 1590-1984, M 1593-1982 (gaps 1596-1609, 1646-54), Banns 1826-1900, B 1591-1984 (SRO)
BT 1607-09,1611-12,1615-18,1622-23,1629-30,1634-35,1640-41,1661-62,1670-71,1732-33,
    1749-51,1754-55,1757,1768,1774-75,1802-05,1807-09,1811-13,1815,1817-20,B1840-50 (SRO)
Cop M 1593-1812 (Ptd, Phillimore 2, 1899); CB 1607-1812 (Ptd, Dwelly 1, 15, 1913-26);
    C 1590-1894 (Index SRO); M 1754-1837 (NSMI); M 1593-1812 (Boyd); B 1591-1904 (SBDB);
    M 1593-1837 (SMI)
Cop (Mf) C 1590-1900, M 1754-1899, Banns 1826-1900, B 1591-1900 (SG, SLC);
    1607-1850 (BT) (SLC, SRO)

BARROW, NORTH St Nicholas (150) (Catsash Hundred; Wincanton Union)
OR C 1568-1812 (gap 1690-1745), M 1568-1991 (gap 1695-1745, 1751-54, 1810-13),
    Banns 1755-1810, B 1569-1812 (gap 1689-1746) (SRO); CB 1813+ (Inc)
BT 1598-99, 1605-08, 1611-12, 1622-23, 1629-30, 1638-40, 1663, 1666-69, 1679, 1712, 1733,
    1740, 1750-52, 1754-57, 1775-76, 1801-37, C 1838, CB 1839-40, C 1842, CB 1843-45,
    B 1846, CB 1848-50, 1852-60, 1916-17 (SRO)
Cop 1598, 1607-1751 (Ptd, Dwelly 1, 15, 1913-26); C 1745-1812 (SCDB); B 1747-1812 (SBDB);
    M 1568-1694, 1754-1837 (SMI)
Cop (Mf) 1598-1917 (BT) (SLC, SRO); C 1568-1689, 1746-64, M 1568-1694, 1746, 1755-1837,
    Banns 1755-1809, B 1569-1688, 1747-1812 (SLC)

BARROW, SOUTH St Peter (139) (peculiar of the Dean and Chapter of Wells) (Catsash Hundred;
    Wincanton Union)
OR C 1679-1812, M 1678-1992 (gap 1809-12), Banns 1754-1807, B 1678-1812 (SRO);
    CB 1813+ (Inc)
BT 1605-09, 1611, 1619-31, 1635-37, 1680, 1749-51, 1753, 1771-82, 1785-86, 1813-37, CB 1838,
    1842-47, C 1848, CB 1849-50, 1852-58, 1860, 1917 (SRO)
Cop 1605-37 (Ptd, Dwelly 5, 15, 1917-26); B 1770-1812 (SBDB); M 1605-1837 (BT & OR) (SMI)
Cop (Mf) 1605-1917 (BT) (SLC, SRO); C 1679-1736, 1747-1812, M 1682-1837, Banns 1754-1815,
    B 1678-1812 (SLC)

BARROW, SOUTH (United Methodist) (K 1931)

BARTON St David (410) (peculiar of the Prebendary of Barton Cathedral Church of Wells)
    (Catsash Hundred; Langport Union)
OR C 1714-1993, M 1755-1985, Banns 1755-1896, B 1714-1992 (SRO)
BT 1598-99, 1603-04, one between 1600-46, 1606-09, 1611-12, 1615-18, 1622-24, 1629-31,
    1634-41, 1663-65, 1678-80, 1704-05, 1733, 1750-54, 1756-57, 1801-04, 1806-21, 1823-24,
    1829-36 (SRO)
Cop 1607-79 (Ptd, Dwelly 1, 1913); B 1784-1888 (SBDB); M 1598-1750 (BT), 1754-1837 (SMI)
Cop (Mf) 1598-1836 (BT) (SLC, SRO); C 1714-1889, M 1755-1887, Banns 1755-1896,
    B 1714-1889 (SLC)

BARTON St David (Independent) b 1804 (K 1931)

BARWICK St Mary Magdalene (415) (Houndsborough, Barwick and Coker Hundred; Yeovil Union)
OR C 1560-1931 (gap 1742-46), M 1560-1977, Banns 1754-1809 (defective), 1824-85, B 1560-1901
    (gaps 1678-1711, 1743-46) (SRO)
BT 1596-1602, 1605-08, two between 1608-29, 1611-12, 1615-16, 1621-22, 1630-31,
    1634-37, 1649-51, 1662-63, 1666-68, 1801-13, 1815-37 (SRO)
Cop 1596-1837 (BT) (SLC, SRO); B 1813-1939 (SBDB); M 1560-1837 (SMI)
Cop (Mf) C 1560-1887, M 1560-1885, Banns 1754-1810, 1823-86, B 1560-1886 (SG, SLC)

BARWICK Stoford (Wesleyan) b 1870 (K 1931)

BATCOMBE St Mary the Virgin (839) (Whitstone Hundred; Shepton Mallet Union)
OR C 1642-1997, M 1673-1994 (gap 1751-53), Banns 1824-84, B 1647-1997 (SRO) (some registers
    include Upton Noble)
BT 1597-98, 1605-09, 1611-13, one between 1613-41, 1616-18, 1629-30, 1633-34,
    1637-39, 1662-63, 1669-70, 1750-52, 1755-57, 1803, 1805, 1808-20, 1822, 1824, 1827-36,
    1838-39, CB 1840 (SRO)
Cop 1597-1669 (Ptd, Dwelly 1, 1913); B 1750-1855 (SBDB); M 1673-1837 (SMI)
Cop (Mf) 1597-1840 (BT) (SLC, SRO); C 1642-1889, M 1642-1902, Banns 1754-1811, 1823-84,
    B 1642-1883 (SLC)

BATCOMBE (Wesleyan) (Lewis 1831) b 1860 (K 1931)

BATH Unitarian Cemetery, Lyncombe Vale opened 1819 (K 1931)

BATH Abbey Cemetery, Lyncombe opened 1844 (5 acres) (K 1931)

BATH Lansdown Cemetery opened 1848 (K 1931)
OR B 1848-1925, 1931-55 (SRO)

BATH Bathwick Cemetery, Smallcombe opened 1856 (K 1931)
OR B 1861-86 (SRO)

BATH Roman Catholic Cemetery, Lyncombe opened 1859 (K 1931)

BATH St Michael's Cemetery, Upper Bristol Road opened 1860 (5 acres) (K 1931)
BT B 1862-78 (SRO)
Cop (Mf) B 1862-78 (SLC)

BATH Lower Bristol Road Cemetery opened 1862 (8 acres) (K 1931)

BATH Walcot Cemetery, Upper Bristol Road, Locksbrook opened 1863 (12 acres) (K 1931)

BATH Twerton Cemetery, Bellott's Road opened 1881 (12¼ acres) (K 1931)

BATH Workhouse
OR DB 1784-1857 (SRO)
BT B 1841-53 (SRO)
Cop (Mf) DB 1784-1857 (SLC, SRO); B 1841-53 (BT) (SLC, SRO)

BATH St Peter and St Paul (Bath Abbey), Abbey Churchyard (Bath Forum Hundred; Bath Union)
OR C 1569-1908, M 1569-1965, Banns 1804-73, B 1569-1945 (SRO)
BT 1609-10, 1624-25, 1629-30, 1667-74, 1695-96, 1774-75, 1784-93, 1796-1837,
    CB 1838-47, 1849-69 (SRO)
Cop 1569-1800 (Ptd, Harleian Society 27-28, 1900-01) 1801-40 (Ts I SG, SRO);
    CMB 1801-1969 (SRO); M 1569-1800 (Boyd); M 1754-1837 (SMI)
Cop (Mf) 1609-1869 (BT) (SLC, SRO); CMB 1569-1901, Banns 1804-73 (SLC)

BATH St James, Stall Street (Bath Forum Hundred; Bath Union)
OR C 1569-1942, M 1569-1942, Banns 1775, 1835-73, B 1569-1859 (SRO)
BT 1603-08, 1623-24, 1635-36, 1662-65, 1674-75, 1696-97, 1739-40, 1743-44, 1755-61, 1768-69,
    1775-76, 1784-93, 1796-1837, CB 1838, CMB 1839, CB 1840-46, 1848-55 (SRO)
Cop CB 1569-1840, M 1718-1840 (Ts I SG, SRO); CMB 1569-1812 (Bath Lib); B 1813-37 (SBDB);
    M 1754-1837 (SMI)
Cop (Mf) 1603-1855 (BT) (SLC, SRO); CM 1569-1901, Banns 1835-73, B 1569-1859 (SLC)

BATH St Michael, Broad Street (Bath Forum Hundred; Bath Union)
OR C 1569-1876, M 1569-1929, Banns 1754-69, B 1569-1851 (SRO)
BT 1607-10, 1613-14, 1623-24, 1629-30, 1635-37, 1639-40, 1662-69, 1704-05, 1739-40, 1743-44,
    1755-56, 1759-61, 1784-85, 1785-90, 1793-1837, CB 1838, CMB 1839, CB 1840-51, 1854-55
    (SRO)
Cop CB 1569-1840, M 1559-1840 (Ts I SG, SRO); CB 1570-1812, M 1559-1812 (Bath Lib,
    British Lib); M 1754-1837 (SMI)
Cop (Mf) 1607-1855 (BT) (SLC, SRO); C 1569-1876, M 1569-1900, Banns 1754-69, B 1570-1851
    (SLC)

BATH Holy Trinity, James Street West (created 1839 as Walcot Holy Trinity from Walcot)
    (Bath Union)
OR C 1840-1925, M 1840-1942, 1948-52 (SRO)
BT C 1840-52, 1854-65 (SRO)
Cop (Mf) 1840-65 (BT) (SLC, SRO)

BATH St Saviour b 1829 (created as Walcot St Saviour 1839, from Walcot) (Bath Union)
OR CM 1840-1955, Banns 1840-98, 1954-57, B 1840-1901 (SRO)
BT CB 1840-62 (SRO)
Cop (Mf) 1840-62 (BT) (SLC, SRO); C 1840-1901, M 1840-1900, Banns 1840-98, B 1840-91
    (SLC)

BATH St Paul, Walcot (created 1869 from Walcot Holy Trinity) (Bath Union)
OR C 1870-1951, M 1874-1952 (SRO)

BATH Christchurch, Montpelier (created 1798 as Walcot Christ Church) (Bath Union)
OR C 1877-1963, M 1888-1949, Banns 1888-1938 (SRO)

BATH St Stephen, Lansdown b 1840 (created 1881 as Lansdown, from Walcot) (Bath Union)
OR C 1880-1958, M 1880-1978 (SRO)

BATH St Peter, Twerton (Bath Union)
OR C 1880-1981, M 1880-1983 (SRO)

BATH St Barnabas, South Down
OR M 1949-77 (SRO)

BATH Frog Lane Chapel, later Trim St. Chapel, Trim Street, Bath St Michael (Presbyterian,
    later Unitarian) f 17th C., b 1795, reb 1860 (K 1931)
OR C 1719-1837, B 1819-37 (PRO: RG 4/55, 85, 2053, 2347, 2348, 2922)
Cop (Mf) C 1719-1837, B 1819-37 (SLC, SRO)

BATH Somerset Street, later Manvers Street (Baptist) f 1720
OR Z 1763-1836, D 1785-1837 (PRO: RG 4/1790, 3195)
Cop (Mf) Z 1763-1836, D 1785-1837 (SLC, SRO)

BATH (Roman Catholic)
OR C 1759, 1780-1825, M 1781-1824, D 1780-1819 (Inc) (chapel burnt 1780, registers lost)
Cop C 1759, 1780-1825, M 1781-1824, D 1780-1819 (Ptd, Catholic Record Society 66, 1976)

BATH Trinity Church, Vineyards (Presbyterian, formerly Countess of Huntingdon's Connexion)
   b 1765 (K 1931)
OR ZC 1788-1837 (PRO: RG 4/1416)
Cop (Mf) ZC 1788-1837 (SLC, SRO)

BATH Monmouth St., Bath St Michael, later Coronation Avenue, Twerton (Moravian)
   f 1765 (K 1931)
OR C 1767-1840, B 1826-40 (PRO: RG 4/1541, 3253)
Cop (Mf) C 1767-1840, B 1826-40 (SLC, SRO)

BATH New King Street (Wesleyan) f 1777 b 1779 reb 1847 (K 1931)

BATH Argyle Chapel, Argyle Street (Independent) b 1788 (K 1931)
OR ZC 1785-1836, B 1800-37 (PRO: RG 4/83, 1356, 1789, 3441)
Cop (Mf) ZC 1785-1836, B 1800-37 (SLC, SRO)

BATH Nelson Place East, Walcot (Wesleyan) f 1815 (K 1931)

BATH Dafford Street, Larkhall (Wesleyan) f 1815 (K 1931)

BATH Thomas Street Chapel, later Westgate Buildings (Primitive Methodist) f 1829 (K 1931)
OR ZC 1813-37 (PRO: RG 4/4445)
Cop (Mf) ZC 1813-37 (SLC, SRO)

BATH Chandos Buildings, later Henry Street (Swedenborgian) f 1829 b 1844 (K 1931)
OR ZC 1830-37 (PRO: RG 4/3969)
Cop (Mf) C 1795-1837 (SLC, SRO)

BATH Our Lady Immaculate, Midford (Roman Catholic) f 1820 cl 1901
OR D 1827-58, 1890-1901 (Bristol RO)
Cop (Mf) D 1827-58, 1890-1901 (Bristol RO, SLC)

BATH Our Lady Help of Christians, Julian Road (Roman Catholic) f 1832 as St Mary, Brunswick
   Place to 1852; Montpelier to 1882; b 1879 (K 1931)
OR C 1832+, M 1858+, DB 1936+ (Inc)

BATH Prior Park College (Roman Catholic) f 1830 cl 1965
OR C 1832+, M 1833+, DB 1919+ (Inc Combe Down)
Cop (Mf) C 1832-55, B 1837-53 (Bristol RO, SLC)

BATH Synagogue, Corn Street (Jewish)
OR M 1838+ (Synagogue)
Cop M 1838-1901 (Ptd, Jewish Historical Studies 29, 1988)

BATH Vineyards (Catholic Apostolic) b 1840 (K 1931)

BATH Sion Church, High Street, Twerton (Methodist) b 1853 (K 1931)

BATH St John the Evangelist, South Parade (Roman Catholic) b 1863 (K 1931)

BATH Shakespeare Avenue (United Methodist) b 1867 (K 1931)

BATH Manvers Hall, Manvers Place (Plymouth Brethren) b 1871 (K 1931)

BATH Denmark Road, Twerton (Independent) b 1883 (K 1931)

BATH Rush Hill Chapel, Bloomfield Road (Independent) b 1885 (K 1931)

BATH Twerton (Salvation Army) b 1885

BATH Oldfield Park (Wesleyan) b 1892 (K 1931)

BATH St Alphege, Oldfield Lane (Roman Catholic) b 1929 reb 1954

BATH Hay Hill (Baptist) (K 1931)

BATH Bethesda Chapel, Weymouth Street, Walcot (Baptist) (K 1931)

BATH Providence Chapel, Lower Bristol Road (Baptist) (K 1931)

BATH Bethel Chapel, Walcot Street (Baptist) (K 1931)

BATH Mill Lane, Twerton (Baptist) (K 1931)

BATH The Triangle, Oldfield Park (Baptist) (K 1931)

BATH York Street (Society of Friends) (K 1931)

BATH Percy Chapel, Charlotte Street (Independent) (K 1931)

BATH First Church of Christ, Scientist, Charlotte Street b 1845 (in place of building of 1765)
(K 1931)

BATHAMPTON St Nicholas (314) (Hampton and Claverton Hundred; Bath Union)
OR C 1765-1901, M 1754-1972, Banns 1824-1972, B 1765-1850 (SRO)
BT 1599, 1605-10, 1615--23, 1629, 1634, 1640-41, 1662-70, 1672, 1676, 1728-29, 1749-50, 1752,
1758-61, 1765-66, 1768-69, 1784, 1788-89, 1790-92, 1798-1809, 1811-31 (SRO)
Cop C 1600-1980, M 1599-1752, 1841-1980, B 1599-1980 (Ts I SG, SRO); M 1754-1837 (NSMI);
M 1749-1837 (SMI)
Cop (Mf) 1599-1831 (BT) (SLC, SRO); CB 1765-1886, M 1754-1887 (SLC)

BATHAMPTON Warminster Road (Wesleyan) b 1929 (K 1931)

BATHEALTON St Bartholomew (98) (Milverton Hundred; Wellington Union)
OR C 1712-1965, M 1742-1979, Banns 1755-1812, B 1712-1976 (SRO)
BT 1606-07, one between 1606-40, 1611, 1613-18, 1621-23, c.1630, 1634-38, 1640-41,
1668, 1679 (may be Bathealton or Combe Florey), 1805, 1813-16 (SRO)
Cop B 1712-1975 (SBDB); M 1606-79 (BT), 1713-1837 (SMI); C 1712-1899, M 1713-1899 (DCI)
Cop (Mf) C 1712-1965, M 1742-1979, Banns 1755-1812, B 1712-1976 (SG, SLC);
1606-79, 1805-16 (BT) (SLC, SRO)

BATHEASTON St John the Baptist (1,783) (part Bath Forum Hundred, part Hampton and Claverton
Hundred; Bath Union)
OR C 1634-1967, M 1634-1934, Banns 1754-1812, B 1634-1942 (SRO)
BT 1598-99, 1605-09, 1611-13, 1615-16, 1622-24, 1629-30, one between 1615-40,
1634-35, 1663-67, 1669-70, 1732-40, 1750-51, 1755, 1758-59, 1765, 1767-68, 1775, 1784-85,
1787-93, 1796, 1798-1829, 1831, 1833, 1835-41, CB 1842-81 (SRO)
Cop 1609-35 (Ptd, Dwelly 1, 1913); 1634-1812 (SG, Bath Lib, British Lib); M 1754-1837 (NSMI);
B 1783-1845 (SBDB); M 1609-35 (BT), 1754-1837 (SMI)
Cop (Mf) 1598-1881 (BT) (SLC, SRO); CMB 1634-1886, Banns 1754-1812 (Ptd on fiche, SRO,
1995 and SLC)

BATHEASTON (Wesleyan) (Lewis 1831) b 1876 (K 1931)

BATHEASTON (Independent) (K 1931)

BATHEASTON St Euphrasia, The Brow (Roman Catholic) b 1948

BATHFORD St Swithun (870) (Bath Forum Hundred; Bath Union)
OR C 1727-1974, M 1730-1990, Banns 1754-1823, B 1729-1967 (SRO)
BT one between 1600-35, 1602-03, 1605-09, 1611, 1613-14, 1617-18, 1622-23, 1629-30,
    1634-38, 1662-79, 1728-29, 1750-52, 1756-58, 1765-69, 1775, 1780, 1783-84, 1785-88,
    1790-94, 1798-1829 (SRO)
Cop 1608-62 (Ptd, Dwelly 1, 1913); 1727-1810 (Ts I SG); CMB 1728-1810 (Bath Lib, British Lib);
    1727-1974 (Ts I SRO); M 1754-1837 (NSMI); M 1608-62 (BT), 1730-1837 (SMI)
Cop (Mf) 1602-1829 (BT) (SLC, SRO); C 1727-1809, M 1730-1810, B 1729-1809 (SG);
    C 1728-1886, M 1730-1886, Banns 1754-1823, B 1729-1886 (SLC)

BATHFORD (Baptist) b 1838 (K 1931)

BATHPOOL All Saints cl 1981
OR C 1897-1981 (SRO in West Monkton deposit)

BATHWICK St Mary the Virgin (4,035) (Bath Forum Hundred; Bath Union)
OR C 1668-70, 1684-1705, 1712, 1722-38, 1745, 1749-54, 1759-1903, M 1669, 1685-1727, 1741,
    1748-1915, Banns 1754-1804, 1809-25, B 1668-72, 1684-1705, 1712, 1718-19, 1722-31,
    1749-1901 (SRO)
BT 1598-1600, 1602, 1607, 1611, 1615, 1619-20, 1622-23, 1629-30, 1634-35, 1664-67, 1669-70,
    1750-51, 1774-78, 1801-37, CB 1838-64, 1866-68 (SRO)
Cop C 1600, 1615, M 1615 (Ptd, Dwelly 1, 1913); C 1668-1840, M 1668-1840, B 1691-1840 (SG);
    B 1801-12 (SBDB); M 1615 (BT), 1754-1837 (SMI)
Cop (Mf) 1598-1868 (BT) (SLC, SRO); CMB 1668-1886, Banns 1754-1825 (Ptd on fiche, 1996)

BATHWICK St John the Baptist, Bathwick Street b 1861 (created 1871 from Bathwick St Mary,
    renamed Bath Bathwick, 1967) (Bath Union)
OR CMB 1861+ (Inc)
BT (Burial Board) B 1861-86 (SRO)

BAWDRIP St Michael (373) (North Petherton Hundred; Bridgwater Union)
OR C 1748-1883, M 1749-1837, Banns 1755-1821, 1824-1900, B 1749-1970 (SRO)
BT 1599-1600, 1602-03, 1605-06, 1609-13, 1615-16, 1621-23, 1629-30, 1634-38, 1662,
    1720-21, 1751-52, 1755-56, 1800-38, CB 1839, CMB 1840, CB 1842-49 (SRO)
Cop 1602-36 (Ptd, Dwelly 1, 1913); B 1749-1900 (SBDB); M 1609-36 (BT), 1754-1837 (SMI)
Cop (Mf) 1599-1849 (BT) (SLC, SRO); C 1748-1883, M 1749-1837, Banns 1755-1821, 1824-1902,
    B 1748-1901 (SLC)

BAWDRIP Sion Chapel, Knowle (Independent, later United Reformed Church) b 1830

BAWDRIP Bradney Chapel (Methodist) b 1842 cl before 1924

BECKINGTON St George (1,340) (Frome Hundred; Frome Union)
OR C 1559-1874, M 1559-1973, Banns 1754-83, 1932-73, B 1559-1954 (SRO)
BT 1599-1600, 1602-03, 1606-07, 1609-14, 1617, 1622-23, 1629-30, 1639-41, 1662-64,
    1668-70, 1737-39, 1751-54, 1801-40, CB 1841 (SRO)
Cop B 1738-1852 (SBDB); M 1559-1837 (SMI)
Cop (Mf) C 1559-1874, M 1559-1900, Banns 1754-83, B 1559-1900 (SLC); C 1559-1874,
    M 1559-1837, Banns 1754-83, B 1559-1900 (SG); 1599-1841 (BT) (SLC, SRO)

BECKINGTON (Baptist) b 1786 (K 1931)
OR CB 1786-1860 (SRO)

BECKINGTON Rudge (Wesleyan) b 1814 (K 1931)
OR B 1966 (Bristol RO)
Cop (Mf) B 1966 (Bristol RO, SLC)

BECKINGTON Rudge (Baptist) b 1817 reb 1850 (K 1931)

BEDMINSTER Board of Guardians
OR Z 1866-1930, D 1866-1930 (SRO)

BEDMINSTER St John the Baptist (13,130) (Hartcliffe with Bedminster Hundred;
  Bedminster Union 1836-99, Long Ashton Union 1899-1930)
OR C 1643-1965, M 1654-1965, B 1656-1965 (Bristol RO)
BT one between 1594-1616, 1598-1600, M 1606, CMB 1611-12, 1616-17, 1619-20,
  1622-24, 1629-30, 1687-88, 1705-06, 1728-29, 1732-34, 1751, 1757, 1759-60, 1764, 1768-69,
  1775, 1784-88, 1790-94, 1796-1830 (Bristol RO)
Cop 1599-1624 (SG); M 1800-37 (Ts SG); B 1813-30 (SBDB); M 1599, 1623 (BT),
  1754-1837 (SMI)
Cop (Mf) 1598-1830 (BT) (Bristol RO, SLC, SRO)

BEDMINSTER St Paul (created 1841 from Bedminster St John) (Bedminster Union 1836-99,
  Long Ashton Union 1899-1930)
OR C 1881-1979, M 1852-1978 (Bristol RO)
BT CB 1843-69 (Bristol RO)
Cop (Mf) C 1881-1901, M 1852-1904 (Bristol RO, SLC); 1843-69 (BT) (Bristol RO, SLC)

BEDMINSTER St Luke (created 1861 from Bedminster St John and Bristol St Mary Redcliffe)
  (Bedminster Union 1836-99, Long Ashton Union 1899-1930)
OR C 1861-1914, M 1861-1900 (Bristol RO)
BT C 1861-67 (Bristol RO)
Cop (Mf) C 1861-1914. M 1861-1900 (Bristol RO, SLC); 1861-67 (BT) (Bristol RO, SLC)

BEDMINSTER St Raphael the Archangel (created 1893 from Bedminster St Paul)
  (Bedminster Union 1836-99, Long Ashton Union 1899-1930)
OR C 1861-1940, M 1894-1932 (Bristol RO)
Cop (Mf) C 1861-1940, M 1894-1932 (Bristol RO, SLC)

BEDMINSTER St Silas
OR C 1867-1959, B 1868-1955 (Bristol RO)

BEDMINSTER St Francis, Ashton Gate (created 1883 from Bedminster St John and Bedminster
  St Paul) (Bedminster Union 1836-99, Long Ashton Union 1899-1930)
OR C 1883-1946, M 1887-1967 (Bristol RO)
Cop (Mf) C 1892-1904 (Bristol RO, SLC)

BEDMINSTER St Aldhelm (created 1902 from Bedminster St John, Bedminster St Paul and
  Bishopsworth) (Long Ashton Union 1899-1930)
OR C 1900-56, M 1907-56 (Bristol RO)
Cop (Mf) C 1900-56, M 1907-56 (Bristol RO, SLC)

BEDMINSTER St Dunstan, Bedminster Down (created 1929 from Bedminster St John)
  (Long Ashton Union 1899-1930)
OR CMB 1929+ (Inc)

BEDMINSTER (Baptist) (Lewis 1831)

BEDMINSTER Ebenezer Chapel (Methodist) (Lewis 1831)
OR C 1837-1964 (Bristol RO)
Cop (Mf) C 1837-1964 (Bristol RO, SLC)

BEDMINSTER (Independent) (Lewis 1831)

BEDMINSTER (United Methodist)
OR C 1843-1961 (Bristol RO)
Cop (Mf) C 1843-1961 (Bristol RO, SLC)

BEDMINSTER Heton Chapel (Methodist)
OR C 1853-1966, M 1899-1967, B 1858-1965 (Bristol RO)
Cop (Mf) C 1853-1966, M 1899-1967, B 1858-1965 (Bristol RO, SLC)

BEDMINSTER Portwall Lane (Methodist)
OR C 1860-1934 (Bristol RO)
Cop (Mf) C 1860-1934 (Bristol RO, SLC)

BEDMINSTER Holy Cross, Dean Lane (Roman Catholic) f 1867

BEDMINSTER (United Methodist)
OR C 1872-1961, M 1901-62 (Bristol RO)
Cop (Mf) C 1872-1961, M 1901-62 (Bristol RO, SLC)

BEDMINSTER (Primitive Methodist)
OR C 1876-1938 (Bristol RO)
Cop (Mf) C 1876-1938 (Bristol RO, SLC)

BEDMINSTER John Millard Memorial Chapel (Free Methodist)
OR C 1901-82 (Bristol RO)
Cop (Mf) C 1901-82 (Bristol RO, SLC)

BEDMINSTER Bath Street, Ashton Gate (Wesleyan)
OR C 1938-77 (Bristol RO)
Cop (Mf) C 1938-77 (Bristol RO, SLC)

BEERCROCOMBE St James (182) (Abdick and Bulstone Hundred; Langport Union)
OR CB 1542-1980 (gaps 1552-62, 1641-51, 1683-1702), M 1542-1979 (gaps 1552-62, 1641-51,
    1683-1703, 1738-50), Banns 1754-1812, 1826-1900 (SRO)
BT 1593-97, 1606-08, 1611-16, 1618, 1621-24, 1629-30, 1636-37, 1662-67, 1731-32, 1749-52,
    1756, 1768-69, 1773-76, 1784-87, 1789, 1800, 1802-39, 1841-43 (SRO)
Cop M 1542-1812 (Ptd, Phillimore 4, 1902); C 1542-1682, 1703-95, M 1703-51, B 1542-1682,
    1703-97 (SRO); CB 1607-36 (Ptd, Dwelly 1, 1913); M 1542-1812 (Boyd); B 1797-1900
    (SBDB); M 1542-1837 (SMI); C 1542-1899, M 1813-99 (DCI)
Cop (Mf) 1593-1843 (BT) (SLC, SRO); CMB 1542-1900, Banns 1755-1900 (SLC)

BERINGTON *see* **BURRINGTON**

BERKLEY St Mary (531) (united with Fayroke, 1460) (Frome Hundred; Frome Union)
OR C 1547-1865, M 1547-1839, Banns 1654-56, 1754-1823, B 1546-1942 (SRO)
BT 1601-02, 1605-18, 1621-23, 1634-36, 1639-40, 1663-64, 1678-79, 1732-33, 1752-57, 1770-76,
    1800-01, 1803-50, CB 1851-52, CMB 1853-54, CB 1855, CMB 1856 (SRO)
Cop B 1770-1902 (SBDB); M 1547-1837 (SMI)
Cop (Mf) C 1547-1865, M 1546-1839, Banns 1754-1823, B 1547-1903 (SG, SLC);
    1601-1856 (BT) (SLC, SRO)

BERROW St Mary (496) (Brent with Wrington Hundred; Axbridge Union)
OR C 1703-12, 1724-1854, M 1700-12, 1724-1967, Banns 1754-64, 1769-91, B 1706-1889 (SRO)
BT one between 1593 & 1609, 1598-99, 1606-07, 1609-14, one between 1613-40, 1617-18,
    1621-22, 1629-30, 1637-38, 1664-65, 1675-76, 1681-82, 1748-52, 1754-57, 1759, 1768-69,
    1772-77, 1780-82, 1787-88, 1802-15, 1817-18, 1820-26, 1828, 1834-36, 1845-46, 1848 (SRO)
Cop C 1800-54 (SCDB); B 1709-1889 (SBDB); M 1598-1638 (BT), 1700-1837 (SMI)
Cop (Mf) C 1703-1854, M 1700-1901, Banns 1754-64, 1769-91, B c1706-1889 (SG, SLC);
    1598-1848 (BT) (SLC, SRO)

BERROW (Wesleyan) b 1809 (K 1931)

BICKENHALL St Paul (270) (chapelry in Staple Fitzpaine) (Abdick and Bulstone Hundred; Taunton Union)
OR C 1682-1971, M 1682-1739, 1755-1967, Banns 1824-1948, B 1682-1991 (SRO)
BT 1603-04, 1613, 1615-16, 1619-22, 1628-29, 1634, 1637, 1640-41, 1663-64, 1680-81, 1749-51, 1754, 1757-59, 1762-65, 1770-73, 1776, 1778-82, 1784-87, 1789-90, 1792-1821, 1824-38, CB 1840-55 (SRO)
Cop M 1682-1812 (Ptd, Phillimore 13, 1910); 1603-41 (Ptd, Dwelly 1, 1913); M 1682-1812 (Boyd); B 1745-1850 (SBDB); M 1615 (BT), 1754-1837 (SMI); C 1682-1899, M 1755-1899 (DCI)
Cop (Mf) 1603-1855 (BT) (SLC, SRO); C 1682-1903, M 1682-1901, Banns 1824-1901, B 1682-1812 (SLC)

BICKNOLLER St George (285) (chapelry in Stogumber until 1770) (Williton and Freemanors Hundred; Williton Union)
OR C 1557-1906, M 1600-99, 1722-1970, Banns 1755-1812, 1824-1900, B 1557-1639, 1677-1973 (SRO)
BT 1605-07, 1609-13, 1617-18, 1621-23, 1629-30, 1634-36, 1638-39, 1704-11, 1721-22, 1726-29, 1741, 1749-51, 1753-56, 1758-59, 1762, 1764-66, 1768-69, 1771-75, 1778, 1781-85, 1800-33 (SRO)
Cop C 1557-1815, M 1558-1888, B 1558-1836 (SRO); 1605-39 (Ptd, Dwelly 1, 1913); B 1758-1921 (SBDB); M 1558-1837 (SMI); C 1557-1899, M 1559-1899 (DCI)
Cop (Mf) C 1557-1900, M 1600-1899, Banns 1755-1812, 1824-1900, B 1557-1639, 1677-1903 (SG, SLC); 1605-1833 (BT) (SLC, SRO)

BICKNOLLER (Methodist)
OR C 1872-1923 (circuit) (SRO)

BIDDISHAM St John the Baptist (158) (peculiar of the Dean and Chapter of Wells) (Bempstone Hundred; Axbridge Union)
OR C 1621-1984, M 1755-1982, Banns 1784-1812, B 1621-1985 (SRO)
BT 1598-99, 1602-06, 1609, 1611-12, 1615, 1617-23, 1629-30, 1634-35, 1639-40, 1663-64, 1803-06, 1808-16, 1822-23, 1825-33 (SRO); 1751, 1753-55, 1757, 1760-61, 1765-67, 1769-71, 1773, 1776-78, 1780-99, 1801 (SRO: D/D/Pd:26/2)
Cop B 1790-1987 (SBDB); M 1602-64 (BT), 1754-1837 (SMI)
Cop (Mf) C 1621-1984, M 1755-1982, Banns 1784-1812, B 1621-1777, 1790-1985 (SG); 1598-1833 (BT) (SLC, SRO)

BIDDISHAM (United Methodist) b 1844

BINEGAR Holy Trinity (376) (peculiar of the Dean and Chapter of Wells) (Wells Forum Hundred; Shepton Mallet Union)
OR C 1809-1874, M 1769-1914, Banns 1769-1832, 1834-1900, B 1809-1922 (SRO) (C from 1717, M from 1724 and B from 1725 survived in 1914)
BT 1605-06, 1608-09, 1611-12, 1616-17, c1619, 1621-24, 1629-31, 1634, 1636-38, 1662-63, 1666-69, 1803-43, 1845-46, CB 1847, CMB 1848-49, CB 1851-57 (SRO); 1749-50, 1753-58, 1760-61 (SRO: D/D/Pd:26/3)
Cop B 1809-99 (SBDB); M 1754-1837 (SMI)
Cop (Mf) C 1809-74, M 1769-1900, Banns 1769-1832, 1834-1900, B 1809-1903 (SG, SLC); 1605-1857 (BT) (SLC, SRO)

BINEGAR Gurney Slade (Wesleyan) b 1834

BISHOPSWORTH or BISHPORT St Peter (created 1852 from Bedminster St John) (Bedminster Union 1836-99, Long Ashton Union 1899-1930)
OR C 1844+, M 1852+, B 1846+ (Inc)
BT C 1844-48, B 1846-48 (Bristol RO)
Cop (Mf) C 1844-48, B 1846-48 (BT) (Bristol RO, SLC)

BISHOPSWORTH Bishpool (Independent) f 1662 b 1840 (K 1931)

BITTON The Tabernacle, Oldland Common (Independent) f 1811 (though listed in the PRO list under Somerset, this chapel is in Gloucestershire, but was missed from the Gloucestershire section of NIPR vol.5)
OR ZC 1822-32 (PRO: RG 4/3855)

BLACKFORD St Michael (near Wincanton) (192) (chapelry in Maperton until 1852) (Whitley Hundred; Wincanton Union)
OR C 1684-86, 1692-1990, M 1692-1975, Banns 1755-1811, 1920-34, B 1693-1991 (gap B 1786-99) (SRO)
BT 1594-95, 1603-06, 1611, 1613, 1615, 1622-24, 1629-30, 1634, 1636-37, 1640-41, 1663, 1667-69, 1678-79, 1705-06, 1732, 1757-58, 1775-76, 1800-31, 1833-37, CB 1848-50, 1860-62 (SRO)
Cop M 1815-37 (Ts SG); M 1594-1641 (BT), 1692-1837 (SMI)
Cop (Mf) C 1684-1812, M 1692-1899, Banns 1755-1811, 1920-34, B 1693-1785, 1800-12 (SG, SLC); 1594-1862 (BT) (SLC, SRO)

BLACKFORD near Wincanton (Wesleyan) b 1837 (K 1931)

BLACKFORD Holy Trinity (created 1844 from Wedmore) (Axbridge Union)
OR M 1826-1960, B 1826-1961 (SRO); C 1831+ (Inc)
BT C 1831-59, B 1829-59 (SRO)
Cop B 1800-1900 (SBDB)
Cop (Mf) M 1845-1901, B 1826-1900 (SG, SLC); 1829-59 (BT) (SLC, SRO)

BLAGDON St Andrew (1,109) (Winterstoke Hundred; Axbridge Union)
OR C 1555-1961, M 1557-1965, Banns 1754-1812, 1827-85, B 1556-1898 (SRO)
BT 1611-16, 1619-23, 1628-30, 1634-41, 1663-69, 1800-06, 1808-19, 1821-24, 1826-37, CB 1838, CMB 1839-49, 1869 (SRO)
Cop M 1754-1837 (NSMI); B 1766-1846 (SBDB); M 1580-1837 (SMI)
Cop (Mf) C 1555-1885, M 1557-1885, Banns 1754-1812, 1827-85, B 1556-1886 (SG, SLC); 1611-1869 (BT) (SLC, SRO)

BLAGDON (Wesleyan) (Lewis 1831) b 1887 (K 1931)

BLAGDON (Baptist) b 1875 (K 1931)

BLEADON St Peter and St Paul (599) (Winterstoke Hundred; Axbridge Union)
OR C 1708-1920, M 1706-1969, B 1706-1893 (all to 1812 defective) (SRO)
BT 1597-98, 1605-10, 1615-17, 1622-24, 1629-30, 1636-38, 1640-41, 1663-64, 1666-67, 1684-85, 1720-21, 1744, 1751-58, 1800-21, 1824-35, 1837, CB 1839 (SRO)
Cop CM 1608-23 (Ptd, Dwelly 1, 1913); 1710-1939 (Ts I SG, SLC); 1706-1949 (SRO); M 1754-1837 (NSMI); C 1813-57 (SCDB); B 1813-85 (SBDB); M 1608-23 (BT), 1717-1837 (SMI)
Cop (Mf) 1597-1839 (BT) (SLC, SRO); C 1708-1887, M 1717-1888, B 1712-1886 (SLC)

BLEADON (United Methodist) b 1846 (K 1931)
OR C 1945-52 (Bristol RO)
Cop (Mf) C 1945-52 (Bristol RO, SLC)

BLEADON (Plymouth Brethren) (K 1931)

BRADFORD ON TONE St Giles (525) (Taunton and Taunton Dean Hundred; Wellington Union)
OR C 1558-1960, M 1561-1990, B 1558-1914 (SRO)
BT 1594-1600, 1605-08, 1611, 1613-17, 1621-24, 1629-31, 1634-40, 1662-64, 1667-70, 1675-76,
    1707-08, 1720-21, 1725-28, 1731-33, 1736-37, 1743-44, 1749-52, 1754-55, 1759, 1768-81,
    1801-37, CB 1838-39, 1842-46 (SRO)
Cop M 1561-1812 (Ptd, Phillimore 7, 1906); CB 1594-1662 (Ptd, Dwelly 1, 1913);
    M 1561-1812 (Boyd); B 1716-1861 (SBDB); M 1558-1837 (SMI); C 1559-1899, M 1812-36
    (DCI)
Cop (Mf) 1594-1846 (BT) (SLC, SRO)

BRADFORD ON TONE (Independent) f 1836 b 1880

BRADLEY, MAIDEN All Saints (659) (part Somerset, Norton Ferris Hundred; which part
    transferred to Wiltshire 1895; part Wiltshire, Mere Hundred; Mere Union)
OR C 1662-1898, M 1662-1837, B 1662-1870 (Wilts RO)
BT 1608-09, 1623-38, 1670-79, 1693-94, 1711-46, 1750-53, 1773-1880 (Wilts RO)
Cop (Mf) 1608-1880 (BT) (SLC)

BRADLEY, MAIDEN (Independent) f 1800 (PRO) f 1780 (K 1939)
OR C 1825-37 (PRO: RG 4/2594)
Cop (Mf) C 1825-37 (SLC)

BRADLEY, WEST (dedication unknown) (132) (chapelry in East Pennard until 1875)
    (Glastonbury Twelve Hides Hundred; Wells Union)
OR C 1633-1955, M 1633-1986, B 1633-1812 (SRO); B 1813+ (Inc)
BT 1598, c.1600, 1605-09, 1623-24, 1629-30, 1638-41, 1662-70, 1673-74, 1734, 1800-33 (SRO)
Cop C 1605-73, M 1605-73, B 1605-73 (Ptd, Dwelly 1, 1913); M 1813-37 (Ts I SG); M 1605-1719
    (OR & BT), 1754-1837 (SMI)
Cop (Mf) 1598-1833 (BT) (SLC, SRO)

BRADLEY, WEST (United Methodist) b 1836 (K 1931)

BRADLEY, WEST (Wesleyan) b 1881 (K 1931)

BRATTON SEYMOUR St Nicholas (59) (Norton Ferris Hundred; Wincanton Union)
OR C 1754-1812, M 1754-1837, Banns 1754-77, B 1755-1810 (SRO); CB 1813+ (Inc)
    (earlier registers lost since 1831)
BT 1595-1600, 1602-04, 1606-09, 1611-13, 1615-17, 1621-23, 1629-30, 1634-37, 1663-64,
    1667-70, 1672-73, 1678-80, 1704-05, 1748-49, 1752, 1756-59, 1767, 1801-18, 1821-30,
    1838-40, 1842, CB 1843, CMB 1844-46, CB 1847, CMB 1848, M 1849, CMB 1850-52,
    1854-55, M 1856, CMB 1857-60 (SRO)
Cop M 1813-51 (SG); B 1755-1810 (SBDB); M 1595-1752 (BT), 1754-1837 (SMI)
Cop (Mf) 1595-1860 (BT) (SLC, SRO)

BREAN St Bridget (134) (Bempstone Hundred; Axbridge Union)
OR C 1731-1976, M 1730-1837, B 1734-1977 (SRO)
BT 1605-09, 1615-17, 1623, 1629-30, 1636-38, 1663-66, 1668, 1675-78, 1744, 1748-52, 1755-56,
    1759, 1802-24, 1829, 1832-35 (SRO)
Cop B 1730-1900 (SBDB); M 1605-23, 1730-1837 (SMI)
Cop (Mf) C 1731-1906, M 1730-1837, B 1730-1900 (SG, SLC); 1605-1835 (BT) (SLC, SRO)

BREAN (Wesleyan) b 1847 (K 1931)

BRENT, EAST St Mary the Virgin (802) (Brent with Wrington Hundred; Axbridge Union)
OR C 1559-1966 (gaps 1623-52, 1658-83), M 1558-1975 (gap 1623-52, 1681-85),
    Banns 1891-1979, B 1558-1928 (gap 1623-52) (SRO)
BT 1597-98, 1621-23, 1630-31, 1636-37, 1639-40, 1644-46, 1678-79, ?1744-46, 1748-52, 1754-60,
    1766-73, 1775-78, 1800-36, CB 1844-46, C 1851 (SRO)
Cop M 1558-1611, B 1558-1622 (Ts SG, SLC, SRO); B 1719-1885 (SBDB); M 1558-1608,
    1754-1837 (SMI)
Cop (Mf) 1597-1851 (BT) (SLC, SRO); CM 1558-1886, B 1558-1885 (SLC)

BRENT, EAST (Wesleyan) b 1871 (Lewis 1831) (K 1931)

BRENT KNOLL or BRENT, SOUTH St Michael (890) (Brent with Wrington Hundred;
    Axbridge Union)
OR C 1679-1711, 1724-1968, M 1679-1709, 1724-1982, B 1678-1711, 1724-73, 1783-1868 (SRO)
BT one between 1588-1610, 1597-98, 1602-03, 1605-07, 1609-10, 1621-24, one between 1621-63,
    1627-28, 1629-30, 1635-40, 1663-64, 1675-76, 1704-05, 1744-49, 1751-52, 1766-73, 1775-80,
    1800-18, 1821-25, 1827-37 (SRO)
Cop C 1622-1800, M 1679-1811, B 1678-1800 (Ts SG, SLC); CMB 1678-1812 (SRO);
    C 1800-12 (SCDB); B 1800-60 (SBDB); M 1748-1837 (SMI)
Cop (Mf) 1597-1837 (BT) (SLC, SRO); CM 1679-1886, Banns 1754-98, B 1678-1868 (SLC)

BRENT KNOLL (United Methodist) (Lewis 1831) b 1837 (K 1931)

BREWHAM, SOUTH and NORTH St John the Baptist (968) (Bruton Hundred; Wincanton Union)
OR C 1668-1868, M 1729-1837, Banns 1754-68, 1783-84, 1824-72, B 1659-1755, 1770-1958 (SRO)
BT 1599-1600, 1602-03, 1606-12, 1615-23, 1629-30, 1634-35, 1662-64, 1666-67, 1669-71,
    1678-79, 1755-57, 1800-37, CB 1838, 1840-47, 1849 (SRO)
Cop C 1607, MB 1607 (Ptd, Dwelly 1, 1913); C 1683-1765, M 1729-1850 (Ts I SRO);
    C 1868-1985 (Ts SG, SRO); B 1770-1902 (SBDB); M 1729-1837 (SMI); M 1599-1678 (BT),
    1729-1837 (SMI)
Cop (Mf) 1599-1849 (BT) (SLC, SRO); C 1683-1867, M 1729-1837, Banns 1754-1872,
    B 1659-1902 (SLC)

BREWHAM, SOUTH and NORTH North Brewham (Wesleyan) b 1841 (K 1931)
OR C 1868-1962 (SRO)

BREWHAM, SOUTH and NORTH North Brewham (Baptist) b 1870 (K 1931)

BRIDGWATER Board of Guardians
OR Z 1866-1931, D 1866-1914 (SRO)

BRIDGWATER Cemetery, Wembdon Road opened 1851 (7 acres)
OR B 1851-1977 (SRO)

BRIDGWATER St John's Cemetery, Bristol Road opened 1878 (13 acres)

BRIDGWATER St Mary, St Mary's Street (7,807) (North Petherton Hundred; Bridgwater Union)
OR C 1558-1972, M 1558-1976, Banns 1754-58, 1780-1978, B 1558-1977 (SRO)
BT 1597-99, 1601-02, 1605-09, 1622-23, 1627-30, 1636-40, 1667-70, 1704-05, 1730-33, 1732-33,
    1737-38, 1800-30 (SRO)
Cop 1597-1669 (Ptd, Dwelly 1, 1913); C 1813-37 (Ts I SRO); C 1813-39 (SCDB);
    B 1800-1900 (SBDB); M 1558-1837 (SMI)
Cop (Mf) 1597-1830 (BT) (SLC, SRO); CM 1558-1901, B 1560-1901 (SLC)

BRIDGWATER Holy Trinity, Taunton Road (created 1841 from Bridgwater St Mary)
    (Bridgwater Union)
OR C 1840-1977, M 1841-1975, B 1849-58 (SRO)
Cop (Mf) C 1840-1901, M 1841-1900, B 1849-58 (SLC)

BRIDGWATER St John the Baptist, Blake Place, Eastover (created 1846 from Bridgwater St Mary) (Bridgwater Union)
OR C 1846-1965, M 1846-1969, B 1846-67, 1962-76 (SRO)
Cop B 1846-67 (SBDB)
Cop (Mf) C 1846-1902, M 1846-1900, B 1846-67 (SLC)

BRIDGWATER All Saints, Westonzoyland Road b 1882 (no separate registers)

BRIDGWATER St Francis (created from Bridgwater, Durleigh, North Petherton and Northmoor Green, 1961)
OR CMB 1961+ (Inc)

BRIDGWATER St Mary Street (Baptist) f 1653 reb 1837 (K 1931)

BRIDGWATER Christ Church Chapel, Dampier Street (Presbyterian, later Unitarian) f 1662 reb 1788 (K 1931)
OR C 1755-1837, B 1833-35 (PRO: RG 4/142); C 1755-1960 (SRO)
Cop (Mf) C 1755-1837, B 1833-35 (SLC, SRO)

BRIDGWATER Meeting House, Friarn Street (Society of Friends) f 1670 b 1722 (K 1931)
OR C 1926-54 (SRO)
BT B 1865-83 (SRO)
Cop B 1796-1837 (SBDB)
Cop (Mf) 1865-83 (BT) (SLC, SRO)

BRIDGWATER King Street (Wesleyan) f 1753 b 1816, reb 1860 cl 1980
OR C 1816-37 (PRO: RG 4/3322); C 1816-42, B 1841-79 (SRO)

BRIDGWATER Sion Chapel, Tuam Street f 1787 reb 1822, later Fore Street (Independent) b 1862 cl 1964
OR ZC 1818-37, B 1823-37 (PRO: RG 4/1825)
Cop (Mf) ZC 1818-37, B 1823-37 (SLC, SRO)

BRIDGWATER Mariners Chapel, St John Street (Independent) f 1837 cl 1960 reb Moorland Road 1961 and became Baptist 1965

BRIDGWATER Dampier Street (Catholic Apostolic) f c1840 in King Street by 1889 cl c1908

BRIDGWATER Friarn Street (Plymouth Brethren) f 1840s (K 1931)

BRIDGWATER St Joseph, Binford Place (Roman Catholic) f 1845 b 1882 (K 1931)
OR C 1848+, M 1849+, DB 1848+ (Inc)

BRIDGWATER St Mary Street (Wesleyan Reform) f 1851 cl 1907

BRIDGWATER Angel Crescent (Primitive Methodist) b 1852

BRIDGWATER West Street (Primitive Methodist) b 1861 Salvation Army by 1880 who moved to Friarn Street 1881 and to Moorland Road 1971

BRIDGWATER Bath Road, later Polden Street (Bible Christian later United Methodist Free) f 1866 cl 1911

BRIDGWATER Monmouth Street (United Methodist) f 1876 b 1911 (K 1931)

BRIDGWATER King's Place (Plymouth Brethren) f by 1897 cl 1940

BRIDGWATER King's Place (National Spiritualist) f 1937

BRIDGWATER West Street Westfield (Independent) b 1966

BRIDGWATER Evangelical Church f 1969

BRIDGWATER Kingdom Hall, Old Taunton Road from 1986 the Drove (Jehovah Witnesses) f 1971

BRIDGWATER Elim Pentecostal Church, George Street f 1973

BRISLINGTON St Luke (1,294) (chapelry in Keynsham until 1786) (Keynsham Hundred; Keynsham Union)
OR C 1566-1963, M 1568-1983, B 1568-1977 (gaps CMB 1597-1614, 1710-13) (Bristol RO)
BT 1629, 1813-34 (SRO); 1606, 1615-22, 1634-40, 1666, 1749-1812 (Bristol RO)
Cop C 1566-1812, M 1568-1808, B 1568-1812 (Ts I SG); CMB 1637-1713 (Ts Bristol RO, SLC); B 1637-1839 (SBDB); M 1754-1837 (SMI)
Cop (Mf) 1629, 1813-34 (BT) (SLC, SRO); 1606-1812 (BT) (Bristol RO, SLC)

BRISLINGTON St Anne (created from Brislington St Luke, 1909) (Keynsham Union)
OR CMB 1909+ (Inc)

BRISLINGTON St Christopher (created from Brislington St Luke, Brislington St Anne and Knowle Holy Nativity, 1932)
OR CMB 1932+ (Inc)

BRISLINGTON St Cuthbert (created from Brislington St Luke and Brislington St Anne, 1930)
OR CMB 1930+ (Inc)

BRISLINGTON (Independent) b 1796 (K 1931)

BRISLINGTON Union Chapel (Baptist and Independent) b 1827

BRISLINGTON (Wesleyan) (K 1931)

BRISTOL for all Bristol parishes *see* Gloucestershire section of the NIPR, vol.5

BROADWAY St Aldhelm and St Eadburga (450) (Abdick and Bulstone Hundred; Chard Union)
OR C 1710-1985, M 1710-1990, B 1678-1930 (SRO)
BT 1598-99, 1606-10, 1612-13, 1616-17, 1621-23, 1628-31, 1636-38, 1640-41, 1662-64, 1668-70, 1672, 1674-75,1742,1749,1756,1758,1768-69,1789-90,1798, 1800-01,1810-11,1813-32 (SRO)
Cop C 1598-1676, M 1599-1669, B 1598-1676 (Ptd, Dwelly 1, 9, 1913, 1922); 1611-1810 (Ptd, Dwelly 15, 1926); C 1700-1837, M 1701-1836, B 1700-1837 (Ts SG); CM 1710-1837, B 1678-1837 (SRO); C 1598-1916 (SCDB); B 1598-1929 (SBDB); M 1599-1837 (SMI); C 1599-1899, M 1599-1836 (DCI)
Cop (Mf) 1598-1832 (BT) (SLC, SRO); C 1710-1916, M 1710-1886, B 1678-1887 (SLC)

BROADWAY Broadway Meeting (Independent) b 1739 (K 1931)
OR ZC 1777-1840 (PRO: RG 4/1418)
Cop C 1774-1840 (SCDB)
Cop (Mf) ZC 1777-1840 (SLC, SRO)

BROCKLEY St Nicholas (171) (Chewton Hundred; Bedminster Union 1836-99, Long Ashton Union 1899-1930)
OR C 1696-1978, M 1699-1833, B 1699-1980 (SRO)
BT 1598-99, 1602-04, 1607, 1609, 1611-12, 1615-18, 1621-24, 1629-30, one between 1630-40, 1634-35, 1636, 1639-41, 1732-33, 1751, 1753, 1775-76, 1801-22, 1824-27, 1829-30, CM 1849, CB 1850-52, C 1853-54 (SRO)
Cop 1598-1640 (Ptd, Dwelly 1, 1913); M 1754-1837 (NSMI); B 1699-1980 (SBDB); M 1598-1640 (BT), 1699-1837 (SMI)
Cop (Mf) 1598-1854 (BT) (SLC, SRO)

BROMPTON RALPH St Mary (424) (Williton and Freemanors Hundred; Williton Union)
OR CM 1557-1978, Banns 1754-1812, B 1558-1914 (SRO)
BT 1602-03, one between 1603-42, 1605-07, 1609, 1611-12, 1617-18, 1621-23, 1629-30, 1634-35,
  1640-41, 1663-56, 1669-70, 1704-11, 1721-24, 1726-27, 1731-32, 1757-58, 1774, 1780-81,
  1782-84, 1786-88, 1788-1836 (SRO)
Cop 1603-42 (SG); CM 1557-1716 (SRO); B 1686-1869 (SBDB); M 1557-1837 (SMI);
  CM 1558-1899 (DCI)
Cop (Mf) 1602-1836 (BT) (SLC, SRO); C 1557-1902, M 1557-1901, B 1558-1900 (SLC)

BROMPTON RALPH (Independent) f 1792 b 1840

BROMPTON REGIS St Mary (802) (Williton and Freemanors Hundred; Dulverton Union)
OR C 1690-1848, M 1690-1954, Banns 1754-1872, B 1690-1870 (1690-1756 damaged) (SRO)
BT 1597-98, 1605, 1608-09, 1611-12, 1616, 1621-22, one between 1624-40, 1629-30, 1634,
  1836-40, 1662-83, 1666-67, 1670, 1672, 1678-79, 1698, 1704-07, ?1731-32, 1753-56, 1758,
  1762-64, 1767-74, 1778-1837, CB 1838-41 (SRO)
Cop 1638 (Ptd, Dwelly 1, 1913); B 1751-1863 (SBDB); M 1638 (BT), 1690-1837 (SMI);
  C 1690-1882, M 1690-1899 (DCI)
Cop (Mf) C 1690-1882, M 1690-1900, Banns 1754-1818, 1824-61, 1885-1901, B 1690-1870
  (SG, SLC); 1597-1841 (BT) (SLC, SRO)

BROMPTON REGIS (United Methodist) f 1822 b 1854
OR ZC 1823-37 (PRO: RG 4/2801)
Cop (Mf) ZC 1823-37 (SLC, SRO)

BROMPTON REGIS Bury (United Methodist) b 1889 (K 1931)

BROOMFIELD All Saints (503) (peculiar of the Dean and Chapter of Wells until 1845)
  (Andersfield Hundred; Bridgwater Union)
OR C 1630-1870, M 1630-1837, Banns 1754-1803, 1824-99, B 1630-1812 (SRO); B 1813+ (Inc)
BT 1598-99, 1605-08, 1611-12, 1621-23, 1629-31, 1634-37, 1640-41, 1813-23, 1828-29 (SRO);
  1745, 1749-59, 1762-64, 1767-68 (SRO: D/D/Pd:26/4)
Cop M 1630-1812 (Ptd, Phillimore 6, 1905); C 1630-1870, B 1630-1812 (SRO);
  M 1630-1812 (Boyd); M 1630-1837 (SMI); C 1630-1870, M 1813-37 (DCI)
Cop (Mf) C 1630-1870, M 1630-1837, Banns 1754-1803, 1824-99, B 1630-1812 (SG, SLC);
  1598-1829 (BT) (SLC, SRO)

BROOMFIELD Shellthorn (Independent) b 1870 cl *c*1949

BRUSHFORD St Nicholas (351) (Williton and Freemanors Hundred; Dulverton Union)
OR C 1558-1894, M 1558-1976, Banns 1754-1815, B 1558-1912 (gap CMB 1624-30) (SRO)
BT 1598-99, 1605-06, 1609-14, 1621-23, 1627-30, 1634-35, 1637-38, 1640-41, 1662-64, 1666-67,
  1667-73, 1678-79, 1698-99, 1704-08, 1721-26, 1728-29, 1731-32, 1735-36, 1744-55, 1757-59,
  1764-85, 1767, 1771-73, 1775, 1777-84, 1786-92, 1794, 1796-97, 1800, 1802-34 (SRO)
Cop 1622 (Ptd, Dwelly 1, 1913); C 1559-1663, M 1559-1753 (SRO); B 1813-1912 (SBDB);
  M 1622 (BT), 1750-1837 (SMI); C 1559-1894, M 1559-1899 (DCI)
Cop (Mf) C 1558-1887, M 1558-1885, Banns 1754-1815, B 1558-1905 (SG, SLC);
  1598-1834 (BT) (SLC, SRO)

BRUSHFORD (Wesleyan) (K 1931)

BRUTON St Mary the Virgin (2,223) (Bruton Hundred; Wincanton Union)
OR C 1554-1876, M 1554-1922, Banns 1883-1934, B 1554-1928 (SRO)
BT 1594-1602, 1615-16, 1629-30, 1636, 1638-39, 1663, 1669-70, 1749-52, 1765, 1768-69, 1786,
  1800-22, 1824-29, 1831-32, CB 1841-42 (SRO)
Cop 1554-1680 (Ptd, PRS 60, 1908); 1681-1812 (Ptd, PRS 78, 1911); M 1554-1812 (Boyd);
  B 1554-1844 (SBDB); M 1554-1837 (SMI)
Cop (Mf) 1594-1842 (BT) (SLC, SRO); C 1554-1876, M 1554-1885, B 1554-1886 (SLC)

BRUTON Union Chapel, High Street (Independent) b 1803 (K 1931)
OR ZC 1802-97 (SRO); ZC 1802-37 (PRO: RG 4/1545)
Cop (Mf) ZC 1802-37 (SLC, SRO)

BRUTON (Wesleyan) b 1848 (K 1931)

BRYMPTON D'EVERCY St Andrew (100) (Stone Hundred; Yeovil Union)
OR CB 1699-1812, M 1701-1836, Banns 1760-98 (SRO); CB 1813+ (Inc)
BT 1602, 1605-07, 1611-15, 1617-19, 1622-23, 1629-30, 1634, 1636-40, 1662-64, 1666-67,
    1669-70, 1678-79, 1695, 1704-05, 1714-15, 1728-33, 1744-45, 1749-52, 1763, 1768-71, 1773,
    1801-21, 1834-35 (SRO)
Cop C 1602-95, M 1602-95, B 1602-95 (Ptd, Dwelly 1, 1913); M 1813-37 (Ts SG);
    B 1785-1812 (SBDB); M 1602-95 (BT), 1699-1837 (SMI)
Cop (Mf) 1602-1835 (BT) (SLC, SRO); CB 1699-1812, M 1701-1836, Banns 1760-98 (SLC)

BUCKLAND DINHAM St Michael and All Angels (532) (peculiar of the Prebendary of Buckland
Dinham until 1845) (Kilmersdon Hundred; Frome Union)
OR C 1540-1973, M 1540-1837, Banns 1754-1812, 1824-82, B 1540-1893 (SRO)
BT 1603-09, 1611-12, 1615-17, 1622-23, 1629-31, one between 1631-60, 1635-37, 1665-66,
    1741-42, 1801-08, 1813-20, 1823-41, CB 1842-53 (SRO); 1686-87, 1694-98, 1700, 1702-18,
    1720-21, 1724-25, 1732-34, 1736, 1740-41, 1743-44, 1750-53, 1755-61 (SRO: D/D/Ppb:17)
Cop 1603-30 (Ptd, Dwelly 1, 1913); B 1800-79 (SBDB); M 1569-1837 (SMI)
Cop (Mf) 1603-1853 (BT) (SLC, SRO); C 1540-1886, M 1540-1837, Banns 1824-82, B 1540-1886
    (SLC)

BUCKLAND DINHAM (Wesleyan) b 1811 (K 1931)

BUCKLAND ST MARY (646) (part Abdick and Bulstone Hundred, part Martock Hundred,
    part South Petherton Hundred; Chard Union)
OR C 1540-1965, M 1538-1978, Banns 1754-1821, B 1538-1990 (gap CMB 1642-1705) (SRO)
BT 1597-1603, one between 1603-35, 1606-14, 1617-23, 1629-30, 1634-40, 1662-64, 1669-70,
    1731-33, 1742-43, 1750-51, 1758, 1767, 1769-79, 1781-87, 1789-90, 1792, 1794-1804,
    1807-28, 1830 (SRO)
Cop M 1538-1812 (Ptd, Phillimore 4, 1902); CB 1599-1617 (Ptd, Dwelly 1, 1913); C 1540-1813,
    B 1538-1812 (SRO); M 1538-1812 (Boyd); B 1813-73 (SBDB); M 1538-1837 (SMI);
    C 1540-1886, M 1813-37 (DCI) (DCI)
Cop (Mf) C 1540-97, 1634-41, 1706-1886, M 1538-1641, 1706-22, 1730-1886, Banns 1754-1821,
    B 1538-1641, 1706-1882 (SG, SLC); 1597-1830 (BT) (SLC, SRO)

BUCKLAND ST MARY Hare (Independent) f 1739 b 1865

BUCKLAND, WEST St Mary (793) (West Kingsbury Hundred; Wellington Union)
OR C 1678-1924, M 1538-1975 (defective 1617-82), B 1538-1944 (1538-1687 defective) (SRO)
BT 1607-08, 1610, 1621-24, 1629-30, 1635-40, 1662-63, 1675-76, 1707-08, 1725-29, 1733-34,
    1748-51, 1755-57, 1759-66, 1770-78, 1780-89, 1791-1802, 1804-24, 1826-38, 1840-41 (SRO)
Cop M 1538-1812 (Ptd, Phillimore 8, 1906); C 1607-29, B 1607-29 (Ptd, Dwelly 1, 1913);
    M 1538-1812 (Boyd); C 1678-1784 (SCDB); B 1538-1862 (SBDB); M 1538-1837 (SMI);
    C 1678-1897, M 1538-1899 (DCI)
Cop (Mf) 1607-1841 (BT) (SLC, SRO); C 1678-1886, M 1538-1617, 1682-1701, 1710-1885,
    Banns 1846-86, B 1538-1645, 1673-87, 1702-1885 (SLC)

BUCKLAND, WEST (Wesleyan) (Lewis 1831)

BUCKLAND, WEST Chelmsine (Plymouth Brethren) b 1868

BURNETT St Michael (82) (Keynsham Hundred; Keynsham Union)
OR CB 1749-1811, M 1749-1833, 1845-46 (SRO); CB 1813+ (Inc)
BT 1592-97, 1599-1600, one between 1600-15, 1603-06, 1611, 1617-18, 1621-23, 1629, 1634-35,
   1639-41, one between 1642-64, 1662, 1667, 1750-51, 1757-58, 1798-1815, 1817-20, 1823,
   1825-34, 1853 (SRO)
Cop 1599-1639 (Ptd, Dwelly 1, 1913); C 1749-1917, M 1749-1812, 1845-1909, B 1749-1815
   (SRO); B 1749-1811 (SBDB); M 1599-1639 (BT), 1749-1837 (SMI)
Cop (Mf) 1592-1853 (BT) (SLC, SRO); CB 1749-1811, M 1749-1833, 1845-46 (SLC)

BURNETT (Wesleyan) (K 1931)

BURNHAM ON SEA Cemetery, Westfield Road opened 1885 (4½ acres)
OR B 1886-1996 (SRO) (with indexes)
Cop B 1881-1996 (SBDB)

BURNHAM ON SEA St Andrew (1,113) (Bempstone Hundred; Axbridge Union)
OR C 1630-1966, M 1630-1985, Banns 1754-97, 1823-91, B 1630-1986 (SRO)
BT two between 1604-60, 1608-09, 1611 defective, c.1611, 1617-18, 1622-23, 1629-30, 1636-37,
   1640-41, 1666-68, one between 1680-1727, 1684-85, 1702-05, 1720-21, 1741-42, 1744-45,
   1748-51, 1754, 1756, 1759, 1768-82, 1789, 1802-28, CB 1846-47 (SRO)
Cop C 1630-1840, M 1630-1837, B 1630-1811 (Ts I SG, SLC, SRO); C 1768-1840 (SCDB);
   B 1768-1850 (SBDB); M 1754-1837 (SMI)
Cop (Mf) 1608-1847 (BT) (SLC, SRO); C 1630-1894, M 1630-1889, Banns 1823-91,
   B 1630-1892 (SLC)

BURNHAM ON SEA St Peter, Highbridge Road b 1928
OR CMB 1928+ (Inc)

BURNHAM ON SEA College Street (Baptist) b 1843 (K 1931)

BURNHAM ON SEA College Street (Wesleyan) (Weston super Mare Circuit) b 1880 (K 1931)

BURNHAM ON SEA Sacred Heart of Jesus, Oxford Street (Roman Catholic) b 1889 (K 1931)

BURRINGTON Holy Trinity (579) (chapelry in Wrington until 1758) (Brent with Wrington
   Hundred; Axbridge Union)
OR C 1687-1945, M 1685-1837, Banns 1754-1810, 1824-86, B 1689-1888 (SRO)
BT 1599-1600, 1606-08, 1611-13, 1616-18, 1621-23, 1628-29, 1634, 1637-41, 1662-63, 1750-51,
   1802-15, 1817, 1819, 1821-25, 1831, 1834-35, CB 1838, CMB 1839-40, CB 1841, CMB 1842,
   CB 1843-44, CMB 1845-46, CB 1847-48, CMB 1849-50, CB 1851, CMB 1852-53,
   CB 1854-57, 1862-66, CMB 1867-68 (SRO)
Cop C 1598-1641, 1662-63, 1687-90, 1695-1841, M 1598-1640, 1663, 1687-1837, B 1598-1641,
   1662-63, 1687-91, 1695-1838 (Ts I SG, SLC, SRO); M 1754-1837 (NSMI); B 1813-78
   (SBDB); M 1598-1663 (BT), 1687-1837 (SMI)
Cop (Mf) 1599-1868 (BT) (SLC, SRO); C 1687-1885, M 1687-1837, Banns 1754-1810, 1824-86,
   B 1687-1888 (SLC)

BURRINGTON Meeting House (Society of Friends) (Monthly Meeting of North Division)
   (Berington in PRO lists)
OR Z 1661-1775, M 1664-1706, 1729-42, B 1663-1767 (PRO: RG 6/1450)

BURROWBRIDGE St Michael (created from Lyng, Othery, Westonzoyland, Middlezoy,
   Bridgwater, North Petherton and Stoke St Gregory, 1840) (Bridgwater Union)
OR C 1838-1954, M 1838-1988, B 1838-1969 (SRO)
BT CB 1838-46, 1848-61 (SRO)
Cop (Mf) 1838-61 (BT) (SLC, SRO)

BURROWBRIDGE Ebenezer Chapel (Baptist) b 1837 (K 1931)
OR M 1931-53 (SRO)

BURTLE St Philip and St James (created from Chilton Polden and Edington, 1856)
(Bridgwater Union)
OR C 1839-1900 (SRO)
Cop (Mf) C 1839-1900 (SLC)

BUTCOMBE St Michael (242) (Hartcliffe with Bedminster Hundred; Axbridge Union)
OR C 1692-1908, MB 1693-1983, Banns 1759-1809, 1827-1901 (gap B 1808-12) (SRO)
BT 1604-12, 1615-18, 1621-24, 1629-30, 1634-38, 1640, 1660-62, 1666-67, 1679, 1732-33,
1801-04, 1806-21, 1823-35 (SRO)
Cop M 1605-1835 (Ptd, E.E. Britten and E.J. Holmyard, 1913); C 1605-79, B 1605-79
(Ptd, Dwelly 1, 1913); CB 1693-1805, M 1693-1754 (SRO); M 1754-1837 (NSMI);
M 1693-1835 (Boyd); B 1692-1906 (SBDB); M 1605-79 (BT), 1693-1837 (SMI)
Cop (Mf) 1604-1835 (BT) (SLC, SRO); C 1692-1903, M 1693-1901, Banns 1759-1809, 1827-1901,
B 1693-1906 (SLC)

BUTCOMBE Meeting House (Society of Friends) 'remains of Quaker burial ground' (K 1931)

BUTLEIGH St Leonard (952) (Whitley Hundred; Wells Union)
OR C 1578-1942, M 1578-1642, 1653-1983 (gap 1713-22), B 1578-1642, 1654-1987 (SRO)
BT one between 1578-1610, 1598-99, 1606-17, 1622-23, 1634-35, 1637-41, 1672-73, 1731-33,
1739-40, 1749-52, 1755-58, 1765-69, 1778-79, 1800-17, 1822-38, M 1839 (SRO)
Cop 1598-1637 (Ptd, Dwelly 1, 1913); B 1786-1857 (SBDB); M 1578-1837 (SMI)
Cop (Mf) 1598-1839 (BT) (SLC, SRO); C 1578-1676, 1714-1886, M 1578-1676, 1723-1885,
B 1578-1676, 1714-1886 (SLC)

BUTLEIGH (Wesleyan) b 1883 (K 1931)

CADBURY, NORTH St Michael (1,109) (Catsash Hundred; Wincanton Union)
OR C 1558-1867, M 1558-1837, 1931-71, Banns 1803-14, 1846-86, B 1558-1905 (SRO)
BT 1598-99, 1605-10, 1611-12 (North or South Cadbury), 1622-24, one between 1628-42, 1636-37,
1639-41, 1663-64, 1667-70, 1678-80, 1732-33, 1748, 1800-37, CB 1838-42 (SRO)
Cop 1558-1734 (SG, SRO); C 1735-1812 (SCDB); B 1735-1970 (SBDB); M 1558-1837 (SMI)
Cop (Mf) 1598-1842 (BT) (SLC, SRO); C 1558-1867, M 1558-1837, Banns 1803-14, 1846-86,
B 1558-1812 (SLC)

CADBURY, NORTH Galhampton (Independent) f 1662 b 1873 (K 1931)

CADBURY, NORTH (Wesleyan) b 1847

CADBURY, SOUTH St Thomas a Becket (231) (Catsash Hundred; Wincanton Union)
OR C 1559-1931, M 1559-1992, Banns 1823-85, B 1559-1993 (SRO)
BT one between 1587-1608, 1601-04, 1607-09, 1611-13, 1617-18, 1621-24, 1629-30, 1636-39,
1663-64, 1666-70, 1672-73, 1678-80, 1800-21, 1824-31, 1833-36, CB 1847-48 (SRO)
Cop C 1607-79, M 1607-79, B 1607-79 (Ptd, Dwelly 1, 1913); M 1800-37 (Ts SG);
B 1790-1837 (SBDB); M 1559-1729, 1754-1837 (SMI)
Cop (Mf) 1601-1848 (BT) (SLC, SRO); C 1559-1887, M 1559-1837, Banns 1823-85,
B 1559-1812 (SLC)

CAMEL, QUEEN St Barnabas (664) (Catsash Hundred; Wincanton Union)
OR C 1703-1899, M 1639-1993 (gap 1754-73), Banns 1774-1800, B 1639-1984 (SRO)
BT 1601-14, 1616-17, 1621-24, 1630-31, 1636-37, 1639-40, 1663-64, one between 1667-97,
1668-69, 1672-73, 1733-34, 1756-57, 1775-76, 1801-24, 1832-37, CB 1838-39, 1841-49 (SRO)
Cop CB 1607 (Ptd, Dwelly 1, 1913); C 1703-32 (SCDB); B 1639-1840 (SBDB);
M 1601-1837 (OR & BT) (SMI)
Cop (Mf) 1601-1849 (BT) (SLC, SRO)

CAMEL, QUEEN (Wesleyan) (Lewis 1831)

CAMEL, WEST All Saints (322) (Somerton Hundred; Yeovil Union)
OR C 1710-1930, M 1710-1993, Banns 1754-1812, B 1678-1993 (SRO)
BT 1597-98, 1607-09, 1613-14, 1622-24, 1627, 1629-30, 1634, 1636-37, 1639-41, 1662-67, 1744,
    1751, 1775, 1806-37, CB 1840-67, 1869-74, 1876 (SRO)
Cop 1597-1629 (Ptd, Dwelly 1, 1913); M 1597, 1607-08, 1613, 1622, 1627, 1629, 1631, 1636,
    1638-40, 1662 (BT), 1710-54, 1774-1837 (SMI)
Cop (Mf) 1597-1876 (BT) (SLC, SRO)

CAMEL, WEST (Wesleyan) (K 1931)

CAMELEY St James (658) (Chewton Hundred; Clutton Union)
OR C 1592-1863, M 1561-1979, Banns 1755-1812, 1824-92, B 1561-1902 (gap B 1620-38) (SRO)
BT 1603, 1605-11, 1613, 1622-24, 1634-40, one between 1640-69 (either Cameley or Hinton
    Blewett), 1663-64, 1666-69, 1678-79, 1734-35, 1749-51, 1755-56, 1800-36 (SRO)
Cop 1605-79 (Ptd, Dwelly 1, 1913); M 1754-1837 (NSMI); C 1750-1812 (SCDB);
    B 1750-1879 (SBDB); M 1561-1837 (SMI)
Cop (Mf) 1603-1836 (BT) (SLC, SRO); C 1592-1862, M 1561-1900, Banns 1755-1812, 1824-92,
    B 1561-1902 (SLC)

CAMERTON St Peter (1,326) (Wellow Hundred; Clutton Union)
OR C 1654-1912, M 1654-1901, B 1654-1941 (CMB 1654-71 defective; gap CMB 1672-99) (SRO)
BT 1601-02, 1606-10, ?1611 (?Camerton), 1613-16, 1623-24, 1634-37, 1639-40, 1663-64, 1666,
    1668-69, 1723-24, 1732-33, 1800-14, 1816-27, 1829-37 (SRO)
Cop 1601-40 (Ptd, Dwelly 1, 1913); 1654-1812 (Ms I SG); M 1754-1837 (NSMI);
    B 1700-1941 (SBDB); M 1607-08 (BT), 1754-1837 (SMI)
Cop (Mf) 1601-1837 (BT) (SLC, SRO); C 1654-79, 1684-98, 1700-11, 1714-1912, M 1654-71,
    1714-1901, Banns 1754-1854, B 1654-78, 1684-85, 1700-06, 1714-1941 (SG)

CAMERTON (Wesleyan) (Somerset Circuit) b 1809 (K 1931)
OR C 1843-1900 (circuit) (Bristol RO); C 1857-1975 (chapel) (Bristol RO)
Cop (Mf) C 1843-1975 (Bristol RO, SLC)

CAMERTON (Baptist) (Lewis 1831)

CAMERTON Carlingcott (Wesleyan)
OR C 1843-1932 (Bristol RO)
Cop (Mf) C 1843-1932 (Bristol RO, SLC)

CAMERTON Tunley (Wesleyan) b 1883

CAMERTON Carlingcott (United Methodist)
OR C 1908-36 (Bristol RO)
Cop (Mf) C 1908-36 (Bristol RO, SLC)

CANNINGTON Cemetery
OR B 1867-1979 (SRO)

CANNINGTON St Mary (1,437) (Cannington Hundred; Bridgwater Union)
OR C 1559-1952 (gap 1645-63), M 1559-1988 (gaps 1648-53, 1655-59), Banns 1768-1902,
    B 1559-1899 (gap 1654-63) (SRO)
BT two between 1582-1618, 1599, 1607-11, 1609-10, 1611, 1621-24, 1636-40, 1663-64, 1771-74,
    1789-90, 1796-97, 1801-25, 1827-35 (SRO)
Cop M 1559-1812 (Ptd, Phillimore 6, 1905); CB 1607-39 (Ptd, Dwelly 1, 1913);
    M 1559-1812 (Boyd); B 1786-1848 (SBDB); M 1559-1837 (SMI)
Cop (Mf) 1599-1835 (BT) (SLC, SRO); C 1559-1901, M 1559-1900, Banns 1823-1902,
    B 1559-1899 (SLC)

CANNINGTON Holy Name (Roman Catholic) chapel of Clifford family in 18th century reb 1830 cl *c*1919
OR C 1780-1838, M 1779-1833, D 1783-1800, 1830 (Inc Bridgewater)
Cop 1779-1838 (Ts I SG, SRO); M 1813-37 (SMI)

CANNINGTON Meeting House (Independent) f 1799 b 1826 (K 1931)

CANNINGTON Combwich (Wesleyan) f 1838 b 1847

CARHAMPTON St John the Baptist (658) (peculiar jurisdiction of Dean of Wells until 1845) (Carhampton Hundred; Williton Union)
OR C 1634-1858, M 1634-1836, Banns 1813-14, 1824-82, B 1634-1888 (gap CMB 1653-76) (SRO)
BT 1598-99, 1606-07, 1609, ?1611-12, 1621-23, 1629-30, 1635-36, 1663-64, 1669-70, 1677-78, 1695-96, 1702-03, 1813, 1816-18, 1820, 1822, 1829-32, CB 1847-64 (SRO); 1741, 1747-51, 1753, 1755, 1758-63, 1765-75, 1778-82, 1785 (SRO: D/D/Pd:26/5)
Cop CMB 1598-1837 (SRO); B 1797-1875 (SBDB); M 1634-1837 (SMI); C 1634-1858, M 1634-1836 (DCI)
Cop (Mf) C 1634-1858, M 1634-1836, Banns 1813-14, 1824-82, B 1634-1888 (SG); 1598-1864 (BT) (SLC, SRO); C 1634-1858, M 1634-1836, Banns 1813-14, 1824-82, B 1634-1888 (SLC)

CARHAMPTON (Methodist) b 1839
OR C 1803-72 (circuit) (SRO)

CASTLE CARY Cemetery opened 1897 (K 1931)

CASTLE CARY All Saints (1,794) (Catsash Hundred; Wincanton Union)
OR C 1564-1889, M 1564-1891, Banns 1754-1823, B 1564-1860 (CMB 1564-1635 defective) (SRO)
BT one between 1592-1623, 1607-08, 1611-13, 1615-18, 1621-24, 1634-35, 1639-40, 1663-64, 1666-69, 1678-80, 1724-25, 1732-33, 1802-37, CB 1838-41, 1843-49, 1851-54 (SRO)
Cop 1607-40 (Ptd, Dwelly 1, 1913); CB 1564-1775, M 1564-1772 (SG, SRO); B 1770-1856 (SBDB); M 1564-1837 (SMI)
Cop (Mf) 1607-1854 (BT) (SLC, SRO); C 1564-1886, M 1564-1749, 1837-85, Banns 1754-1823, B 1564-1860 (SLC)

CASTLE CARY (Independent) b 1816 (K 1931)

CASTLE CARY (Wesleyan) (Lewis 1831) b 1839 (K 1931)
OR C 1850-1927, B 1858-1966 (SRO)

CATCOTT St Peter (651) (chapelry in Moorlinch until 1903) (Whitley Hundred; Bridgwater Union)
OR C 1691-1928, M 1733-1838, Banns 1754-1807, 1824-77, B 1691-1892 (SRO)
BT 1597-1600, 1603-04, 1607-18, 1621-22, 1634-41, 1662, 1720-21, 1732-33, 1756-58, 1781, 1784, 1787-1811, 1813-31, CB 1840-48 (SRO)
Cop 1597-1640 (Ptd, Dwelly 1, 1913); C 1733-1812 (SCDB); B 1733-1872 (SBDB); M 1597-1640 (BT), 1733-1837 (SMI)
Cop (Mf) C 1691-1901, M 1733-36, 1746-1805, 1813-38, 1902, Banns 1754-1812, 1824-77, B 1691-1893 (SG, SLC); 1597-1848 (BT) (SLC, SRO)

CATCOTT Burtle (Primitive Methodist) b 1859 (K 1931)

CATCOTT (Wesleyan) b 1877 (K 1931)
OR C 1848-1925 (SRO)

CATCOTT (Primitive Methodist) b 1880

CHAFFCOMBE St Michael (243) (South Petherton Hundred; Chard Union)
OR C 1680-1906, M 1682-1984, B 1680-1992 (SRO)
BT 1598-1600, 1606-09, 1611-12, 1621-24, 1634-40, 1663-64, 1672, 1728, 1732-33,
    1749-50, 1763-68, 1773-74, 1789-90, 1800-03, 1805-10, 1812-13, 1815-36 (SRO)
Cop C 1623-38, M 1623-38, B 1623-38 (Ptd, Dwelly 1, 1913); M 1700-1837 (Ts I SG);
    B 1679-1992 (SBDB); M 1623-38 (BT), 1680-1837 (SMI); C 1680-1890, M 1680-1837 (DCI)
Cop (Mf) 1598-1836 (SLC, SRO); C 1680-1887, M 1680-1757, 1785-1885, B 1678-1812 (SLC)

CHANTRY Holy Trinity (created from Whatley, Elm and Mells, 1846) (Frome Union)
OR CMB 1846+ (Inc)

CHANTRY (Primitive Methodist) (K 1931)

CHAPEL ALLERTON *see* **ALLERTON, CHAPEL**

CHARD Board of Guardians
OR Z 1848-1914, D 1848-1914 (SRO)

CHARD Cemetery opened 1857 (5½ acres)

CHARD St Mary the Virgin (5,141) (East Kingsbury Hundred; Chard Union)
OR C 1649-1981, M 1540-44, 1652-1981, Banns 1798-1810, 1814-1960, B 1649-1916,
    1961-81 (SRO)
BT one between 1605-35, 1609-13, 1621-24, 1629-30, 1636-40, 1662-63, 1675-76, 1701-02,
    1705-06, 1731-34, 1750 (? or 1730), 1756-57, 1763-64, 1774-76, 1806-23, 1825 (SRO)
Cop C 1649-1729, M 1540-44, 1652-1729, B 1649-1711 (Ts I SG, SRO); B 1731-1833 (SBDB);
    M 1540-44 (OR), 1621-39 (BT), 1652-1837 (SMI); C 1649-1899, M 1540-1889 (DCI)
Cop (Mf) 1609-1825 (BT) (SLC, SRO); C 1649-1900, M 1540-44, 1652-1899, Banns 1798-1901,
    B 1649-1895 (SLC)

CHARD The Good Shepherd, East Street, Furnham b 1872 (created from Chard, 1897)
OR C 1893-1963, M 1893-1971 (SRO)

CHARD Holyrood Street (Baptist) f 1653 (K 1931)
OR Z 1786-1837, B 1786-93 (PRO: RG 4/34, 2869)
Cop (Mf) Z 1786-1837, B 1786-93 (SLC, SRO)

CHARD Fore Street (previously High Street) (Independent) f 1672 (K 1931)
OR C 1786-1903, M 1968-74, B 1812-82 (SRO); ZC 1786-1837, B 1812-18 (PRO: RG 4/1546,
    2690)
Cop (Mf) ZC 1786-1837, B 1812-18 (SLC, SRO)

CHARD Meeting House (Society of Friends)
Cop B 1795-1807 (SBDB)

CHARD Fore Street (Wesleyan) f 1878 b 1895 (K 1931)

CHARD (Plymouth Brethren) b 1884

CHARD The English Martyrs, East Street (Roman Catholic) f 1920 (K 1931)

CHARLCOMBE St Mary (107) (Hampton and Claverton Hundred; Bath Union)
OR C 1712-1812, M 1719-1980, Banns 1815, B 1709-1812 (SRO); CB 1813+ (Inc)
BT 1607-08, 1611-13, 1622-23, 1629-30, 1634-39, 1663-69, 1732-33, 1746-50, 1756-57, 1796,
    1798-1815, 1817-19, 1822 (SRO)
Cop 1607-39 (Ptd, Dwelly 1, 1913); C 1709-1812, M 1709-1837, B 1710-1812 (Ts I SG, Bath Lib,
    SRO); M 1754-1837 (NSMI); M 1638 (BT), 1756-1837 (SMI)
Cop (Mf) 1607-1822 (BT) (SLC, SRO); C 1712-1812, M 1723-1900, B 1709-1900 (SLC)

CHARLTON ADAM alias EAST CHARLTON St Peter and St Paul (480) (Somerton Hundred; Langport Union)
OR C 1704-1877, M 1707-1837, Banns 1828-69, B 1704-1927 (SRO)
BT 1607-10, 1612-13, 1615-16, 1623-24, 1629-30, 1634-41, 1661-62, 1664-65, 1668-70, 1704-05, 1748-49, 1805-16, 1819, 1821-25, 1827-30 (SRO)
Cop M 1707-1812 (Ptd, Phillimore 1, 1898); C 1607-39, M 1607-39, B 1607-39 (Ptd, Dwelly 1, 1913); M 1707-1812 (Boyd); B 1704-1900 (SBDB); M 1607-39 (BT), 1707-1837 (SMI)
Cop (Mf) 1607-1830 (BT) (SLC, SRO); C 1704-1877, M 1704-1837, Banns 1828-69, B 1704-1901 (SLC)

CHARLTON ADAM (Wesleyan) b 1883 (K 1931)

CHARLTON HORETHORNE St Peter and St Paul (485) (Horethorne Hundred; Wincanton Union)
OR C 1695-1988 (gap 1734-38), M 1695-1987 (gap 1733-54), Banns 1754-86, 1870-1902, B 1695-1988 (gaps 1734-38, 1743-62) (SRO)
BT 1598-99, 1602-03, 1605-08, 1611-12, 1615-17, 1621-23, 1628-30, 1635-37, 1640-41, 1662-65, 1668-70, 1733-34, 1743-44, 1749-52, 1756-58, 1765, 1775-84, 1802-37, CB 1838-39, CMB 1846, CB 1847-49, CMB 1850, CB 1851, CMB 1852-53, CB 1855-63 (SRO)
Cop B 1734-1876 (SBDB); M 1598-1641 (BT), 1695-1736, 1753-1837 (SMI)
Cop (Mf) C 1695-1860, M 1695-1806, 1813-37, Banns 1754-86, 1870-1902, B 1695-1743, 1762-1889 (SG, SLC); 1598-1863 (BT) (SLC, SRO)

CHARLTON HORETHORNE (Wesleyan) b 1861 cl 1928

CHARLTON MACKRELL alias WEST CHARLTON St Mary the Virgin (366) (Somerton Hundred; Langport Union)
OR C 1575-1874, M 1575-1837, Banns 1754-1820, 1824-1900, 1909-66, B 1575-1813 (SRO); B 1813+ (Inc)
BT 1599-1603, 1605-08, 1615-18, 1621-24, 1629-30, 1634-37, 1639-40, 1662-64, 1704-08, 1730-32, 1748-49, 1751-52, 1806-13, 1815-18, 1821-26 (SRO)
Cop M 1575-1812 (Ptd, Phillimore 1, 1898); C 1599-1663, B 1599-1663 (Ptd, Dwelly 1, 1913); CMB 1575-1847 (SRO); M 1575-1812 (Boyd); C 1783-1812 (SCDB); B 1783-1812 (SBDB); M 1575-1837 (SMI)
Cop (Mf) 1599-1826 (BT) (SLC, SRO); C 1575-1874, M 1575-1837, Banns 1754-1820, 1824-1900, B 1575-1813 (SLC)

CHARLTON MUSGROVE St Stephen (415) (Norton Ferris Hundred; Wincanton Union)
OR C 1534-1959, M 1534-1985, Banns 1754-1819, 1925-83, B 1534-1940 (SRO)
BT 1598-99, 1602-03, 1606-09, 1611-24, one between 1617-60, 1621-22, 1623-24, 1629, 1634-40, 1663-64, 1667-69, 1672-73, 1678-80, 1704-05, 1707-08, 1732-33, 1748-49, 1752, 1756, 1800-27, 1829-30, 1840, CB 1842 (SRO)
Cop 1615-79 (Ptd, Dwelly 1, 1913); B 1790-1861 (SBDB); M 1541-1837 (SMI)
Cop (Mf) 1598-1842 (BT) (SLC, SRO)

CHARLTON MUSGROVE (Baptist) b 1830 (K 1931)

CHARLTON, QUEEN St Margaret (168) (chapelry in Keynsham until 1741) (Keynsham Hundred; Keynsham Union)
OR CB 1562-1812, M 1562-1889, Banns 1823+ (SRO); CB 1813+ (Inc)
BT 1602-03, 1606-07, 1611-14, 1621-24, 1629-30, 1634-37, 1639-40, 1663-64, 1798-1854 (SRO)
Cop C 1568-1754, M 1567-1754, B 1562-1754 (Ms and Ts I SG, Bath Lib, British Lib); 1562-1915 (SRO); M 1750-1837 (SMI)
Cop (Mf) 1602-1854 (BT) (SLC, SRO); CB 1562-1812, M 1562-1889 (SLC)

CHARLYNCH St Mary (199) (Cannington Hundred; Bridgwater Union)
OR CB 1744-1981, M 1754-79, 1839-1982 (SRO)
BT 1594-97, 1599, 1605-09, 1617, 1621-22, 1629-31, 1635-37, 1639-40, 1662-64, 1666-68,
    1678-80, 1705-10, 1718-21, 1725-26, 1731-32, 1753, 1790-91, 1796-97, 1799-1806, 1810-27,
    1834 (SRO)
Cop M 1754-79 (Ptd, Phillimore 6, 1905); C 1607-63, M 1607-1779, B 1607-63 (Ptd, Dwelly 1,
    1913); CM 1593-1946, B 1593-1981 (Ts I SRO); M 1754-79 (Boyd); B 1744-1977 (SBDB);
    M 1593-1812 (SMI)
Cop (Mf) 1594-1834 (BT) (SLC, SRO)

CHARTERHOUSE (Winterstoke Hundred; Axbridge Union) (extra-parochial place, divided in
    1933 between Blagdon and Cheddar)

CHEDDAR St Michael burial ground
BT B 1886-89 (SRO)
Cop (Mf) 1886-89 (BT) (SLC, SRO)

CHEDDAR St Andrew (1,980) (peculiar of the Dean of Wells until 1845) (Winterstoke Hundred;
    Axbridge Union)
OR CMB 1678+, Banns 1823+ (Inc)
BT 1601-02, 1605-18, 1621-24, 1631, 1635-38, one between 1640-61, 1662-65, 1675-76, 1678,
    1684-85, 1695-96, 1747, 1749-51, 1753-55, 1757-59, 1769-84, 1786-89, 1791-1802, 1813-34
    (1701-02, 1748 in peculiar series) (SRO)
Cop 1608-75 (Ptd, Dwelly 1, 1913); B 1739-1841 (SBDB); M 1608-75 (BT), 1754-1834 (SMI)
Cop (Mf) 1601-1834 (BT) (SLC, SRO); C 1601-1875, M 1601-1907, B 1601-1920 (SRO)

CHEDDAR (Baptist) b 1831 (K 1931)

CHEDDAR (Wesleyan) (Lewis 1831) b 1853 reb 1897 (K 1931)
OR C 1838-68 (Bristol RO)
Cop (Mf) C 1838-68 (Bristol RO, SLC)

CHEDDAR (Reformed Episcopal) b 1853

CHEDDAR (Plymouth Brethren) b 1870 and 1875

CHEDDAR Our Lady Queen of the Apostles, The Barrows (Roman Catholic) b 1945

CHEDDON FITZPAINE St Mary (325) (Taunton and Taunton Dean Hundred; Taunton Union)
OR C 1558-1898, M 1559-1836, Banns 1754-1812, B 1558-1959 (SRO)
BT 1602-11, ?1613, 1621-22, 1629-30, 1635-41, 1663-64, 1667-70, 1707-08, 1720-21, 1726-29,
    1732-33, 1739-40, 1749-51, 1754, 1759, 1762, 1768, 1770, 1775, 1789, 1801-37, CB 1838-59
    (SRO)
Cop M 1559-1812 (Ptd, Phillimore 8, 1906); C 1607-37, B 1607-37 (Ptd, Dwelly 1, 1913);
    C 1637-66, M 1637-44, B 1637-56 (SRO); M 1559-1812 (Boyd); B 1813-1903 (SBDB);
    M 1559-1837 (SMI); C 1558-1898, M 1813-36 (DCI)
Cop (Mf) 1602-1859 (BT) (SLC, SRO); C 1558-1898, M 1559-1836, Banns 1754-1812,
    B 1558-1900 (SRO)

CHEDZOY St Mary (549) (North Petherton Hundred; Bridgwater Union)
OR C 1559-1969, M 1558-1970, Banns 1754-1815, 1824-1923, B 1558-1897 (SRO)
BT 1597-1600, 1607-08, 1613-14, 1619-20, 1629-30, 1635-41, 1672-73, 1679-80, 1704-07,
    1719-21, 1725-26, 1732-33, 1740-43, 1748-53, 1758-59, 1764-65, 1768-71, 1773-75, 1777-81,
    1783, 1786-1837, CB 1839, 1842-49 (SRO)
Cop M 1558-1812 (Ptd, Phillimore 12, 1910); CB 1597-1639 (Ptd, Dwelly 1, 1913);
    M 1558-1812 (Boyd); B 1695-1848 (SBDB); M 1558-1837 (SMI)
Cop (Mf) 1597-1849 (BT) (SLC, SRO)

CHEDZOY (Wesleyan) b 1864 cl 1927

CHELVEY St Bridget (70) (Hartcliffe with Bedminster Hundred; Bedminster Union 1836-99,
    Long Ashton Union 1899-1930)
OR C 1574-1980, M 1574-1925, B 1574-1977 (SRO)
BT 1599-1600, 1603-04, 1607-09, 1611-16, 1622-23, 1629-30, 1635-37, 1639-41, 1662-64,
    1732, 1749-51, 1800-18, 1820, 1824-25 (SRO)
Cop 1599-1663 (Ptd, Dwelly 1, 1913); B 1737-1805 (SBDB); M 1575-1837 (SMI)
Cop (Mf) 1599-1825 (BT) (SLC, SRO)

CHELWOOD St Leonard (246) (Keynsham Hundred; Clutton Union)
OR C 1720-1984, M 1738-1973, Banns 1755-1814, B 1720-1973 (SRO)
BT 1603-04, one between 1609-28, 1611, 1613-14, 1617, 1622-23, 1630, 1634-40, 1662-64,
    1747-48, 1800-15, 1817-39, CB 1840, CMB 1841-42 (SRO)
Cop C 1720-1984, M 1738-1973, Banns 1755-1814, B 1720-1973 (SRO); M 1754-1837 (NSMI);
    B 1813-1903 (SBDB); M 1603-64 (BT), 1738-1837 (SMI)
Cop (Mf) CB 1720-1903, M 1738-1899 (SG, SLC); 1603-1842 (BT) (SLC, SRO)

CHELWOOD Whitley Batch and Chelwood (Independent) f 1721
OR C 1721-1837 (PRO: RG 4/4079)
Cop (Mf) C 1721-1837 (SLC, SRO)

CHERITON, NORTH Cemetery opened 1893 (K 1931)

CHERITON, NORTH St John the Baptist (246) (Horethorne Hundred; Wincanton Union)
OR C 1558-1964, M 1558-1728, 1744, 1756-83, 1795-1836, Banns 1756-83, 1795-1810,
    B 1558-1988 (SRO)
BT 1599-1600, 1602-09, one between 1620-40, 1622-23, 1635-39, 1662-65, 1667-69, 1730-31,
    1733-34, 1801-37, CB 1838-40, 1842-61 (SRO)
Cop 1558-1670 (SRO); B 1813-37 (SBDB); M 1754-1837 (SMI)
Cop (Mf) 1599-1861 (BT) (SLC, SRO); C 1558-1728, 1738-72, 1784-1940, M 1558-1728,
    1744-1836, Banns 1756, 1763, 1804-08, 1828-1901, B 1558-1728, 1738-72, 1783-1894 (SLC)

CHEW MAGNA St Andrew (2,048) (Chew Hundred; Clutton Union)
OR C 1560+, M 1558+, Banns 1823+, B 1559+ (Inc)
BT 1598-99, 1601-02, 1605-06, 1611-12, 1616-17, 1621-24, 1627-28, one between 1629-39,
    1635-38, 1663-64, 1800-42, CB 1845-66 (SRO)
Cop 1598-1638 (Ptd, Dwelly 1, 1913); 1562-1812 (Ts I SG, SRO); M 1754-1837 (NSMI);
    B 1813-45 (SBDB); M 1605-21 (BT), 1754-1837 (SMI)
Cop (Mf) 1598-1866 (BT) (SLC, SRO); C 1562-1937, M 1560-1989, Banns 1754-83, 1790-91,
    1823-1957, B 1562-1913 (SRO); CMB 1562-1780 (Weston Super Mare Lib)

CHEW MAGNA (United Methodist) (Lewis 1831) b 1874 (K 1931)
OR C 1867-1968 (Bristol RO)
Cop (Mf) C 1867-1968 (Bristol RO, SLC)

CHEW MAGNA (Baptist) b 1868 (K 1931)

CHEW STOKE St Andrew (693) (Chew Hundred; Clutton Union)
OR C 1663-1975 (gap 1739-53), M 1664-1837 (gap 1742-55), Banns 1791-1812, 1876-98,
    B 1663-1872 (gap 1742-53) (SRO)
BT 1598-99, 1603-09, 1611-12, 1615-18, 1621-23, 1629-31, 1634-35, 1639-40, c.1641, 1685-86,
    1690-91, 1695-99, 1702-03, 1800-16 (SRO)
Cop 1605-23 (Ptd, Dwelly 1, 1913); M 1754-1837 (NSMI); C 1787-1812 (SCDB);
    B 1813-65 (SBDB); M 1605-23 (BT), 1664-1837 (SMI)
Cop (Mf) C 1663-1888, M 1664-1837, Banns 1791-1812, 1876-98, B 1672-1872 (SG, SLC);
    1598-1816 (BT) (SLC, SRO)

CHEW STOKE (Wesleyan) f 1820 (K 1931)
OR B 1822-36 (PRO: RG 4/3258)
Cop (Mf) B 1822-36 (SLC, SRO)

CHEWTON MENDIP St Mary Magdalene (1,315) (Chewton Hundred; Wells Union)
OR C 1554-1858 (gap 1664-66), M 1554-1957 (gap 1673-78), Banns 1754-1812, B 1554-1901
(gap 1664-74) (SRO)
BT one between 1585-1635, 1597-98, 1605-12, 1616-17, 1623-24, 1629-30, 1636-37,
1639-41, 1667-68, 1753, 1761, 1802-38, CB 1839 (SRO)
Cop 1623-39 (Ptd, Dwelly 1, 1913); B 1783-1843 (SBDB); M 1554-1837 (SMI)
Cop (Mf) 1597-1839 (BT) (SLC, SRO); C 1554-1858, M 1554-1900, B 1554-1901 (SLC)

CHEWTON MENDIP (Wesleyan) (Lewis 1831) b 1862 (K 1931)
OR M 1955-64 (Bristol RO)
Cop (Mf) M 1955-64 (Bristol RO, SLC)

CHILCOMPTON St John (487) (peculiar of the Dean of Wells until 1845) (Chewton Hundred;
Clutton Union)
OR C 1649-87, 1702-1968, M 1654-78, 1729-1968, Banns 1754-82, 1902-53, B 1653-82,
1710-1981 (SRO)
BT 1599-1600, 1603-14, 1621-22, 1629-30, 1634, 1636-39, 1663, 1666-70, 1712-13, 1801-04,
1813-24, 1828, 1832, CB 1841-45 (SRO); 1753, 1800 (SRO: D/D/Pd:26/6)
Cop 1607-31 (Ptd, Dwelly 1, 1913); B 1653-1845 (SBDB); M 1607-31 (BT), 1652-1837 (SMI)
Cop (Mf) 1599-1845 (BT) (SLC, SRO)

CHILCOMPTON Norton Down (Wesleyan) b 1888 (Lewis 1831) (K 1931)
OR C 1843-1900 (in Circuit register) (Bristol RO)
Cop (Mf) C 1843-1900 (Bristol RO, SLC)

CHILCOMPTON St Aldhelm, Bowden Hill (Roman Catholic) f 1939

CHILLINGTON St James (311) (chapelry in South Petherton until 1750) (South Petherton Hundred;
Chard Union)
OR C 1750-1913, M 1757-1984, B 1750-1984 (SRO)
BT 1599-1600, 1607-10, 1612-13, 1615-16, 1619-20, 1622-24, 1629-31, 1634, 1636-37, 1639-41,
1678-79, 1681, 1687, 1707-08, 1755, 1789-90, 1800, 1805-30, 1833 (SRO)
Cop 1599-1681 (Ptd, Dwelly 1, 1913); B 1750-1984 (SBDB); M 1599-1640 (BT), 1754-1837 (SMI);
C 1750-1887, M 1757-1805 (DCI)
Cop (Mf) 1599-1833 (BT) (SLC, SRO); C 1750-1913, M 1757-1885, Banns 1756-1833,
B 1750-1812 (SG, SLC)

CHILLINGTON (Bible Christian) f 1824 cl 1851

CHILTHORNE DOMER St Mary (236) (Stone Hundred; Yeovil Union)
OR C 1678-1949 (gap 1746-67), M 1693-1951 (gap 1746-64), B 1678-1980 (gap 1746-67) (SRO)
BT 1599-1600, 1602-07, 1611-12, 1615-16, 1621-23, 1629-30, 1634-37, 1639-40, 1662-64,
1667-70, 1704-05, 1730-32, 1768, 1803, 1806-36, CB 1840 (SRO)
Cop 1615-36 (Ptd, Dwelly 1, 1913); B 1768-1879 (SBDB); M 1615-36 (BT), 1686-1837 (SMI)
Cop (Mf) 1599-1840 (BT) (SLC, SRO)

CHILTON CANTELO St James (127) (Houndsborough, Barwick and Coker Hundred;
Yeovil Union)
OR CB 1714-1812, M 1714-1836 (SRO); CB 1813+ (Inc)
BT 1599-1600, 1603-04, 1606-09, 1611, 1615-18, 1622-24, 1629, 1634-37, 1640-41, 1661-67,
1733-34, 1737, 1751, 1756-57, 1762, 1765, 1775-76, 1802-15, 1818-21, 1829-30, CB 1840-42,
1846, CMB 1847 (SRO)
Cop 1607-66 (Ptd, Dwelly 1, 1913); B 1714-1812 (SBDB); M 1607-66 (BT), 1714-1837 (SMI)
Cop (Mf) 1599-1847 (BT) (SLC, SRO); CB 1714-1812, M 1714-1836 (SLC)

CHILTON COMMON (North Petherton Hundred; Bridgwater Union) (extra-parochial place, became part of Chilton Trinity for civil purposes, 1907, for ecclesiastical, 1966)

CHILTON POLDEN St Edward (423) (chapelry in Moorlinch until 1828) (Whitley Hundred; Bridgwater Union)
OR C 1710-1884, M 1710-71, B 1710-1953 (SRO) (CB 1722-23 in Moorlinch register) (registers from 1654 survived in 1914)
BT 1605-09, 1611, 1615, 1617-18, 1621-24, 1635-40, 1668, 1720-21, 1749-50, 1752, 1756, 1775, 1800-07, 1810-27, 1830-31, 1833-37, CB 1838, 1840-49 (SRO)
Cop B 1728-1812 (SBDB); M 1621-23 (BT), 1731-71 (SMI)
Cop (Mf) C 1710-1884, M 1731-71, B 1728-1921 (SG); C 1728-1884, M 1734-54, B 1728-1921 (SLC); 1605-1849 (BT) (SLC, SRO)

CHILTON POLDEN (Independent) b 1840 (K 1931)

CHILTON TRINITY The Holy Trinity (49) (part Andersfield Hundred, part North Petherton Hundred, part Whitley Hundred; Bridgwater Union) (other registrations at Bridgewater)
OR C 1732-46, 1845-1993, M 1732-46, B 1732-46, 1845-1993 (SRO)
BT 1599, 1602-03, 1605, 1607-11, 1615, 1621-23. 1629-30, 1634-36, 1639-40, one between 1661-85, 1662-65, 1666-67; 1813-37 see Bridgwater St Mary (SRO)
Cop 1661-85 (Ptd, Dwelly 1, 1913)
Cop (Mf) 1599-1667 (BT) (SLC, SRO); 1732-46 (SLC)

CHINNOCK, EAST St Mary (673) (Houndsborough, Barwick and Coker Hundred; Yeovil Union)
OR C 1647-1846, M 1648-1837, Banns 1754-1934, B 1647-1872 (1647-1763 defective) (SRO)
BT 1599-99, 1602-04, 1606-07, 1610-14, 1616-17, 1622-23, 1635-37, 1639-40, 1663-66, 1695-96, 1730-31, 1745-48, 1754-55, 1800-36, CB 1839 (SRO)
Cop B 1764-1871 (SBDB); M 1597-1640 (BT), 1648-1837 (SMI)
Cop (Mf) C 1647-64, 1686-89, 1716-1846, M 1648-64, 1682-87, 1711-1837, Banns 1754-1889, B 1647-64, 1686-89, 1716-1872 (SG, SLC); 1598-1839 (BT) (SLC, SRO)

CHINNOCK, EAST (Wesleyan) b 1868 (K 1931)

CHINNOCK, MIDDLE St Margaret (173) (Houndsborough, Barwick and Coker Hundred; Yeovil Union)
OR CB 1695-1812, M 1695-1837, 1841 (SRO); CB 1813+ (Inc)
BT 1599-1600, 1605-08, 1611-13, 1619-24, 1629-30, 1636-37, 1639-40, 1663-64, 1668-69, one between 1660-82, 1720, 1734-35, 1737-47, 1749-50, 1800-36, CB 1839 (SRO)
Cop C 1813-1996 (SCDB); B 1813-1992 (SBDB); M 1599-1669 (BT), 1695-1837 (SMI)
Cop (Mf) 1599-1839 (BT) (SLC, SRO); CB 1695-1812, M 1695-1837, 1841 (SLC)

CHINNOCK, WEST St Mary (523) (chapelry in Chiselborough until 1970) (Houndsborough, Barwick and Coker Hundred; Yeovil Union)
OR C 1683-1862, M 1744-1966, B 1678-1955 (SRO)
BT 1636-41, 1664, 1748-51, 1753, 1758-60, 1762-63, 1765-81, 1783-86, 1800-38, CB 1840 (SRO)
Cop B 1686-1887 (SBDB); M 1636-41, 1664 (BT), 1695-1837 (SMI)
Cop (Mf) 1636-1840 (BT) (SLC, SRO); C 1683-1862, M 1695-1886, B 1678-1888 (SLC)

CHINNOCK, WEST (Wesleyan) b 1825 (K 1931)

CHIPSTABLE All Saints (343) (Williton and Freemanors Hundred; Wellington Union)
OR C 1695-1876, M 1694-1992, B 1695-1812 (SRO); B 1813+ (Inc)
BT 1601-02, 1605-12, 1615-18, 1621-23, 1630-31, 1634-35, 1639-42, c.1642, 1662-63, 1666-73, 1694, 1705-10, 1720-22, 1726-27, 1731-33, 1746-47, 1750-51, 1755-58, 1768-69, 1771-72, 1775-77, 1779-81, 1783-84, 1789-90, 1798-1817, 1828-30, 1832-34 (SRO)
Cop 1607-23 (Ptd, Dwelly 1, 1913); 1611, 1694-1837 (Ptd, Dwelly 8, 15, 1921-26); M 1607-23 (BT), 1695-1837 (SMI); C 1694-1876, M 1695-1837 (DCI)
Cop (Mf) 1601-1834 (BT) (SLC, SRO)

CHIPSTABLE Water Row (Independent) f 1823 b 1887

CHIPSTABLE Bethel Chapel (Dissenting) b 1890 (K 1931)

CHISELBOROUGH St Peter and St Paul (483) (Houndsborough, Barwick and Coker Hundred; Yeovil Union)
OR C 1558-1862, M 1558-1979, Banns 1824-1901, B 1558-1948 (SRO)
BT 1598-99, 1605-06, 1610-16, 1621-24, 1629-30, 1634-41, 1663-65, 1667, 1748-49, 1752-53, 1756-58, 1760, 1765-81, 1800-03, 1805-37, CB 1838-41 (SRO)
Cop 1558-1979 (Ts I SG, SRO); B 1813-92 (SBDB); M 1558-1837 (SMI)
Cop (Mf) 1598-1841 (BT) (SLC, SRO); C 1558-1663, 1695-1862, M 1558-1633, 1750-1901, Banns 1824-1901, B 1558-1633, 1698-1731, 1750-1902 (SLC)

CHISELBOROUGH (Independent) f 1816 b 1872

CHRISTON St Mary (83) (Winterstoke Hundred; Axbridge Union)
OR C 1559-1812, M 1549-1701, 1707, 1718-1978, Banns 1756-1812, B 1548-1713, 1716-1985 (SRO); C 1813+ (Inc)
BT 1605-06, 1617-18, 1622-23, 1628-29, 1634-37, 1640-41, 1663-64, 1800-09, 1811-15, 1817-21, 1824-26, 1828-1831, 1833-35 (SRO)
Cop C 1559-1710, M 1550-1722, B 1549-1712 (Ts I SG, SLC); B 1717-1906 (SBDB); M 1754-1837 (SMI)
Cop (Mf) 1605-1835 (BT) (SLC, SRO); C 1559-1812, M 1599-1699, 1718-1812, 1826-87, Banns 1756-1812, B 1559-1902 (SLC)

CHURCHILL St John the Baptist (985) (chapelry in Banwell until 1749) (peculiar of Banwell) (Winterstoke Hundred; Axbridge Union)
OR C 1653-1845, M 1653-1976, Banns 1755-1812, 1829-80, B 1653-1866 (all to 1812 defective) (SRO)
BT 1605-06, 1609-12, 1621-23, 1634-36, 1638-41, 1663-65, 1667-68, 1773-74, 1776-91, 1802-23, 1832-37 (1775-76 and 1807-08 in peculiar series) (SRO)
Cop 1609-67 (Ptd, Dwelly 1, 1913); C 1813-46 (Ts I SRO); M 1754-1837 (NSMI); B 1653-1866 (SBDB); M 1609-41 (BT), 1653-1837 (SMI)
Cop (Mf) 1605-1837 (BT) (SLC, SRO); C 1653-95, 1738-1845, M 1653-94, 1748-1886, Banns 1781-1812, 1829-80, B 1653-99, 1748-1866 (SLC)

CHURCHILL Langford (Independent) f 1662 b 1848 (K 1931)

CHURCHILL (Wesleyan) b 1881 (K 1931)

CHURCHSTANTON St Paul (977) (Diocese of Exeter, transferred to Diocese of Bath and Wells, 1970) (Hemyock Hundred; Taunton Union) (transferred from Devon to Somerset, 1896)
OR C 1662-1918, M 1662-1960, B 1662-1941 (SRO)
BT 1606-c1840 (Devon RO)
Cop B 1662-1902 (SBDB); M 1662-1837 (SMI); C 1662-1899, M 1662-1836 (DCI)

CHURCHSTANTON (Methodist)
OR C 1848-83 (SRO)

CHURCHSTANTON Churchinford (Baptist) (K 1931)

CLANDOWN Holy Trinity (created from Midsomer Norton, 1849) (Clutton Union)
OR C 1841-1986, M 1850-1982, Banns 1850-1982, B 1848-1921 (SRO)

CLANDOWN (Wesleyan) b 1874 (K 1931)
OR C 1874-1982 (SRO); C 1956-79 (Springfield) (SRO)

CLANDOWN (Primitive Methodist) b 1880 (K 1931)

CLAPTON in GORDANO St Michael (167) (Portbury Hundred; Bedminster Union 1836-99, Long Ashton Union 1899-1930)
OR C 1558-1942, M 1559-1956, Banns 1813-1948, B 1558-1812 (SRO); B 1813+ (Inc)
BT 1599-1600, 1602, 1605-06, 1608-10, 1615-18, 1621-23, 1634-37, 1636-37, 1639-41, 1662-65, 1732-33, 1750-51, 1775, 1800-01, 1803-37, CB 1838, 1842-49 (SRO)
Cop 1599-1663 (Ptd, Dwelly 1, 1913); M 1754-1837 (NSMI); B 1558-1812 (SBDB); M 1559-1837 (SMI)
Cop (Mf) 1599-1849 (BT) (SLC, SRO)

CLATWORTHY St Mary (246) (Williton and Freemanors Hundred; Williton Union)
OR C 1561-1922, M 1561-1937, B 1561-1812 (SRO); B 1813+ (Inc)
BT 1598-99, 1605-08, 1611-16, 1621-24, 1629-30, 1634-36, 1639-41, 1662-70, 1672-73, 1679-80, 1704-10, 1713, 1721-22, 1731-33, 1736-38, 1743-44, 1749-51, 1753-56, 1758, 1764-65, 1768-81, 1783-84, 1786-87, 1790-1817, 1819-25, 1827-30, 1832-37 (SRO)
Cop C 1558-1764, M 1558-1953 (SRO); B 1764-1812 (SBDB); M 1754-1837 (SMI); CM 1561-1899 (DCI)
Cop (Mf) C 1561-1922, M 1561-1857, Banns 1755-1813, B 1561-1812 (SG); 1598-1837 (BT) (SLC, SRO)

CLAVERTON St Mary (156) (Hampton and Claverton Hundred; Bath Union)
OR C 1582-1945, M 1582-1991, Banns 1823-1947, B 1581-1944 (SRO)
BT 1613-16, 1622-24, 1630-31, 1634-37, 1639-40, 1664-70, 1737-38, 1749-51, 1754-57, 1763-76, 1782, 1785-1825, 1828-37, CB 1838-46, 1848, 1850-55, B 1856, CB 1857-67 (SRO)
Cop 1582-1812 (Ts I SG; Bath Lib, British Lib); 1582-1707 (SRO); M 1754-1837 (NSMI); B 1813-1944 (SBDB); M 1636 (BT), 1750-1837 (SMI)
Cop (Mf) 1613-1867 (BT) (SLC, SRO); C 1582-1945, M 1582-1929, Banns 1823-1947, B 1581-1944 (SLC)

CLEEVE Holy Trinity (chapelry in Yatton until 1841) (Winterstoke Hundred; Bedminster Union 1836-99, Long Ashton Union 1899-1930)
OR C 1840-1937, M 1844-1965, B 1840-1971 (SRO)
BT CB 1840-48, 1853, 1855-70 (SRO)
Cop (Mf) 1840-70 (BT) (SLC, SRO)

CLEEVE (Plymouth Brethren) b 1867

CLEEVE, OLD St Andrew (1,347) (Williton and Freemanors Hundred; Williton Union)
OR C 1661-1965, M 1661-1923, B 1661-1897 (SRO)
BT 1602-03, 1606-07, 1609-13, 1616-17, 1621-24, 1629-30, 1636-38, one between 1663-76, 1666-67, 1669-70, 1700-01, 1704-06, c1706-07, 1709-10, 1721-24, 1759-61, 1764-69, 1771, 1774-75, 1778-80, 1800-13, 1815-17, 1819-29, 1831-33 (SRO)
Cop C 1661-1869, M 1661-1813, B 1661-1861 (SRO); B 1813-55 (SBDB); M 1602-1837 (SMI); CM 1661-1899
Cop (Mf) 1602-1833 (BT) (SLC, SRO)

CLEEVE, OLD (Roman Catholic) chapel b 1627 in house of Poyntz family at Leigh and used to c1908

CLEEVE, OLD Washford (Wesleyan) f 1792 b 1811 (K 1931)
OR C 1803-1923 (SRO)

CLEEVE, OLD Ebenezer Chapel, Roadwater (Bible Christian later United Methodist) b 1841 reb 1907 (K 1931)

CLEEVE, OLD Beulah Chapel, Brendon Hill (Bible Christian) b 1861

CLEVEDON Cemetery, Old Church Road opened 1882 (3 acres)
OR B 1882-1943 (SRO)

CLEVEDON St Andrew (1,147) (Portbury Hundred; Bedminster Union 1836-99,
  Long Ashton Union 1899-1930)
OR C 1727-1965, M 1731-1969, Banns 1757-1900, B 1727-1976 (SRO)
BT 1607-08, 1611-12, 1622-24, 1629-30, 1634-36, 1639-41, 1662-66, 1749-51, 1753, 1757,
  1800-37, CB 1838-70 (SRO)
Cop 1607-66 (Ptd, Dwelly 1, 1913); C 1607-1934, M 1731-1923, Banns 1757-1862, B 1607-1941
  (SRO); M 1754-1837 (NSMI); B 1607-1941 (SBDB); M 1635-66 (BT), 1731-1837 (SMI)
Cop (Mf) 1607-1870 (BT) (SLC, SRO); C 1727-1901, M 1731-1900, Banns 1757-1900,
  B 1727-1903 (SLC)

CLEVEDON Christ Church b 1839 (created from Clevedon St Andrew, 1940)
  (Bedminster Union 1836-99, Long Ashton Union 1899-1930)
OR C 1880-1954, M 1940-72 (SRO)

CLEVEDON All Saints, East Clevedon (created from Clevedon St Andrew, 1861)
  (Bedminster Union 1836-99, Long Ashton Union 1899-1930)
OR C 1860-93, B 1860-1930 (SRO)
Cop C 1860-80, B 1860-1930 (SRO); B 1860-1930 (SBDB)

CLEVEDON St John the Evanglist, South Clevedon (created from Clevedon St Andrew, 1876)
  (Bedminster Union 1836-99, Long Ashton Union 1899-1930)
OR CMB 1876+ (Inc)

CLEVEDON Hill Road (Plymouth Brethren) b 1851 (K 1931)

CLEVEDON Copse Road (Independent) b 1851 (K 1931)

CLEVEDON Meeting House, Albert Road (Society of Friends) b 1868 (K 1931)

CLEVEDON Lower Linden Road (Wesleyan) b 1882 (K 1931)

CLEVEDON Immaculate Conception, Marine Hill (Roman Catholic) b 1886 (K 1931)

CLEVEDON Station Road (Baptist) (K 1931)

CLEVEDON Old Street (Salvation Army) (K 1931)

CLEVEDON Old Church Road (Christadelphian) (K 1931)

CLOFORD St Mary (302) (Frome Hundred; Frome Union)
OR CB 1561-1812, M 1561-1979 (gap 1778-83), Banns 1824-1986 (SRO); CB 1813+ (Inc)
BT 1594-9, 1605-16,1618-9,1635-40,1678-9, 1737-8,1749-50, 1802-3,1806-17,1820,1822-9 (SRO)
Cop B 1783-1812 (SBDB); M 1561-1754, 1784-1837 (SMI)
Cop (Mf) CB 1561-1812, M 1561-1754, 1784-1903, Banns 1824-1951 (SG, SLC);
  1594-1829 (BT) (SLC, SRO)

CLOFORD Leighton (Primitive Methodist) (Lewis 1831) b 1863 (K 1931)

CLOSWORTH All Saints (195) (Houndsborough, Barwick and Coker Hundred; Yeovil Union)
OR C 1685-1982, M 1685-1965, Banns 1755-89, B 1685-1978 (SRO) (C 1534-1670, M from 1531
  and B from 1543 survived in 1914)
BT 1594-99, 1602-05, 1608-09, 1611-12, 1616-17, 1621-24, 1629-30, 1634-37, 1639-40, 1662-65,
  1667-68, 1672-73, 1803, 1805-06, 1808-19, 1821-25, 1827-37, CB 1840, 1842-45,
  CMB 1846-48, CB 1849, CMB 1850, 1852, CB 1853-66, 1868-73, 1875 (SRO)
Cop 1598-1603 (Ptd, Dwelly 1, 1913); M 1813-36 (Ts SG); B 1784-1890 (SBDB);
  M 1598-1603 (BT), 1685-1837 (SMI)
Cop (Mf) 1594-1875 (BT) (SLC, SRO)

CLUTTON Board of Guardians
OR Z 1839-1933, C 1874-1929, D 1838-1927 (SRO)

CLUTTON St Augustine (1,287) (Chew Hundred; Clutton Union)
OR C 1693-1884, M 1693-1837, Banns 1754-1812, 1823-56, B 1691-1890 (SRO)
BT 1609, 1611-12, 1615-16, 1619-24, 1629-31, 1634-41, 1662-63, one between 1663-65, 1666-69, 1798-1814 (SRO)
Cop 1609-38 (Ptd, Dwelly 1, 1913); M 1754-1837 (NSMI); C 1693-1812 (SCDB); B 1691-1843 (SBDB); M 1609-38 (BT), 1694-1837 (SMI)
Cop (Mf) 1609-1814 (BT) (SLC, SRO); C 1693-1884, M 1693-1837, Banns 1799-1812, 1823-56, B 1691-1890 (SG, SLC)

CLUTTON (Wesleyan) (Lewis 1831) b 1808 (K 1931)
OR C 1843-1900 (circuit) (Bristol RO); C 1840-1929 (chapel) (Bristol RO)
Cop (Mf) C 1843-1929 (Bristol RO, SLC)

CLUTTON (Independent) (Lewis 1831) b 1878 (K 1931)

CLUTTON (Primitive Methodist) b 1852 (K 1931)

COKER, EAST St Michael (1,330) (Houndsborough, Barwick and Coker Hundred; Yeovil Union)
OR C 1560-1950, M 1560-1980, Banns 1754-83, 1795-1812, B 1560-1892 (SRO)
BT one between 1594-99, one between 1595-97, 1597-1800, 1611-12, 1615-16, 1629-30, 1635-36, 1640-41, 1662-67, 1669-70, 1801-37 (SRO)
Cop 1560-1714 (SRO); M 1560-1714 (Boyd); B 1765-1844 (SBDB); M 1560-1837 (SMI)
Cop (Mf) C 1560-1753, 1765-1888, M 1560-1885, Banns 1754-83, 1795-1812, B 1560-1753, 1765-1885 (SG, SLC); 1597-1837 (BT) (SLC, SRO)

COKER, EAST (Wesleyan) (K 1931)

COKER, EAST (Plymouth Brethren) (K 1931)

COKER, WEST St Martin (1,013) (Houndsborough, Barwick and Coker Hundred; Yeovil Union)
OR C 1697-1953, M 1697-1973 (gap 1749-54), Banns 1754-1901, B 1697-1952 (SRO)
BT 1602-03, 1605-14, 1619-20, 1623-24, 1629-31, 1636-37, 1639-41, 1662-64, one between 1664-90, 1667-68, 1733-34, 1740-41, 1801, 1806-14, 1817-36 (SRO)
Cop 1608-39 (Ptd, Dwelly 1, 1913); B 1771-1845 (SBDB); M 1608-39 (BT), 1697-1748, 1755-1837 (SMI)
Cop (Mf) 1602-1836 (BT) (SLC, SRO); CM 1697-1900, Banns 1754-1901, B 1697-1804, 1813-1901 (SLC)

COKER, WEST (Wesleyan) b 1839 (K 1931)

COKER, WEST (Plymouth Brethren) (K 1931)

COLEFORD Holy Trinity (chapelry in Kilmersdon until 1834) (Kilmersdon Hundred; Frome Union)
OR C 1831-1972, M 1842-1972, Banns 1842-1956, B 1831-1967 (SRO)
Cop B 1831-68 (SBDB)
Cop (Mf) C 1831-1901, M 1842-1901, Banns 1842-1901, B 1831-1901 (SLC)

COLEFORD (Wesleyan) b 1866

COLEFORD (Primitive Methodist) b 1868
OR C 1880-1932 (SRO)

COMBE St Nicholas (1,202) (peculiar of the Dean of Wells until 1845) (East Kingsbury Hundred; Chard Union)
OR C 1678-1942, M 1678-1984, Banns 1823-57, 1887-1901, B 1678-1965 (SRO)
BT one between 1579-94, 1605-06, 1608-09, 1611-12, one between 1618-40, 1629-30, 1636-37, 1639-40, 1662-63, 1666-67, 1749, 1751-65, 1767-76, 1778-80, 1782-95, 1803-26, 1828-36 (1714-16 in peculiar series) (SRO)
Cop M 1678-1812 (Ptd, Phillimore 14, 1913); C 1636-39, M 1636-39, B 1636-39 (Ptd, Dwelly 1, 1913); C 1606-63, 1678-1942, M 1813-1924, B 1678-1965 (SRO); M 1678-1812 (Boyd); B 1678-1845 (SBDB); M 1636-39 (BT), 1678-1837 (SMI); C 1678-1841, M 1678-1927, B 1678-1930 (DCI)
Cop (Mf) 1605-1836 (BT) (SLC, SRO); C 1678-1901, MB 1678-1900, Banns 1823-57, 1887-1901 (SLC)

COMBE St Nicholas Taunton Road (Wesleyan) b 1891 (K 1931)

COMBE St Nicholas Wadeford (Baptist) (K 1931)

COMBE ABBAS AND TEMPLECOMBE St Mary (448) (Horethorne Hundred; Wincanton Union)
OR C 1563-1871, M 1563-1981, B 1563-1902 (SRO)
BT 1597-98, 1602-24, 1629-30, 1663-68, 1749-51, 1770-76, 1801-37, CB 1838-59, 1861-69 (SRO)
Cop 1597-1812 (Ptd, Dwelly 1, 3, 15, 1913, 1915, 1926); C 1872-1989, B 1813-1988 (Ts I SRO); B 1694-1846 (SBDB); M 1563-1837 (SMI)
Cop (Mf) 1597-1869 (BT) (SLC, SRO)

COMBE ABBAS AND TEMPLECOMBE Templecombe (Independent) f 1700
OR C 1816-36 (PRO: RG 4/3610)
Cop (Mf) C 1816-36 (SLC, SRO)

COMBE DOWN Holy Trinity (created from Monkton Combe, 1839) (Bath Union)
OR CMB 1839+ (Inc)
BT C 1854, 1877-79 (SRO)
Cop (Mf) 1854-79 (BT) (SLC, SRO)

COMBE DOWN Union Chapel b 1815 (K 1931)

COMBE DOWN St Peter and St Paul (Roman Catholic) b 1919

COMBE FLOREY St Peter and St Paul (316) (Taunton and Taunton Dean Hundred; Taunton Union)
OR C 1566-1906, M 1566-1837, Banns 1754-1813, 1824-1960, B 1566-1814 (SRO); B 1814+ (Inc)
BT 1594-98, 1603-04, 1606-08, 1613-16, 1621-26, 1628-29, 1634, 1636-37, 1639-41, 1663-65, 1668-70, 1672-73, 1707, 1725-28, 1732-33, 1741-42, 1749-53, 1764, 1767-70, 1771-73, 1775, 1777-81, 1789, 1800-18, 1820-36 (SRO)
Cop 1566-1837 (Ts I SG, SRO); M 1566-1837 (SMI); C 1566-1899, M 1569-1837 (DCI)
Cop (Mf) 1594-1836 (BT) (SLC, SRO); C 1566-1901, M 1566-1837, Banns 1754-1813, 1824-1900, 1940-44, B 1566-1814 (SLC)

COMBE HAY (dedication unknown) (260) (Wellow Hundred; Bath Union)
OR C 1539-1938, M 1539-1836, Banns 1754-81, B 1540-1811 (SRO); B 1813+ (Inc)
BT 1594-98, 1602-03, 1605-12, 1615-16, 1621-23, 1630-31, 1634-40, 1664-69, 1672, 1732-33, 1737-38, 1750-52, 1757, 1775, 1781-85, 1797-1801, 1803-04, 1806-19, CB 1846-47, CMB 1851-52, CB 1853, 1868-71 (SRO)
Cop 1538-1777 (Ms I SG); M 1754-1837 (NSMI); B 1777-1812 (SBDB); M 1539-1837 (SMI)
Cop (Mf) 1594-1871 (BT) (SLC, SRO)

COMBE, MONKTON St Michael (1,031) (Bath Forum Hundred; Bath Union)
OR C 1561-1753, 1771-1842, M 1563-1666, 1792-97, B 1561-1708, 1771-1853 (SRO)
  (marriages also in South Stoke registers)
BT 1599-1600, 1605-08, 1611, 1623, 1630-31, 1634-36, 1639-40, 1662-63, 1666-69, 1802-03,
  [1803-12 in South Stoke returns], 1814-31, 1833-37, CB 1838-52, 1854 (SRO)
Cop C 1561-1708, 1771-1812, M 1559-1639, 1792-97, B 1561-1699, 1771-1812 (Ts I SG,
  Bath Lib, British Lib, SRO); M 1792-97 (NSMI); B 1813-37 (SBDB); M 1778-99 (SMI)
Cop (Mf) 1599-1854 (BT) (SLC, SRO)

COMBE, MONKTON (Independent) f 1815 b 1870

COMPTON BISHOP St Andrew (554) (peculiar of the Prebendary of Compton Bishop until 1845)
  (Winterstoke Hundred; Axbridge Union)
OR C 1641-1927, M 1641-1706, 1732-1943, B 1641-1717, 1727-1926 (SRO)
BT 1603-04, 1606-09, 1611-12, 1615-17, 1621-23, 1629-30, 1635-37, 1639-40, 1664-65, 1813-18,
  1820-37, CB 1838-58 (SRO)
Cop 1606-21 (SG); C 1813-61 (SCDB); B 1641-1852 (SBDB); M 1603-1837 (SMI)
Cop (Mf) 1603-1858 (BT) (SLC, SRO)

COMPTON DANDO St Mary (382) (Keynsham Hundred; Keynsham Union)
OR C 1652-1895, M 1654-1973, B 1654-1965 (SRO)
BT 1602-03, 1605-07, 1612-13, 1616, 1621-24, 1629-30, 1634-37, 1639-40, 1668-69, 1678-79,
  1683, 1733-34, 1747-48, 1750-51, 1753, 1757, 1799, 1800-28 (SRO)
Cop 1616-79 (Ptd, Dwelly 1, 1913); C 1652-1895, M 1654-1973, B 1654-1965 (SRO);
  M 1754-1837 (NSMI); B 1739-1899 (SBDB); M 1616-1836 (SMI)
Cop (Mf) 1602-1828 (BT) (SLC, SRO); C 1652-1895, MB 1654-1900 (SLC)

COMPTON DANDO (Wesleyan) (Lewis 1831) b 1857 (K 1931)

COMPTON DUNDON St Andrew (623) (peculiar of the Prebendary of Compton Dundon until
  1845) (part Whitley Hundred, part Somerton Hundred; Langport Union)
OR C 1682-1962, M 1696-1967, Banns 1755-1811, B 1696-1995 (SRO)
BT c.1610, 1611-14, 1616, 1621-24, 1629-30, 1635-40, 1666-68, 1678, c.1679, 1707-08, 1749-51,
  1753, 1813-14, 1816-26, 1828-37 (SRO); 1735-36, 1744-45, 1747, 1752, 1756-92, 1797-99,
  1807-11 (SRO: D/D/Ppb:28)
Cop B 1696-1861 (SBDB); M 1610-40 (BT), 1696-1837 (SMI)
Cop (Mf) C 1682-1962, M 1696-1906, B 1696-1882 (SG); 1610-1837 (BT) (SLC, SRO)

COMPTON DUNDON Dundon (Wesleyan) b 1887 (K 1931)

COMPTON MARTIN St Michael (572) (Chewton Hundred; Clutton Union)
OR C 1559-1982, M 1559-1965, Banns 1857-86, B 1559-1894 (gap CMB 1642-53) (SRO)
BT 1601-02, 1605-08, 1611-12, 1616-17, 1621-24, 1629-30, 1636, 1639-43, 1660-70, 1695-96,
  1732-33, 1749-51, 1776, 1800-36 (SRO)
Cop 1559-1812 (Ms I SG); M 1754-1837 (NSMI); C 1654-1812 (SCDB); B 1854-77 (SBDB);
  M 1569-1837 (SMI)
Cop (Mf) 1601-1836 (BT) (SLC, SRO); C 1559-1641, 1654-1885, M 1569-1641, 1654-1850,
  Banns 1857-86, B 1559-1641, 1654-1894 (SLC)

COMPTON MARTIN (Wesleyan) b 1850 (K 1931)
OR C 1877-1977 (Bristol RO)
Cop (Mf) C 1877-1977 (Bristol RO, SLC)

COMPTON PAUNCEFOOT St Mary the Virgin (228) (Catsash Hundred; Wincanton Union)
OR CB 1559-1993, M 1559-1911 (SRO)
BT one between 1590-1639, 1601-04, 1606-08, 1611, 1613, 1615-18, 1621-22, 1629-31, 1635-41,
    1683, 1800-18, 1820-37, 1841, CB 1842-51 (SRO)
Cop C 1590-1638, M 1590-1638, B 1590-1638 (SG); M 1813-37 (Ts I SG); B 1761-1837 (SBDB);
    M 1559-1837 (SMI)
Cop (Mf) 1601-1851 (BT) (SLC, SRO)

CONGRESBURY St Andrew (1,327) (Winterstoke Hundred; Axbridge Union)
OR C 1543-1953, M 1543-1957, B 1543-1955 (SRO)
BT 1605-11, 1613-18, 1621-24, 1629-30, 1683-84, 1686-87, 1719-20, 1735-36, 1746-51, 1754-55,
    1777-78, 1802-17, CB 1837-53 (SRO)
Cop CM 1543-1837, B 1563-1837 (Ts I SG, SRO); M 1754-1800 (SLC); M 1754-1837 (NSMI);
    B 1763-1852 (SBDB); M 1543-1837 (SMI)
Cop (Mf) 1605-1853 (BT) (SLC, SRO)

CONGRESBURY St Ann, Hewish (created from Congresbury, Wick St Lawrence, Banwell and
    Puxton, 1865) (Axbridge Union)
OR C 1865-1968, M 1865-1979, B 1866-1979 (SRO)

CONGRESBURY Hewish (United Methodist) b 1838 (K 1931)
OR C 1926-70 (Bristol RO)
Cop (Mf) C 1926-70 (Bristol RO, SLC)

CONGRESBURY (United Methodist) b 1878 (K 1931)

CORFE St Nicholas (271) (chapelry in Taunton St Mary Magdalene until 1826)
    (Taunton and Taunton Dean Hundred; Taunton Union)
OR C 1566-1894, MB 1566-1979, Banns 1779-1901, 1913-36 (SRO) (earliest register recovered,
    1942)
BT 1603-24, 1629, 1634-40, 1663-64, 1666, 1701-08, 1728-29, 1752, 1800-28, 1836-38 (SRO)
Cop M 1687-1812 (Ptd, Phillimore 7, 1906); C 1567-1839, M 1556-1663, 1813-40,
    B 1566-1839 (Ts SG, SRO); M 1687-1812 (Boyd); B 1678-1899 (SBDB); M 1603-66 (BT),
    1687-1837 (SMI); C 1567-1894, M 1813-99 (DCI)
Cop (Mf) 1603-1838 (BT) (SLC, SRO); C 1566-1894, M 1566-1682, 1776-1900, Banns 1779-1901,
    1913-36, B 1566-1899 (SLC)

CORFE (Baptist) b 1870 (K 1931)

CORSTON All Saints (433) (Wellow Hundred; Keynsham Union)
OR C 1568-1950, M 1568-1837, Banns 1756-1816, B 1568-1904 (SRO)
BT 1598, 1603-04, 1606-13, 1615-17, 1622-23, 1629-30, 1634-36, 1639-41, 1663-64, 1746-48,
    1750-51, 1800-16, 1819-20, 1822-34, 1836-37, 1842 (SRO)
Cop C 1567-1812, M 1586-1811, B 1569-1812 (Ts I SG, Bath Lib); M 1754-1837 (NSMI);
    B 1724-1849 (SBDB); M 1568-1689, 1704-1837 (SMI)
Cop (Mf) 1598-1842 (BT) (SLC, SRO)

CORSTON (Wesleyan) b 1837 (K 1931)

CORTON DENHAM St Andrew (494) (Horethorne Hundred; Wincanton Union)
OR C 1538-1992, M 1538-1988, Banns 1784-1812, B 1560-1937 (SRO)
BT 1603, 1605-08, 1611-13, 1615-17, 1623-24, 1629-30, 1635-37, 1662-70, 1672-73, 1733-34,
    1747-48, 1801-31 (SRO)
Cop B 1755-1837 (SBDB); M 1538-1837 (SMI)
Cop (Mf) C 1538-1865, M 1538-1836, Banns 1754-1812, B 1560-1937 (SG);
    1603-1831 (BT) (SLC, SRO)

CORTON DENHAM (Wesleyan) b 1861

COSSINGTON St Mary (280) (Whitley Hundred; Bridgwater Union)
OR C 1675-1942, M 1675-1984 (defective 1738-54), Banns 1793-1812, B 1675-1812 (SRO);
B 1813+ (Inc)
BT 1606-08, 1621-22, 1629-30, 1634-37, 1639-41, 1664-65, 1740-41, 1749-52, 1755-56, 1761-62,
1800-30, 1832, CB 1844-47, 1861 (SRO)
Cop 1606-40 (Ptd, Dwelly 1, 1913); B 1675-1812 (SBDB); M 1606-65 (BT), 1675-1837 (SMI)
Cop (Mf) 1606-1861 (BT) (SLC, SRO)

COTHELSTONE St Thomas of Canterbury (120) (chapelry in Kingston until 1729) (Taunton and
Taunton Dean Hundred; Taunton Union)
OR C 1658-1719, M 1664-1836, B 1658-1719, 1813-1993 (SRO); C 1813+ (Inc) (CB 1720-52
survived in 1914)
BT 1594-7, 1605-8, 1611-5, 1623, 1635-40, 1667-8, 1678-9, 1707-8, 1720-1, 1725-8, 1739-41,
1748-52, 1754-5, 1757-8, 1763-6, 1768-75, 1782-4, 1786-8, 1802-26, CB 1855-64 (SRO)
Cop M 1664-1715 (Ptd, Phillimore 8, 1906); CMB 1607-79 (Ptd, Dwelly 1, 1913);
M 1664-1715 (Boyd); B 1813-37 (SBDB); M 1595-1837 (SMI); C 1658-1719, M 1813-36 (DCI)
Cop (Mf) 1594-1864 (BT) (SLC, SRO); CB 1664-1718, M 1664-1715, 1816-36 (SLC)

COXLEY Christ Church b 1839 (created from Wells St Cuthbert, 1844) (Wells Union)
OR C 1845-1917, B 1845-1945 (SRO)
Cop (Mf) C 1845-1901, M 1845-1900 (SLC)

COXLEY (Wesleyan) b 1878
OR C 1891-1966, M 1895-1937, B 1900-45 (Bristol RO)
Cop (Mf) C 1891-1966, M 1895-1937, B 1900-45 (Bristol RO, SLC)

CRANMORE, EAST St James (64) (chapelry in Doulting) (Liberty of Cranmore, Frome Hundred;
Shepton Mallet Union)
OR C 1783-1944, M 1813-1946, Banns 1900-45, B 1785-1944 (SRO) (1716+ survived in 1914)
BT 1598, 1607, 1611-12, 1615, 1621-23, 1628, 1635-36, 1639-41, 1663-64, 1669-70, 1753-54,
1800-20 (SRO)
Cop 1597-1663 (Ptd, Dwelly 1, 1913); M 1754-1806 (SRO, copied 1954, register no longer extant);
B 1813-1908 (SBDB); M 1598, 1607, 1679 (BT), 1754-1837 (SMI)
Cop (Mf) 1598-1820 (BT) (SLC, SRO); C 1783-1901, M 1754-1898, B 1785-1908 (SLC)

CRANMORE, WEST St Bartholomew (298) (chapelry in Doulting) (Liberty of Cranmore,
Wells Forum Hundred; Shepton Mallet Union)
OR C 1578-1931, M 1562-1837, Banns 1754-1811, B 1569-1937 (gap CMB 1635-94) (SRO)
BT 1597-8, 1606-8, 1611-2, 1621-3, 1629-30, 1636-41, 1661-4, 1669-70, 1800-21, 1824-31 (SRO)
Cop 1597-1663 (Ptd, Dwelly 1, 1913); C 1580-1634, M 1563-70 (SRO); B 1813-1902 (SBDB);
M 1566-1837 (SMI)
Cop (Mf) 1597-1831 (BT) (SLC, SRO); C 1578-1634, 1695-1901, M 1562-1634, 1696-1837,
Banns 1754-1811, B 1569-1633, 1695-1711, 1721-1903 (SLC)

CRANMORE, WEST (Wesleyan) reb 1899 (K 1931)

CREECH St Michael (1,116) (Andersfield Hundred; Taunton Union)
OR C 1668-1978, M 1665-1991, Banns 1754-1804, 1823-60, 1872-75, B 1665-1992 (CB 1749-70
defective) (SRO)
BT one between 1575-1627, 1606-08, 1611-12, 1616-17, 1619-26, one between 1627-41, 1629-30,
1639-40, 1662-64, 1681-86, 1697-98, 1721-28, 1736-44, 1746-47, 1749-52, 1754, 1759,
1769-70, 1777-78, 1783-84, 1800-15, 1824 (SRO)
Cop M 1665-1814 (Ptd, Phillimore 7, 1906); C 1607-39, M 1607-39, B 1607-39 (Ptd, Dwelly 1,
1913); CB 1836-65 (Bath Lib); 1606-1837 (I SRO); M 1665-1814 (Boyd); B 1665-1864
(SBDB); M 1607-39 (BT), 1665-1837 (SMI)
Cop (Mf) 1606-1824 (BT) (SLC, SRO); C 1668-1901, M 1665-1901, Banns 1754-1804, 1823-60,
1872-75, B 1665-1901 (SLC)

CREECH St Michael Meeting House, North End (Society of Friends) f 1674 cl 1804

CREECH St Michael Independent Chapel, Adsborough f 1701 b 1868

CREECH St Michael Zion Chapel(Baptist) f 1816 b 1831 reb 1983

CREECH St Michael Ham (Wesleyan) f 1832 b by 1899 cl 1915

CREECH St Michael North End (Wesleyan) b 1842 cl 1855

CREWKERNE Cemetery opened 1874 (7¼ acres) (K 1931)

CREWKERNE St Bartholomew, Church Street (3,789) (Crewkerne Hundred; Chard Union)
OR C 1558-1972, M 1558-1967, B 1558-1938 (SRO)
BT 1594-1602, 1605-09, 1611, 1619-24, 1629-30, 1638-41, 1668, 1707-09, 1727-28, 1731-32,
    1737-38, 1741-44, 1746-47, 1749-53, 1755-56, 1759-60, 1762-65, 1767-69, 1772-74, 1778-81,
    1783-86, 1788-95, 1797-1815, 1817-23, 1825-35, 1837-38, CB 1840, 1842-44, 1849, 1851-67,
    1869-72 (SRO)
Cop M 1559-1812 (Ptd, Phillimore 5, 1904); C 1599, B 1599 (Ptd, Dwelly 1, 1913);
    CB 1668, 1690-1764 (Ts SLC); M 1559-1812 (Boyd); C 1795-1830 (SCDB); B 1795-1839
    (SBDB); M 1559-1837 (SMI); C 1558-1899, M 1813-99 (DCI)
Cop (Mf) 1594-1872 (BT) (SLC, SRO); C 1550-1900, M 1558-1901, B 1558-1901 (SLC)

CREWKERNE Meeting House (Society of Friends) f by 1668 cl c1750

CREWKERNE Hermitage Street (Presbyterian, later Unitarian) f c1670, b 1733, reb 1811
OR C 1785-1967, M 1809-1967, B 1834-1967 (SRO); C 1785-1836, B 1834 (PRO: RG 4/1547)
Cop (Mf) C 1785-1836, B 1834 (SLC, SRO)

CREWKERNE North Street (Strict Baptist) f 1810 reb 1880 (K 1931)
OR C 1831-37 (PRO: RG 4/2699); M 1983-85 (SRO)
Cop (Mf) C 1831-37 (SLC, SRO)

CREWKERNE Ebenezer Chapel (Bible Christian) f 1821, cl 1831, again f 1835, cl 1838, f again
    1851, reb 1872 West Street, reb 1890 Hermitage Street, cl 1962
OR ZC 1823-37 (PRO: RG 4/1419)
Cop (Mf) ZC 1823-37 (SLC, SRO)

CREWKERNE South Street (Wesleyan) (South Petherton Circuit) f 1831 b 1874 (K 1931)

CREWKERNE South Street (Latter-day Saints) f 1851 cl c1860

CREWKERNE East Street (Plymouth Brethren) f 1859 b 1863 (K 1931)

CREWKERNE Oxen Lane (Salvation Army) f 1884 Rose Lane reb c1887, reb 1959 North Street

CREWKERNE Hermitage Street (United Methodist) b 1890 (K 1931)

CREWKERNE St Peter, South Street (Roman Catholic) b 1935

CRICKET MALHERBIE St Mary Magdalen (28) (Abdick and Bulstone Hundred; Chard Union)
OR C 1723-1809, 1846-1992, M 1731-1984, Banns 1754-1892, B 1732-1992 (SRO)
BT 1598-1600, 1602-09, 1611-18, 1621-24, 1629-30, 1634-38, 1659-62, 1666-68, 1738, 1742-43,
    1746-52, 1754-57, 1804-05, 1807-09, 1811, 1813-18, 1820-23, 1826-28 (SRO)
Cop C 1604-37, M 1604-37, B 1604-37 (Ptd, Dwelly 1, 1913); M 1754-1837 (Ts I SG);
    B 1775-1992 (SBDB); M 1604-37 (BT), 1731-1837 (SMI); C 1598-1807, M 1599-1837 (DCI)
Cop (Mf) 1598-1828 (BT) (SLC, SRO); C 1723-1807, M 1731-1837, 1845-83, Banns 1754-1892,
    B 1732-1807 (SLC)

CRICKET ST THOMAS (86) (South Petherton Hundred; Chard Union)
OR C 1564-1992, M 1567-1836, Banns 1803-38, 1840, 1853-1954, B 1567-1988 (SRO)
BT 1599-1600, 1605-16, 1621-24, 1629, 1635-36, 1639-40, 1662-63, 1668-69, 1678-79, 1704-05,
    1731-32, 1743-44, 1750-52, 1770, 1796-1823, 1825, 1829-36 (SRO)
Cop C 1599-1678, M 1599-1678, B 1599-1678 (Ptd, Dwelly 1, 1913); M 1813-51 (SG);
    C 1564-1901, M 1567-1836, B 1567-1908 (SRO); B 1768-1837 (SBDB); M 1567-1837 (SMI);
    C 1554-1901, M 1567-1836 (DCI)
Cop (Mf) 1599-1836 (BT) (SLC, SRO); C 1564-1812, M 1618-1798, 1815-36, Banns 1803-98,
    B 1614-1812 (SLC)

CROSCOMBE St Mary (803) (Whitstone Hundred; Shepton Mallet Union)
OR C 1558-1953, M 1558-1992, Banns 1823-1901, B 1558-1933 (SRO)
BT 1606-10, 1613-15, one between 1616-39, 1619-24, 1626-27, 1635-37, 1639-40, 1662-65,
    one between 1666-68, 1669-70, 1672-73, 1690-91, 1696, 1704-05, 1800-41, CB 1842-49, 1851
    (SRO)
Cop 1607-72 (Ptd, Dwelly 1, 1913); M 1558-1753 (SRO); B 1783-1858 (SBDB); M 1558-1837
    (SMI)
Cop (Mf) 1606-1851 (BT) (SLC, SRO); C 1558-1901, MB 1558-1900, Banns 1823-1901

CROSCOMBE (Baptist) b 1723 (K 1931)

CROSCOMBE (Wesleyan) b 1890 (but by 1931 used by Seventh-Day Adventists) (K 1931)

CROWCOMBE Holy Ghost (691) (Williton and Freemanors Hundred; Williton Union)
OR C 1641-1948, M 1641-1837, B 1641-1900 (SRO)
BT 1594-97, 1606-09, 1611-14, 1616, 1623-24, 1634-35, 1638-40, 1663-64, 1670-71, 1679-80,
    1704-O5, 1708-09, 1718-21, 1725-26, 1728-29, 1732-33, 1742-43, 1748-51, 1755, 1759, 1761,
    1764-65, 1768-71, 1773-75, 1778-83, 1786-87, 1789-90, 1798-1829, 1831, 1833-37,
    CB 1840-42 (SRO)
Cop M 1594-1812 (Ptd, Phillimore 12, 1910); CB 1594-1670 (Ptd, Dwelly 1, 1913);
    M 1594-1812 (Boyd); C 1729-1812 (SCDB); B 1729-1847 (SBDB); M 1594-1641 (BT),
    1653-1837 (SMI); C 1641-1899, M 1813-37 (DCI)
Cop (Mf) 1594-1842 (BT) (SLC, SRO)

CROWCOMBE (Baptist) b 1890 cl 1916

CUCKLINGTON St Lawrence (280) (Norton Ferris Hundred; Wincanton Union)
OR C 1568-1904, M 1559-1985, Banns 1754-90, B 1558-1992 (SRO)
BT one between 1590-1606, 1605-08, 1615-18, 1622-25, 1629-31, 1634-41, 1663-64, 1667-70,
    1674-75, 1685-86, 1732-36, 1746-52, 1754, 1756-57, 1759-60, 1765-71, 1800-20, 1822-25,
    1827-37, CB 1838-61 (SRO)
Cop CMB 1558-1837 (SRO); M 1558-1837 (Boyd); B 1706-1837 (SBDB); M 1559-1837 (SMI)
Cop (Mf) C 1558-1904, M 1559-1836, Banns 1754-90, B 1558-1690, 1706-1812 (SG, SLC);
    1605-1861 (BT) (SLC, SRO)

CUDWORTH St Michael (146) (peculiar of the Prebendary of Cudworth in the Cathedral of Wells
until 1845) (South Petherton Hundred; Chard Union)
OR CB 1699-1992, M 1699-1984, Banns 1790-1806, 1923 (SRO)
BT 1607-09, 1611-13, 1615-18, 1621, 1629-30, 1634-40, 1813-27 (SRO); 1704, 1707-09, 1711-14,
    1718 (SRO: D/D/Ppb:35)
Cop M 1813-36 (Ts SG); B 1778-1837 (SBDB); M 1607-40 (BT), 1699-1837 (SMI); C 1699-1812,
    M 1699-1816 (DCI)
Cop (Mf) CB 1754-1812, M 1755-1836, Banns 1790-1806 (SG, SLC); 1607-40, 1813-27
    (BT) (SLC, SRO)

CULBONE alias KITNOR St Culbone (62) (Carhampton Hundred; Williton Union)
OR C 1683-1812, M 1699-1836, Banns 1754-1980, B 1695-1784 (SRO); CB 1813+ (Inc)
(register B 1784-1812 lost between 1914 and 1935)
BT 1605-07, 1609, 1613, 1621-23, 1630, 1635-37, 1640, 1662-64, 1669-70, 1673-74, 1678-79,
1701-02, 1705-08, 1721-22, 1726-27, 1731-33, 1732-33, 1737, 1749-55, 1757-59, 1762, 1764,
1767-69, 1771-73, 1775, 1777-84, 1787-90, 1802-06, 1808-30, 1836, B 1838, CB 1844 (SRO)
Cop M 1699-1808, 1818-1951 (Ts I SG); C 1683-1750, M 1699-1749 (SRO); B 1685-1784 (SBDB);
M 1699-1837 (SMI); C 1683-1812, M 1699-1836 (DCI)
Cop (Mf) 1605-1844 (BT) (SLC, SRO); C 1683-1812, M 1699-1749, 1764-85, 1818-36,
Banns 1754-1831, 1935-64, B 1685-1784 (SLC)

CURLAND All Saints (167) (chapelry in Curry Mallet) (Abdick and Bulstone Hundred;
Langport Union)
OR C 1634-1963, M 1634-1956, B 1634-1854 (SRO)
BT 1605-09, 1611-13, 1615-16, 1619-20, 1622, 1624-25, 1629-31, 1635-37, 1639-41, 1664-69,
1731, 1742, 1749-52, 1755-57, 1763-65, 1784-86, 1788-1801, 1803-16, 1819-23, 1826-37,
C 1854 (SRO)
Cop CMB 1605 (Ptd, Dwelly 1, 1913); B 1772-1901 (SBDB); M 1605 (BT), 1634-1752 (SMI);
CM 1634-1899 (DCI)
Cop (Mf) C 1634-1724, 1740-1900, M 1634-1753, 1847-1900, B 1634-1724, 1740-1901 (SG, SLC);
1605-1854 (BT) (SLC, SRO)

CURLAND (Wesleyan) b 1821 (K 1931)
OR M 1979-82, B 1898-1924 (SRO)

CURRY MALLET All Saints (496) (Abdick and Bulstone Hundred; Langport Union)
OR C 1682-1961, M 1684-1990, Banns 1754-1812, B 1682-1995 (SRO)
BT 1597-1600, 1607-16, 1619-20, 1622-23, 1629-30, 1634-37, one between 1640-63, 1662-64,
1667-69, 1725-26, 1731-32, 1736-38, 1745-46, 1749-50, 1752, 1755-56, 1758-60, 1762,
1764-65, 1773-75, 1777-79, 1800-04, 1807-20, 1822-25, 1827-37, CB 1838 (SRO)
Cop 1597-1615 (Ptd, Dwelly 1, 1913); 1682-1750 (Ts I SG); M 1597-1615 (BT), 1684-1837 (SMI);
C 1682-1899, M 1683-1899 (DCI)
Cop (Mf) 1597-1838 (BT) (SLC, SRO); C 1682-1900, M 1684-1807, 1813-1900, Banns 1754-1812,
B 1751-1812 (SLC)

CURRY MALLET (Baptist) b 1874 (K 1931)

CURRY, NORTH St Peter and St Paul (1,833) (peculiar of the Dean and Chapter of Wells until
1845) (North Curry Hundred; Taunton Union)
OR C 1539-1946, M 1539-1986, Banns 1754-1812, 1840-1901, B 1539-1928 (SRO)
BT 1599-1611, 1618-19, 1621-23, 1640-41, 1697-1700, 1748-52, 1754-58, 1761, 1763-64,
1770-82, 1785-1805, 1807-08 (with Stoke St Gregory & West Hatch), 1813-16, 1822, 1826-31,
1833-37, CB 1838-62 (1784-85, 1808-09, 1817-24 in peculiar series) (SRO)
Cop M 1539-1812 (Ptd, Phillimore 2, 1899); C 1618-21, B 1618-21 (Ptd, Dwelly 1, 1913);
M 1539-1812 (Boyd); B 1784-1838 (SBDB); M 1539-1837 (SMI)
Cop (Mf) 1599-1862 (BT) (SLC, SRO); CM 1539-1901, Banns 1754-1812, 1840-1901,
B 1539-1720, 1784-1901 (SLC)

CURRY, NORTH (Baptist) b 1825 (K 1931)

CURRY, NORTH (Wesleyan) (Lewis 1831) b 1833 (K 1931)
OR B 1898-1924 (SRO)

CURRY RIVEL St Andrew (1,444) (Abdick and Bulstone Hundred; Langport Union)
OR C 1628, 1637-1956, M 1642, 1653-1972, Banns 1813-23, B 1606, 1642, 1653-1983 (SRO)
BT one between 1601-28, 1607-09, 1611-12, 1616-17, 1623-24, 1629-30, one between 1632-42,
    1635-40, 1662-63, 1666-68, 1731-32, 1742-43, 1749-51, 1754-55, 1757, 1769, 1789-90,
    1800-37, CB 1838-50, CMB 1851-63 (SRO)
Cop M 1642-1812 (Ptd, Phillimore 3, 1901); C 1607-38, M 1607-38, B 1607-38 (Ptd, Dwelly 1,
    1913); M 1642-1812 (Boyd); B 1709-1847 (SBDB); M 1607-40 (BT), 1642-1837 (SMI);
    C 1628-1899, M 1813-99 (DCI)
Cop (Mf) 1607-1863 (BT) (SLC, SRO); C 1628-1886, M 1653-1886, Banns 1812-23, B 1642-1886
    (SLC)

CURRY RIVEL Wiltown (Independent) f 1840 b 1866 (K 1931)

CUTCOMBE St John (709) (Carhampton Hundred; Williton Union)
OR C 1636-1897, M 1638-1971, Banns 1754-1819, B 1638-1880 (SRO) (1935 list has from 1576;
    1914 list from 1624)
BT one between 1592-1606, 1598-1600, 1602-11, 1613-18, 1622-23, 1629-30, 1634-41, one
    between 1660-67, 1661-62, 1678-80, 1685-86, 1695-96, 1704-07, 1709-10; 1721-22, 1728-29,
    1731-32, 1749-52, 1755, 1757-59, 1762, 1764-65, 1767-69, 1771-75, 1778-84, 1786-1831,
    1835-37, CB 1838-39 (SRO)
Cop 1636-1703 (SRO); B 1783-1870 (SBDB); M 1638-1837 (SMI); C 1636-1897, M 1638-1899
    (DCI)
Cop (Mf) C 1636-1886, M 1638-1886, Banns 1754-1823, B 1638-1880 (SG, SLC); 1598-1839
    (BT) (SLC, SRO)

CUTCOMBE Wheddon Cross (Wesleyan) f 1839 b 1896 (K 1931)
OR C 1803-72 (circuit) (SRO)

DINDER St Michael and All Angels (210) (peculiar of the Dean of Wells until 1845)
    (Wells Forum Hundred; Wells Union)
OR C 1695-1954, M 1695-1986, Banns 1756-1900, B 1578-1636, 1695-1992 (SRO)
BT 1598-99, 1602-03, 1605-09, 1611, 1613-14, 1621-22, 1630-31, 1635-37, 1640-41, 1813-19,
    1821-23, 1825, M 1841 (1753 in peculiar series) (SRO)
Cop 1598-1640 (Ptd, Dwelly 1, 1913); M 1598-1753 (SRO); B 1695-1992 (SBDB);
    M 1598-1640 (BT), 1695-1837 (SMI)
Cop (Mf) 1598-1841 (BT) (SLC, SRO); C 1695-1901, M 1695-1836, Banns 1756-1900,
    B 1578-1636, 1695-1812 (SLC)

DINNINGTON St Nicholas (187) (chapelry in Seavington St Michael, in 1920s included in
    Hinton St George) (South Petherton Hundred; Chard Union)
OR C 1592-1812, M 1592-1837, Banns 1754-82, 1785-1808, B 1608-1812 (gaps C 1613-91,
    1753-56, M 1594-1751, B 1593-1732) (SRO); CB 1813+ (Inc)
BT 1599-1600, 1606-08, 1611-13, 1621-24, 1629-30, 1634, 1636-40, 1663-64, 1667-69, 1674,
    1678-80, 1734 or 1735, 1748-49, 1770-72, 1802-06, 1808-18, 1820-32, 1834-36, CB 1837-43
    (SRO)
Cop 1599-1674 (SG); C 1592-1611, 1757-80, M 1592-1611, 1784-97, 1800-37, Banns 1790,
    B 1592-1612, 1757-79 (Ts SG); C 1592-1812 (SBDB); M 1592-1837 (SMI); C 1592-1812,
    M 1592-1837 (DCI)
Cop (Mf) 1599-1843 (BT) (SLC, SRO); C 1592-1611, 1693-1812, M 1592-1611, 1700-17,
    1734-1837, 1895, Banns 1754-75, 1785-1808, B 1592-1611, 1733-1812 (SLC)

DINNINGTON Wesleyan f 1809 cl c1822 (Bible Christian) f 1824 b 1862 cl 1956

DINNINGTON Elim Pentecostal Church f c1964 in old Methodist Chapel

DITCHEAT St Mary Magdalene (1,238) (Whitstone Hundred; Shepton Mallet Union)
OR C 1562-1958, M 1562-1974, Banns 1783-1812, 1823-89, B 1562-1900 (SRO)
BT 1605-08, 1611-12, 1616-17, 1622-24, 1629-31, 1635-37, 1663-64, 1666-67, 1679-80, 1704-05, 1732-33, 1746-51, 1755-57, 1800-36 (SRO)
Cop 1605-23 (Ptd, Dwelly 1, 1913); C 1562-1653 (SRO); B 1783-1843 (SBDB); M 1562-1837 (SMI)
Cop (Mf) 1605-1836 (BT) (SLC, SRO); C 1562-1886, MB 1562-1885, Banns 1754-1812, 1823-89 (SLC)

DITCHEAT (Wesleyan) b 1808 (K 1931)
OR Z 1865-78 (SRO) (in parish registers)

DODINGTON All Saints (93) (Williton and Freemanors Hundred; Williton Union)
OR CB 1538-1805, M 1538-1835 (gap 1634-53), 1886, Banns 1754-98 (SRO); CB 1813+ (Inc) (the registers 1538-1740 were recovered between 1831 and 1914)
BT 1597-1600, 1603-10, 1612-13, 1615, 1617-18, 1621-23, 1630-31, 1634-36, 1639-41, 1662-64, 1666-67, 1670, 1672, 1679-80, 18th century, 1704-06, 1712, 1718-20, 1725, 1730-34, 1736, 1742-43, 1748-52, 1755, 1757-59, 1802-05, 1807-37 (SRO)
Cop M 1538-1805 (Ptd, Phillimore 6, 1905); C 1597-1679, B 1597-1679 (Ptd, Dwelly 1, 1913); M 1538-1805 (Boyd); B 1741-1805 (SBDB); M 1538-1837 (SMI)
Cop (Mf) 1597-1837 (BT) (SLC, SRO); C 1538-1634, 1652-1804, M 1538-1634, 1652-1730, 1743-1805, 1814-35, 1886, Banns 1754-98, B 1538-1634, 1652-1805 (SLC)

DONYATT St Mary (557) (Abdick and Bulstone Hundred; Chard Union)
OR C 1712-1882, M 1719-1837, Banns 1754-1885, B 1719-1868 (SRO)
BT one between 1592-1623, 1598-99, one between 1600-22, 1605-09, 1611-12, 1622-24, 1629-30, one between 1632-40, 1635-36, 1640-41, 1756-58, 1800-03, 1807-34 (SRO)
Cop 1600-29 (Ptd, Dwelly 1, 1913); C 1712-1837, MB 1719-1837 (Ts I SG, SRO); B 1813-60 (SBDB); M 1600-29 (BT), 1719-1837 (SMI); C 1712-1882, M 1603-1837 (DCI)
Cop (Mf) 1598-1834 (BT) (SLC, SRO); C 1712-1882, M 1719-1837, Banns 1754-1885, B 1719-1868 (SLC)

DOULTING St Aldhelm (630) (Whitstone Hundred; Shepton Mallet Union)
OR C 1668-1912, M 1634-1994, Banns 1754-1812, 1886-1955, B 1634-1978 (SRO) (registers from 1563 survived in 1914)
BT 1602-09, 1611-18, 1621-22, 1629-30, 1632-36, 1640-41, one between 1635-40, 1663-64, one between 1662-67, 1667-69, 1672-75, 1679-80, 1736-37, 1800-21 (SRO)
Cop 1615-29 (Ptd, Dwelly 1, 1913); C 1663-99, 1733-83, M 1634-85, B 1634-83, 1774-83 (SRO); B 1783-1870 (SBDB); M 1615-29 (BT), 1634-83, 1754-1837 (SMI)
Cop (Mf) 1602-1821 (BT) (SLC, SRO); C 1668-1901, M 1634-1901, Banns 1754-1812, 1886-1901, B 1634-1901 (SLC)

DOULTING Priestleigh (Wesleyan) b 1865 (K 1931)

DOULTING Waterlip (Primitive Methodist) b 1875

DOULTING Waterlip (Plymouth Brethren) (K 1931)

DOWLISH WAKE St Andrew (380) (South Petherton Hundred; Chard Union)
OR C 1644-1878, M 1645-1984, Banns 1760-1837, B 1644-1942, 1966-71 (SRO)
BT 1599-1600, 1605-12, 1615, 1617-20, 1622-23, 1630-31, 1635-37, 1639-41, 1667-68, 1674-75, 1729-32, 1734-36, 1740, 1746-47, 1751-52, 1756-57, 1764-65, 1768, 1772-73, 1775, 1789-90, 1800-05, 1809-25, 1827-35, C 1836 (SRO)
Cop 1599-1619 (Ptd, Dwelly 1, 1913); B 1761-1907 (SBDB); M 1599-1619 (BT), 1646-1837 (SMI); C 1644-1878, M 1646-1837 (DCI)
Cop (Mf) 1599-1836 (BT) (SLC, SRO); C 1644-1878, M 1644-1886, Banns 1760-1837, B 1644-1907 (SLC)

DOWLISH WAKE (sect of Joanna Southcott) f c1811, cl c1850

DOWLISH, WEST (38) (Abdick and Bulstone Hundred; Chard Union) (incorporated into Dowlish Wake, 1933, but had had no church for several centuries, and no separate register sequence)

DOWNHEAD St Nicholas (221) (chapelry in Doulting) (Whitstone Hundred; Shepton Mallet Union)
OR C 1708, 1720, 1730-1812, M 1730, 1733-49, 1756-1978, Banns 1755-61, 1770-1805, 1824-89,
    B 1695, 1730-54, 1764-1812 (SRO); CB 1813+ (Inc)
BT 1608-09, 1613-18, 1622-24, 1630-31, 1635-36, 1639-41, 1663, 1667-69, 1750, 1801-26,
    1829-30 (SRO)
Cop 1615-30 (Ptd, Dwelly 1, 1913); M 1608-1745 (SRO); B 1783-1812 (SBDB); M 1615-30 (BT),
    1756-1837 (SMI)
Cop (Mf) 1608-1830 (BT) (SLC, SRO); C 1711-1812, M 1733-1836, Banns 1824-94,
    B 1695, 1730-1812 (SLC)

DOWNHEAD (Primitive Methodist) b 1863 (K 1931)

DOWNSIDE Christ Church (created from Midsomer Norton, 1840) (Clutton Union)
OR C 1839-1980, M 1846-1980, Banns 1846-84, B 1839-1984 (SRO)
Cop (Mf) C 1839-86, M 1846-86, Banns 1846-84, B 1839-85 (SLC)

DOWNSIDE St Gregory (Roman Catholic) f 1814 (K 1931)
OR C 1919+ (Inc)

DOWNSIDE (Wesleyan) (K 1931)

DRAYCOTT St Peter (created from Cheddar, Nyland and Rodney Stoke, 1862) (Wells Union)
OR C 1861-1966, M 1863-1981, Banns 1863-1902, B 1861-1973 (SRO)
Cop (Mf) C 1861-1900, M 1863-1900, Banns 1863-1902, B 1861-1901 (SG, SLC)

DRAYCOTT (United Methodist) b 1876 (K 1931)

DRAYCOTT (Wesleyan) b 1887

DRAYTON St Catherine (519) (part Abdick and Bulstone Hundred, part East Kingsbury Hundred;
    Langport Union)
OR C 1558-1958, M 1558-1979, Banns 1754-1818, 1823-1900, B 1558-1918 (SRO)
BT 1599-1600, 1605-10, 1615, 1621-24, 1635-36, 1639-41, 1660-62, 1666-70, 1731-33, 1735-36,
    1741-43, 1749-52, 1757, 1769, 1789-90, 1800-37, CB 1838-49 (SRO)
Cop M 1577-1812 (Ptd, Phillimore 3, 1901); C 1599-1639, B 1599-1639 (Ptd, Dwelly 1, 1913);
    M 1577-1812 (Boyd); B 1708-1900 (SBDB); M 1577-1837 (SMI); C 1558-1899, M 1813-99
    (DCI)
Cop (Mf) 1599-1849 (BT) (SLC, SRO); CM 1558-1901, Banns 1754-1900, B 1558-1900 (SLC)

DULVERTON Board of Guardians
OR Z 1866-1927, D 1866-1930 (SRO)

DULVERTON All Saints (1,285) (Williton and Freemanors Hundred; Dulverton Union)
OR C 1558-1601, 1616-50, 1653-1967, M 1559-1649, 1654-1967, Banns 1757-1814, 1823-85,
    B 1558-1618, 1641-42, 1648, 1653-1923 (SRO)
BT 1598-99, one between 1598-1602, 1602-03, 1605-12, 1616-17, 1621-24, 1629-30, 1636-37,
    1639-41, 1662-65, one between 1665-67, 1678-79, 1694-95, 1698-99, 1701-02, one between
    1702-04, 1704-05, 1721-22, 1728-29, 1731-33, 1749-50, 1752, 1754-57, 1759, 1762-65,
    1767-69, 1789-92, 1794-95, 1797, 1799-1801, 1803-38, CB 1851-56 (SRO)
Cop B 1766-1844 (SBDB); M 1558-1837 (SMI); C 1558-1899, M 1559-1899 (DCI)
Cop (Mf) CMB 1558-1886, Banns 1757-1814, 1823-85 (SG, SLC); 1598-1856 (BT) (SLC, SRO)

DULVERTON (Independent) f 1672 reb 1831 (K 1931)
OR ZC 1831-36 (PRO: RG 4/2056)
Cop (Mf) ZC 1831-36 (SLC, SRO)

DULVERTON (United Methodist) (Tiverton and Bampton Circuit) b 1902 (K 1931)

DULVERTON St Stanislaus, High Street (Roman Catholic) b 1955

DUNDRY St Michael (583) (chapelry in Chew Magna until 1855) (Chew Hundred;
   Bedminster Union 1836-99, Long Ashton Union 1899-1930)
OR CMB 1654+ (Inc) (C from 1560, M from 1558 and B from 1559 survived in 1914)
BT 1603-06, 1611-12, 1615-16, 1622-24, 1630-31, 1635-37, 1639-41, 1663-64, 1695-96, 1800-37,
   CB 1838-39, CMB 1840, CB 1841 (SRO)
Cop 1603-95, 1800-12 (from BT only) (Ts I SG); M 1754-1837 (NSMI); M 1754-1837 (SMI)
Cop (Mf) 1603-1841 (BT) (SLC, SRO)

DUNDRY (Baptist) b 1828 (K 1931)

DUNKERTON All Saints (718) (Wellow Hundred; Bath Union)
OR C 1724, 1748-1858, M 1748-1837, Banns 1754-1812, B 1752-1888 (SRO)
BT 1601-04, 1606-09, 1611-16, 1622, 1629-31, 1634-37, 1639-40, 1663-64, 1732-33, 1735-37,
   1743-44, 1750-52, 1754, 1756-57, 1800-06, 1808-23 (SRO)
Cop 1608-15 (Ptd, Dwelly 1, 1913); M 1754-1837 (NSMI); B 1752-1879 (SBDB); M 1608-15 (BT),
   1748-1837 (SMI)
Cop (Mf) C 1748-1858, M 1748-1837, Banns 1754-1812, B 1752-1888 (SG, SLC);
   1601-1823 (BT) (SLC, SRO)

DUNKERTON (Baptist) b 1821 (K 1931)

DUNKERTON (Methodist)
OR C 1843-1900 (circuit register) (Bristol RO)
Cop (Mf) C 1843-1900 (Bristol RO, SLC)

DUNSTER Cemetery opened 1880 (2 acres)
OR B 1880-98 (SRO)

DUNSTER St George (983) (Carhampton Hundred; Williton Union)
OR C 1559-1956, M 1559-1979, Banns 1754-1812, B 1560-1864 (SRO)
BT 1594-99, 1605-07, 1621-22, 1635-36, 1639-41, 1662-63, 1669-70, 1690-91, 1694-95, 1697-98,
   1701-02, 1704-05, 1708-09, 1721-22, 1726-27, 1732-37, 1740-41, 1749-51, 1755-58, 1781,
   1789, 1800, 1804-12, 1814-36, CB 1848-70 (SRO)
Cop 1559-1680 (SRO); C 1767-98 (SCDB); B 1767-1864 (SBDB); M 1750-1837 (SMI);
   CM 1559-1899 (DCI)
Cop (Mf) C 1559-1903, M 1559-1901, Banns 1754-1812, B 1560-1864 (SG, SLC);
   1594-1870 (BT) (SLC, SRO)

DUNSTER (Wesleyan) b 1878 (K 1931)
OR C 1803-72 (circuit) (SRO); C 1803-37 (chapel) (PRO: RG 4/2182)
Cop (Mf) C 1803-37 (SLC, SRO)

DURLEIGH (dedication unknown) (139) (Andersfield Hundred; Bridgwater Union)
OR CB 1683-1980, M 1683-1935, Banns 1756-1801, 1823-1920 (SRO)
BT 1599-1607, 1609-19, one between 1611-13, 1621-24, 1629-31, 1635-41, 1666, 1668-71,
   1678-80, 1704-07, 1709-10, 1712-13, 1718-20, 1725-26, 1728-29, 1732-35, 1741-44, 1747-52,
   1806-25, 1827-38 (SRO)
Cop M 1683-1807 (Ptd, Phillimore 6, 1905); CB 1599-1679, M 1599-1679 (Ptd, Dwelly 1, 1913);
   M 1683-1807 (Boyd); B 1820-1980 (SBDB); M 1599-1837 (OR & BT) (SMI)
Cop (Mf) 1599-1838 (BT) (SLC, SRO); CM 1683-1901, Banns 1823-1920, B 1683-1905 (SLC)

DURSTON St John (226) (North Petherton Hundred; Taunton Union)
OR C 1712-1906, M 1712-1946, Banns 1755-1812, 1824-99, B 1712-1813 (SRO); B 1813+ (Inc)
BT 1606-16, 1622, 1629-31, 1634, 1636-37, 1639-41, 1666-67, 1678-80, 1732-33, 1740-41,
    1748-49, 1752-53, 1759-60, 1764-65, 1767-82, 1789, 1795-97, 1801-31, 1833-37, 1839,
    CB 1840-41, CMB 1842, 1844, CB 1845, CMB 1846-47, CB 1848, CMB 1849, CB 1850,
    CMB 1851, CB 1852-54 (SRO)
Cop 1606-1812 (Ptd, Dwelly 1, 9, 15, 1922-26); M 1712-1812 (Boyd); B 1712-1813 (SBDB);
    M 1606-80 (BT), 1712-1837 (SMI)
Cop (Mf) 1606-1854 (BT) (SLC, SRO)

EARNSHILL (12) (chapelry in Curry Rivel until temp.Henry VIII; incorporated into Hambridge,
    1844, no separate registers) (Abdick and Bulstone Hundred; Langport Union)

EASTHAMS a sinecure rectory until 1925 when it became part of Crewkerne

EASTON St Paul (created from Wells St Cuthbert, 1844) (Wells Union)
OR M 1845-1978 (SRO)

EASTON (Wesleyan) b 1831 (K 1931)

EASTON in GORDANO Cemetery, Greenbank
OR B 1871-1901 (Bristol RO)
Cop (Mf) B 1871-1901 (Bristol RO, SLC)

EASTON in GORDANO St George (2,255) (peculiar of the Prebendary of Easton, in the Cathedral
    Church of Wells until 1845) (Portbury Hundred; Bedminster Union 1836-99, Long Ashton
    Union 1899-1930)
OR C 1559-1898, M 1559-1906, Banns 1754-76, B 1559-1919 (SRO)
BT after 1589, 1605, 1611-12, 1636-37, 1640-41, 1662-65, 1813-17, 1820, 1824-26, 1828-37,
    CB 1838-44, CMB 1845, CB 1846-47 (1708-09 in peculiar series) (SRO)
Cop C 1700-17 (SRO); M 1754-1837 (NSMI); B 1791-1837 (SBDB); M 1559-1837 (SMI)
Cop (Mf) C 1559-1898, M 1559-1837, B 1559-1919 (SG); 1605-1847 (BT) (SLC, SRO)

EASTON in GORDANO St Mark
OR CB 1848+, M 1849+ (Inc)
BT CB 1848-72, M 1849-72 (Bristol RO)
Cop (Mf) 1848-72 (BT) (Bristol RO, SLC)

EASTON in GORDANO (Wesleyan) (Lewis 1831)
OR M 1937-66 (Bristol RO)
Cop (Mf) M 1937-66 (Bristol RO, SLC)

EASTOVER St John the Baptist *see* **BRIDGWATER St John the Baptist**

EASTRIP (extra-parochial until 1933 when became part of Bruton) (Bruton Hundred;
    Wincanton Union)

EDINGTON St George (1,112) (chapelry in Moorlinch until 1828) (Whitley Hundred; Bridgwater
    Union) (registers united with those of Sutton Mallet, Stawell, Moorlinch and Chilton Polden)
OR C 1552-1909, M 1571-1769, B 1555-1812 (SRO) (Z 1653-55 and CMB 1722-23 in Moorlinch
    register); B 1813+ (Inc)
BT 1599-1600, 1605-06, 1608-09, 1611-12, 1615-18, 1622-23, 1635-37, 1639-40, 1662-63,
    1667-68, 1678-79, 1720-21, 1744-45, 1768-70, 1775-76, 1778-79, 1782-83, 1803-05, 1809-10,
    1812-13, 1830-31, 1833-37, CB 1838-49 (SRO)
Cop C 1679-1812 (SCDB); B 1678-1812 (SBDB); M 1679-1812 (SMI)
Cop (Mf) C 1552-1900, M 1571-1769, B 1555-1811 (SG, SLC); 1599-1849 (BT) (SLC, SRO)

EDSTOCK and BEER hamlet in Cannington, divided between Cannington and Otterhampton, 1886 (Cannington Hundred; Bridgwater Union)

ELM St Mary (427) (Frome Hundred; Frome Union)
OR C 1697-1912, M 1697-1958, B 1697-1812 (SRO); B 1813+ (Inc)
BT 1598-99, 1601-03, 1606-07, 1609-10, 1615-16, 1618-23, 1628-31, 1634-37, 1639-41, 1663-66, 1749-52, 1755-58, 1803-24, 1831, 1834-37, CB 1838-53 (SRO)
Cop M 1698-1753 (SRO); M 1598-1666 (BT), 1698-1837 (SMI)
Cop (Mf) 1598-1853 (BT) (SLC, SRO); C 1697-1903, M 1698-1901, B 1698-1812 (SLC)

ELM (Wesleyan) b 1823 (Little Elm) b 1835 (Great Elm) (K 1931)

ELWORTHY St Martin (210) (Williton and Freemanors Hundred; Williton Union)
OR C 1685-1978, M 1686-1974, Banns 1754-1807, 1873-88, B 1685-1978 (SRO)
BT one between 1589-99, 1599-1800, 1605-12, 1615-18, 1621-24, 1630-31, 1635-36, 1639-40, 1662-65, 1678-80, 1701-02, 1704-07, 1711, 1721-22, one between 1721-28, 1731-33, 1735-36, 1746, 1751, 1753-55, 1759, 1763-64, 1770-71, 1786, 1788-1825, 1827, 1833, 1835-37 (SRO)
Cop C 1685-1758, M 1686-1752 (SRO); B 1758-1887 (SBDB); M 1686-1837 (SMI); C 1685-1894, M 1686-1898 (DCI)
Cop (Mf) C 1685-1887, M 1686-1888, Banns 1754-1807, 1873-88, B 1685-1887 (SG, SLC); 1599-1837 (BT) (SLC, SRO)

EMBOROUGH St Mary (207) (chapelry in Chewton Mendip) (Chewton Hundred; Shepton Mallet Union)
OR C 1569-1977, M 1569-1974, Banns 1770-80, 1784-1812, 1854, 1856, 1913-58, B 1569-1812 (SRO); B 1813+ (Inc Chewton Mendip)
BT 1598-99, 1605-12, 1622-23, 1629-31, 1634-36, 1639-41, 1749-50, 1754-56, 1758-59, 1802-03, 1805-27, 1829, 1832, 1834-36, CB 1850-55 (SRO)
Cop 1569-1769 (Ts I SG); C 1738-1812 (SCDB); B 1741-1812 (SBDB); M 1570-1837 (SMI)
Cop (Mf) 1598-1855 (BT) (SLC, SRO); C 1569-1886, M 1570-1884, B 1569-1812 (SLC)

ENGLISHCOMBE (dedication unknown) (388) (Wellow Hundred; Bath Union)
OR C 1728-1987, M 1756-1980, Banns 1756-1812, B 1749-1909 (SRO)
BT 1605-14, 1618-19, 1622-23, 1635-37, 1639, 1662-64, 1667-69, 1673-74, 1692-94, 1797-1815, 1817-21, 1823-37, CB 1838-40, CMB 1841, CB 1842, CMB 1843-66 (SRO)
Cop C 1609-73, M 1609-73, B 1609-73 (Ptd, Dwelly 1, 1913); C 1728-1812, M 1756-1812, B 1749-1812 (Ts I SG, Bath Lib, British Lib); M 1754-1837 (NSMI); B 1813-53 (SBDB); M 1605-68 (BT), 1754-1837 (SMI)
Cop (Mf) 1605-1866 (BT) (SLC, SRO)

ENGLISHCOMBE (Independent) f 1838 (K 1931)

ENGLISHCOMBE (Wesleyan) b 1845 (K 1931)

ENMORE St Michael (294) (Andersfield Hundred; Bridgwater Union)
OR C 1653-1886, M 1655-1979, Banns 1754-1811, 1825-1901, B 1653-1812 (SRO); B 1813+ (Inc)
BT one between 1578-1601, one between 1602-06, 1606-16, 1619-23, 1630, 1635-37, 1639-41, 1666-67, 1670-73, 1678-79, 1704, 1706-07, 1712-13, 1719-21, 1732-33, 1742-46, 1748-51, 1759-60, 1764-65, 1767-68, 1770-76, 1802-05, 1807-23, 1825-26, 1828, 1831-37, CB 1838-39, 1843-48, 1850-54 (SRO)
Cop M 1653-1812 (Ptd, Phillimore 6, 1905); CB 1607-79, M 1607-41 (Ptd, Dwelly 1, 1913); M 1655-1812 (Boyd); B 1750-1812 (SBDB); M 1607-41 (BT), 1655-1837 (SMI)
Cop (Mf) 1606-1854 (BT) (SLC, SRO); C 1653-1886, M 1655-1901, Banns 1754-1811, 1825-1901, B 1653-1812 (SLC)

ENMORE (Bible Christian) f before 1867 cl 1889

ENMORE Gospel Hall, Bridgwater Road b 1901 since 1930's Plymouth Brethren

EVERCREECH St Peter with CHESTERBLADE St Mary (1,490) (peculiar of the Dean of Wells until 1845) (Wells Forum Hundred; Shepton Mallet Union)
OR C 1540-1969, M 1540-1967, Banns 1754-1814, B 1540-1873 (SRO)
BT one between 1619-36, 1621-24, 1629-30, 1636-37, 1639-41, one between c.1661-90, 1663, 1676-77, 1679, 1801-05, 1807-31 (SRO); 1753-61, 1765-66, 1771-74, 1800-02 (SRO: D/D/Pd:26/8)
Cop 1629-39 (Ptd, Dwelly 1, 1913); CMB 1540-1707 (SRO); C 1540-1881, M 1540-1889, B 1540-1890 (Ts I SLC); B 1790-1838 (SBDB); M 1540-1837 (SMI)
Cop (Mf) C 1540-1969, M 1540-1908, Banns 1754-1814, B 1540-1873 (SG, SLC); 1621-1831 (BT) (SLC, SRO)

EVERCREECH (Wesleyan) (Lewis 1831) b 1873 (K 1931)

EXFORD St Mary Magdalene (447) (Carhampton Hundred; Dulverton Union)
OR C 1618, 1632-1951, M 1642-1986, Banns 1754-1810, B 1642-1916 (SRO)
BT 1594-96, 1598-99, 1605-12, 1621-24, 1629-31, 1635-37, 1639-41, 1662-64, 1667-70, 1672-73, 1678-80, 1701-09, 1711-13, 1721-22, 1731-33, 1745, 1749-60, 1762, 1764-65, 1767-69, 1771-75, 1777-79, 1782, 1784, 1786. 1788, 1790-1830, 1832-35 (SRO)
Cop C 1618-1716, M 1642-1716, B 1642-1715 (SRO); B 1768-1900 (SBDB); M 1642-1837 (SMI); C 1609-1899, M 1642-1899 (DCI)
Cop (Mf) C 1618, 1632-1901, M 1642-1902, Banns 1754-1810, B 1642-1901 (SG, SLC); 1594-1835 (BT) (SLC, SRO)

EXFORD (Wesleyan) b 1885 (K 1931)
OR C 1803-72 (circuit) (SRO)

EXMOOR St Luke (52) (extra-parochial place, mainly in Somerset with a small part in Devon, until created a parish in 1857) (parts in Williton and Freemanors Hundred, Somerset and South Molton Hundred, Devon; parts in Dulverton Union, Somerset and South Molton Union, Devon)
OR M 1856-1960 (SRO); CB 1857+ (Inc)
Cop M 1856-99 (DCI)
Cop (Mf) M 1856-99 (SG, SLC)

EXTON St Peter (347) (part Carhampton Hundred, part Williton and Freemanors Hundred; Dulverton Union)
OR C 1559-1864, M 1559-1975, Banns 1794-1813, 1824-84, B 1559-1812 (SRO); B 1813+ (Inc)
BT 1603-09, 1611-12, 1615-16, 1621-23, 1635-36, 1639-41, 1662-63, one between 1662-68, 1668-70, 1672-73, 1678-80, 1697-98, 1703-08, 1711-12, 1722, 1728, 1743, 1745-46, 1751, 1753-59, 1762-64, 1767-69, 1771-1811, 1813-22, 1827-32, 1834-36 (SRO)
Cop CM 1559-1686 (SRO); B 1785-1812 (SBDB); M 1558-1666, 1750-1837 (SMI); C 1558-1864, M 1558-1899 (DCI)
Cop (Mf) C 1559-1864, M 1559-1901, Banns 1794-1813, 1824-84, B 1559-1644, 1684-1812 (SG, SLC); 1603-1836 (BT) (SLC, SRO)

EXTON Bridgetown (Wesleyan) b 1849 (K 1931)
OR C 1803-72 (circuit) (SRO)

FAILAND (created from Portbury, 1887) (Portbury Union; Bedminster Union 1836-99, Long Ashton Union 1899-1930)
OR C 1887-1937, M 1920-41 (SRO)

FARLEIGH HUNGERFORD St Leonard (168) (Wellow Hundred; Frome Union)
OR C 1673-1995, M 1675-1996, B 1673-1995 (SRO)
BT 1602-03, 1605, 1611-14, 1616-17, 1622, 1635-36, 1639-40, one between 1662-65, 1732-37, 1748, 1775, 1800-29, 1831 (SRO)
Cop 1616 (Ptd, Dwelly 1, 1913); 1674-1947 (Index SRO); M 1675-1753 (SRO); B 1759-1813 (SBDB); M 1616 (BT), 1675-1837 (SMI)
Cop (Mf) 1602-1831 (BT) (SLC, SRO); CB 1674-1812, M 1674-1836 (SLC)

FARLEIGH HUNGERFORD (Independent or Baptist) f 1850 (K 1931)

FARMBOROUGH All Saints (924) (Keynsham Hundred; Clutton Union)
OR C 1559-1924 (defective 1647-61), M 1559-1987 (defective 1599-1604, 1645-62),
    Banns 1754-1812, B 1559-1933 (defective 1646-61) (SRO)
BT 1605-13, 1615-16, 1621-24, 1629-30, 1635-37, 1639-41, 1663-66, 1668-69, 1671, 1675-76,
    1678-79, 1681-83, 1732-33, 1738-39, 1749-50, 1798-1838, 1841-61 (SRO)
Cop CB 1559-1812, M 1562-1812 (Ts I SG, Bath Lib, British Lib); M 1561-1753 (SRO);
    M 1754-1837 (NSMI); B 1733-1863 (SBDB); M 1561-1837 (SMI)
Cop (Mf) 1605-1861 (BT) (SLC, SRO); C 1559-1924, MB 1559-1901 (SLC)

FARMBOROUGH (Wesleyan) b 1812 (United Methodist) b 1866 (K 1931)
OR M 1933-87 (Bristol RO)
Cop (Mf) M 1933-87 (Bristol RO, SLC)

FARRINGTON GURNEY St John the Baptist (568) (chapelry in Chewton Mendip until 1867 when
    united with Ston Easton) (Chewton Hundred; Clutton Union)
OR C 1681-1729, 1732-54, 1761-1918, M 1695-1704, 1740-1976, Banns 1755-1809, 1823-1951,
    B 1681-1704, 1711, 1729-54, 1761-1896 (SRO)
BT 1599-1600, 1606-09, 1611-12, 1619-24, 1629-31, 1635-36, 1638-41, 1732-33, 1746-48,
    1751-52, 1756-57, 1801-05, 1808-17, 1819-23, 1825-34, 1836 (SRO)
Cop CB 1754-61, 1810-99, M 1775-1899 (SRO); M 1754-1837 (NSMI); B 1754-1878 (SBDB);
    M 1599-1641 (BT), 1695-1837 (SMI)
Cop (Mf) 1599-1836 (BT) (SLC, SRO); C 1681-1704, 1720-1901, M 1695-1704, 1736-1900,
    Banns 1755-1809, 1823-1901, B 1693-1704, 1711, 1729-1896 (SLC)

FARRINGTON GURNEY (Wesleyan) (Lewis 1831) b 1881 (K 1931)

FELTON COMMON HILL St Katharine and the Noble Army of Martyrs (created from Winford,
    Backwell and Wrington, 1873) (Bedminster Union 1836-99, Long Ashton Union 1899-1930)
OR CMB 1873+ (Inc)

FIDDINGTON St Martin (210) (Cannington Hundred; Bridgwater Union)
OR C 1706-1939, M 1706-1836, B 1706-1812 (SRO); B 1813+ (Inc)
BT 1597-1602, 1605-14, 1621-23, 1629-31, 1635-37, 1640-41, 1661-67, 1670-73, 1678-80,
    1704-07, 1744-45, 1765, 1768-69, 1790, 1801-05, 1807-36, 1843-46, 1848, CB 1849,
    CMB 1850, CB 1851 (SRO)
Cop M 1706-1812 (Ptd, Phillimore 12, 1910); 1706-1922 (Ms I SG); B 1804-1922 (SRO);
    M 1706-1812 (Boyd); B 1706-1812 (SBDB); M 1597-1680 (BT), 1706-26, 1738-1837 (SMI)
Cop (Mf) 1597-1851 (BT) (SLC, SRO)

FIDDINGTON Providence Chapel, Whitnell (General Baptist) b 1835 cl c1925

FIDDINGTON Coultings (Independent) f by 1861 cl c1900

FIDDINGTON (Wesleyan) b c1874 cl by 1900

FITZHEAD St James (311) (chapelry in Wiveliscombe until 1737) (peculiar of the Prebendary of
    Wiveliscombe in the Cathedral of Wells until 1845) (West Kingsbury Hundred;
    Wellington Union)
OR C 1558-1913 (gap 1654-61), M 1558-1861 (gap 1646-53), Banns 1762-1809, B 1558-1812
    (SRO); B 1813+ (Inc)
BT 1598-1600, 1605-07, 1609-11, 1622-24, 1629-30, 1636-37, 1639-41, 1662-64, 1667-68,
    1672-73, 1677-80, 1743-44, 1811-37, CB 1838-51 (1779-83 in peculiar series) (SRO)
Cop 1609-63 (Ptd, Dwelly 1, 1913); M 1559-1762 (SRO); B 1705-1812 (SBDB); M 1559-1837
    (SMI); C 1558-1899, M 1559-1837 (DCI)
Cop (Mf) 1598-1851 (BT) (SLC, SRO); C 1558-1905, M 1558-1861, Banns 1762-1809,
    B 1558-1812 (SLC)

FIVEHEAD St Martin (387) (part Abdick and Bulstone Hundred, part Williton and Freemanors Hundred; Langport Union)
OR C 1654-1898, M 1656-1983, Banns 1754-1821, B 1654-1981 (SRO)
BT 1598-1600, 1606-13, 1621-24, 1630-31, 1635-39, 1663, 1667-69, 1728-29, 1736-37, 1742-43, 1745-46, 1749-53, 1760-61, 1764-65, 1775-76, 1765-70, 1774-75, 1778-80, 1782, 1789-90, 1801, 1803-04, 1806-56, B 1857 (SRO)
Cop M 1656-1812 (Ptd, Phillimore 5, 1904); CB 1598-1636, M 1598-1636 (Ptd, Dwelly 1, 1913); M 1813-37 (Ts I SG); M 1656-1812 (Boyd); B 1803-86 (SBDB); M 1598-1639 (BT), 1656-1837 (SMI); C 1654-1898, M 1813-99 (DCI)
Cop (Mf) 1598-1857 (BT) (SLC, SRO); C 1654-1725, 1733-38, 1748-1898, M 1656-1725, 1733-38, 1754-1885, B 1654-1725, 1733-38, 1754-1887 (SLC)

FIVEHEAD (Baptist) b 1828 (K 1931)

FLAX BOURTON St Michael (219) (chapelry in Wraxall until 1841) (Portbury Hundred; Bedminster Union 1836-99, Long Ashton Union 1899-1930)
OR C 1702-1967, M 1707-1983, Banns 1759-95, 1825, 1831-99, B 1701-1984 (SRO)
BT 1838, CB 1839-43, CMB 1844-45, CB 1846-57, CMB 1860 (SRO)
Cop B 1701-1902 (SBDB); M 1701-1837 (SMI)
Cop (Mf) 1838-60 (BT) (SLC, SRO); C 1702-1900, M 1707-30, 1749-1902, Banns 1759-90, 1825, 1831-99, B 1701-77, 1794, 1811-1902 (SLC); M 1754-1837 (NSMI)

FOXCOTE alias FORSCOTE St James the Less (102) (Wellow Hundred; Frome Union)
OR C 1691-1816, M 1691-1836, Banns 1757-80, B 1691-1812 (SRO); CB 1813 + (Inc)
BT 1595-99, 1602-12, 1615-16, 1622-23, 1630-31, 1635-36, 1639-40, 1733-34, 1747, 1751-52, 1755-57, 1797, 1801-29, 1831-33 (SRO)
Cop 1598-1639 (Ptd, Dwelly 1, 1913); M 1696-1751 (SRO); M 1623-39 (BT), 1696-1837 (SMI)
Cop (Mf) 1595-1833 (BT) (SLC, SRO)

FRESHFORD Cemetery
OR B 1873 + (Cemetery)
BT B 1873-76 (SRO)
Cop (Mf) B 1873-76 (SLC)

FRESHFORD St Peter (666) (Bath Forum Hundred; Bradford Union 1836-82, Bath Union 1882-1930)
OR C 1678-1944, M 1653-85, 1699-1958, Banns 1823-1901, B 1705-1906 (SRO)
BT 1601-03, 1605-15, 1617, 1622-24, 1635-37, 1639-41, 1666-70, 1688, 1736-37, 1749-52, 1755-57, 1759-61, 1765-69, 1784-93, 1796-1817, CB 1850-53, 1873-74 (SRO)
Cop C 1601-1763, 1783-1812, M 1601-1812, B 1601-88, 1705-63, 1783-1812 (Ts I SG); CMB 1656-1812 (Bath Lib, British Lib); M 1653-1753 (SRO); M 1754-1837 (NSMI); B 1783-1867 (SBDB); M 1601-41 (BT), 1653-1837 (SMI)
Cop (Mf) 1601-1874 (BT) (SLC, SRO); C 1653-1761, 1783-1902, M 1653-1901, Banns 1823-1901, B 1653-1763, 1783-1906 (SLC)

FRESHFORD (Wesleyan) f 1809 (K 1931)
OR accounts 1809-78, C 1849-1908, M 1838-82 (Wilts RO)

FRESHFORD (Primitive Methodist) b 1873 (K 1931)

FROME Board of Guardians
OR Z 1836-1932, D 1836-1947 (SRO)

FROME Cemetery, Vallis Road opened 1851
OR B 1851 + (Cemetery)
Cop B 1851-1909 (SBDB)

FROME St John the Baptist (12,240) (Frome Hundred; Frome Union)
OR CMB 1558+, Banns 1767-79, 1815-23 (Inc)
BT one between 1595-1605, 1598, 1602, 1606-07, 1611, 1613-15, 1621-22, 1635, 1663, 1668-70, 1672, 1679, 1752-53, 1802-37, CB 1838-46 (SRO)
Cop CB 1558-1812, M 1558-1897, Banns 1767-79 (Ts I SG, SRO); B 1813-37 (SBDB); M 1598 (BT), 1754-1837 (SMI)
Cop (Mf) 1598-1846 (BT) (SLC, SRO); CB 1558-1846, M 1558-1837 (SRO)

FROME Christ Church, Christ Church Street West (created from Frome St John and Marston Bigot, 1844) (Frome Union)
OR CMB 1844+ (Inc)
Cop B 1819-37 (SBDB)

FROME Holy Trinity, Trinity Street (created from Frome St John, 1840) (Frome Union)
OR C 1838-86, M 1838-1909, B 1838-95 (SRO)
Cop C 1838-45 (Index SRO); CB 1838-46 (SLC)

FROME Rook Lane, Bath Street (Independent) f 1662, b 1707, reb 1862 (K 1931)
OR CB 1793-1836 (PRO: RG 4/1548, 1730)
Cop (Mf) CB 1793-1836 (SLC, SRO)

FROME Badcox Lane, later Catherine Street (Baptist) f 1669, reb 1814 (K 1931)
OR Z 1801-37, B 1785-1837 (PRO: RG 4/1550, 3261, 3264)
Cop (Mf) Z 1801-37, B 1785-1837 (SLC, SRO); Z 1834-1961 (SG)

FROME Sheppard's Barton (Baptist) b 1705, reb 1850 (K 1931)
OR Z 1785-1836, B 1764-1837 (PRO: RG 4/1551, 2925, 3262, 3263); M 1837-54, 1899-1960, B 1763-1855 (SRO)
Cop (Mf) Z 1785-1836, B 1764-1837 (SLC, SRO)

FROME Zion Chapel, Whittox Lane, Frome Selwood (Independent) f 1773 reb 1810, 1889 (K 1931)
OR ZC 1786-1836 (PRO: RG 4/1549, 3260)
Cop (Mf) ZC 1786-1836 (SLC, SRO)

FROME off Christchurch Street (Wesleyan) b 1811 (K 1931)
OR ZCB 1812-37 (PRO: RG 4/2924, 3218, 3760); C 1841-63 (circuit), C 1837-81 (chapel) (SRO); M 1908-79, B 1812-60 (Bristol RO)
Cop B 1812-60 (SBDB)
Cop (Mf) ZCB 1812-37 (SLC, SRO); M 1908-79, B 1812-60 (Bristol RO, SLC)

FROME Sun Street, Whittox Lane (Primitive Methodist) f 1828 b 1834 (K 1931)
OR ZC 1827-37 (PRO: RG 4/2872); C 1838-1961, M 1939-82 (SRO)
Cop (Mf) ZC 1827-37 (SLC, SRO)

FROME Meeting House, South Parade (Society of Friends) (Lewis 1831) (K 1931)
BT B 1866 (SRO)
Cop (Mf) 1866 (BT) (SLC, SRO)

FROME St Catherine, Park Road (Roman Catholic) f 1853 (K 1931)
OR C 1853+, M 1879+, B 1856+ (Inc)

FROME Blatchbridge (Primitive Methodist) b 1854

FROME Portway (United Methodist) f 1858 b 1910 (K 1931)

FROME (Christadelphian) b 1879

FROME Blue Ribbon Gospel Association Chapel b 1885

FROME Naish's Street (Salvation Army) (K 1931)

FROME SELWOOD St Mary the Virgin, Innox Hill (created from Frome St John, 1873)
(Frome Union)
OR CMB 1873+ (Inc)

FURNHAM *see* **CHARD Good Shepherd**

GLASTONBURY Cemetery opened 1854 (6 acres 1 rood 35 perches)

GLASTONBURY St John the Baptist (2,984) (peculiar of Glastonbury until 1845)
(Glastonbury Twelve Hides Hundred; Wells Union)
OR C 1603-31, 1648-1980, M 1603-31, 1652-1971, Banns 1754-1901, B 1603-31, 1652-1922 (SRO)
BT 1597-98, 1601-05, 1607-13, 1616-24, 1629-30, 1636-37, 1639-40, 1663-64, 1732-33, 1800-44,
    CB 1845-61 (SRO)
Cop C 1603-30, M 1603-31, B 1603-21 (Ptd, Dwelly 1, 1913); CMB 1686-1800 (SRO);
    B 1746-1849 (SBDB); M 1603-31 (BT), 1686-1837 (SMI)
Cop (Mf) 1597-1861 (BT) (SLC, SRO); C 1603-1901, M 1603-1900, Banns 1754-1901,
    B 1603-1901 (SLC)

GLASTONBURY St Benedict (created 1726 from Glastonbury St John the Baptist) (a donative,
    peculiar jurisdiction of the bishop of Bath and Wells until 1845) (Glastonbury Twelve Hides
    Hundred; Wells Union)
OR C 1663-1950, M 1663-1952, Banns 1813-1901, B 1663-1932 (SRO)
BT 1607-29, 1663, 1732, 1800-37, CB 1841-43 (SRO)
Cop 1607-63 (Ptd, Dwelly 1, 1913); 1680-1812 (SRO); B 1741-1881 (SBDB); M 1607-63 (BT),
    1680-1837 (SMI)
Cop (Mf) 1607-1843 (BT) (SLC, SRO); C 1662-97, 1708-1900, M 1680-97, 1708-1900,
    Banns 1813-1901, B 1664-97, 1708-1901 (SLC)

GLASTONBURY High Street (Independent) f 1662, b 1813 (K 1931)

GLASTONBURY Lambrook Street (Wesleyan) b 1866 (K 1931)
OR C 1814-37 (PRO: RG 4/1552); C 1814-1959 (SRO)
Cop (Mf) C 1814-37 (SLC, SRO)

GLASTONBURY Meeting House, High Street (Society of Friends) (Lewis 1831) (K 1931)

GLASTONBURY Bovetown (Plymouth Brethren) b 1825 and 1871 (K 1931)

GLASTONBURY (Baptist) (Lewis 1831)

GLASTONBURY Northload Street (Primitive Methodist) b 1844 (K 1931)
OR C 1862-1969, M 1940-53 (SRO)

GLASTONBURY Our Lady, Magdalene Street (Roman Catholic) b 1926

GOATHILL St Peter (35) (Horethorne Hundred; Sherborne Union) (transferred to Dorset, 1895)
OR C 1699-1707, 1771-1810, M 1702-44, 1765-1811, 1822-37, B 1749-50, 1773-1807,
    Banns 1783-86 (Dorset RO) (rectors also of Purse Caundle, Dorset 1603-95 where registrations
    are to be found); CB 1813+ (Inc)
BT 1607, 1613, 1621, 1803-17, 1819, 1821-25, 1827-28, 1830-37, CB 1838-39, 1841-75 (SRO)
Cop M 1702-1837 (SG); M 1702-1837 (SMI)
Cop (Mf) 1607-1875 (BT) (SLC, SRO)

GOATHURST St Edward King and Martyr (349) (Andersfield Hundred; Bridgwater Union)
OR C 1539-1910, M 1547-1979, Banns 1754-1817, B 1539-1812 (SRO); B 1813+ (Inc)
BT 1597-99, 1603, 1606-13, 1621-24, 1629-30, 1635-37, 1639-41, 1662-64, 1666-68, 1670,
   1672-73, 1679-80, 1704-09, 1719-21, 1726, 1730-31, 1737, 1742, 1749-52, 1755, 1758-59,
   1764-65, 1767-71, 1773-75, 1781-84, 1786-90, 1801-38, CB 1839-40 (SRO)
Cop M 1547-1812 (Ptd, Phillimore 12, 1910); CB 1598-1679 (Ptd, Dwelly 1, 1913);
   M 1547-1812 (Boyd); B 1749-1812 (SBDB); M 1539-1837 (SMI)
Cop (Mf) 1597-1840 (BT) (SLC, SRO); CM 1539-1901, B 1539-1812 (SLC)

GODNEY Holy Trinity (chapelry in Meare until 1740) (Glastonbury Twelve Hides Hundred;
   Wells Union)
OR C 1741-57, 1760, 1770-83, 1836-69, M 1742, B 1839-64, 1867-69 (SRO)
Cop B 1839-69 (SBDB)

GREEN OARE (extra-parochial place until 1966 when became part of Chewton Mendip)

GREINTON St Michael and All Angels (219) (Whitley Hundred; Bridgwater Union)
OR C 1655-56, 1667-71, 1728-1988, M 1665, 1671, 1730-1987, Banns 1772-1807, B 1665,
   1777-1989 (SRO)
BT 1606-10, 1616, 1621-23, 1635-36, 1639-41, 1650-51, 1662-63, 1667, 1675-76, 1780-84,
   1787-1804, 1807-25, 1827-37, CB 1838-50 (SRO)
Cop M 1665-1754 (SRO); B 1728-1917 (SBDB); M 1754-1837 (SMI)
Cop (Mf) 1606-1850 (BT) (SLC, SRO); C 1667-71, 1728-1900, M 1665, 1730-54, 1772-1897,
   Banns 1772-1807, B 1665-71, 1728-1900 (SLC)

HALCON All Saints (created from Taunton Holy Trinity, West Monkton, Taunton St James and
   Cheddon Fitzpaine, 1967, renamed Taunton All Saints 1972)
OR CMB 1967+ (Inc)

HALSE St John the Baptist (444) (Williton and Freemanors Hundred; Taunton Union)
OR C 1558-1862, M 1558-1970, Banns 1755-1813, B 1558-1853 (gap CMB 1696-1761) (SRO)
   (register 1558-1654 recovered between 1831 and 1914)
BT 1599, 1603-11, 1621-24, 1636, 1639-40, 1662-64, 1666-67, 1669-70, 1674, 1682-83, 1687-88,
   1725-29, 1732-41, 1747-48, 1750-52, 1754, 1757-59, 1762, 1764-65, 1767-75, 1777-80,
   1782-1832, CB 1833-40, 1842-43 (SRO)
Cop M 1559-1812 (Ptd, Phillimore 10, 1907); CB 1599 (Ptd, Dwelly 1, 1913);
   M 1559-1812 (Boyd); C 1761-1812 (SCDB); B 1761-1852 (SBDB); M 1559-1837 (SMI);
   C 1558-1862, M 1813-99 (DCI)
Cop (Mf) 1599-1843 (BT) (SLC, SRO); C 1558-1862, M 1559-1886, Banns 1755-1813,
   B 1558-1853 (SLC)

HALSE (Bible Christian later United Methodist) b 1840 cl 1964

HAM, HIGH St Andrew (1,027) (part Pitney Hundred, part Whitley Hundred, part Williton and
   Freemanors Hundred; Langport Union)
OR C 1569-1964, M 1569-1968, Banns 1849-1900, B 1569-1902 (SRO)
BT 1597-98, 1607, 1609-14, 1621-25, 1629-30, one between 1631-35, 1635-36, 1639-41, 1663-64,
   1668-70, 1705-06, 1728-36, 1747-48, 1751-53, 1755-58, 1760-63, 1765-82, 1784-89, 1793-95,
   1798-99, 1801-22, 1824, 1837, CB 1838 (SRO)
Cop M 1569-1812 (Ptd, Phillimore 1, 1898); CB 1597-1670 (Ptd, Dwelly 1, 1913);
   M 1569-1812 (Boyd); B 1680-1853 (SBDB); M 1569-1837 (SMI)
Cop (Mf) 1597-1838 (BT) (SLC, SRO); CB 1569-1901, M 1569-1900, Banns 1849-1900 (SLC)

HAM, HIGH Henley (Independent) f 1662 b 1841 (K 1931)

HAM, HIGH (Wesleyan) (Lewis 1831)

HAM, HIGH Low Ham (Independent) b 1860 reb 1884 (K 1931)

68

HAM, HIGH (United Methodist) (K 1931)

HAMBRIDGE with EARNSHILL St James (created by uniting Earnshill, Nidon and parts of
    Curry Rivel, Isle Brewer, Barrington and Drayton, 1844) (Langport Union)
OR C 1844-83, M 1845-1982, B 1844-1941 (SRO)
BT CB 1844-47 (SRO)
Cop (Mf) C 1844-83, M 1845-1982, B 1844-1941 (SG); 1844-47 (BT) (SLC, SRO)

HAMBRIDGE (United Methodist) b 1852 (K 1931)

HARDINGTON St Mary (28) (Kilmersdon Hundred; Frome Union)
OR M 1756, 1763, 1841-1951, Banns 1756, 1758, 1927-73 (SRO) (most registrations in
    Hemington, q.v.)
Cop (Mf) M 1841-78, 1890-92, 1902, Banns 1756-58 (SLC)

HARDINGTON MANDEVILLE St Mary (603) (Houndsborough, Barwick and Coker Hundred;
    Yeovil Union)
OR C 1687-1893, M 1687-1840 (CM defective 1687-1783), Banns 1754-83, 1795-1811, 1860-1957,
    B 1687-1878 (SRO)
BT 1598-99, 1602-03, 1605-09, one between 1605-14, 1611-12, 1614-15, 1622-24, 1635-40,
    1666-70, 1698, 1732, 1737-38, 1746-47, 1754-56, 1799-1840, CB 1842, CMB 1843-51 (SRO)
Cop 1598-1649 (Ptd, Dwelly 1, 1913); B 1688-1869 (SBDB); M 1598-1649 (BT), 1687-1837 (SMI)
Cop (Mf) C 1813-93, M 1813-40, Banns 1860-1900, B 1813-78 (SG); 1598-1851 (BT) (SLC, SRO);
    C 1688-1893, M 1709-1840, Banns 1860-1900, B 1688-1878 (SLC)

HARDINGTON MANDEVILLE (United Methodist) b 1865 (K 1931)

HARPTREE, EAST St Laurence (695) (peculiar of the Prebendary of East Harptree until 1845)
    (Winterstoke Hundred; Clutton Union)
OR C 1663-1980, M 1663-1969 (defective 1710-23), Banns 1754-1814, 1852-1905, B 1663-1968
    (SRO)
BT 1595-96, one between 1597-1626, 1605-14, 1621-23, 1630-31, 1635-38, 1640-41, 1814-21,
    1829-30, CB 1853-64 (1727-29 in peculiar series) (SRO)
Cop 1597-1635 (Ptd, Dwelly 1, 1913); M 1754-1837 (NSMI); C 1772-1812 (SCDB);
    B 1772-1865 (SBDB); M 1597-1635 (BT), 1663-1837 (SMI)
Cop (Mf) 1595-1864 (BT) (SLC, SRO); CM 1663-1901, Banns 1754-1905, B 1663-1900 (SLC)

HARPTREE, EAST (Methodist) f 1815
OR ZC 1816-34 (PRO: RG 4/3259)
Cop (Mf) ZC 1816-34 (SLC, SRO)

HARPTREE, EAST (United Methodist) b 1866, reb 1899 (K 1931)

HARPTREE, EAST St Michael (Roman Catholic) f 1806 as Shortwood St Michael
    (in Hinton Blewitt, q.v.) b 1883 (K 1931)

HARPTREE, WEST St Mary (536) (Chewton Hundred; Clutton Union)
OR C 1656-1979, M 1661-1976 (gap 1794-1812), B 1661-1972 (SRO)
BT one between 1595-1621, 1598-99, 1606-10, 1623-24, 1627-30, 1636-41, 1662-65, 1667-70,
    1672-73, 1678-80, 1732-33, 1747-49, 1775-76, 1801-20, 1822-36 (SRO)
Cop 1598-1680 (Ptd, Dwelly 1, 1913); M 1754-1837 (NSMI); C 1794-1812 (SCDB);
    B 1794-1886 (SBDB); M 1598-1680 (BT), 1800-34 (SMI)
Cop (Mf) 1598-1836 (BT) (SLC, SRO); C 1656-1903, M 1655-1900, B 1661-1901 (SLC)

HASLEBURY PLUCKNETT St Michael (826) (peculiar of the Prebendary of Haslebury until 1845) (Houndsborough, Barwick and Coker Hundred; Yeovil Union)
OR C 1672-1951, M 1673-1729, 1751-1841, Banns 1754-1812, B 1672-1956 (SRO) (C from 1650 survived in 1914)
BT 1598-99, 1607-16, 1621-24, 1635-36, one between 1633-39, 1640-41, 1747, 1749, 1751-53, CB 1847-67, 1870-74 (1762-77 in peculiar series) (SRO)
Cop 1813-36, M 1754-1805 (Ts I SG); B 1764-1857 (SBDB); M 1598-1641 (BT), 1673-1837 (SMI)
Cop (Mf) 1598-1874 (BT) (SLC, SRO); C 1764-1886, M 1754-1841, Banns 1754-98, 1805-10, B 1678-1886 (SLC)

HASLEBURY PLUCKNETT (United Methodist) reb 1887 (K 1931)

HATCH BEAUCHAMP St John the Baptist (324) (Abdick and Bulstone Hundred; Taunton Union)
OR C 1760-1922, M 1760-1994, Banns 1779-1813, 1823, ML 1816-70, B 1760-1995 (SRO)
BT 1605-11, 1619-20, 1622-24, 1629-31, 1635-40, 1669-70, 1725, 1732-37, 1740-42, 1749-50, 1752, 1755, 1757, 1764-73, 1775-76, 1778-85, 1789-90, 1799-1822, 1824-28, CB 1852-59, 1861-67 (SRO)
Cop 1609-38 (Ptd, Dwelly 1, 1913); M 1609 (BT), 1754-1840 (SMI); CM 1605-1899 (DCI)
Cop (Mf) 1605-1867 (BT) (SLC, SRO); CB 1760-1812, M 1779-1812 (SRO)

HATCH BEAUCHAMP (Baptist) f 1742 (K 1931)
OR C 1742-1845 (SRO)

HATCH, WEST St Andrew (396) (chapelry in North Curry until 1850) (peculiar of the Dean and Chapter of Wells) (North Curry Hundred; Taunton Union)
OR C 1606-1992, M 1604-1980, Banns 1823-1903, B 1682-1975 (SRO)
BT 1602-03, 1606-10 [with North Curry returns], 1612-13, 1623-24, 1629-30, 1636-41, 1663, 1679-80, 1764, 1807-08 [with North Curry returns], 1813, 1815-16, 1822, 1824, 1826-28, 1830-37, CB 1838, 1840-52 (1817-24 in peculiar series) (SRO)
Cop M 1604-1812 (Ptd, Phillimore 3, 1901); C 1606-1812, B 1604-1812 (Ts I SG, SRO, SLC); M 1604-1812 (Boyd); B 1604-1901 (SBDB); M 1604-53, 1698-1837 (SMI); C 1606-1889, M 1813-99 (DCI)
Cop (Mf) 1602-1852 (BT) (SLC, SRO); C 1604-1889, M 1604-1901, Banns 1823-1903, B 1604-1901 (SLC)

HATCH, WEST (Wesleyan) b 1886 (K 1931)

HAWKRIDGE St Giles (67) (Williton and Freemanors Hundred; Dulverton Union)
OR CB 1653-1811, M 1655-1911 (SRO); CB 1813+ (Inc)
BT 1598-99, 1601, 1603, 1605-09, 1611, 1613, 1621-24, 1630-31, 1635-41, 1662-66, 1669, 1678-80, 1701-02, 1704-113, 1721-23, 1726-27, 1731-33, 1735-38, 1740-41, 1746, 1750-57, 1759-60, 1762-63, 1778-82, 1800-13, 1816, 1818-29, 1831-33, 1836-37 (SRO)
Cop 1598-1623 (Ptd, Dwelly 1, 1913); CB 1653-1775, M 1655-1748 (SRO); B 1778-1811 (SBDB); M 1598-1623 (BT), 1655-1837 (SMI); C 1653-1811, M 1655-1899 (DCI)
Cop (Mf) 1598-1837 (BT) (SLC, SRO); CB 1653-1811, M 1653-1899 (SLC)

HEATHFIELD St John the Baptist (136) (Taunton and Taunton Dean Hundred; Taunton Union)
OR C 1703-1991, M 1700-1987, Banns 1756-96, 1807-12, B 1698-1992 (SRO)
BT 1607-08, 1611, 1621-24, 1630-31, 1636-37, 1639-40, 1662-63, 1707-08, 1720-21, 1726-29, 1732-34, 1738-40, 1745-52, 1754-55, 1757-60, 1764-83, 1785-95, 1797-1816, 1818-26, 1828-29, 1831-36, CB 1838 (SRO)
Cop M 1700-56 (Ptd, Phillimore 8, 1906); M 1700-56 (Boyd); B 1751-1992 (SBDB); M 1607-63 (BT), 1700-1837 (SMI); C 1702-1812, M 1813-37 (DCI)
Cop (Mf) 1607-1838 (BT) (SLC, SRO); C 1703-1812, M 1700-1837, Banns 1756-96, B 1698-1812 (SLC)

HEMINGTON St Mary (384) (united with Hardington, 1748, and contains almost all registrations of that parish) (Kilmersdon Hundred; Frome Union)
OR C 1539-1950, M 1539-1837, B 1539-1919 (SRO)
BT one between 1577-1628, 1597-98, 1611-14, 1616-17, 1621-24, 1635-36, 1638-41, 1663-68, 1671-73, 1706-07, 1798-1821, 1830, 1832-35 (SRO)
Cop C 1774-1812 (SCDB); B 1774-1901 (SBDB); M 1750-1837 (SMI)
Cop (Mf) 1597-1835 (BT) (SLC, SRO); C 1539-1901, M 1539-1837, B 1539-1902 (SLC)

HEMINGTON Falkland (Wesleyan) b 1842
OR C 1840-1978 (Bristol RO)
Cop (Mf) C 1840-1978 (Bristol RO, SLC)

HEMINGTON (Primitive Methodist) b 1868 (K 1931)

HEMINGTON Hebron Chapel (United Methodist) b 1875 (K 1931)
OR C 1843-1900 (circuit), C 1875-1955 (chapel) (Bristol RO)
Cop (Mf) C 1843-1955 (Bristol RO, SLC)

HENDFORD Holy Trinity (created from Yeovil, 1846, renamed Yeovil Holy Trinity, 1972) (Yeovil Union)
OR C 1846-1960, M 1846-1994, B 1860-1968 (SRO)

HENGROVE Christ Church (created from Brislington and Brislington St Christopher, 1940)
OR CMB 1940+ (Inc)

HENSTRIDGE St Nicholas (1,074) (peculiar of the Prebendary of Henstridge until 1845) (Horethorne Hundred; Wincanton Union)
OR C 1653-1889, M 1653-1910, Banns 1754-72, 1775-1813, B 1653-1892 (SRO)
BT 1605-06, 1609-11, 1621-24, 1636-37, 1639-41, 1662-64, 1667-69, 1678-79, 1682-83, 1814-22 (SRO); 1702-05, 1707-11, 1718, 1745-49, 1758-78, 1782-84 (SRO: D/D/Ppb:63)
Cop B 1748-1812 (SBDB); M 1750-1837 (SMI)
Cop (Mf) 1605-1822 (BT) (SLC, SRO); C 1653-1889, M 1653-1900, Banns 1754-72, 1775-1813, B 1653-1892 (SLC)

HENSTRIDGE (Independent) f 1792 (K 1931)

HENSTRIDGE (Wesleyan) b 1845 (K 1931)

HENSTRIDGE Yenston (Wesleyan) b 1845 (K 1931)

HENTON Christ Church (created from Wookey and Meare, 1848) (Wells Union)
OR CMB 1848+ (Inc)

HENTON Bleadney (United Methodist) b 1838 (K 1931)

HEWISH St Ann see **CONGRESBURY St Ann**

HIGHBRIDGE Cemetery opened 1885 (2 acres) (K 1931)
OR B 1885-1996 (SRO and indexes)
Cop B 1888-1996 (SBDB)

HIGHBRIDGE St John the Evangelist b 1859 (chapelry in Burnham until 1860) (Bempstone Hundred; Axbridge Union)
OR C 1859-1950, M 1860-1978, Banns 1861-1910 (SRO)
Cop (Mf) C 1859-1901, M 1860-1900, Banns 1861-1910 (SLC)

HIGHBRIDGE Church Street (Wesleyan) (Bridgewater Circuit) b 1865 (K 1931)
OR M 1964-86 (SRO)

HIGHBRIDGE Hope Chapel, Church Street (Baptist) b 1820 reb 1868 (K 1931)

HIGHBRIDGE Burnham Road (Salvation Army) (K 1931)

HILLFARANCE Holy Cross (579) (Taunton and Taunton Dean Hundred; Wellington Union)
OR C 1701-1991, M 1701-1992, Banns 1755-1812, 1832-41, B 1701-1950 (gap CMB 1742-51) (SRO)
BT 1594-97, 1602, 1605-11, 1615-16, 1619-24, 1635-37, 1639-41, 1662-64, 1667, 1669-70, 1672-73, 1679-80, 1682-83, 1707-08, 1732-33, 1738-41, 1745-52, 1757, 1765-68, 1771-74, 1800-16, 1818-23, 1825-36 (SRO)
Cop M 1701-1812 (Ptd, Phillimore 8, 1906); CB 1594-1682 (BT) (Ts SG); M 1701-1812 (Boyd); B 1752-1886 (SBDB); M 1594-1683 (BT), 1701-1837 (SMI); C 1707-1881, M 1813-99 (DCI)
Cop (Mf) 1594-1836 (BT) (SLC, SRO); C 1701-1881, M 1701-1885, Banns 1754-1812, 1832-41, B 1701-39, 1752-1887 (SLC)

HILLFARANCE Hillcommon (United Methodist) b 1846 and 1886

HINTON St George (850) (Crewkerne Hundred; Chard Union)
OR C 1632-1844, M 1632-1837, B 1632-1955 (SRO)
BT 1598-99, 1602-03, 1605-08, 1611-12, 1615-16, 1622-24, 1635-36, 1639-41, one between 1663-83, 1666-70, 1802-16, 1818-32, 1834-37, CB 1838, 1865-68 (SRO)
Cop M 1632-1837 (Ptd, Phillimore 13, 1910); CMB 1597-1669 (Ptd, Dwelly 2, 1914); M 1632-1837 (Boyd); C 1632-1780 (SCDB); B 1632-1859 (SBDB); M 1597-1837 (OR & BT) (SMI); C 1632-1844 (DCI)
Cop (Mf) 1598-1868 (BT) (SLC, SRO); C 1632-1844, M 1632-1837, B 1632-1902 (SLC)

HINTON St George (Wesleyan) f 1843 cl c1925

HINTON St George High Street (Plymouth Brethren) f before 1851 b 1874 cl c1972

HINTON BLEWITT St Margaret (325) (Chewton Hundred; Clutton Union)
OR C 1565-1979, M 1563-1976, Banns 1806-11, 1824-1901, B 1580-1975 (SRO)
BT 1599, 1605-06, 1611-12, 1623-24, 1629-31, 1635-37, 1639-41, one between 1640-63, 1667-70, 1675-76, 1678-79, 1748, 1801-14, 1826 (SRO)
Cop 1623-29 (Ptd, Dwelly 2, 1914); M 1754-1837 (NSMI); C 1735-1812 (SCDB); B 1735-1902 (SBDB); M 1563-1837 (SMI)
Cop (Mf) 1599-1826 (BT) (SLC, SRO); CM 1563-1901, Banns 1824-1901, B 1580-1902 (SLC)

HINTON BLEWITT St Michael, Shortwood (Roman Catholic) f 1806
OR C 1795-1881, M 1839-67, D 1838-79 (Bristol RO)
Cop (Mf) C 1795-1881, M 1839-67, D 1838-79 (Bristol RO, SLC)

HINTON CHARTERHOUSE St John the Baptist (735) (chapelry in Norton St Philip until 1824) (Wellow Hundred; Bath Union)
OR C 1546-1914, M 1546-1950, Banns 1750-1814, 1872-1901, B 1546-1883 (SRO)
BT 1598-1600, 1602-03, 1605-13, 1615-16, 1622-23, 1629-30, 1634-36, 1639-40, 1643-70, 1672-73, 1682-83, 1687-88, 1693, 1732-33, 1737-38, 1749-52, 1754, 1797-98, 1800-14, 1816-25, 1827, 1829-30 (SRO)
Cop 1546-1733 (Ms I SG, SRO); M 1754-1837 (NSMI); B 1734-1869 (SBDB); M 1549-1837 (SMI)
Cop (Mf) 1598-1830 (BT) (SLC, SRO); C 1546-1902, M 1546-1900, Banns 1750-1814, 1872-1901, B 1546-1884 (SLC)

HINTON CHARTERHOUSE (Wesleyan) b 1814 (K 1931)

HOLCOMBE St Andrew (538) (Kilmersdon Hundred; Shepton Mallet Union)
OR C 1698-1911, M 1698-1754, 1784-1982, B 1698-1900 (SRO)
BT 1599-1600, 1604-09, 1611-12, 1621-24, 1629-30, 1635-36, 1639-40, 1663-64, 1704-08, 1800, 1802-37, CB 1838-70, 1874 (SRO)
Cop 1604-39 (Ptd, Dwelly 2, 1914); C 1783-1813 (SCDB); B 1784-1885 (SBDB); M 1604-39 (BT), 1698-1837 (SMI)
Cop (Mf) 1599-1874 (BT) (SLC, SRO); C 1692-1901, M 1698-1754, 1784-1901, Banns 1784-88, 1824-1901, B 1698-1900 (SLC)

HOLCOMBE (Wesleyan) f 1774, reb 1893 (K 1931)

HOLFORD St Mary (188) (Whitley Hundred; Williton Union)
OR C 1558-1977, M 1558-1837, Banns 1755-82, B 1558-1812 (SRO); B 1813+ (Inc)
BT 1598-99, 1605-11, 1615-16, 1622-24, 1630-32, 1635-37, 1639-40, 1662-64, 1666-67, 1672-73, 1678-80, 1707-08, 1718-21, 1725-28, 1732-34, 1737-38, 1740-43, 1745-46, 1776-77, 1790-95, 1802-16, 1818-20, 1824-28, 1830-31 (SRO)
Cop M 1558-1812 (Ptd, Phillimore 12, 1910); CB 1615-78 (Ptd, Dwelly 2, 1914); M 1558-1812 (Boyd); M 1558-1837 (SMI)
Cop (Mf) 1598-1831 (BT) (SLC, SRO); C 1558-1904, M 1558-1837, B 1558-1810 (SLC)

HOLTON St Nicholas (209) (Whitley Hundred; Wincanton Union)
OR CB 1558-1714, 1777-1993, M 1558-1705, 1778-1965 (all defective) (SRO)
BT 1602-04, 1606-08, 1611, 1613-14, 1622-24, 1629-31, 1636-37, 1639-41, 1663-69, 1672-73, 1678-79, 1801-37, CB 1838-60 (SRO)
Cop M 1813-37 (SG); B 1777-1837 (SBDB); M 1558-1678, 1778-1837 (SMI)
Cop (Mf) 1602-1860 (BT) (SLC, SRO); CB 1558-1702, 1777-1812, M 1558-1702, 1778-1898 (SLC)

HOLTON (Baptist) b 1820 (K 1931)

HOLWELL (transferred to Dorset, 1844, see Dorset NIPR)

HORNBLOTTON St Peter (118) (Whitstone Hundred; Shepton Mallet Union)
OR C 1763-1993, M 1768-1990, Banns 1824-87, B 1767-1991 (SRO)
BT 1605-09, 1611, 1615-16, 1621-23, 1629-30, 1635-36, 1640-41, 1663, 1666-67, 1669-70, 1675-76, 1695, 1701, 1703-09, 1800-25, 1827-33, C 1834, CMB 1836 (SRO)
Cop M 1768-1849 (Ts I SG); B 1767-1837 (SBDB); M 1750-1837 (SMI)
Cop (Mf) 1605-1836 (BT) (SLC, SRO); C 1763-1812, M 1768-1832, Banns 1824-87, B 1763-1812 (SLC)

HORRINGTON, EAST St John the Evangelist (created from Wells St Cuthbert, 1844)
(Wells Union)
OR C 1845-1974, M 1845-1975, Banns 1845-1901, B 1868-1975 (SRO)
Cop (Mf) C 1845-97, M 1845-1900, Banns 1845-1901, B 1845-1901 (SLC)

HORRINGTON, EAST (Baptist) b 1876

HORSINGTON Cemetery opened 1885 (¾ acre) (K 1931)

HORSINGTON St John the Baptist (968) (Horethorne Hundred; Wincanton Union)
OR C 1559-1904, M 1559-1978, B 1558-1863 (SRO)
BT 1599-1600, 1602-04, 1606-11, 1613-14, 1622-24, 1640-41, 1644, 1662-64, 1666-69, 1733-35, 1749-52, 1769-70, 1800-31, 1833-37, CB 1838-39, 1841-52 (SRO)
Cop 1558-1836 (Ptd, W.E. Daniel, 1907); C 1904-88, B 1864-1923 (SRO); M 1558-1836 (Boyd); B 1813-62 (SBDB); M 1599, 1607-09 (BT), 1750-1837 (SMI)
Cop (Mf) 1599-1852 (BT) (SLC, SRO)

HORSINGTON (Baptist) b 1700 (K 1931)

HORSINGTON South Cheriton (Independent) b 1816 (K 1931)

HORSINGTON South Cheriton (Wesleyan) b 1844 (K 1931)

HUISH CHAMPFLOWER St Peter (345) (Williton and Freemanors Hundred; Dulverton Union)
OR C 1559-1873, M 1605-1982, Banns 1755-1813, B 1558-1957 (SRO)
BT 1597-99, 1603-04, 1611-12, 1616-17, 1621-24, 1636-41, 1662-64, 1669-70, 1691-98, 1701-04,
 1707-08, 1710-12, 1721-22, 1726-28, 1731-34, 1736-38, 1745-46, 1753, 1757-59, 1762,
 1764-80, 1782-84, 1786-88, 1790-92, 1795-98, 1800-30 (SRO)
Cop 1597-1638 (Ptd, Dwelly 2, 1914); C 1597-1788, M 1597-1753 (SRO); B 1637-1902 (SBDB);
 M 1597, 1616, 1623, 1638, 1754-1837 (SMI); C 1785-1873, M 1755-1899 (DCI)
Cop (Mf) 1597-1830 (BT) (SLC, SRO); C 1559-1873, M 1559-1900, Banns 1755-1813,
 B 1559-1903 (SLC)

HUISH EPISCOPI St Mary (574) (peculiar of the Archdeacon of Wells until 1845) (part Pitney
 Hundred, part East Kingsbury Hundred, Williton and Freemanors Hundred; Langport Union)
OR C 1692-1963, M 1698-1985, Banns 1754-1812, 1823-1919, B 1678-1989 (SRO) (the first
 register to 1726 was recovered shortly before 1914)
BT one between 1571-1624, one between 1600-23, 1611-16, 1623-24, 1635-36, 1639-41, 1669-75,
 1679-80, 1775-76, 1789-90, 1804-11, 1813-26, 1828-34, 1836, CB 1838-40, 1842-46,
 CMB 1847-49, CB 1850, CMB 1851-65 (SRO)
Cop M 1698-1812 (Ptd, Phillimore 1, 1898); CMB 1615-23 (Ptd, Dwelly 2, 1914);
 M 1698-1812 (Boyd); B 1758-1812 (SBDB); M 1615-23 (BT), 1698-1726, 1754-1837 (SMI);
 C 1698-1854, M 1813-99 (DCI)
Cop (Mf) 1611-1865 (BT) (SLC, SRO); C 1678-1727, 1758-1901, M 1678-1727, 1754-1900,
 Banns 1754-1812, 1823-1900, B 1678-1727, 1758-1871 (SLC)

HUISH EPISCOPI (Wesleyan) (K 1931)

HULL, BISHOPS St Peter and St Paul (1,155) (chapelry in Taunton St Mary Magdalene until 1729;
 parish went into the centre of Taunton, and should be searched for Taunton registrations)
 (Taunton and Taunton Dean Hundred; Taunton Union)
OR C 1562-1964, M 1562-1988 (gap 1672-94), Banns 1754-1812, 1843-1900, B 1562-1972 (SRO)
BT 1593-9,1602-10,1615-6,1619-20,1622-4,1631-2,1635-6,1639-41,1707-8,1727-30,1732-6,
 1749-50,1752,1754-5,1757-60,1762-5,1767-76,1778-84,1788-90,1800-37, B 1838-40 (SRO)
Cop M 1562-1812 (Ptd, Phillimore 10, 1907); M 1813-37 (Ts I SG, SRO); M 1562-1812 (Boyd);
 B 1735-1869 (SBDB); M 1562-1837 (SMI); C 1562-1899, M 1813-99 (DCI)
Cop (Mf) 1593-1840 (BT) (SLC, SRO); C 1562-1901, M 1562-1900, Banns 1754-1812, 1843-1901,
 B 1562-1902 (SLC)

HULL, BISHOPS St John the Evangelist (created from Bishops Hull, Wilton and
 Taunton St Mary Magdalene, 1864, later known as Taunton St John) (Taunton Union)
OR C 1859-1966, M 1864-1977, Banns 1864-1900, B 1866-1955 (SRO)
Cop (Mf) C 1859-1901, M 1864-1901, Banns 1864-1900, B 1866-84 (SLC)

HULL, BISHOPS (Congregational, later United Reformed Church) f 1662 b 1868 (K 1931)
OR C 1734-1837, B 1774-1837 (PRO: RG 4/1542,1543,2054); C 1891-1957, M 1895-1957,
 B 1892-1957 (SRO)
Cop (Mf) C 1734-1837, B 1774-1837 (SLC, SRO)

HUNTSPILL St Peter (1,503) (Huntspill and Puriton Hundred; Bridgwater Union)
OR C 1654-1994, M 1654-1968, Banns 1754-1826, B 1654-1992 (SRO)
BT 1623-24, 1664-65, 1720-21, 1735-38, 1740-42, 1744-48, 1751-52, 1757-58, 1762-63, 1765-79,
 1781-82, 1800-37, CB 1838, 1841 (SRO)
Cop 1623 (Ptd, Dwelly 2, 1914); C 1712-1848, M 1712-1837, Banns 1754-1820, B 1712-1838
 (Ts I, SLC); C 1800-12 (SCDB); B 1654-1884 (SBDB); M 1623, 1654-1837 (SMI)
Cop (Mf) 1623-1841 (BT) (SLC, SRO); C 1654-1840, M 1654-1915, Banns 1754-1826,
 B 1654-1884 (SLC)

HUNTSPILL (Baptist) (Lewis 1831)

HUNTSPILL (Wesleyan) b 1851 (K 1931)

HUNTSPILL, EAST All Saints (created from Huntspill, 1845) (Bridgwater Union)
OR C 1846-1951, M 1846-1967 (SRO)
Cop (Mf) C 1846-1951, M 1846-1967 (Ptd on fiche, 1995)

HUNTSPILL, EAST (United Methodist) b 1840 (K 1931)

HUTTON St Mary (381) (Winterstoke Hundred; Axbridge Union)
OR C 1715-17, 1743-1974, M 1715-17, 1747-1836, Banns 1825-1927, B 1715-16, 1743-1916 (SRO)
BT 1597-99, 1611-12, 1621-24, 1629, 1636-37, 1640-41, 1663-64, 1668-70, 1676-77, 1679-80,
    1704-05, 1746-52, 1754-59, 1769-70, 1777-78, 1799-1804, 1806-16, 1818, 1820-37,
    CB 1838-40 (SRO)
Cop C 1621-68, M 1621-68, B 1621-68 (Ptd, Dwelly 2, 1914); M 1813-37 (Ts I SG); M 1754-1837
    (SRO); M 1754-1837 (NSMI); B 1743-1902 (SBDB); M 1621-29 (BT), 1754-1837 (SMI)
Cop (Mf) 1597-1840 (BT) (SLC, SRO); C 1715-17, 1743-1901, M 1715-17, 1747-1836,
    Banns 1825-1901, B 1715-16, 1743-1903 (SLC)

ILCHESTER Cemetery, Limington Hill opened 1901 (½ acre) (K 1931)

ILCHESTER St Mary (1,095) (Tintinhull Hundred; Yeovil Union)
OR C 1690-1963 (gap 1740-48), M 1690-1979, Banns 1765-1812, B 1690-1901 (SRO)
BT 1594-98, 1602-03, 1607-08, 1611-12, 1616-17, 1619-24, 1629, 1635-36, 1640-41, 1663-64,
    1666-70, 1704-05, 1731-32, 1750-53, 1755, 1760, 1768, 1802-30, 1835-37, CB 1846-48 (SRO)
Cop 1594-1666 (Ptd, Dwelly 9, 15, 1922-26 and Ilchester & District LHS Occ Papers 67, 1986);
    B 1776-1846 (SBDB); M 1594-1666 (BT), 1690-1837 (SMI)
Cop (Mf) 1594-1848 (BT) (SLC, SRO); C 1690-1739, 1748-1902, M 1690-1739, 1748-54,
    1765-1901, Banns 1765-1803, B 1690-1739, 1748-1901 (SLC)

ILCHESTER Providence Chapel (Independent) f 1799 (K 1931)
OR C 1807-37, B 1806-36 (PRO: RG 4/1553); C 1807-43, B 1807-41 (SRO)
Cop (Mf) C 1807-37, B 1806-36 (SLC, SRO)

ILCHESTER (Wesleyan) b 1850 (K 1931)

ILMINSTER Cemetery opened 1859 (2 acres, later increased to 3¾ acres) (K 1931)
Cop B 1760-1982 (SBDB)

ILMINSTER St Mary with HORTON St Peter (2,957) (Royal peculiar of the Manor of Ilminster
    until 1845) (Abdick and Bulstone Hundred; Chard Union). Horton St Peter consecrated 1900.
OR C 1652-1944, M 1662-1956 (gap 1711-17), Banns 1848-1910, B 1660-1898 (SRO)
BT 1605-08, 1621-24, 1635-37, 1639-40, 1663-64, 1669-70, 1813 (SRO)
Cop M 1662-1812 (Ptd, Phillimore 13, 1910); 1660-1837 (Ts SG, SRO); M 1662-1811 (Boyd);
    B 1813-49 (SBDB); M 1662-1837 (SMI); C 1652-1883, M 1653-1899 (DCI)
Cop (Mf) 1605-70, 1813 (BT) (SLC, SRO); C 1652-1901, M 1662-1900, Banns 1754-1901,
    B 1660-1914 (SLC)

ILMINSTER Old Meeting, East Street (Presbyterian, then Unitarian) f 1670 reb 1718, 1894
    (K 1931)
OR C 1718-1881, B 1785-1896 (SRO); ZC 1718-1837, B 1786-1837 (PRO: RG 4/1554, 3265)
Cop (Mf) ZC 1718-1837, B 1786-1837 (SLC, SRO)

ILMINSTER Broadway Hill (Wesleyan) (South Petherton Circuit) f 1795 b 1838 (K 1931)
OR ZC 1780-1837 (PRO: RG 4/1555)

ILMINSTER Meeting House (Society of Friends)
Cop B 1800-27 (SBDB)

ILMINSTER Zion Chapel (Independent) f 1812
OR ZC 1814-37 (PRO: RG 4/2500); C 1837-1964, M 1837-1945, B 1859-1943 (SRO)

ILMINSTER West Street (Wesleyan) (South Petherton Circuit) f 1857 b 1887 (K 1931)

ILMINSTER (Independent) reb 1926 (K 1931)
OR C 1969-73 (SRO)

ILMINSTER St Joseph, Station Road (Roman Catholic) b 1953

ILTON St Peter (530) (peculiar jurisdiction of Dean of Wells until 1845)
  (Abdick and Bulstone Hundred; Chard Union)
OR C 1642-1967, M 1645-1982, Banns 1754-1811, 1823-1974, B 1642-1903 (SRO)
BT 1598-99, 1605-09, 1611-12, 1616-17, 1619-24, 1629, 1635-37, 1662-64, 1666-67, 1670-71,
  1679-80, 1813-37, CB 1838-39 (1761-64 in peculiar series) (SRO)
Cop M 1642-1811 (Ptd, Phillimore 4, 1902); 1616-35 (Ptd, Dwelly 2, 1914); B 1813-55 (SBDB);
  1642-1837 (Ts SG, SRO); M 1642-1811 (Boyd); M 1616-35 (BT), 1645-1837 (SMI);
  C 1642-1899, M 1813-99 (DCI)
Cop (Mf) 1598-1839 (BT) (SLC, SRO)

ILTON (Wesleyan) b 1874 (K 1931)

ISLE ABBOTS St Mary the Virgin (380) (Abdick and Bulstone Hundred; Langport Union)
OR C 1561-1991, M 1562-1979, B 1561-1992 (SRO)
BT 1593-99, 1604-11, 1616, 1621-24, 1629-30, 1635-37, 1640-41, 1662-63, 1667-70, 1679-80,
  1707-08, 1731-32, 1740-42, 1749-50, 1752, 1759, 1762-63, 1765, 1768, 1773, 1775, 1777-82,
  1789-91, 1797-1800, 1803-13, 1822-23, 1834-35 (SRO)
Cop M 1562-1837 (Ptd, Phillimore 14, 1913); 1593-1679 (Ptd, Dwelly 2, 1914);
  M 1562-1837 (Boyd); B 1775-1837 (SBDB); M 1562-1837 (SMI); C 1561-1812 (DCI)
Cop (Mf) 1593-1835 (BT) (SLC, SRO)

ISLE ABBOTS (Baptist) b 1815 (K 1931)
OR ZB 1777-1864 (SRO)

ISLE BREWERS All Saints (254) (Abdick and Bulstone Hundred; Langport Union)
OR C 1705-1994, M 1705-1982 (gap 1731-54), B 1705-1993 (SRO)
BT 1598-1600, 1603-13, 1622-24, 1629-30, 1635-37, 1639-40, 1663-64, 1667-68, 1672-73, 1707,
  1725-26, 1731-33, 1736, 1741, 1750-52, 1756-57, 1764-65, 1769-70, 1775-76, 1778-81,
  1784-89, 1800-02, 1804-35, CB 1840-49 (SRO)
Cop M 1705-1812 (Ptd, Phillimore 4, 1902); C 1598-1667 (Ptd, Dwelly 2, 1914); C 1705-1828,
  M 1813-37, B 1705-1812 (Ts SG, SRO); C 1705-1828, M 1705-1836, B 1705-1812 (SRO);
  M 1705-1812 (Boyd); B 1705-1812 (SBDB); M 1598-1667 (BT), 1705-32, 1754-1837 (SMI);
  C 1705-1899, M 1813-99 (DCI)
Cop (Mf) 1598-1849 (BT) (SLC, SRO)

KEINTON MANDEVILLE St Mary (459) (Catsash Hundred; Langport Union)
OR C 1728-1993, M 1728-1982, Banns 1754-1812, 1823-95, B 1728-1993 (SRO)
BT 1598, 1606-08, 1611-13, 1622-23, 1628-31, 1635, 1639-41, 1663-64, 1667-69, 1673-74,
  1704-05, 1755-56, 1759-60, 1803-25 (SRO)
Cop CB 1629, M 1629, 1736-1851 (Ts I SG); B 1812-1903 (SBDB); M 1750-1837 (SMI)
Cop (Mf) 1598-1825 (BT) (SLC, SRO); C 1728-60, 1783-1902, M 1736-1900, Banns 1823-95,
  B 1736-60, 1803-1903 (SLC)

KEINTON MANDEVILLE (Wesleyan) b 1843 (K 1931)

KEINTON MANDEVILLE (United Methodist) b 1881 (K 1931)

KELSTON alias KELVESTON St Nicholas (274) (Bath Forum Hundred; Keynsham Union)
OR CMB 1538+ (gap C 1582-85, M 1575-84, 1643-64, 1715-20, 1731-35, B 1586-94, 1644-64, 1740-43), Banns 1754-1812, 1824+ (Inc)
BT 1593-98, 1606-11, 1615-16, 1621-24, 1629-30, 1635-37, 1639-40, 1662-63, 1666-70, 1672-74, 1676-77, 1744-46, 1750-51, 1753-54, 1765-69, 1775-76, 1784-88, 1791-93, 1796-1830, CB 1856-71 (SRO)
Cop 1538-1812 (Ts I SG, Bath Lib, British Lib); M 1754-1837 (NSMI); M 1754-1830 (SMI)
Cop (Mf) 1593-1871 (BT) (SLC, SRO)

KENN St John the Evangelist (273) (chapelry in Yatton until 1846) (peculiar of the Prebendary of Yatton until 1845) (Winterstoke Hundred; Bedminster Union 1836-99, Long Ashton Union 1899-1930)
OR C 1544-1891, M 1542-1950, B 1540-1812 (SRO); B 1813+ (Inc)
BT 1607-14, one between 1621-23, 1623-24, 1630-31, 1635-37, 1639-41, 1746-50, 1752-53, 1813-18, 1820-24, 1825 (in Yatton), 1828-35 (SRO); 1690, 1692-93 (SRO: D/D/Ppb:113)
Cop 1607-21 (Ptd, Dwelly 2, 1914); M 1754-1837 (NSMI); B 1689-1812 (SBDB); M 1542-1837 (SMI)
Cop (Mf) 1607-1835 (BT) (SLC, SRO); CB 1544-1887, M 1544-1688, 1708-1886, Banns 1824-86 (SLC)

KENN (Independent) f 1680 b 1861 (K 1931)

KEWSTOKE St Paul (467) (Winterstoke Hundred; Axbridge Union)
OR C 1667-1863, M 1667-1958, Banns 1755-90, 1844-1902, B 1667-1894 (SRO)
BT 1607-08, 1621-22, 1624-25, 1629-31, 1635-37, 1639-41, 1664-65, 1704-05, 1738-39, 1750-51, 1755-56, 1798-1823, 1826-30, 1835-37, CB 1838-39 (SRO)
Cop M 1754-1837 (NSMI); B 1783-1855 (SBDB); M 1607-65 (BT), 1667-1837 (SMI)
Cop (Mf) 1607-1839 (BT) (SLC, SRO)

KEWSTOKE (Plymouth Brethren) (K 1931)

KEYNSHAM Board of Guardians
OR Z 1836-90, 1906-49, C 1890-1915, 1944, D 1906-50 (SRO)

KEYNSHAM Cemetery opened 1877 (2½ acres) (K 1931)

KEYNSHAM St John the Baptist (2,142) (Keynsham Hundred; Keynsham Union)
OR C 1628-1885, M 1628-88, 1697-1912, B 1628-1858 (SRO)
BT 1593-97, 1606-09, 1611-12, 1622-24, 1630-31, 1636-37, 1640-41, 1662-63, 1732-33, 1749, 1751-55, 1762, 1775-76, 1784-85, 1790-94, 1796-1824, 1826-33 (SRO)
Cop CB 1628-1807, M 1629-1812 (Ts I SG, SRO, Bath Lib); M 1754-1837 (NSMI); B 1808-32 (SBDB); M 1754-1837 (SMI)
Cop (Mf) 1593-1833 (BT) (SLC, SRO); C 1628-1885, M 1629-97, 1703, 1713-1901, B 1628-84, 1697-1858 (SLC)

KEYNSHAM (Baptist) b 1807 (K 1931)
OR Z 1787-1837, B 1803-75, D 1830-50 (Bristol RO)
Cop (Mf) Z 1787-1837, B 1803-75, D 1830-50 (Bristol RO, SLC)

KEYNSHAM Chewton (Wesleyan) (Lewis 1831) (K 1931)
OR C 1807-1940 (Bristol RO)
Cop (Mf) C 1807-1940 (Bristol RO, SLC)

KEYNSHAM (United Methodist) b 1860 (K 1931)

KEYNSHAM Bethesda Chapel (Reformed Methodist) (K 1931)
OR C 1865-1934, M 1953-66 (Bristol RO)
Cop (Mf) C 1865-1934, M 1953-66 (Bristol RO, SLC)

KEYNSHAM St Dunstan, Bristol Road (Roman Catholic) b 1935

KILMERSDON St Peter and St Paul (2,129) (Kilmersdon Hundred; Frome Union)
OR C 1653-1902, M 1653-1987, Banns 1754-1899, B 1653-1888 (gap CMB 1708-24) (SRO)
BT one between 1590-1623, 1598-1600, 1602-04, 1607-12, 1615-16, 1620-21, 1623-24, 1629-30,
    1635-37, 1640, 1663-65, 1668-69, early 18th century, 1732-38, 1749-53, 1757-58, 1800-37,
    CB 1838-39 (SRO)
Cop 1603-35 (Ptd, Dwelly 2, 1914); 1603-1708 (SRO); B 1780-1877 (SBDB); M 1603-35 (BT),
    1654-1837 (SMI)
Cop (Mf) 1598-1839 (BT) (SLC, SRO); C 1653-1708, 1725-1898, M 1654-77, 1690-1707,
    1725-1900, Banns 1754-1899, B 1653-1708, 1725-1888 (SLC)

KILMERSDON (Presbyterian) (Lewis 1831)

KILMERSDON Charlton (Primitive Methodist) b 1861 (K 1931)
OR C 1900-57 (Bristol RO)
Cop (Mf) C 1900-57 (Bristol RO, SLC)

KILMERSDON (Wesleyan) (Lewis 1831) b 1857 (K 1931)
OR C 1843-1900 (circuit), C 1845-1968 (chapel) (Bristol RO)
Cop (Mf) C 1843-1968 (Bristol RO, SLC)

KILMERSDON (Primitive Methodist) b 1864 (K 1931)

KILMINGTON St Mary the Virgin (580) (Norton Ferris Hundred; Mere Union)
    (transferred to Wiltshire, 1896)
OR C 1596-1670, 1686-88, 1705-1954, M 1582-1648, 1655-70, 1687, 1705-1837, B 1582-1641,
    1653, 1655-88, 1705-1886 (Wilts RO)
BT 1605-09, 1611-13, 1616-17, 1621-24, 1635-37, 1639-40, 1670, 1732-33, 1744-45, 1748-52,
    1754, 1756-58, [transcripts for the years 1804-06 'were removed from the bundle, 1956'],
    1807-32, 1851-54 (SRO)
Cop M 1582-1837 (Ptd, Phillimore 14, 1913); CB 1655-87 (Ts I SG); M 1582-1837 (Boyd);
    B 1778-1841 (SBDB); M 1582-1837 (SMI)
Cop (Mf) 1605-1854 (BT) (SLC, SRO); C 1596-1670, 1686-88, 1705-1954, M 1582-1648, 1655-70,
    1687, 1705-1837, B 1582-1641, 1653, 1655-88, 1705-1886 (SRO, SLC)

KILMINGTON (Wesleyan) b 1847
OR C 1841-63 (Frome circuit), C 1868-1945 (chapel) (SRO); M 1900-08 (Wilts RO: acc.1420)
Cop (Mf) C 1841-63, 1868-1945 (SLC, SRO)

KILTON St Nicholas (141) (Williton and Freemanors Hundred; Williton Union) (part of the parish
    merged with Lilstock, 1881, as Kilton with Lilstock, the rest incorporated into Stringston and
    Holford)
OR CB 1683-1812, M 1683-1835 (SRO); CB 1813+ (Inc)
BT 1607-12, 1621-24, 1630-31, 1635-41, 1662-66, 1670-73, 1678-80, 1704-06, 1709, 1719-20,
    1730-1, 1733, 1741-3, 1745-6, 1748-50, 1769, 1790-7, 1800-16, 1818-20, 1824-5, 1833 (SRO)
Cop M 1683-1812 (Ptd, Phillimore 12, 1910); 1621-64 (Ptd, Dwelly 2, 1914); M 1683-1812 (Boyd);
    C 1753-1810 (SCDB); B 1764-1812 (SBDB); M 1621-64 (BT), 1683-1837 (SMI)
Cop (Mf) 1607-1833 (BT) (SLC, SRO)

KILVE St Mary (233) (Williton and Freemanors Hundred; Williton Union)
OR CB 1538-1812, M 1538-1837, Banns 1754-86, 1824-25, 1878 (SRO); CB 1813+ (Inc)
BT 1605-12, 1617-18, 1621-24, 1629-31, 1635-36, 1638-40, 1662-68, 1670-73, 1704-07, 1719-20,
    1730-33, 1738-39, 1741-43, 1783-93, 1801-27, 1829, 1832 (SRO)
Cop M 1638-1812 (Ptd, Phillimore 12, 1910); 1618-38 (Ptd, Dwelly 2, 1914); M 1638-1812 (Boyd);
    B 1784-1812 (SBDB); M 1618-1837 (OR & BT) (SMI)
Cop (Mf) 1605-1832 (BT) (SLC, SRO); C 1539-1812, M 1632-1812, Banns 1754-86, 1824-25,
    1878, B 1539-1812 (SLC)

KILVE Putsham (Independent) b 1807 cl 1888

KINGSBURY EPISCOPI St Martin (1,695) (peculiar of the Dean of Wells until 1845)
    (East Kingsbury Hundred; Langport Union)
OR C 1557-1917, M 1557-1992, B 1557-1869 (SRO)
BT 1601-02, 1607-09, 1611-12, 1615-16, 1621-24, 1629-30, 1635-36, 1639-41, 1785-91, 1813-21
    (1773-82 in peculiar series) (SRO)
Cop M 1557-1812 (Ptd, Phillimore 5, 1904); C 1557-1850, M 1813-50, B 1581-1869 (Ts I SG);
    M 1557-1812 (Boyd); B 1580-1869 (SBDB); M 1557-1743, 1754-1837 (SMI); C 1557-1855,
    M 1812-37 (DCI)
Cop (Mf) 1601-1821 (BT) (SLC, SRO)

KINGSBURY EPISCOPI Mid Lambrook (Independent) f 1687 b 1841 (K 1931)
OR ZC 1681-97, 1794-1837, M 1688-94 (PRO: RG 4/1556, 2055, 2057); M 1688-1875,
    B 1744-1877 (SRO)
Cop C 1681-97 (SCDB)
Cop (Mf) ZC 1681-97, 1794-1837, M 1688-94 (SLC, SRO)

KINGSBURY EPISCOPI (Wesleyan) f 1810 b 1900 (K 1931)

KINGSDON All Saints (610) (Somerton Hundred; Langport Union)
OR C 1538-1863, M 1540-1955 (gap 1594-1614), Banns 1810-11, 1823-37, 1861-1925,
    B 1538-1906 (SRO)
BT 1599-1600, 1602-08, one between 1610-25, 1611-14, 1616-17, 1619-20, 1622-24, 1630-31,
    1635-41, 1662-64, 1666-71, 1678-79, 1695-96, 1704-05, 1720-21, 1749-53, 1755, 1765,
    1800-02, 1804-17, 1819-25, 1828-34 (SRO)
Cop M 1540-1812 (Ptd, Phillimore 1, 1898); CB 1540-1659 (C of A); M 1540-1812 (Boyd);
    B 1758-1882 (SBDB); M 1540-97, 1615-1837 (SMI)
Cop (Mf) 1599-1834 (BT) (SLC, SRO); C 1538-1863, M 1538-1900, Banns 1823-1903,
    B 1538-1906 (SRO)

KINGSDON (Independent) f 1665, enlarged 1824 (K 1931)
OR C 1809-34 (PRO: RG 4/2349)
Cop (Mf) C 1809-34 (SLC, SRO)

KINGSTON St Mary (892) (Taunton and Taunton Dean Hundred; Taunton Union)
OR C 1677-1926, M 1677-1977, Banns 1754-87, B 1677-1927 (SRO)
BT 1597-1600, 1606-08, 1621, 1623-24, 1629-30, one between 1629-35, 1636-37, 1639-41,
    1662-64, 1666-67, 1669-70, 1707-08, 1720-21, 1727-28, 1732-33, 1737-39, 1743, 1749-52,
    1754-55, 1759, 1764, 1767-75, 1777-87, 1789-90, 1800-35 (SRO)
Cop 1677-1840 (Ts SG, SRO); C 1772-1812 (SCDB); B 1763-1856 (SBDB); M 1677-1837 (SMI);
    CM 1677-1899 (DCI)
Cop (Mf) 1597-1835 (BT) (SLC, SRO); C 1677-1900, M 1677-1900, Banns 1754-87,
    B 1677-1901 (SLC)

KINGSTON (Independent) b 1821 (K 1931)
OR ZC 1823-37, B 1828-37 (PRO: RG 4/3266)
Cop (Mf) ZC 1823-37, B 1828-37 (SLC, SRO)

KINGSTON PITNEY sinecure rectory included in Yeovil after 1937

KINGSTON SEYMOUR All Saints (368) (Chewton Hundred; Bedminster Union 1836-99, Long Ashton Union 1899-1930)
OR C 1727-1883, M 1728-1982, Banns 1754-1885, B 1727-1983 (SRO)
BT 1602-03, 1606-13, 1621-24, 1635-37, 1639-41, 1662-63, 1732-33, 1748-56, 1800-37, CB 1849-64 (SRO)
Cop 1622-39 (Ptd, Dwelly 2, 1914); M 1754-1837 (NSMI); B 1727-1868 (SBDB); M 1622, 1635-36, 1639, 1754-1837 (SMI)
Cop (Mf) 1602-1864 (BT) (SLC, SRO); C 1727-1883, M 1728-1885, Banns 1754-1885, B 1727-1888 (SLC)

KINGSTON SEYMOUR (Plymouth Brethren) b 1865 (K 1931)

KINGSTONE All Saints (292) (Tintinhull Hundred; Chard Union)
OR C 1715-1897, M 1715-39, 1754-1984, Banns 1755-1810, 1848-1966, B 1715-1992 (SRO)
BT 1598-1600, 1606-14, 1622-24, 1629-31, 1635-36, 1639-40, 1668-69, 1678-79, 1737-38, 1768, 1789-90, 1800-12, 1814 (SRO)
Cop 1714-1837 (Ts I SG, SRO); M 1714-1837 (SMI); C 1715-1897, M 1714-1837 (DCI)
Cop (Mf) 1598-1814 (BT) (SLC, SRO); C 1717-1897, M 1715-1885, Banns 1754-1809, 1848-85, B 1715-1812 (SLC)

KINGWESTON All Saints (122) (Catsash Hundred; Langport Union)
OR C 1653-1992, M 1660-1984, Banns 1753-1810, B 1653-1993 (SRO)
BT 1598-99, 1605-09, 1611, 1613-14, 1619-20, 1622-23, 1629-31, 1635-37, 1639-41, 1663-64, 1667-70, 1699-1701, 1704, 1733-34, 1751-52, 1800-17, 1823-24, CB 1841-48 (SRO)
Cop B 1786-1993 (SBDB); M 1660-1837 (SMI)
Cop (Mf) 1598-1848 (BT) (SLC, SRO); CB 1653-1812, M 1660-1885, Banns 1753-1810 (SLC)

KITNOR St Culbone *see* **CULBONE**

KITTISFORD St Nicholas (171) (Milverton Hundred; Wellington Union)
OR C 1694-1978, M 1695-1977, Banns 1754-1812, B 1694-1978 (SRO)
BT 1598-1600, 1606-07, 1621-24, 1629-30, 1635-36, 1639-41, 1663-73, 1678-79, 1720, 1725-26, 1737, 1750, 1757-60, 1762-66, 1768-75, 1777-90, 1800-O5, 1807-21, 1823-32, 1834-35 (SRO)
Cop M 1695-1812 (Ptd, Phillimore 14, 1913); CB 1694-1837 (Ptd, Dwelly 8, 1919); 1621-78 (Ptd, Dwelly 2, 1914); M 1695-1812 (Boyd); C 1694-1812 (SCDB); B 1694-1878 (SBDB); M 1621-78 (BT), 1695-1837 (SMI); C 1694-1899, M 1813-99 (DCI)
Cop (Mf) 1598-1835 (BT) (SLC, SRO)

KNOWLE ST GILES (108) (chapelry in Cudworth umtil 1731) (South Petherton Hundred; Chard Union)
OR C 1695-1976, M 1695-1750, 1813-1964, B 1695-1981 (SRO) (registers from 1784 only listed in 1914)
BT 1607-09, 1611-13, 1615-23, 1630, 1635-37, 1639-41, 1662-63, 1813, 1821, 1834-35 (SRO); 1704, 1707-08, 1711-14, 1717 (SRO: D/D/Ppb:35)
Cop M 1813-34 (Ts SG); B 1695-1897 (SBDB); M 1611-1744, 1813-37 (SMI); C 1607-1883, M 1611-1940, B 1607-1782 (with gaps) (DCI)
Cop (Mf) 1607-1835 (BT) (SLC, SRO); C 1695-1783, 1813-1912, M 1813-85, B 1695-1783, 1813-98 (SLC)

KNOWLE Holy Nativity (created from Bedminster St John, 1883) (Chard Union)
OR C 1874-1907, M 1883-1906 (Bristol RO)
Cop (Mf) C 1874-1907, M 1883-1906 (Bristol RO, SLC)

KNOWLE St Katherine (chapelry of Holy Nativity Knowle)
OR C 1889-1957 (Bristol RO)
Cop (Mf) C 1889-1957 (Bristol RO, SLC)

KNOWLE St Martin (created from Knowle Holy Nativity, 1906) (Chard Union)
OR CMB 1906+ (Inc)

KNOWLE St Barnabas (created from Bedminster and Knowle St Martin, 1935)
OR CMB 1935+ (Inc)

KNOWLE St Gerard Majella, Talbot Road (Roman Catholic) b 1909

KNOWLE (United Methodist)
OR C 1914-69, M 1939-68 (Bristol RO)
Cop (Mf) C 1914-69, M 1939-68 (Bristol RO, SLC)

LAMBROOK, EAST St James (united with Kingsbury Episcopi, 1931) (peculiar of the Chancellor
of Wells until 1845) (East Kingsbury Hundred; Langport Union)
OR C 1771-1888, M 1933-46 (SRO) (MB took place at Kingsbury Episcopi)
BT 1607, 1814-15 (C 1785-91 in peculiar series) (SRO)
Cop C 1770-1860 (Ts SG); C 1771-1821 (DCI)
Cop (Mf) 1607, 1814-15 (BT) (SLC, SRO); C 1771-1822 (SLC)

LAMYATT St Mary and St John (204) (Whitstone Hundred; Shepton Mallet Union)
OR CB 1608-1993, M 1608-1993, Banns 1755-1811, 1825-30, 1844-61, 1884-1961 (SRO)
BT 1602-03, 1606-08, 1613, 1621-23, 1630-31, 1636-37, 1640-41, 1663-68, 1672, 1678-79,
1704-05, 1707-10, 1754, 1756, 1800-28, 1830, 1833-37, CB 1841-52 (SRO)
Cop CB 1608-1783 (Ms SRO); B 1813-40 (SBDB); M 1608-1837 (SMI)
Cop (Mf) 1602-1852 (BT) (SLC, SRO); C 1613-1812, M 1613-1753, 1755-1838, Banns 1772-1811,
1825-30, 1844-61, 1884-1905, B 1613-1812 (SLC)

LAMYATT (Wesleyan) b 1865 (K 1931)

LANGFORD BUDVILLE St James (608) (chapelry in Milverton until 1863) (peculiar of the
Archdeacon of Taunton) (Milverton Hundred; Wellington Union)
OR C 1537-1934 (gap 1599-1604), M 1607-1837 (gap 1615-64), Banns 1754-1812, B 1552-1973
(gap 1654-64) (SRO)
BT 1605-13, 1622-24, 1629-31, 1636-37, 1639-41, 1662-63, 1669-70, 1672-73, 1813-35 (SRO)
Cop M 1607-1812 (Ptd, Phillimore 8, 1906); C 1537-1765, B 1552-1765 (C of A); C 1537-1814,
M 1601-13, 1665-1809, B 1552-1801 (SRO); M 1607-1812 (Boyd); C 1766-1816 (SCDB);
B 1766-1845 (SBDB); M 1607-1837 (SMI); C 1538-1899, M 1813-37 (DCI)
Cop (Mf) 1605-1835 (BT) (SLC, SRO)

LANGPORT Board of Guardians
OR Z 1866-93, 1914-31, D 1914-31 (SRO)

LANGPORT Cemetery opened 1880 (1¼ acres) (K 1931)

LANGPORT All Saints (1,245) (chapelry in Huish Episcopi until 1876) (peculiar of the Archdeacon
of Wells as the Prebendary of Huish cum Brent until 1845) (Pitney Hundred; Langport Union)
OR C 1619-22, 1728-1981, M 1619-22, 1728-1992, Banns 1754-1812, 1823-1902, B 1619-22,
1728-1940 (SRO)
BT 1605-13, 1622-26, 1628, 1630-31, 1635-36, 1639-40, 1753-59, 1770-76, 1779-80, 1804-11,
1813-36, CB 1838-40, 1842-45, 1854, CMB 1856-57 (SRO)
Cop M 1728-1812 (Ptd, Phillimore 1, 1898); M 1728-1812 (Boyd); B 1728-1812 (SBDB);
M 1728-1837 (SMI); C 1728-1857, M 1813-99 (DCI)
Cop (Mf) 1605-1857 (BT) (SLC, SRO); C 1619-22, 1728-1901, M 1619-22, 1728-1900,
Banns 1754-1812, 1823-1902, B 1619-22, 1728-1911 (SLC)

LANGPORT (Independent) b 1821 (K 1931)
OR ZC 1832-37, B 1833-36 (PRO: RG 4/2501)
Cop (Mf) ZC 1832-37, B 1833-36 (SLC, SRO)

LANGPORT St Joseph, The Hill (Roman Catholic) b 1905

LANGRIDGE St Mary Magdalene (109) (Bath Forum Hundred; Bath Union)
OR C 1763-1812, M 1756-1970, Banns 1756+, B 1763-1811 (SRO); CB 1813+ (Inc)
BT 1603-07, 1609, 1611, 1622-23, 1630, 1635-37, 1639-40, 1663-64, 1666-70, 1765-66, 1785-86, 1797-1823 (SRO)
Cop 1609-39 (Ptd, Dwelly 2, 1914); CB 1763-1840, M 1813-38 (Ts SG); 1813-40 (SRO); CB 1763-1812 (Bath Lib); B 1801-11 (SBDB); M 1609, 1635, 1756-1837 (SMI)
Cop (Mf) 1603-1823 (BT) (SLC, SRO)

LANSDOWN St Stephen *see* **BATH St Stephen**

LAVERTON St Mary (196) (Frome Hundred; Frome Union)
OR C 1693-1812, M 1695-1836 (gap 1810-12), Banns 1754-1809, 1823-1900, B 1678-1812 (SRO); CB 1813+ (Inc) (earlier registers destroyed by fire)
BT 1598, 1602-03, 1606-15, 1622-24, 1628-30, 1635-36, 1639-40, 1660-64, 1667-69, 1732-33, 1750-52, 1768-70, 1802-37, CB 1839-40, CMB 1841-44, CB 1845, CMB 1846, CB 1847-49, CMB 1850-51 (SRO)
Cop 1609-39 (Ptd, Dwelly 2, 1914); B 1777-1812 (SBDB); M 1609-39 (BT), 1695-1837 (SMI)
Cop (Mf) 1598-1851 (BT) (SLC, SRO); C 1693-1812, M 1695-1836, Banns 1755-1809, 1823-1900, B 1678-1812 (SLC)

LAVERTON (Baptist) (Lewis 1831)

LEIGH, ABBOTS Holy Trinity (360) (chapelry in Bedminster until 1852) (Portbury Hundred; Bedminster Union 1836-99, Long Ashton Union 1899-1930)
OR C 1656-1991, M 1656-1837, B 1656-1933 (Bristol RO)
BT 1831-34 (SRO); 1673-1881 (Bristol RO)
Cop M 1754-1837 (NSMI); C 1703-1840 (SBDB); M 1769-1837 (SMI)
Cop (Mf) 1673-1881 (BT) (SLC, SRO); C 1656-1991, M 1656-1837, B 1656-1933 (Bristol RO, SLC)

LEIGH upon MENDIP St Giles (640) (chapelry in Mells until 1860) (Frome Hundred; Frome Union)
OR C 1575-1973, M 1568-1836, Banns 1755-1814, B 1566-1888 (SRO)
BT 1594-97, 1601-02, 1607-09, 1618, 1622-24, 1630-31, 1639-41, 1662, 1666-67, 1802-37, CB 1838-43, B 1844-45, 1847-50 (SRO)
Cop 1607-22 (Ptd, Dwelly 2, 1914); B 1771-1871 (SBDB); M 1568-1837 (SMI)
Cop (Mf) 1594-1850 (BT) (SLC, SRO); C 1575-1903, M 1568-1643, 1650-63, 1680-1836, Banns 1754-1814, B 1566-1888 (SLC)

LEIGH upon MENDIP (Wesleyan) b 1811 (K 1931)

LEIGH upon MENDIP (Primitive Methodist) b 1836 (K 1931)

LEIGH WOODS St Mary the Virgin (created from Long Ashton, 1893) (Bedminster Union 1836-99, Long Ashton Union 1899-1930)
OR CMB 1893+ (Inc)

LEIGHLAND St Giles (created from Old Cleeve, 1724, refounded 1865) (Williton and Freemanors Hundred; Williton Union)
OR C 1783-1976, M 1755-1931, Banns 1755-1803, 1824-1934, B 1813-1946 (SRO) (previous entries at Old Cleeve)
BT 1800-09, 1811-13, 1818 (SRO)
Cop M 1755-1812 (SRO); C 1784-1812 (SCDB); B 1783-1863 (SBDB); M 1754-1837 (SMI); C 1784-1899, M 1755-1899 (DCI)
Cop (Mf) 1800-18 (BT) (SLC, SRO)

LEIGHLAND (Independent) (K 1931)

LEIGHLAND Roadwater (United Methodist) (K 1931)

LILSTOCK St Andrew (64) (Williton and Freemanors Hundred; Williton Union) (chapelry in
Stogursey, until 1881, when detached and united with Kilton)
OR C 1654-1881, M 1661-1869, B 1657-1974 (SRO)
BT 1606-09, 1613-14, 1621-23, 1628-30, 1635-36, 1640-41, 1663, 1666-68, 1672-73, 1678-80,
1704-06, 1725, 1732, 1742-43, 1746-52, 1759, 1802-04, 1808-17, 1820, 1833 (SRO)
Cop M 1661-1812 (Ptd, Phillimore 12, 1910); 1607-79 (Ptd, Dwelly 2, 1914); M 1661-1812 (Boyd);
B 1657-1928 (SBDB); M 1607-41 (BT), 1661-1750, 1763-1837 (SMI)
Cop (Mf) 1606-1833 (BT) (SLC, SRO); C 1654-1881, M 1654-1785, 1812-34, 1845-69,
Banns 1760-87, 1825-32, B 1654-1928 (SLC)

LIMINGTON Virgin Mary (313) (Stone Hundred; Yeovil Union)
OR C 1684-1926, M 1695-1979, Banns 1754-1812, B 1684-1812 (SRO); B 1813+ (Inc)
BT 1594-97, 1601-02, 1607-09, 1618, 1622-24, 1630-31, 1639-41, 1662, 1666-67,
1802-37, CB 1838-43, B 1844-45, 1847-50 (SRO)
Cop M 1695-1812 (Ptd, Phillimore 2, 1899); 1684-1800 (Index SRO); M 1695-1812 (Boyd);
C 1684-1812 (SCDB); B 1688-1812 (SBDB); M 1695-1710, 1730-1837 (SMI)
Cop (Mf) 1594-1850 (BT) (SLC, SRO)

LIMINGTON (Primitive Methodist) b 1871 (K 1931)

LITTLETON, HIGH Holy Trinity (911) (Chewton Hundred; Clutton Union)
OR C 1654-1948 (gap 1728-36), M 1654-84, 1699-1714, 1737-1957, Banns 1823-1900, B 1634-36,
1656-66, 1720-1961 (SRO)
BT 1599-1602, 1607-08, 1611-13, 1621-24, 1630-31, 1635-37, 1640-41, 1662-63, 1666-70,
1679-80, 1685-86, 1800-37, CB 1838 (SRO)
Cop C 1599-1640, 1653-1992, M 1599-1640, 1654-1957, B 1599-1641, 1654-1991 (Ts I SG, SRO);
M 1754-1837 (NSMI); B 1601-1907 (SBDB); M 1599-1640 (BT), 1654-1837 (SMI)
Cop (Mf) 1599-1838 (BT) (SLC, SRO); C 1654-1901, M 1654-84, 1699-1714, 1737-1812,
Banns 1823-1900, B 1634-36, 1654-66, 1720-1902 (SLC)

LITTLETON, HIGH (Wesleyan) b 1821 (K 1931)
OR C 1841-1955 (Bristol RO)
Cop C 1841-1955 (Ts I SG)
Cop (Mf) C 1841-1955 (Bristol RO, SLC)

LITTLETON, HIGH (Primitive Methodist) f 1868 b 1909 (K 1931)

LITTON St Mary (414) (Wells Forum Hundred; Clutton Union)
OR C 1587+, M 1583+, B 1582+ (gap C 1696-1713, MB 1696-1732) (Inc)
BT 1622-24, 1630-31, 1635-37, 1639-40, 1813-36 (SRO); 1749-54, 1776-80 (SRO: D/D/Ppb:76)
Cop C 1713-1812, M 1733-97, 1813-37, B 1733-1820 (SRO); B 1813-37 (SBDB); M 1754-1837
(SMI)
Cop (Mf) 1622-40, 1813-36 (BT) (SLC, SRO); C 1587-1696, 1713-1917, M 1583-1693, 1733-1966,
B 1582-1696, 1733-1992 (SRO)

LOCKING St Augustine (212) (Winterstoke Hundred; Axbridge Union)
OR C 1750-1960, M 1755-1836, Banns 1972-85, B 1778-1812 (SRO); B 1813+ (Inc)
BT 1598-99, 1602-04, 1606-09, C 1610, 1611, 1613-14, 1621-24, 1629-31, 1636, 1638-41, 1666,
1668-70, 1748-52, 1754-59, 1777, 1798, 1801-11, 1813-33, 1835-37, CB 1837-38, CMB 1839,
CB 1840-41, CMB 1842, CB 1843-48 (SRO)
Cop M 1755-1837 (NSMI); B 1788-1993 (SBDB); M 1755-1837 (SMI)
Cop (Mf) 1598-1848 (BT) (SLC, SRO)

LONG ASHTON *see* **ASHTON, LONG**

LONG LOAD Christ Church (chapelry in Martock until 1733, refounded 1867) (Martock Hundred; Yeovil Union)
OR C 1749-1878, M 1749-1981, Banns 1774-1808, B 1749-1978 (SRO) (CB from 1711 listed, 1914)
Cop M 1749-1808 (Ptd, Phillimore 3, 1901); 1731-1821 (SRO); M 1749-1808 (Boyd); B 1813-87 (SBDB); M 1749-1837 (SMI); C 1736-1878, M 1813-99 (DCI)
Cop (Mf) C 1749-1878, M 1749-58, 1774-75, 1790-1808, 1813-85, Banns 1774-1808, B 1749-1888 (SG, SLC)

LONG LOAD (Wesleyan) b 1884

LOPEN All Saints (502) (chapelry in South Petherton until 1747) (South Petherton Hundred; Chard Union)
OR C 1693-1866, M 1696-1837 (gap 1724-53), Banns 1754-1812, B 1693-1925 (gap CMB 1696-1704) (SRO)
BT 1607-10, 1612-13, 1621-24, 1629-31, 1636-37, 1639-41, 1669-70, 1672-73, 1678-79, 1729, 1731, 1742-43, 1757-61, 1766, 1789-90, 1800-31, CB 1859-61 (SRO)
Cop M 1723-1812 (Ptd, Phillimore 13, 1910); 1609-39 (Ptd, Dwelly 2, 1914); M 1723-1812 (Boyd); B 1755-1889 (SBDB); M 1609-39 (BT), 1723-1837 (SMI); C 1693-1866, M 1813-37 (DCI)
Cop (Mf) 1607-1861 (BT) (SLC, SRO); C 1693-1867, M 1696, 1711, 1719, 1754-1837, Banns 1754-1812, B 1693-1902 (SLC)

LOPEN (Independent) f 1825 b 1863 cl 1952

LOTTISHAM St Mary the Virgin (created from West Bradley)
OR CB 1872+, M 1884+ (Inc)

LOVINGTON St Thomas a Becket (214) (peculiar of the Dean of Wells until 1845) (Catsash Hundred; Wincanton Union)
OR C 1677-1955, M 1681-1987, Banns 1755-1810, 1824-85, B 1678-1992 (SRO)
BT 1605-08, 1611-12, 1621-24, 1629-30, 1636-41, 1663-64, 1666-69, 1676, 1679-80, 1749-51, 1754-57, 1813-35, CB 1837, 1842, 1844-45, 1849, 1862-63, 1866-69 (SRO)
Cop C 1674-1812 (SCDB); B 1678-1837 (SBDB); M 1681-1837 (SMI)
Cop (Mf) 1605-1869 (BT) (SLC, SRO); C 1674-1888, M 1681-1701, 1711-36, 1748-1837, Banns 1755-1810, 1824-85, B 1678-1812 (SLC)

LOVINGTON (United Methodist) b 1896 (K 1931)

LOXTON St Andrew (148) (Winterstoke Hundred; Axbridge Union)
OR CB 1558-1981, M 1560-1982, Banns 1754-1808 (pre-1800 registers defective) (SRO)
BT 1608-14, 1621-24, 1629-31, 1640, 1664-66, 1678, 1685, 1688-89, 1748, 1750-51, 1803, 1805-12, 1814-19, 1821-22, 1824-26, 1828-31, 1833-37, CB 1838-40 (SRO)
Cop M 1754-1837 (NSMI); C 1568-1801 (SCDB); B 1558-1892 (SBDB); M 1560-1837 (SMI)
Cop (Mf) 1608-1840 (BT) (SLC, SRO); C 1568-1789, 1801-88, M 1560-1885, Banns 1754-1808, 1823-88, B 1558-1789, 1801-92 (SLC)

LUCCOMBE St Mary (546) (Carhampton Hundred; Williton Union)
OR C 1690-1934, M 1653-64, 1690-1959, Banns 1754-98, 1835-1900, B 1666, 1690-1704, 1709-1966 (SRO)
BT 1594-99, 1603, 1605-09, 1611-12, 1621-23, 1662-70, 1672-73, 1678-79, 1701-02, 1704-08, 1721-22, 1727, 1729-32, 1751-58, 1762, 1764-65, 1767-69, 1771-73, 1775, 1777-84, 1786-87, 1789-1816, 1820, 1825, 1829-37, CB 1838-48, 1851-55 (SRO)
Cop C 1594-1611, 1621-23, 1662-75, 1690-1839, M 1594-1611, 1621-23, 1656-57, 1662-75, 1690-1837, Banns 1754-98, B 1594-1611, 1621-23, 1662-75, 1690-1837 (Ptd, T.L. Stoate, 1995); B 1690-1902 (SBDB); M 1652-1837 (SMI); C 1690-1899, M 1653-1899 (DCI)
Cop (Mf) 1594-1855 (BT) (SLC, SRO); CM 1653-64, 1690-1901, Banns 1754-1810, 1835-1900, B 1653-64, 1690-1903 (SLC)

LUCCOMBE (Methodist)
OR C 1803-72 (circuit) (SRO)

LUFTON St Peter and St Paul (20) (Stone Hundred; Yeovil Union)
OR C 1748, 1764, 1780-1811, M 1760-1823, 1836, Banns 1760-1823, B 1759-1811 (SRO);
   CB 1813+ (Inc)
BT 1598-99, 1602, 1606-07, 1609, 1613-14, 1622, 1629, 1635-36, 1638-40, 1666-67, 1705, 1748,
   1759-60, 1763, 1767, 1770-71, 1780, 1784-85, 1790-92, 1795-96, 1798, 1811, 1814-15, 1821,
   1831-36, CB 1840-45, CMB 1846, CB 1848-49 (SRO)
Cop 1598 (Ptd, Dwelly 2, 1914); M 1754-1837 (SMI)
Cop (Mf) 1598-1849 (BT) (SLC, SRO); C 1748, 1764, 1780, 1785, 1792-98, 1807, 1811,
   M 1760-71, 1792, 1795, 1811, 1823, 1836, B 1759-73, 1784, 1790, 1808-11 (SLC)

LULLINGTON All Saints (146) (Frome Hundred; Frome Union)
OR C 1713-1812, M 1713-1837, Banns 1754-1812, B 1712-1812 (SRO); CB 1813+ (Inc)
BT 1598-99, one between 1598-1639, 1607-09, 1611, 1613, 1616, 1621-24, 1629-31, 1635-36,
   1639-40, 1750-53, 1801-26, 1828-36 (SRO)
Cop 1598-1639 (Ptd, Dwelly 2, 1914); 1712-1840 (Ms SG); C 1713-1837, M 1713-52, B 1712-1812
   (SRO); M 1639, 1713-1837 (SMI)
Cop (Mf) 1598-1836 (BT) (SLC, SRO); C 1713-1805, M 1713-1837, B 1712-1812 (SLC)

LUXBOROUGH St Mary (391) (Carhampton Hundred; Williton Union)
OR C 1590-1866, M 1590-1968, Banns 1757-1906, B 1590-1945 (SRO) (registers from 1557 in
   1914 list)
BT 1598-99, 1606-08, 1610-12, 1621, 1623, 1630, 1636, 1639-40, 1663-64, 1668-69, 1678-79,
   1695-96, 1701, 1703-11, 1721-22, 1726-282, 1732-33, 1744-52, 1755-61, 1764-66, 1768-75,
   1777-81, 1783-1831, 1834, 1836-37, CB 1838 (SRO)
Cop C 1590-1712, M 1591-1711 (SRO); B 1587-1904 (SBDB); M 1541-1837 (SMI); C 1590-1866,
   M 1541-1899 (DCI)
Cop (Mf) 1590-1838 (BT) (SLC, SRO); C 1590-1866, M 1590-1900, Banns 1824-1900,
   B 1590-1845 (SLC)

LUXBOROUGH (United Methodist) b 1856 (K 1931)

LYDEARD, BISHOPS St Mary (1,295) (peculiar of the Dean of Wells until 1845)
   (West Kingsbury Hundred; Taunton Union)
OR C 1674-1896, M 1674-1978, Banns 1781-1814, B 1674-1949 (SRO)
BT one between 1595-1613, 1598-1600, 1603, 1605-06, 1608-10, 1613-14, 1620-24, 1635-36,
   1638-40, 1695-96, 1701-02, 1714-15, 1748-51, 1753-63, 1767-71, 1773, 1775, 1777-81,
   1813-15, 1819-37, CB 1838-65 (SRO)
Cop 1595-1638 (Ptd, Dwelly 2, 1914); B 1739-1853 (SBDB); M 1595-1638 (BT), 1674-1837 (SMI);
   CM 1674-1899
Cop (Mf) 1598-1865 (BT) (SLC, SRO)

LYDEARD, BISHOPS (Independent) f 1834 b 1837 (K 1931)
OR C 1873-1968, M 1849-1970, B 1886-1969 (SRO)

LYDEARD ST LAWRENCE (654) (Taunton and Taunton Dean Hundred; Taunton Union)
OR C 1573-1915, M 1573-1837, Banns 1754-1812, 1879-1989, B 1573-1883 (gap CMB 1644-52)
   (SRO)
BT 1599-1600, 1602-05, 1607, 1611-12, 1618-19, 1621-24, 1626-27, 1630-31, 1639-41, 1707-08,
   1720-21, 1725-26, 1728, 1749-52, 1754, 1759-60, 1764, 1767, 1769-70, 1773, 1778-91,
   1799-1817, 1821-27, 1829-38, CB 1840-53 (SRO)
Cop C 1573-1640, M 1573-1751 (SRO); C 1754-1812 (SCDB); B 1754-1869 (SBDB); M 1573-1837
   (SMI); C 1573-1899, M 1573-1837 (DCI)
Cop (Mf) 1599-1853 (BT) (SLC, SRO); C 1573-1900, M 1573-1837, Banns 1754-1812, 1879-1900,
   B 1573-1883 (SLC)

LYDEARD ST LAWRENCE Scarr (Independent) f 1676 b 1870 (K 1931)

LYDEARD ST LAWRENCE (Independent) f 1687 b 1861 (K 1931)

LYDFORD, EAST alias LYDFORD on FOSSE St Mary (166) (Somerton Hundred;
  Shepton Mallet Union)
OR C 1730-1989, M 1750-51, 1754-1966, Banns 1754-1812, 1824-1901, B 1730-1990 (SRO)
BT 1602-09, 1611-12, 1615, 1621-22, 1628, 1630-31, 1639-40, 1663-64, 1667-69, 1704-05, 1746,
  1750-51, 1801, 1803-17, 1819-21, 1823-24, 1833-37, CB 1838 (SRO)
Cop 1615-28 (Ptd, Dwelly 2, 1914); B 1730-1837 (SBDB); M 1615 (BT), 1754-1837 (SMI)
Cop (Mf) CB 1730-1812, M 1750-1902 (SG); 1602-1838 (BT) (SLC, SRO); C 1730-1900,
  M 1750-51, 1754-1900, Banns 1754-1812, 1824-1901, B 1730-1812 (SLC)

LYDFORD on FOSSE (created from union of East Lydford, Wheathill and West Lydford, 1971)
OR CMB 1971+ (Inc)

LYDFORD, WEST St Peter (357) (peculiar of West Lydford at Wells until 1845) (Catsash Hundred;
  Shepton Mallet Union)
OR C 1733-1993, M 1739-1981 (gap 1754-78), B 1750-1993 (SRO)
BT 1611-12, 1623, 1663-64, 1814-25, CB 1866-67 (SRO)
Cop 1623 (Ptd, Dwelly 2, 1914); M 1623 (BT), 1754-1837 (SMI)
Cop (Mf) 1611-64, 1814-25, 1866-67 (BT) (SLC, SRO); C 1733-1900, M 1739-54, 1779-1900,
  B 1750-88, 1790-1855 (SLC)

LYDFORD, WEST (Wesleyan) b 1830 (K 1931)

LYMPSHAM St Christopher (521) (Brent with Wrington Hundred; Axbridge Union)
OR C 1737-1929, M 1754-1973, Banns 1755-69, B 1737-1884 (SRO)
BT 1605-10, 1613-14, one between 1619-21, 1621-24, 1640-41, 1704, 1720-21, 1748-50, 1754-57,
  1759-60, 1801-15 (SRO)
Cop CB 1737-1841, M 1754-1840, Banns 1755-69 (Ts I SG); CB 1737-1901, M 1754-1900
  (Ts I SRO); B 1813-67 (SBDB); M 1754-1837 (SMI)
Cop (Mf) 1605-1815 (BT) (SLC, SRO); CM 1737-1885, B 1737-1884 (SLC)

LYMPSHAM (Wesleyan) f 1770 reb 1902 (K 1931)

LYNCOMBE St Mark (created from Widcombe with Lyncombe, 1856, renamed Bath Lyncombe,
  1967) (Bath Union)
OR C 1843-1963, M 1856-1969, B 1843-1931 (SRO)
BT 1813-37, CB 1838-50 (SRO)
Cop 1813-40 (Ts I SG); M 1813-37 (SMI)
Cop (Mf) 1813-50 (BT) (SLC, SRO)

LYNCOMBE, SOUTH St Luke (created from Lyncombe, 1868, renamed Bath St Luke, 1967)
  (Bath Union)
OR C 1860-1962, M 1868-1973 (SRO)

LYNG St Bartholomew (363) (Andersfield Hundred; Bridgwater Union)
OR C 1691-1879, M 1692-1967, Banns 1825-1938, B 1692-1992 (SRO)
BT one between 1596-1621, 1597, 1599-1800, 1607-09, 1611, 1621-24, 1629-31, 1666-67,
  1678-80, 1705-06, 1720-21, 1732-33, 1737-38, 1740, 1742-43, 1750-51, 1753, 1755, 1759-60,
  1764-65, 1767-88, 1790-98, 1800-30, CB 1838-42, 1845-61 (SRO)
Cop M 1813-37 (Ts I SG); B 1692-1992 (SBDB); M 1597-1680 (BT), 1692-1837 (SMI)
Cop (Mf) 1597-1861 (BT) (SLC, SRO); C 1691-1879, M 1692-1900, Banns 1825-1900,
  B 1692-1811 (SLC)

LYNGFORD St Peter (created from Rowbarton, 1957, renamed Taunton St Peter, Lyngford, 1972)
OR C 1955-95, M 1957-70, Banns 1957-71 (SRO)

MAPERTON St Peter and St Paul (187) (Catsash Hundred; Wincanton Union)
OR C 1559-1992, M 1567-1983, B 1558-1991 (SRO)
BT 1599-1600, 1603-08, 1611, 1613-14, 1621-24, 1629-31, 1636-37, 1639-40, 1663-64, 1667-70,
    1672-73, 1678-80, 1704-05, after 1715, 1732, 1735-36, 1739-41, 1775-76, 1800-24, 1826-37,
    CB 1838-39, 1841-45, 1848-51 (SRO)
Cop 1613-79 (Ptd, Dwelly 2, 1914); M 1566-1837 (Phil Ms); C 1559-1838, M 1566-1837,
    B 1558-1839 (SRO); M 1566-1837 (Boyd); M 1613, 1621, 1678, 1754-1837 (SMI)
Cop (Mf) 1599-1851 (BT) (SLC, SRO); C 1559-1812, M 1566-1837, B 1558-1808 (SLC)

MARK St Mark (1,289) (chapelry in Wedmore until 1816) (peculiar of the Consistorial Decanal
    Court of Wells until 1845) (Bempstone Hundred; Axbridge Union)
OR C 1646-1972, M 1654-1987, Banns 1755-1813, 1823-53, B 1568-74, 1584-1602, 1654-1877
    (SRO)
BT 1606-08, 1611, 1621-24, 1636-37, 1639-40, 1676-77, 1685-86, 1695-96, 1721-22, 1780, 1801,
    1803-37, CB 1838, 1840-51, 1860-77 (SRO); 1740, 1746, 1749-55, 1759-65, 1767-79, 1781,
    1783-88, 1790-1800 (SRO: D/D/Pd:26/9)
Cop B 1755-1838 (SBDB); M 1606-40 (BT), 1647-1837 (SMI)
Cop (Mf) C 1646-1748, M 1646-1756, B 1568-1601 (SG); 1606-1877 (BT) (SLC, SRO);
    C 1646-1886, M 1654-1886, Banns 1755-1813, 1823-53, B 1584-1877 (SLC)

MARK (Wesleyan) (Lewis 1831) b 1869 (K 1931)

MARK (Baptist) b 1866 (K 1931)

MARKSBURY St Peter (371) (Keynsham Hundred; Keynsham Union)
OR C 1563-1949, M 1563-1836 (gap 1743-53), Banns 1754-1812, B 1563-1981 (SRO)
BT 1603-04, 1606-08, 1611-14, 1616, 1619-24, 1630-31, 1636-37, 1639-41, 1662-70, one between
    1663-73, 1678-80, 1690, 1730-36, 1743, 1746-52, 1798-1813, 1815, 1817-20, 1822-23, 1825,
    1835-36, CB 1837, CMB 1843, CB 1844-48 (SRO)
Cop 1563-1812 (Ts I SG, Bath Lib, British Lib); M 1754-1837 (NSMI); B 1741-1887 (SBDB);
    M 1563-1837 (SMI)
Cop (Mf) 1603-1848 (BT) (SLC, SRO); C 1563-1887, M 1563-1836, Banns 1754-1812,
    B 1563-1888 (SLC)

MARKSBURY (Wesleyan) b 1841 (K 1931)

MARSTON BIGOT St Leonard (485) (Frome Hundred; Frome Union)
OR C 1654-1883, M 1654-1993, B 1654-1981 (SRO)
BT 1598-99, 1603-04, 1607-10, 1622-24, 1636-37, 1639-40, 1733-34, 1800-17, 1820-34,
    CB 1848-49 (SRO)
Cop 1607-39 (Ptd, Dwelly 2, 1914); C 1784-1812 (SCDB); B 1784-1850 (SBDB); M 1598-1640
    (BT), 1654-1750, 1788-1837 (SMI)
Cop (Mf) 1598-1849 (BT) (SLC, SRO); C 1654-1883, M 1654-1901, B 1654-1906 (SLC)

MARSTON BIGOT Gaer Hill (Wesleyan) b 1850 (K 1931)

MARSTON MAGNA St Mary (346) (Horethorne Hundred; Sherborne Union 1835-94,
    Yeovil Union 1894-1930)
OR C 1565-1894, M 1562-1838, Banns 1754-82, 1788-1819, B 1563-1946 (gaps B 1611-15,
    1677-80) (SRO)
BT 1602-04, 1606-09, 1611-14, 1617-18, 1621-26, 1629-31, 1636-37, 1639-41, 1663-65, 1673-74,
    1773-76, 1800-32, 1834-38, CB 1839-42, 1844 (SRO)
Cop 1561-1735 (Ms I SG); C 1681-1812 (SCDB); B 1681-1863 (SBDB); M 1602-74 (BT),
    1681-1837 (SMI)
Cop (Mf) 1602-1844 (BT) (SLC, SRO)

MARSTON MAGNA (Wesleyan) b 1882

MARTOCK All Saints (2,841) (Martock Hundred; Yeovil Union)
OR C 1559-1986, M 1558-1971, Banns 1754-1901, B 1558-1960 (SRO)
BT 1598-99, 1601-02, 1605-08, 1623-24, 1638-40, 1662-63, 1695-97, 1705-06, 1720-21, 1730-38, 1740-43, 1745-47, 1749-52, 1755-57, 1760-61, 1765-1837, CB 1838, 1840-49 (SRO)
Cop M 1559-1812 (Ptd, Phillimore 3, 1901); C 1559-1812, B 1558-1912 (SRO); M 1559-1812 (Boyd); C 1756-1812 (SCDB); B 1760-1844 (SBDB); M 1559-1837 (SMI); C 1559-1894, M 1813-99 (DCI)
Cop (Mf) C 1558-1894, MB 1558-1901, Banns 1754-1901 (SG, SLC); 1598-1849 (BT) (SLC, SRO)

MARTOCK Holy Trinity f 1841
OR CMB 1841+ (Inc)

MARTOCK Bower Hinton Chapel later Pound Lane Chapel (Presbyterian later Independent) f c1669, reb 1791 cl 1908
OR ZC 1685-98, 1788-1837 (PRO: RG 4/1420)
Cop C 1685-98, 1818-36 (SCDB); B 1834-1936 (SBDB)
Cop (Mf) ZC 1685-98, 1788-1837 (SLC, SRO)

MARTOCK (Wesleyan) b 1791 reb Long Load 1855 cl 1960; North Street b 1868 reb 1886
OR C 1968-82, M 1978-83 (SRO)

MARTOCK Ebenezer Chapel (Independent) f 1824 became Martock United Reformed Church 1973

MARTOCK Gospel Hall, Church Street (Plymouth Brethren) b 1893

MEARE St Mary (1,296) (Glastonbury Twelve Hides Hundred; Wells Union)
OR C 1559-1902, M 1559-1681, 1713-1975, Banns 1754-1901, B 1559-1691, 1713-1928 (SRO)
BT 1605-12, 1616-17, 1619-20, 1623-24, 1630-31, 1639-40, 1663, 1668-69, 1720-21, 1731-32, 1734-37, 1743-45, 1747-50, 1752, 1758, 1765-73, 1779-82, 1784-85, 1801-27, 1829-35 (SRO)
Cop 1605-68 (Ptd, Dwelly 2, 1914); CB 1559-1676, M 1559-1672 (SRO); C 1559-1757 (SCDB); B 1558-1840 (SBDB); M 1559-1669, 1750-1837 (SMI)
Cop (Mf) C 1559-1902, M 1559-1680, 1714-1900, Banns 1754-1901, B 1559-1901 (SG, SLC); 1605-1835 (BT) (SLC, SRO)

MEARE (Independent) f 1826 (K 1931)

MEARE Westhay (Primitive Methodist) b 1859 (K 1931)

MEARE (Baptist) b 1861

MELLS St Andrew (1,259) (Frome Hundred; Frome Union)
OR C 1565-1954, M 1565-1970, Banns 1754-1813, 1823-1901, B 1565-1901 (SRO)
BT 1594-99, 1601-02, 1606-08, 1611-12, 1621-24, 1637-38, 1663-67, 1669-70, 1679-80, 1733-35, 1747-48, 1775-76, 1800-35, 1837, CB 1839-41, B 1842 (SRO)
Cop C 1826-40, B 1807-40 (Ts I SG); B 1678-1901 (SBDB); M 1754-1837 (SMI)
Cop (Mf) CB 1565-1901, M 1565-1900, Banns 1754-1813, 1823-1901 (SG, SLC); 1594-1842 (BT) (SLC, SRO)

MERRIOTT All Saints (1,405) (Crewkerne Hundred; Chard Union)
OR C 1646-1876, M 1653, 1662-1939, B 1678-1952 (SRO)
BT 1598-99, 1605-09, 1613, 1621-23, one between 1627-40, 1636-41, 1666-71, 1695-96, 1701-02, 1708-09, 1732-37, 1740-46, 1755-56, 1764-65, 1768-75, 1778, 1782-83, 1803-34, 1836-50, CB 1851-66 (SRO)
Cop M 1653-1812 (Ts I SG); M 1653-1813 (Boyd); B 1775-1842 (SBDB); M 1598-1641 (BT), 1653-1837 (SMI); C 1646-1876, M 1653-1899 (DCI)
Cop (Mf) 1598-1866 (BT) (SLC, SRO)

MERRIOTT Lower Street (Wesleyan) f 1811 b 1857 (K 1931)
OR M 1911-78 (SRO)

MERRIOTT Union or Unity Chapel, Lower Street (Baptist and Independent, Independent only by 1903) f 1839 b 1879 cl 1964

MERRIOTT Broadway Chapel, Broadway (Plymouth Brethren) f 1846 b 1847 (K 1931)

MERRIOTT Four-Square Gospel Mission Hall later Elim Pentecostal Church f 1937

MIDDLEZOY Holy Cross (679) (Whitley Hundred; Bridgwater Union)
OR C 1653-1904, M 1653-1837, Banns 1823-85, B 1653-1886 (SRO) (registers only from 1758 were listed in 1914)
BT 1603-06, 1610-14, 1621-24, 1636-37, 1640-41, 1666-69, 1720-21, 1727, 1731-37, 1744-47, 1751-52, 1755-56, 1758-59, 1765-71, 1775, 1778-79, 1782, 1784-85, 1787-88, 1791-92, 1794-1829, CB 1846-52 (SRO)
Cop B 1756-1845 (SBDB); M 1754-1837 (SMI)
Cop (Mf) 1603-1852 (BT) (SLC, SRO); CB 1653-1886, M 1653-1885, Banns 1823-85, (SLC)

MIDDLEZOY (Wesleyan) b 1847, new one b 1898 (K 1931)

MIDSOMER NORTON St John the Baptist (2,942) (Chewton Hundred; Clutton Union)
OR C 1697-1968 (gap 1737-39, 1773-83), M 1700-1974, Banns 1952-84, B 1697-1960 (SRO)
BT one between 1579-1614, 1594-95, 1599-1601, 1605-09, 1611-12, 1616, one between 1616-37, 1621-24, 1629-31, 1636-40, 1664-65, 1667, 1733-34, 1746-47, 1749-50, 1802-37, CB 1838-40 (SRO)
Cop M 1701-1837 (Ptd, Phillimore 14, 1913); 1616-30 (Ptd, Dwelly 2, 1914); M 1754-1837 (NSMI); M 1701-1837 (Boyd); B 1794-1839 (SBDB); M 1616-30 (BT), 1701-1837 (SMI)
Cop (Mf) 1594-1840 (BT) (SLC, SRO)

MIDSOMER NORTON (Wesleyan) reb 1859 (K 1931)
OR C 1801-57 (PRO: RG 4/1732, 3267); C 1843-1900 (circuit) (Bristol RO)
Cop (Mf) C 1801-57 (SLC, SRO); C 1843-1900 (Bristol RO, SLC)

MIDSOMER NORTON Welton (Primitive Methodist) b 1858 (K 1931)
OR M 1935-87 (SRO)

MIDSOMER NORTON Dunkerton Street (Wesleyan) b 1859
OR C 1883-1926 (Bristol RO)
Cop (Mf) C 1883-1926 (Bristol RO, SLC)

MIDSOMER NORTON Clapton (Wesleyan) b 1864 (K 1931)
OR C 1838-74 (Bristol RO)
Cop (Mf) C 1838-74 (Bristol RO, SLC)

MIDSOMER NORTON (United Methodist Free) b 1876

MIDSOMER NORTON (Primitive Methodist) b 1877 (K 1931)
OR C 1926-44 (Bristol RO)
Cop (Mf) C 1926-44 (Bristol RO, SLC)

MIDSOMER NORTON (United Methodist)
OR C 1880-89, 1959-67 (Bristol RO)
Cop (Mf) C 1880-89, 1959-67 (Bristol RO, SLC)

MIDSOMER NORTON Holy Ghost, High Street (Roman Catholic) b 1913

MIDSOMER NORTON (Salvation Army) (K 1931)

MIDSOMER NORTON Welton (Baptist) (K 1931)

MIDSOMER NORTON Reckfield Road (Methodist)
OR C 1942-55 (Bristol RO)
Cop (Mf) C 1942-55 (Bristol RO, SLC)

MIDSOMER NORTON Stones Cross (Methodist)
OR M 1956-62 (Bristol RO)
Cop (Mf) M 1956-62 (Bristol RO, SLC)

MILBORNE PORT Cemetery, Wheathill Lane opened 1901 (1½ acres) (K 1931)

MILBORNE PORT St John the Evangelist (2,072) (Horethorne Hundred; Wincanton Union)
OR CMB 1538+, Banns 1823-1964, ML 1888-1921 (Inc)
BT 1598-99, 1602-05, 1607-09, 1613-14, 1623-24, 1630-31, 1636-41, 1664-65, 1667-70, 1734-35, 1749-53, 1756-57, 1760, 1762, 1765-90, 1797-1801, 1803-37, CB 1838, CMB 1839-40, CB 1841-60 (SRO)
Cop CB 1538-1813, M 1538-1754 (Ts SG, SLC); CB 1538-1813, M 1538-1837 (SRO); B 1813-37 (SBDB); M 1562-1837 (SMI)
Cop (Mf) 1598-1860 (BT) (SLC, SRO); C 1538-1907, M 1538-1924, Banns 1823-1964, ML 1888-1921, B 1538-1891 (SRO)

MILBORNE PORT (Independent) f 1662, b 1749, reb 1844 cl c1990.
OR ZC 1787-1837, DB 1780-1837 (PRO: RG 4/1751); C 1835-1911, B 1780-1909 (SRO)
Cop (Mf) ZC 1787-1837, DB 1780-1837 (SLC, SRO)

MILBORNE PORT (Wesleyan) b 1866 (K 1931)

MILTON St Jude (created from Kewstoke, 1892)
OR C 1896-1960, M 1892-1964 (SRO)

MILTON St Peter (created from Kewstoke, Worle, Weston super Mare Christ Church and Weston super Mare St Saviour, 1965)
OR CMB 1965+ (Inc)

MILTON CLEVEDON St James (242) (Bruton Hundred; Shepton Mallet Union)
OR C 1596-1982, M 1596-1843, Banns 1754-1811, B 1596-1982 (gap CMB 1631-71) (SRO)
BT 1592-93, 1607-08, 1611-14, 1622-24, 1629-31, 1636-41, 1663-64, 1668-69, 1698-99, 1704-07, 1732-33, 1751-52, 1754, 1756-57, 1759-60, 1801-37, CB 1838-39, CMB 1840-42, CB 1843-49 (SRO)
Cop 1607-68 (Ptd, Dwelly 2, 1914); M 1596-1622, 1671-1712, 1715-1884, B 1783-1865 (SRO); B 1727-1899 (SBDB); M 1595-1837 (SMI)
Cop (Mf) 1592-1849 (BT) (SLC, SRO)

MILVERTON St Michael (2,344) (peculiar of the Archdeacon of Taunton as Prebendary of Milverton in the Cathedral Church of Wells until 1845) (Milverton Hundred; Wellington Union)
OR C 1538-1925, M 1538-1942, Banns 1754-1812, 1824-59, 1878-1901, B 1538-1917 (SRO)
BT 1605-07, 1611-14, 1623-24, 1638-40, 1707-08, 1743-45, 1813-22 (SRO)
Cop M 1538-1812 (Ptd, Phillimore 13, 1910); M 1538-1812 (Boyd); C 1779-1812 (SCDB); B 1779-1852 (SBDB); M 1539-1837 (SMI); C 1539-1899, M 1837-99 (DCI)
Cop (Mf) 1605-1822 (BT) (SLC, SRO); C 1538-1901, M 1538-1792, 1813-1900, Banns 1754-1812, 1824-59, 1878-1901, B 1538-1901 (SLC)

MILVERTON (Independent) f 1770 (K 1931)
OR C 1784-1837 (PRO: RG 4/2926); C 1784-1955, M 1906-49, B 1810-1953 (SRO)
Cop (Mf) C 1784-1837 (SLC, SRO)

MILVERTON Meeting House (Society of Friends) (Lewis 1831)
Cop B 1780-1832 (SBDB)

MILVERTON (Wesleyan) b 1830 (K 1931)
OR C 1784-1837 in Wellington chapel registers; C 1876-1920 (SRO)

MILVERTON Hounds Moor (United Methodist) b 1836 (K 1931)

MINEHEAD St Michael (1,481) (Carhampton Hundred; Williton Union)
OR C 1559-1950, M 1559-1979, Banns 1823-1974, B 1548-1964 (SRO)
BT 1591-98, 1603-04, 1611-12, 1622-24, 1636-37, 1639-40, 1663-64, one between 1667-80,
    1673-74, 1676-77, 1704-06, 1721-22, 1725-26, 1731-37, 1740-53, 1756-60, 1762-75, 1777-84,
    1787-93, 1796-97, 1800-14, 1818-24, 1826-36, CB 1838-87, 1889, 1891-93 (SRO)
Cop CM 1559-1840, B 1548-1840 (Ts I SG, SRO); B 1807-43 (SBDB); M 1639, 1754-1837 (SMI)
Cop (Mf) 1591-1893 (BT) (SLC, SRO); C 1559-1901, M 1559-1900, Banns 1823-1901,
    B 1548-1901 (SLC)

MINEHEAD Meeting House (Society of Friends)
Cop C 1718-65 (SCDB); B 1741-1813 (SBDB)

MINEHEAD The Parks (Baptist) b 1791, reb 1902 (K 1931)

MINEHEAD The Avenue (Wesleyan) b 1876 (K 1931)
OR C 1803-72 (circuit) (SRO)

MINEHEAD Sacred Heart, Townsend Road and Alcombe Road (Roman Catholic) b 1896

MINEHEAD Bancks Street (Independent) b 1902 (K 1931)
OR C 1905-60, B 1905-09 (SRO)

MISTERTON St Leonard (460) (Crewkerne Hundred; Beaminster Union 1835-96,
    Chard Union 1896-1930)
OR C 1558-1906, M 1558-1977, Banns 1756-1812, 1824-86, B 1558-1894 (SRO)
BT 1605-14, 1622-24, 1629, 1639-40, 1663-64, 1666-68, 1728-29, 1731-32, 1734-35, 1740-53,
    1757, 1764-69, 1771-1816, 1818-21, 1826, 1828-29, C 1832-35, CB 1849 (SRO)
Cop 1613-39 (Ptd, Dwelly 2, 1914); B 1762-1882 (SBDB); M 1613, 1639, 1754-1837 (SMI);
    C 1558-1899, M 1561-1899 (DCI)
Cop (Mf) CB 1558-1886, M 1558-1885, Banns 1754-1812 (SG); CB 1558-1886, M 1558-1885,
    Banns 1754-1812, 1824-86 (SLC); 1605-1849 (BT) (SLC, SRO)

MISTERTON Quaker Burial Ground, Cathole Mead f before 1705 cl late 18th or early 19th century

MISTERTON Mission Chapel, Middle Street (Baptist) b 1866 (K 1931)

MISTERTON Mission Chapel, Main Street (Wesleyan) b 1891 cl 1931

MONKSILVER All Saints (322) (Williton and Freemanors Hundred; Williton Union)
OR C 1653-1884, M 1653-1978, Banns 1754-1805, 1825-28, 1871-91, B 1653-1979 (SRO)
BT 1602, 1605-13, 1621-25, 1629-31, 1636-37, 1640-41, 1662-64, 1672-73, 1679-80, 1704-07,
    1721-22, 1728-29, 1731-38, 1743-46, 1753-56, 1759-60, 1764-1825 (SRO)
Cop CM 1653-89, 1754-1837, B 1653-89 (SRO); B 1797-1903 (SBDB); M 1653-98, 1754-1837
    (SMI); C 1653-1884, M 1653-1897 (DCI)
Cop (Mf) 1602-1825 (BT) (SLC, SRO); C 1653-1884, M 1653-1888, Banns 1754-1805, 1825-28,
    1871-91, B 1653-1904 (SLC)

MONKSILVER (Wesleyan) b 1897

MONKTON COMBE *see* **COMBE MONKTON**

MONKTON, WEST St Augustine (1,155) (Whitley Hundred; Taunton Union)
OR C 1710-1961, M 1710-1975, Banns 1754-1816, B 1710-1953 (SRO)
BT 1599-1600, 1605-08, 1613-14, 1618-20, 1623, 1625-26, 1629-31, 1636-37, 1639-40, 1663-64,
    1707-08, 1726-28, 1732-33, 1746-54, 1759-60, 1762-66, 1772-76, 1781-82, 1789-90,
    1795-1816, 1818-29, 1831-35 (SRO)
Cop M 1710-1812 (Ptd, Phillimore 8, 1906); 1599-1639 (Ptd, Dwelly 2, 1914);
    M 1710-1837 (Boyd); B 1813-52 (SBDB); M 1710-1837 (SMI); C 1710-1894, M 1813-99 (DCI)
Cop (Mf) 1599-1835 (BT) (SLC, SRO); C 1710-1901, M 1710-1900, Banns 1754-1816,
    B 1710-1900 (SLC)

MONKTON, WEST (Wesleyan) (Lewis 1831)

MONKTON, WEST (Baptist) (Lewis 1831)

MONKTON, WEST Bathpool (Independent) (K 1931)

MONTACUTE St Katherine (1,028) (Tintinhull Hundred; Yeovil Union)
OR C 1558-1844, M 1558-1949, Banns 1754-1810, 1879-1943, B 1558-1926 (SRO)
BT 1597-1600, 1605-07, 1609-13, 1619, 1622-23, 1631-32, 1639-40, 1669, 1695-96, 1704-05,
    1728, 1731, 1741-50, 1755, 1760, 1765-67, 1769, 1771-72, 1776-81, 1802, 1808-37,
    CB 1838-50, 1859 (SRO)
Cop CB 1558-1812, M 1558-1837 (SRO); B 1813-44 (SBDB); M 1754-1837 (SMI); M 1559-1837
    (SMI)
Cop (Mf) 1597-1859 (BT) (SLC, SRO); C 1559-1844, M 1560-1900, Banns 1754-88, 1879-1900,
    B 1559-1901

MONTACUTE (Baptist) b 1880 (K 1931)
OR C 1813-37 (SRO)

MONTACUTE (Wesleyan) (Lewis 1831)

MOORLAND *see* **NORTHMOOR GREEN**

MOORLINCH St Mary (2,192) (Whitley Hundred; Bridgwater Union)
OR C 1654-1906, M 1662-1839, Banns 1781-1877, B 1653-1935 (SRO)
BT 1598-1600, 1602-03, 1605-12, 1619-24, 1629-31, 1636-37, *c*.1661-67, 1678-80, 1690, 1720-21,
    1732-33, 1745-46, 1749-50, 1752, 1800-27, 1829-37, CB 1839-40, 1846-51 (SRO)
Cop 1598-1623 (Ptd, Dwelly 2, 1914); B 1743-1885 (SBDB); M 1598-1623 (BT), 1654-1837 (SMI)
Cop (Mf) 1598-1851 (BT) (SLC, SRO); CB 1653-1731, 1743-1886, M 1653-1731, 1754-1839,
    Banns 1781-1877 (SLC)

MOORLINCH (Independent) f 1791 b 1840, reb 1894 (K 1931)

MUCHELNEY St Peter and St Paul (310) (Pitney Hundred; Langport Union)
OR C 1702-1900, M 1703-1977, Banns 1754-1812, 1824-85, B 1702-1813 (SRO); B 1813+ (Inc)
BT 1607-08, 1611, *c*.1619, one between 1620-29, 1623-24, 1627-31, 1636-37, 1639-41, 1661-62,
    1666-67, 1682-83, 1695-97, 1730-32, 1734-38, 1741-47, 1750-52, 1782-83, 1800-13, 1819-37,
    CB 1838-49 (SRO)
Cop M 1703-1812 (Ptd, Phillimore 1, 1898); 1620-96 (Ptd, Dwelly 2, 1914); B 1813-1984
    (Ts SRO); M 1703-1812 (Boyd); B 1722-1813 (SBDB); M 1620-96 (BT), 1703-1837 (SMI);
    C 1704-1899, M 1814-37 (DCI)
Cop (Mf) 1607-1849 (BT) (SLC, SRO); C 1702-1887, M 1702-48, 1754-1885, Banns 1754-1812,
    1824-85, B 1702-1813 (SLC)

MUDFORD St Mary (422) (Stone Hundred; Yeovil Union)
OR C 1563-1638, 1776-1867, M 1563-1638, 1776-1842, Banns 1787, 1823-1900, B 1563-1638,
    1776-1941 (SRO)
BT 1594-98, 1603-09, 1613-14, 1622-24, 1630-31, 1636-37, 1639-40, 1662-63, 1667-68, 1733-37,
    1745-46, 1756, 1801-21, 1823-36 (SRO)
Cop M 1563-1638, 1755-1836 (Phil Ms); M 1563-1837 (Boyd); C 1784-1812 (SCDB);
    B 1784-1902 (SBDB); M 1754-1837 (SMI)
Cop (Mf) 1594-1836 (BT) (SLC, SRO); C 1563-1638, 1776-1903, M 1563-1638, 1776-1842,
    Banns 1787, 1823-1901, B 1563-1638, 1780-1900 (SLC)

MUDFORD (Wesleyan) b 1845

NAILSEA Holy Trinity (2,114) (chapelry in Wraxall until 1811) (Portbury Hundred;
    Bedminster Union 1836-99, Long Ashton Union 1899-1930)
OR C 1554-1874, M 1554-1911, Banns 1754-1803, 1813-14, 1822-1921, B 1554-1895 (SRO)
BT 1593-96, 1602-03, 1607-08, 1611-14, 1621-24, 1639-40, 1732-33, 1800-37, CB 1838-66 (SRO)
Cop CMB 1554-1663 (C of A); M 1754-1837 (NSMI); B 1756-1840 (SBDB); M 1754-1837 (SMI)
Cop (Mf) 1593-1866 (BT) (SLC, SRO)

NAILSEA Christ Church (created from Nailsea Holy Trinity, 1844) (Bedminster Union 1836-99,
    Long Ashton Union 1899-1930)
OR CMB 1844+ (Inc)
BT C 1843-44, CB 1874-77 (SRO)
Cop (Mf) 1843-77 (BT) (SLC, SRO)

NAILSEA (Independent) b 1830 (K 1931)

NAILSEA (Wesleyan) (K 1931)
OR C 1840-1964 (Bristol RO)
Cop (Mf) C 1840-1964 (Bristol RO, SLC)

NAILSEA Ebenezer Chapel (United Methodist Free) b 1856 (K 1931)
OR C 1862-1962 (Bristol RO)
Cop (Mf) C 1862-1962 (Bristol RO, SLC)

NEMPNETT THRUBWELL St Mary the Virgin (225) (chapelry in Compton Martin until 1859)
    (Keynsham Hundred; Clutton Union)
OR C 1556-1807, M 1556-1836, Banns 1744-53, B 1557-1807 (SRO); CB 1813+ (Inc)
BT 1611-12, 1621-24, 1629-30, 1636-37, 1639-41, 1663-66, 1669-70, 1675-76, 1732-33, 1776-77,
    1800-18, 1820-36 (SRO)
Cop 1611-1812 (BT) (Ts I SG); M 1754-1837 (NSMI); C 1744-1807 (SCDB); B 1744-1807 (SBDB);
    M 1754-1837 (SMI)
Cop (Mf) 1611-1836 (BT) (SLC, SRO)

NEMPNETT THRUBWELL (Baptist) b 1842 (K 1931)

NETTLECOMBE St Mary (325) (Williton and Freemanors Hundred; Williton Union)
OR C 1548-1925, M 1540-1977, Banns 1754-1901, B 1540-1979 (gap CMB 1646-52) (SRO)
BT 1598-99, 1605-12, 1622-24, 1629-30, 1636-40, 1663, 1669-70, 1676-78, 1703-05, 1721-22,
    1726-28, 1731-33, 1740-41, 1751-59, 1762-63, 1765, 1767-69, 1771-81, 1783-97, 1799-1814,
    1816-17, 1830, 1832-33, 1835, 1837 (SRO)
Cop 1598-1673 (Ptd, Dwelly 2, 1914); 1540-98 (SRO); B 1795-1887 (SBDB); M 1540-98 (OR),
    1598-1673 (BT), 1754-1837 (SMI); CM 1540-1899 (DCI)
Cop (Mf) 1598-1837 (BT) (SLC, SRO); CB 1540-1887, M 1540-1884, Banns 1754-1886 (SLC)

NETTLECOMBE (Methodist)
OR C 1872-1923 (circuit) (SRO)

NEWTON, NORTH St Peter (created from North Petherton 1743, refounded 1880)
(North Petherton Hundred; Bridgwater Union)
OR C 1778-1915, Banns 1880-1900, B 1780-1943 (SRO)
BT 1640, 1813-22 (SRO)
Cop B 1761-1900 (SBDB)
Cop (Mf) 1640, 1813-22 (BT) (SLC, SRO); C 1778-1809, 1815-1901, Banns 1880-1900,
    B 1780-1807, 1813-1901 (SLC)

NEWTON, NORTH Meeting House (Independent) f 1851 Free Chapel b 1865, cl by 1972

NEWTON ST LOE Holy Trinity (477) (Wellow Hundred; Keynsham Union)
OR C 1538-1654, 1660-62, 1701-1875, M 1538-1641, 1649, 1661-1838, B 1538-1645, 1649-1890
    (SRO)
BT one between 1585-1616, 1605, 1607-08, 1611-12, 1616-17, one between 1616-40, 1621-23,
    1636-37, 1639-41, 1664-71, 1673-74, 1750-51, 1798-1837, CB 1838-39, C 1840, CB 1841,
    1862, 1864-77 (SRO)
Cop 1538-1812 (Ts I SG, Bath Lib, British Lib); M 1754-1837 (NSMI); B 1805-69 (SBDB);
    M 1754-1837 (SMI)
Cop (Mf) 1605-1877 (SLC, SRO); C 1538-1875, M 1538-1838, Banns 1824-87, B 1538-1888 (SLC)

NORTHMOOR GREEN St Peter and St John (created from North Petherton, 1845)
(Bridgwater Union)
OR M 1846-1966, B 1844-1993 (SRO); C 1846+ (Inc)
Cop (Mf) M 1846-1901 (SLC)

NORTHOVER St Andrew (138) (Tintinhull Hundred; Yeovil Union)
OR C 1534-1982, M 1541-1979, B 1543-1982 (gap CMB 1715-21) (SRO) (first M is dated 1531 but
    probably in error for 1541)
BT one between 1590-1620, 1598-1600, 1602-03, 1605-12, 1621-24, 1629-30, 1634-37, 1640-41,
    1663-64, 1668-69, 1704, 1731-32, 1735-36, 1740-41, 1802-20, 1831-33 (SRO)
Cop 1598-1812 (Ptd, Dwelly 9, 15, 1922-26); M 1531-1812 (Ptd, Phillimore 1, 1898);
    CB 1598-1810, M 1816-50 (Ts I SG); M 1531-1812 (Boyd); C 1723-1812 (SCDB);
    B 1722-1905 (SBDB); M 1541-1837 (SMI)
Cop (Mf) 1598-1833 (BT) (SLC, SRO); C 1534-1909, M 1531-1903, B 1543-1906 (SLC)

NORTON FITZWARREN All Saints (545) (Taunton and Taunton Dean Hundred; Taunton Union)
OR C 1556-1863, M 1565-1980, Banns 1754-1812, 1906-73, B 1566-1988 (SRO)
BT 1594-97, 1602-03, 1605-09, 1619-24, 1630-31, 1636-37, 1639-41, 1662-64, 1667, 1697-98,
    1707-08, 1725-29, 1731, 1739-41, 1745-46, 1749-52, 1754, 1759-60, 1767-69, 1776,
    1791-1823, 1825-36 (SRO)
Cop M 1565-1812 (Ptd, Phillimore 8, 1906); C 1556-1726, B 1566-1725 (Ts SG, SLC, SRO);
    M 1565-1657, 1683-1725 (SRO); M 1565-1812 (Boyd); C 1726-1812 (SCDB); B 1726-1850
    (SBDB); M 1565-1837 (SMI); C 1556-1863, M 1813-99 (DCI)
Cop (Mf) 1594-1836 (BT) (SLC, SRO)

NORTON FITZWARREN (Independent) b 1821 (K 1931)
OR C 1826-37 (PRO: RG 4/2873)
Cop (Mf) C 1826-37 (SLC, SRO)

NORTON HAWKFIELD (Chew Hundred; Clutton Union) (tithing in Chew Magna,
    transferred to Norton Malreward, 1896)

NORTON MALREWARD Holy Trinity (110) (Chew Hundred; Clutton Union)
OR C 1554-1814 (gap 1642-65), M 1554-1835 (gap 1642-68 ex 1647), B 1557-1812 (gaps 1574-77,
    1584-86, 1641-66 ex 1656) (SRO); C 1814+, B 1813+ (Inc)
BT 1603-7, 1612, 1629, 1636-41, 1672, 1678, 1681-2, 1695-6, 1721-1814, 1833-7, CB 1838 (SRO)
Cop M 1754-1837 (NSMI); C 1721-1814 (SCDB); B 1721-1812 (SBDB); M 1754-1837 (SMI)
Cop (Mf) 1603-1838 (BT) (SLC, SRO); C 1554-1814, M 1554-1806, 1816-35, B 1554-1812 (SLC)

NORTON ST PHILIP St Philip and St James (767) (Wellow Hundred; Frome Union)
OR C 1585-1851, M 1585-1968, Banns 1754-1812, 1823-74, B 1585-1973 (gap CMB 1654-67)
   (SRO)
BT 1591-1600, one between 1592-1663, 1602-14, 1621-24, 1629-30, 1635-40, 1663-64, 1666-68,
   1738, 1800-36 (SRO)
Cop 1584-1812 (Ts I SG); B 1740-1858 (SBDB); M 1609, 1613, 1621, 1639, 1754-1837 (SMI)
Cop (Mf) 1591-1836 (BT) (SLC, SRO); C 1585-1851, M 1585-1901, Banns 1754-1811, 1823-74,
   B 1585-1902 (SLC)

NORTON ST PHILIP (Baptist) (Lewis 1831) (K 1931)

NORTON ST PHILIP (Wesleyan) b 1836 (K 1931)
OR C 1840-1918 (SRO)

NORTON ST PHILIP Our Lady (Roman Catholic) b 1923

NORTON SUB HAMDON St Mary the Virgin (513) (Houndsborough, Barwick and Coker
   Hundred; Yeovil Union)
OR C 1558-1936, M 1558-1948, Banns 1754-1812, B 1558-1899 (SRO)
BT one between 1575-1601, 1595-97, one between 1601-25, 1606-13, 1616-18, 1621-24, 1636-40,
   c1663-92, 1669-70, 1730-32, 1740-42, 1749-52, 1755, 1769-70, 1798-1814, 1816-37,
   CB 1838-49 (SRO)
Cop C 1558-1837, MB 1558-1850 (Ts I SG); C 1558-1936, M 1588-1948, B 1558-1899 (SRO);
   M 1754-1837 (SMI)
Cop (Mf) 1595-1849 (BT) (SLC, SRO); CM 1558-1901, B 1558-1899 (SLC)

NORTON SUB HAMDON (Independent) f 1665 b 1871

NORTON SUB HAMDON (Wesleyan) b 1842 (K 1931)
OR C 1859-1904 (SRO)

NORTON SUB HAMDON (Plymouth Brethren) b 1868

NUNNEY All Saints (1,204) (Frome Hundred; Frome Union)
OR C 1547-1655, 1665-1920, M 1547-1641, 1645-1652, 1659-1993, Banns 1755-1812, 1823-1946,
   B 1547-1641, 1646-55, 1665-1911 (SRO) (registers started 1614 in 1914 list)
BT 1601-03, 1607-13, 1622-24, 1628, 1630-31, 1634-37, 1639-40, 1663-64, 1668, 1737-40,
   1750-57, 1759-60, 1802-06, 1809-22, 1824-34 (SRO)
Cop 1636-39 (Ptd, Dwelly 2, 1914); B 1783-1848 (SBDB); M 1636, 1639, 1754-1837 (SMI)
Cop (Mf) 1601-1834 (BT) (SLC, SRO); CM 1547-1901, Banns 1755-1812, 1823-1901, B 1547-1900
   (SLC)

NUNNEY Trudox Hill (Independent) (K 1931)
OR C 1760-1866, B 1800-87 (SRO)

NUNNEY (Wesleyan) b 1812 (K 1931)

NUNNEY (Primitive Methodist) b 1852

NUNNEY (Plymouth Brethren) (K 1931)

NYLAND cum BATCOMBE parish united to Glastonbury before 1535

NYNEHEAD All Saints (311) (Taunton and Taunton Dean Hundred; Wellington Union)
OR C 1670-1977, M 1670-1987, Banns 1754-1819, 1825-1947, B 1670-1994 (SRO)
BT 1598-1600, 1605-08, 1611-13, one between 1611-38, 1621-22, 1630-31, 1636-37, 1639-41,
  1662-64, 1669-70, 1739-41, 1749-52, 1756, 1763-64, 1767-70, 1779-80, 1801-37, CB 1838-40,
  CMB 1841, CB 1842, CMB 1843, 1850-59, CB 1897 (SRO)
Cop M 1670-1812 (Ptd, Phillimore 8, 1906); 1605-69 (Ptd, Dwelly 2, 1914); CB 1813-93
  (Index SRO); M 1670-1812 (Boyd); C 1769-1812 (SCDB); B 1769-1877 (SBDB); M 1605-1837
  (OR & BT) (SMI); C 1670-1899, M 1813-99 (DCI)
Cop (Mf) 1598-1897 (BT) (SLC, SRO)

OAKE St Bartholomew (147) (Taunton and Taunton Dean Hundred; Wellington Union)
OR C 1630-1991, M 1630-1959, Banns 1757-1810, B 1631-1991 (SRO)
BT 1594-95, 1599-1600, 1605-08, 1611-12, 1621-26, 1629-31, 1636-40, 1662-64, 1667-70, 1672,
  1679, 1683-84, 1725-28, 1732-34, 1744-45, 1750-52, 1775, 1801-16, 1818-37, CB 1840,
  1842-45, 1847-52, 1854-59 (SRO)
Cop 1594-1629 (BT) (Ts SG); C 1793-1812 (SCDB); B 1793-1991 (SBDB); M 1754-1837 (SMI);
  C 1630-1812, M 1630-1899 (DCI)
Cop (Mf) 1594-1859 (BT) (SLC, SRO)

OAKHILL All Saints (created from Shepton Mallet, Ashwick and Stoke Lane, 1866)
  (Shepton Mallet Union)
OR M 1866-1983 (SRO); CB 1866+ (Inc)
Cop (Mf) M 1866-1901 (SLC)

OAKHILL (Wesleyan) b 1825 (K 1931)

OAKHILL (Independent) f 1840 b 1873 (K 1931)
OR C 1837-1959, M 1860-1906, B 1868-1958 (SRO) (for earlier registrations *see* Shepton Mallet,
  Paul Street)

OARE St Mary (70) (Carhampton Hundred; Williton Union)
OR C 1690-1743, 1765-86, 1799-1987, M 1674-88, 1693-1743, 1765-86, 1799-1826, B 1691-1744,
  1765-84, 1791, 1800-12 (SRO); B 1813+ (Inc)
BT 1599-1600, 1603-08, 1611-14, 1621-24, 1630, 1634-37, 1639-40, 1663, 1665-72, 1678-79,
  1701-12, 1721-22, 1724-27, 1731-33, 1749, 1753-60, 1762-64, 1768-69, 1771-75, 1778-83,
  1786-88, 1790, 1801-05, 1807-28, 1830, CB 1848-49 (SRO)
Cop CB 1599-1670, M 1599-1670 (Ptd, Dwelly 2, 1914); M 1813-51 (Ts SG); C 1674-1812,
  M 1675-1729 (SRO); B 1800-12 (SBDB); M 1599-1670 (BT), 1674-1837 (SMI); C 1674-1812,
  M 1675-1826 (DCI)
Cop (Mf) 1690-1826 (SG); 1599-1849 (BT) (SLC, SRO); C 1690-1743, 1766-1808, 1814-91,
  M 1674-88, 1693-1743, 1766-1803, 1813-26, B 1691-1743, 1766-1808 (SLC)

ODCOMBE St Peter and St Paul (616) (Houndsborough, Barwick and Coker Hundred;
  Yeovil Union)
OR C 1669-1926, M 1669-1966 (gaps 1730-44, 1753-55), Banns 1755-1813, 1864-1931,
  B 1669-1877 (SRO)
BT 1598-1600, 1605-13, 1615-16, 1619-20, 1622-24, 1629-31, 1636-41, 1662-63, 1669-70, 1720,
  1801-03, 1806-14, 1816-21, 1823-25, 1827-29, 1830-35 (SRO)
Cop C 1669-1857, M 1669-1838, B 1864-77 (SRO); B 1813-62 (SBDB); M 1669-1837 (SMI)
Cop (Mf) 1598-1835 (BT) (SLC, SRO); C 1669-1903, M 1669-1727, 1744-1900, Banns 1755-1805,
  1827-1805, B 1669-1729, 1735-1877 (SLC)

ODCOMBE (Baptist) b 1860

ODCOMBE (Primitive Methodist) b 1878 (K 1931)

ODD DOWN St Philip and St James (created from South Lyncombe, 1964, renamed
Bath Odd Down, 1967)
OR M 1957-71 (SRO); CB 1964+ (Inc)

ORCHARDLEIGH St Mary (27) (Frome Hundred; Frome Union)
OR C 1623-1800, M 1625-1807, 1819-20, Banns 1765-99, B 1625-1807 (SRO); C 1813+,
   M 1837+, B 1813+ (Inc)
BT 1634, 1636-37, 1663-64, 1671, 1830 (SRO)
Cop 1623-1839 (Ms SG); C 1623-1800, M 1623-1761, B 1623-1807 (SRO); M 1625-34 (OR),
   1636-71 (BT), 1750-1837 (SMI)
Cop (Mf) 1634-71, 1830 (BT) (SLC, SRO); C 1624-66, 1676, 1695-1707, 1733-95, 1837,
   M 1625-39, 1659, 1674-75, 1700, 1730-1807, 1819-20, Banns 1765-99, B 1625-68, 1678-79,
   1700-05, 1733-99, 1807, 1837 (SLC)

ORCHARD PORTMAN St Michael (112) (Taunton and Taunton Dean Hundred; Taunton Union)
OR C 1538-1991, M 1538-1984 (gap 1712-14), B 1539-1991 (SRO)
BT 1597-99, 1602-04, 1606-12, 1623-24, 1635-41, 1662-63, 1667-70, 1676-77, 1707-08, 1727-28,
   1749-52, 1754, 1759, 1764, 1767-71, 1775-78, 1800-03, 1805-06, 1808-17, 1819-22, 1824-26,
   1828-35, 1838, CB 1840-55 (SRO)
Cop M 1538-1812 (Ptd, Phillimore 7, 1906); CB 1538-1840, M 1813-42 (Ms SG, SRO);
   M 1538-1812 (Boyd); B 1813-40 (SBDB); M 1538-1837 (SMI); C 1539-1812, M 1813-36 (DCI)
Cop (Mf) 1597-1855 (BT) (SLC, SRO); C 1538-1812, M 1538-1897, Banns 1759-1823,
   B 1539-1812 (SLC)

OTHERY St Michael (581) (Whitley Hundred; Bridgwater Union)
OR C 1560-1961, M 1560-1994, Banns 1756-94, 1805-08, 1823-85, B 1560-1893 (SRO)
BT 1603-13, one between 1615-39, 1621-24, 1629-30, 1636-38, 1666, 1731-33, 1752-59, 1765,
   1768-70, 1775, 1778-79, 1781-82, 1785, 1787, 1791, 1795-1822, 1824-40, M 1841-45,
   CMB 1846-50, CB 1851, CMB 1852-62, 1864-69 (SRO)
Cop 1608 (Ptd, Dwelly 7, 1919); B 1792-1893 (SBDB); M 1754-1837 (SMI)
Cop (Mf) 1603-1869 (BT) (SLC, SRO); CB 1560-1887, M 1560-1838, Banns 1756-94, 1805-08,
   1823-85 (SLC)

OTHERY (Independent) f 1807 b 1836 (K 1931)

OTTERFORD St Leonard (406) (Taunton and Taunton Dean Hundred; Taunton Union)
OR C 1558-1986, M 1558-1984, Banns 1754-1815, 1824-1902, B 1558-1975 (SRO)
BT 1603-08, 1611, 1618-24, 1629-31, 1636-41, 1662-64, 1669, 1697-98, 1707-08, 1724-26,
   1749-54, 1757-59, 1764, 1767-70, 1775, 1777-78, 1800-05, 1807-37 (SRO)
Cop M 1558-1812 (Ptd, Phillimore 11, 1908); M 1800-37 (Ts I SG); M 1558-1812 (Boyd);
   C 1752-1812 (SCDB); B 1760-1902 (SBDB); M 1558-1837 (SMI); C 1558-1863, M 1813-37
   (DCI)
Cop (Mf) 1603-1837 (BT) (SLC, SRO); CM 1558-1900, Banns 1824-1902, B 1558-1903 (SLC)

OTTERFORD (Plymouth Brethren) b 1862

OTTERFORD Bishops Wood (Plymouth Brethren) b 1874 (K 1931)

OTTERHAMPTON All Saints with COMBWICH St Peter (240) (Cannington Hundred;
Bridgwater Union)
OR C 1656-1903, M 1656-1973, B 1656-1981 (gap CB 1745-71) (SRO)
BT 1607-14, 1623-24, 1636-38, 1640-41, 1666-67, 1670-71, 1679, 1703-10, 1719-20, 1730-33,
   1738-39, 1748-50, 1804-11, 1813-30, 1832-33, 1835-36, CB 1838, 1840-41 (SRO)
Cop 1656-1749 (Ptd, Phillimore 6, 1905); C 1723-1810 (SRO); M 1646-1749 (Boyd);
   B 1745-1901 (SBDB); M 1656-1748, 1771-1837 (SMI)
Cop (Mf) 1607-1841 (BT) (SLC, SRO); C 1656-1748, 1771-1903, M 1656-1748, 1751, 1813-1901,
   Banns 1871-1901, B 1656-1748, 1771-1902 (SLC)

OTTERHAMPTON Bethel Chapel, Combwich (Independent, after 1879 Wesleyan) b 1838 (K 1931)

OVERSTOWEY *see* **STOWEY, OVER**

PAULTON Cemetery opened 1880 (2 acres) (K 1931)
OR B 1882-1966 (SRO)

PAULTON Holy Trinity (1,784) (chapelry in Chewton Mendip until 1841) (Chewton Hundred; Clutton Union)
OR C 1728-1973, M 1716, 1732-1990, Banns 1801-15, 1872-1900, B 1737-1987 (SRO)
BT 1594-97, 1599, 1602, 1605-09, 1611, 1613, 1616, 1623, c1625, 1629-30, 1636-37, 1639-40, 1663, 1732, 1749, 1800-34, 1841-42 (SRO)
Cop M 1754-1837 (NSMI); B 1751-1857 (SBDB); M 1754-1837 (SMI)
Cop (Mf) 1594-1842 (BT) (SLC, SRO); C 1730-1901, M 1754-1900, Banns 1754-1815, 1872-1900, B 1730-1902

PAULTON (Baptist) f 1655 (K 1931)
OR Z 1785-1836, B 1830-35 (PRO: RG 4/1733); M 1933-54 (SRO)
Cop (Mf) Z 1785-1836, B 1830-35 (SLC, SRO)

PAULTON High Street (Wesleyan) b 1826 (K 1931)
OR C 1839-1953 (chapel), C 1843-1900 (Somerset circuit), C 1959-64 (Paulton circuit) (Bristol RO)
Cop (Mf) C 1839-1964 (Bristol RO, SLC)

PAULTON (Primitive Methodist) b 1850 and another 1868 (K 1931)

PAULTON Our Lady Help of Christians (Roman Catholic) b 1961

PAWLETT St John the Baptist (577) (North Petherton Hundred; Bridgwater Union)
OR C 1667-1943, M 1668-1837, Banns 1754-1812, 1824-91, B 1667-1904 (SRO)
BT 1597, 1602-03, 1605, 1607, 1611, 1622-23, 1629-30, 1634, 1638, 1662-63, 1667, 1736-37, 1742, 1748-52, 1754-57, 1761-70, 1772-76, 1784-85, 1800, 1802-04, 1806-15, 1817-27, CB 1848-50 (SRO)
Cop 1597-1623 (Ptd, Dwelly 2, 1914); B 1730-1875 (SBDB); M 1668-1837 (SMI)
Cop (Mf) 1597-1850 (BT) (SLC, SRO); C 1667-1886, M 1668-1837, Banns 1754-1812, 1824-85, B 1667-1885 (SLC)

PAWLETT Carter Memorial Chapel (Wesleyan) f 1803 b 1855 (K 1931)

PEASEDOWN St John (created from Wellow, Dunkerton and Camerton, 1874)
OR C 1874-1961, M 1875-1959, B 1893-1961 (SRO)

PEASEDOWN (two Primitive Methodist) b 1840 (K 1931)

PEASEDOWN Carlingcott (Wesleyan) b 1844 (K 1931)
OR C 1915-60 (Bristol RO)
Cop (Mf) C 1915-60 (Bristol RO, SLC)

PEASEDOWN Carlingcott (United Methodist) b 1851 (K 1931)

PEASEDOWN Ashgrove St John (Baptist) b 1908 (K 1931)

PEASEDOWN St Joseph, Bath Road (Roman Catholic) b 1926

PEASEDOWN Ashgrove St John (Christadelphian) (K 1931)

PEASEDOWN Bath Road (Methodist)
OR C 1955-66 (Bristol RO)
Cop (Mf) C 1955-66 (Bristol RO, SLC)

PENDOMER St Roch (98) (Houndsborough, Barwick and Coker Hundred; Yeovil Union)
OR C 1729-1812, M 1730-1839, Banns 1754-1811, 1827-1963, B 1729-1812 (SRO);
    CB 1813+ (Inc)
BT 1593-95, 1598-99, 1602-03, 1605-07, 1609-12, 1623, 1627-28, 1630-31, 1634-39, 1662-63,
    1704, 1720-21, 1799-1812, 1811-20, 1823-37, CB 1838-39, C 1840, CMB 1842, CB 1844,
    C 1845, MB 1846, CB 1847, 1849, CMB 1850-52, M 1853 (SRO)
Cop 1609-23 (Ptd, Dwelly 2, 1914); M 1730-54 (SG); B 1728-1992 (SBDB); M 1754-1837 (SMI)
Cop (Mf) 1593-1853 (BT) (SLC, SRO); C 1729-1812, M 1730-1839, Banns 1754-1811, 1827-62,
    B 1729-1812 (SLC)

PENNARD, EAST All Saints (726) (Whitstone Hundred; Shepton Mallet Union)
OR C 1608-1928, M 1608-1962, Banns 1824-1921, B 1608-1871 (SRO)
BT 1599-1600, 1607-09, 1621-23, 1629-31, 1635-41, 1663-65, 1674-75, 1679-80, 1733, 1748-49,
    1756-58, 1800-12, 1814-32 (SRO)
Cop M 1608-1812 (Ptd, Phillimore 14, 1913); 1599-1679 (Ptd, Dwelly 2, 1914);
    M 1608-1812 (Boyd); B 1747-1858 (SBDB); M 1608-1837 (SMI)
Cop (Mf) 1599-1832 (BT) (SLC, SRO); C 1608-1859, M 1608-1901, Banns 1824-86,
    B 1608-1871 (SLC)

PENNARD, EAST Huxham (Wesleyan) b 1840 (K 1931)

PENNARD, WEST St Nicholas (920) (chapelry in Glastonbury until 1824)
    (Glastonbury Twelve Hides Hundred; Wells Union)
OR C 1538-1874, M 1538-1980, Banns 1789-1852, B 1538-1859 (SRO)
BT 1607-08, 1610-13, 1621-24, 1629-30, 1637-41, 1664-65, 1668-69, 1732-34, 1749-50, 1774-75,
    1802, 1806-37, CB 1838, CMB 1840-44, CB 1845-48 (SRO)
Cop 1607-39 (Ptd, Dwelly 2, 1914); B 1721-1904 (SBDB); M 1607-39 (BT), 1750-1837 (SMI)
Cop (Mf) 1607-1848 (BT) (SLC, SRO); C 1538-1874, M 1538-1900, Banns 1789-1852,
    B 1538-1859 (SLC)

PENNARD, WEST (Wesleyan) b 1820 and another b 1847 (K 1931)

PENNARD, WEST (United Methodist) reb 1903 (K 1931)

PENSELWOOD St Michael (361) (Norton Ferris Hundred; Wincanton Union)
OR C 1721-1892, M 1722-1837, Banns 1754-1803, B 1720-1924 (SRO)
BT 1593-97, 1599-1602, 1605-09, 1611, 1613, 1621-24, 1627, 1629-31, 1636-38, 1663-70,
    1678-79, 1704, 1732-33, 1748-52, 1755-57, 1762, 1765-67, 1800-19, 1822-24, 1827-28, 1830,
    1832, 1834-37 (SRO)
Cop 1597-1623 (Ptd, Dwelly 2, 1914); CB 1721-1801, M 1722-73 (SRO); C 1800-12 (SCDB);
    B 1800-98 (SBDB); M 1599, 1722-1837 (SMI)
Cop (Mf) 1593-1837 (BT) (SLC, SRO); C 1721-1892, M 1722-1837, Banns 1754-1803,
    B 1720-1900 (SLC)

PENSELWOOD (Primitive Methodist) (K 1931)

PENSFORD St Thomas a Becket (355) (chapelry in Stanton Drew until 1920s, renamed Publow with
    Pensford, 1972) (Keynsham Hundred; Clutton Union)
OR C 1651-1963 (gap 1755-59), M 1651-1963 (gap 1727-53), Banns 1754-1812, B 1654-1967
    (gap 1755-59) (SRO)
BT 1605-06, 1611-13, 1621-24, 1627-31, 1636-41, 1662-64, 1800-34 (SRO)
Cop C 1651-1906, M 1651-1963, B 1654-1813 (SRO); M 1651-65, 1754-1831 (SMI)
Cop (Mf) 1605-1834 (BT) (SLC, SRO); C 1651-1902, M 1651-65, 1754-1904, Banns 1754-1812,
    B 1654-83, 1760-1902 (SLC)

PENSFORD (Wesleyan) f 1757 (K 1931)
OR C 1794-1837 (PRO: RG 4/1558)
Cop (Mf) C 1794-1837 (SLC, SRO)

PENSFORD (Independent) f 1730 b 1760

PERROT, NORTH St Martin (454) (Houndsborough, Barwick and Coker Hundred; Yeovil Union)
OR C 1648-1873, M 1684-1837, Banns 1754-1812, B 1684-1937 (SRO)
BT 1598-1600, 1602-04, 1606-08, 1611-14, 1621-24, 1636-41, 1660-64, 1669-70, 1695-97,
1728-29, 1731-32, 1749-53, 1755-56, 1770-71, 1800-01, 1805-11, 1813, 1815-37, CB 1838-50,
1852-54 (SRO)
Cop 1599-1637 (Ptd, Dwelly 2, 1914); B 1787-1812 (SBDB); M 1599-1637 (BT), 1684-1837 (SMI)
Cop (Mf) 1598-1854 (BT) (SLC, SRO); C 1648-1888, M 1684-1730, 1754-1837, Banns 1754-1812,
B 1684-1832 (SLC)

PETHERTON, NORTH Cemetery opened 1856 (K 1931)
OR B 1913-34, 1940-88 (SRO)

PETHERTON, NORTH St Mary (3,566) (North Petherton Hundred; Bridgwater Union)
OR C 1558-1963, M 1558-1631, 1645-1980, Banns 1754-1877, B 1558-1954 (SRO)
BT 1597-1600, 1607-08, 1621-24, 1635-38, 1663-64, 1703-04, 1709-10, 1718-21, 1725-26,
1732-33, 1740-45, 1748-49, 1752, 1755-58, 1760, 1764-65, 1770-71, 1773-75, 1777-81,
1783-84, 1786-94, 1799-1834 (SRO)
Cop 1558-1837 (Ptd, Dwelly 10-13, 15, 1922-26, index in Dwelly 14, never printed, Ms at SG);
M 1558-1837 (Boyd); B 1709-1838 (SBDB); 1558-1600, 1754-1837 (SMI)
Cop (Mf) 1597-1834 (BT) (SLC, SRO); CMB 1558-1901, Banns 1754-1877 (SLC)

PETHERTON, NORTH Bridgwater Road (Congregational, later URC) f 1795 b 1833

PETHERTON, NORTH Tappers Lane (Wesleyan) b 1832 cl 1961
OR C 1842-1916 (SRO)

PETHERTON, NORTH Northmoor Green (Baptist) f 1839 b 1844 cl between 1939-65

PETHERTON, NORTH Union Chapel, Hedging b 1863 cl c1964

PETHERTON, NORTH Fordgate (Independent) b 1863 cl by 1944

PETHERTON, NORTH Somerset Bridge (Independent) b 1865 cl c1916

PETHERTON, SOUTH Cemetery opened 1868 (3½ acres, 1½ acres added, 1897) (K 1931)

PETHERTON, SOUTH St Peter and St Paul (2,294) (South Petherton Hundred; Yeovil Union)
OR C 1574-1970, M 1574-1985, Banns 1784-92, 1823-1905, B 1574-1947
(gap CMB 1644-69) (SRO)
BT one between 1569-1617, 1606-07, 1613-14, 1621-22, 1629-30, 1636-39, one between 1661-70,
1663-67, 1695-96, 1728-29, 1768-69, 1779, 1789-92, 1800-35 (SRO)
Cop B 1737-1844 (SBDB); M 1754-1837 (SMI); C 1574-1881, M 1574-1899 (DCI)
Cop (Mf) C 1574-1901, MB 1574-1900, Banns 1823-1900 (SG, SLC); 1606-1835 (BT) (SLC, SRO)

PETHERTON, SOUTH St Michael, Lightgate Road f 1934 b 1961

PETHERTON, SOUTH Round Well Street (Presbyterian by 1839 Independent) f 1752 b 1775
reb 1863
OR ZC 1773-1837 (PRO: RG 4/1563, 2503); C 1777-1850, M 1864-92, B 1868-74 (SRO)
Cop C 1777-1837 (SCDB)
Cop (Mf) ZC 1773-1837 (SLC, SRO)

PETHERTON, SOUTH Old Meeting, Palmer Street (Presbyterian by 1747 Independent) f 1663
  b 1705 cl 1844
OR ZC 1694-1837, B 1821-35 (PRO: RG 4/43, 2351, 4491)
Cop C 1694-1837 (SCDB)
Cop (Mf) ZC 1694-1837, B 1821-35 (SLC, SRO)

PETHERTON, SOUTH Coke Memorial Church (Wesleyan) f North Street 1753 b 1809, reb 1882
OR C 1813-37, 1843-57 (PRO: RG 4/2927, 3268); C 1813-1979 (SRO)
Cop C 1813-57 (SCDB)
Cop (Mf) C 1813-37, 1843-57 (SLC, SRO)

PETHERTON, SOUTH Mount Calvary Chapel, Over Stratton (Bible Christian later Methodist)
  f 1807 b 1861 (K 1931)
OR C 1813-1979 (SRO)

PETHERTON, SOUTH Pitway (Bible Christian) f 1826 b 1849 cl c1884

PETHERTON, SOUTH (Baptist) (Lewis 1831)

PETHERTON, SOUTH St Michael, Lightgate Road (Roman Catholic) b 1961

PILL Christ Church (created from Easton in Gordano and Portbury, 1861)
  (Bedminster Union 1836-99, Long Ashton Union 1899-1930)
OR C 1860-1983, M 1861-1965 (SRO)

PILL Union Chapel f 1787, reb 1815 (K 1931)

PILL (Wesleyan) b 1871 (K 1931)

PILL (Salvation Army) (K 1931)

PILL St Anthony of Padua (Roman Catholic) b 1959

PILTON St John the Baptist (1,118) (peculiar of the Precenter of Wells until 1845) (part Glastonbury
  Twelve Hides Hundred, part Whitstone Hundred; Shepton Mallet Union)
OR C 1558-1879, M 1558-1992, Banns 1783-1815, B 1558-1913 (SRO)
BT 1616-17, 1621-24, 1628-31, 1636-41, 1663-64, 1666-70, 1695-96, 1807-08, 1811-12, 1814-37,
  CB 1838-39 (SRO); 1701-04, 1707, 1709, 1712-14, 1803-07 (SRO: D/D/Ppr:8)
Cop 1616-69 (Ptd, Dwelly 2, 1914); C 1783-1812 (SCDB); B 1784-1845 (SBDB); M 1616, 1621,
  1623, 1629, 1636-37, 1639-40, 1663, 1667-69 (BT), 1754-1837 (SMI)
Cop (Mf) 1616-1839 (BT) (SLC, SRO); C 1558-1879, M 1558-1900, B 1558-1910 (SLC)

PILTON Ebenezer Chapel (Wesleyan) (Lewis 1831) b 1886 (K 1931)
OR M 1917-62 (SRO)

PILTON (United Methodist) (K 1931)

PITCOMBE St Leonard (480) (chapelry in Bruton until 1784) (Bruton Hundred; Wincanton Union)
OR C 1538-1957 (gaps 1653-55, 1695-1703, 1767-82), M 1567-1837 (gap 1653-1703),
  Banns 1783-1812, 1823-91, B 1538-1958 (gap 1767-82) (SRO)
BT 1597-98, 1605-06, 1616-17, 1622-24, 1629-31, 1636-40, 1663-69, 1679, 1750-51, 1800-12,
  1814-33, 1835-37, CB 1838-39, 1841-44 (SRO)
Cop 1567-1836 (Ptd, Dwelly 8, 1921); B 1813-62 (SBDB); M 1750-1837 (SMI)
Cop (Mf) 1597-1844 (BT) (SLC, SRO)

PITMINSTER St Mary and St Andrew (1,426) (Taunton and Taunton Dean Hundred; Taunton Union)
OR C 1544-1979, M 1542-1994, Banns 1754-1888, B 1542-1966 (SRO)
BT 1597-99, 1602-04, one between 1605-20, 1608-09, 1621-24, 1636-40, 1662-64, 1667-70, 1672-73, 1678-79, 1707-08, 1720-21, 1725-29, 1732-33, 1750-52, 1800-36 (SRO)
Cop M 1542-1812 (Ptd, Phillimore 7, 1906); 1542-1836 (Ts I SG, SRO); M 1542-1812 (Boyd); C 1701-1886 (SCDB); B 1683-1886 (SBDB); M 1542-1837 (SMI); C 1544-1899, M 1813-99 (DCI)
Cop (Mf) 1597-1836 (BT) (SLC, SRO); C 1545-1885, M 1542-1885, Banns 1754-1886, B 1542-1886 (SLC)

PITMINSTER Fulwood Chapel (Independent) b 1732 (K 1931)
OR C 1708-1836 (PRO: RG 4/1421, 2874); C 1705-93 (SRO)
Cop (Mf) C 1708-1836 (SLC, SRO)

PITMINSTER Blagdon (Independent) b 1877 (K 1931)

PITMINSTER (Plymouth Brethren) (K 1931)

PITNEY St John the Baptist (368) (peculiar of Dean of Wells until 1845) (Pitney Hundred; Langport Union)
OR C 1623-1880 (gap 1725-33), M 1625-1974 (gap 1725-34), Banns 1823-1979, B 1623-1976 (gap 1726-34) (SRO)
BT 1606-12, one between 1615-23, 1622-23, 1627-29, 1636-40, 1663-64, 1779-80, 1802-11, 1813-15, 1817, 1819-21, 1823-36 (SRO)
Cop M 1623-1812 (Ptd, Phillimore 2, 1899); M 1623-1812 (Boyd); B 1735-1812 (SBDB); M 1623-1837 (SMI)
Cop (Mf) 1606-1836 (BT) (SLC, SRO); C 1623-1880, M 1623-1900, Banns 1823-1901, B 1623-1903 (SLC)

PITNEY (Independent) f 1836 b 1875

PODYMORE alias PODIMORE MILTON St John (175) (Whitley Hundred; Yeovil Union)
OR C 1635-1978 (gap 1747-62), M 1744-1970 (gap 1747-55), Banns 1756-1811, 1823-1970, B 1635-1979 (gap 1747-62) (SRO)
BT 1601-03, 1605-07, 1610-14, 1622-24, 1630, 1636-40, 1662, 1756, 1806-09, 1811-14, 1816-19, 1821, 1823-30, 1832-37 (SRO)
Cop M 1744-1812 (Ptd, Phillimore 2, 1899); M 1813-51 (Ts and Ms I SG); M 1744-1812 (Boyd); C 1763-1812 (SCDB); B 1764-1899 (SBDB); M 1744-46, 1756-1837 (SMI)
Cop (Mf) 1601-1837 (BT) (SLC, SRO); C 1635-1905, M 1744-46, 1756-1897, Banns 1756-1810, 1823-1902, B 1654-1900 (SLC)

POLDOWN HILL (Quaker) *see* **SUTTON MALLET**

PORLOCK Cemetery opened 1889 (1 acre) (K 1931)

PORLOCK St Dubricius (830) (Carhampton Hundred; Williton Union)
OR C 1618-1970 (gap 1670-79), M 1618-1968 (gap 1669-79), B 1621-1927 (gap 1670-79) (SRO)
BT 1594-97, c.1600, 1603-12, 1616-17, 1619-24, 1629-30, 1636-41, 1663-64, 1667-70, 1672-73, 1678-79, 1697-98, 1703-13, 1721-22, 1728-29, 1733-34, 1751-55, 1757-59, 1764-65, 1767-68, 1771-75, 1778-84, 1789-90, 1801-03, 1806-33, 1835, CB 1838-55 (SRO)
Cop C 1618-93, M 1618-92, B 1621-92 (SRO); B 1730-1859 (SBDB); M 1618-92, 1750-1837 (SMI); C 1618-1897, M 1618-1899 (DCI)
Cop (Mf) M 1837-1957 (SG); 1594-1855 (BT) (SLC, SRO)

PORLOCK (Wesleyan) b 1837 (K 1931)
OR C 1803-72 (circuit) (SRO)

PORTBURY St Mary (621) (Portbury Hundred; Bedminster Union 1836-99, Long Ashton Union 1899-1930)
OR C 1559-1626, 1720-1875, M 1592-1641, 1720-1913, Banns 1812, 1823-1938, B 1559-1639, 1720-1895 (SRO)
BT 1599-1600, one between 1602-20, 1605-08, 1611-12, 1621-24, 1630-31, 1637-40, 1662, 1664-65, 1732-33, 1755, 1757, 1775, 1800-13, 1816-19, 1822-28, 1828-31, 1838-54, CB 1855, CMB 1856 (SRO)
Cop 1637 (Ptd, Dwelly 2, 1914); M 1754-1837 (NSMI); B 1775-1895 (SBDB); M 1754-1837 (SMI)
Cop (Mf) 1599-1856 (BT) (SLC, SRO)

PORTBURY (Wesleyan) (K 1931)

PORTISHEAD St Peter (800) (Portbury Hundred; Bedminster Union 1836-99, Long Ashton Union 1899-1930)
OR C 1554-1615, 1682-1963, M 1561-71, 1580-1602, 1682-1972, Banns 1754-1823, B 1555-1617, 1681-1971 (SRO)
BT 1607-08, 1611-12, 1622-24, 1629-30, 1636-37, 1639-40, 1678-79, 1750, 1800, 1802-37 (SRO)
Cop M 1754-1837 (NSMI); B 1791-1868 (SBDB); M 1754-1837 (SMI)
Cop (Mf) 1607-1837 (BT) (SLC, SRO); C 1554-1615, 1682-1901, M 1561-1602, 1682-1901, Banns 1754-1823, B 1555-1901 (SLC)

PORTISHEAD Nautical School Chapel (admission registers to school 1878-1913, 1940-43 at Bristol RO)
OR C 1913-82 (SRO)

PORTISHEAD Meeting House (Society of Friends) (Monthly Meeting of North Division) f 1648 (K 1931)
OR Z 1648-1773, M 1686-1816, B 1659-1832 (PRO: RG 6/1354)
BT B 1865-67, 1872-74, 1894 (SRO)
Cop (Mf) 1865-94 (BT) (SLC, SRO)

PORTISHEAD High Street (Wesleyan) (Clevedon Circuit) (Lewis 1831) b 1886 (K 1931)

PORTISHEAD (Independent) b 1877 (K 1931)

PORTISHEAD Roath Road Chapel (Plymouth Brethren) b 1886 (K 1931)

PORTISHEAD St Joseph, West Hill (Roman Catholic) b 1887

POYNTINGTON All Saints (165) (Horethorne Hundred; Sherborne Union) (transferred to Dorset, 1895)
OR C 1618-1897, M 1618-1843, Banns 1754-1812, 1823-1964, B 1618-1813 (Dorset RO); B 1813+ (Inc)
BT 1599-1600, 1602-03, 1605-09, 1611-13, 1622-23, 1627, 1629-31, 1636-37, 1813-14, 1816-20, 1822-40 (SRO)
Cop M 1618, 1623-36, 1646, 1651-62, 1694-1843 (Ts I SG); CB 1618-1836, M 1618-1843 (Dorset RO); B 1813-37 (SBDB); M 1754-1837 (SMI)
Cop (Mf) 1599-1840 (BT) (SLC, SRO)

PRESTON PLUCKNETT St James (347) (chapelry in Yeovil) (Stone Hundred; Yeovil Union)
OR C 1741-1981, M 1742-1979, Banns 1754-83, 1796, 1823-1949, B 1741-1925 (SRO)
BT 1622-24, 1629-31, 1638-41, 1662-65, 1744-52, 1756-57, 1769, 1778, 1798, 1800-O1, 1806-37, CB 1838-39, 1841-52 (SRO)
Cop B 1793-1901 (SBDB); M 1754-1837 (SMI)
Cop (Mf) 1622-1852 (BT) (SLC, SRO); CB 1741-1902, M 1745-1902, Banns 1754-91, 1823-1900 (SLC)

PRIDDY St Lawrence (202) (chapelry in Westbury until 1862, when created a parish including parts
of West Harptree, East Harptree, Chewton Mendip, Wells St Cuthbert, Wookey and Easton)
(peculiar of the Archidiaconal Court of Wells until 1845) (Wells Forum Hundred; Wells Union)
OR C 1761-1868, M 1759-1987, Banns 1759-1812, B 1761-1971 (SRO)
BT 1605-10, 1619-24, 1629-31, 1635-40, 1663-65, 1813-17, 1819-20, 1825-33 (SRO)
Cop M 1813-36 (Ts SG); B 1761-1900 (SBDB); M 1754-1837 (SMI)
Cop (Mf) 1605-1833 (BT) (SLC, SRO); C 1761-1868, M 1759-1901, Banns 1761-1812,
    B 1761-1901 (SLC)

PRIDDY (United Methodist) b 1881

PRISTON St Luke (308) (Keynsham Hundred; Keynsham Union)
OR C 1723-87, 1790-1910, M 1723-1930, Banns 1754-67, 1775-94, 1812, 1824-47, 1935, 1970-73,
    B 1723-74, 1782-85, 1789-1812 (SRO); B 1813+ (Inc)
BT 1598-99, 1603-06, 1611-12, 1621-24, 1627-30, 1634-41, 1667-69, 1671-72, 1679-80, 1736-39,
    1746-47, 1749-50, 1793-94, 1800-19, CB 1871 (SRO)
Cop 1723-1812 (Ts I SG, Bath Lib); M 1754-1837 (NSMI); B 1764-1812 (SBDB); M 1723-1837
    (SMI)
Cop (Mf) 1598-1819, 1871 (BT) (SLC, SRO); C 1723-1903, M 1724-1901, Banns 1754-1845, 1873,
    B 1723-1812 (SLC)

PUBLOW All Saints (839) (chapelry in Stanton Drew until 1864, united with Penslow in 1920s)
    (Keynsham Hundred; Clutton Union)
OR C 1569-1971, M 1569-1644, 1655-1972, Banns 1822-1972, B 1569-1878 (SRO)
BT 1606-08, 1616-17, 1619-24, 1629-30, 1636-41, 1805-17, 1819-27, 1834-37, CB 1838-49,
    B 1850-51, CB 1852-53, B 1854-55, CB 1856 (SRO)
Cop M 1754-1837 (NSMI); B 1755-1863 (SBDB); M 1734-1837 (SMI)
Cop (Mf) 1606-1856 (BT) (SLC, SRO); C 1569-1901, M 1569-1693, 1754-1900, Banns 1764,
    1822-1901, B 1569-1732, 1762-1880 (SLC)

PUBLOW Meeting House (Society of Friends) (Monthly Meeting of North Division)
OR Z 1640-1776, M 1665-1773, B 1668-1767 (PRO: RG 6/1222)

PUCKINGTON St Andrew (182) (Abdick and Bulstone Hundred; Langport Union)
OR C 1694-1812, M 1695-1834, Banns 1754-1844, B 1692-1811 (SRO); CB 1813+ (Inc)
BT 1594-99, 1606-12, 1621-24, 1627-31, 1635-40, 1662-63, 1758, 1789-90, 1800-38, CB 1839
    (SRO)
Cop M 1695-1812 (Ptd, Phillimore 4, 1902); M 1813-36 (Ts I SG); M 1695-1812 (Boyd);
    M 1695-1837 (SMI); C 1694-1812, M 1813-34 (DCI)
Cop (Mf) 1594-1839 (BT) (SLC, SRO); C 1694-1812, M 1695-1834, Banns 1754-1844,
    B 1693-1811 (SLC)

PURITON St Michael (509) (Huntspill and Puriton Hundred; Bridgwater Union)
OR C 1558-1912 (gap 1711-28, 1730-50), M 1558-1837 (gap 1704-29), Banns 1754-1893,
    B 1558-1904 (gap 1711-28, 1730-50) (SRO)
BT 1599-1600, 1607-8, 1622-24, 1629-31, 1664-67, 1745-46, 1748-51, 1754-56, 1763, 1766,
    1800-04, 1807-37, CB 1839-40, B 1842, CB 1848 (SRO)
Cop B 1640-1884 (SBDB); M 1754-1837 (SMI)
Cop (Mf) 1599-1848 (BT) (SLC, SRO); C 1558-1886, M 1558-1837, Banns 1754-1886,
    B 1558-1886 (SLC)

PURITON (Independent) b 1872 (K 1931)
OR C 1872-1967, M 1881-1965, B 1856-1960 (SRO)

PUXTON St Saviour (145) (chapelry in Banwell until 1749) (peculiar of Banwell in the Cathedral Church of Wells) (Winterstoke Hundred; Axbridge Union)
OR C 1543-1980, M 1543-1723, 1747-1980, Banns 1755-96, B 1543-1709, 1731-1981 (SRO) (registers start 1728 in 1914 list)
BT 1608-12, 1621-24, 1630-31, 1636-40, 1664-67, 1774-1818, 1820-22, 1824-27, CB 1832-37, CMB 1838, CB 1839 (1775-76 and 1807-08 in peculiar series) (SRO)
Cop M 1754-1837 (NSMI); B 1732-1977 (SBDB); M 1754-1837 (SMI)
Cop (Mf) 1608-1839 (BT) (SLC, SRO)

PUXTON (United Methodist) (K 1931)

PYLLE St Thomas a Becket (205) (Whitstone Hundred; Shepton Mallet Union)
OR C 1591-1968, M 1591-1976, B 1591-1812 (SRO); B 1813+ (Inc)
BT 1605-09, 1613-14, 1621-23, 1627-28, 1630-31, 1637-41, 1663-64, 1683-84, 1800-06, 1808-37, CB 1838-39, 1841-52, 1854-56 (SRO)
Cop 1622-27 (Ptd, Dwelly 2, 1914); CMB 1591-1840 (C of A); M 1627, 1754-1837 (SMI)
Cop (Mf) 1605-1856 (BT) (SLC, SRO); C 1591-1901, M 1591-1902, B 1591-1812 (SLC)

PYLLE (Wesleyan) b 1864 (K 1931)

QUAKER RECORDS (Society of Friends) Quarterly Meeting of Bristol and Somersetshire
OR ZMB 1776-1837 (PRO: RG 6/109-112, 131, 281-284, 300, 619, 1058-1060, 1154)
Cop M 1754-1837 (NSMI); M 1754-1837 (SMI)

Monthly Meeting of Middle Division (comprising Frome, Yeovil, Glastonbury etc.)
OR Z 1652-1752, M 1658-1774, B 1656-1762 (PRO: RG 6/1170, 1176)
Cop M 1754-1837 (SMI)
see also registers for Alford, Poldown Hill (under Sutton Mallet) and Street

Monthly Meeting of North Division (comprising Bath, Claverham, Sidcot, etc.)
OR Z 1648-1836, M 1687-1837, B 1655-1775 (PRO: RG 6/11, 38-39, 124, 166, 291-292, 1550)
Cop M 1754-1837 (SMI)
see also registers for Berington, Claverham (in Yatton) and Publow

Monthly Meeting of West Division (comprising Bridgwater, Taunton, Wellington, etc.)
OR Z 1648-1837, M 1659-1837, B 1654-1837 (PRO: RG 6/13, 42-43, 169, 307, 308, 1194, 1226)
BT B 1884-91, 1894-95 (SRO); M 1754-1837 (SMI)
Cop (Mf) 1884-95 (BT) (SLC, SRO)
see Gloucestershire NIPR for Bristol Monthly Meeting

QUANTOXHEAD, EAST St Mary (277) (Williton and Freemanors Hundred; Williton Union)
OR CB 1559-1812, M 1559-1836, Banns 1755-1823 (SRO); CB 1813+ (Inc) (register starts in 1654 in 1914 list)
BT 1598-1600, 1605-09, 1611, 1615-16, 1621-22, 1635-37, 1639-41, 1662-64, 1666-68, 1679-82, one between 1681-99, 1703-07, 1718-20, 1726-27, 1730-33, 1742-43, 1748-55, 1759, 1765, 1789-90, 1799-1800, 1802-15 (SRO)
Cop M 1654-1812 (Ptd, Phillimore 12, 1910); 1608-98 (Ptd, Dwelly 2, 1914); M 1654-1812 (Boyd); B 1700-1812 (SBDB); M 1598-1641 (BT), 1654-1837 (SMI)
Cop (Mf) 1598-1815 (BT) (SLC, SRO); CB 1559-1812, M 1559-1836, Banns 1755-1823 (SLC)

QUANTOXHEAD, WEST St Etheldreda (222) (Williton and Freemanors Hundred; Williton Union)
OR CB 1559-1986, M 1558-1992, Banns 1755-1840, 1907-30 (SRO)
BT 1599-1600, 1603, 1606-14, 1623-24, 1629-31, 1636-37, 1662-67, 1671-72, 1699-1700, 1704-07, 1720-22, 1725-27, 1731-33, 1743-44, 1769-70, 1775, 1800-18, 1820, 1822-26 (SRO)
Cop 1613 (Ptd, Dwelly 2, 1914); M 1613 (BT), 1754-1837 (SMI); C 1559-1812, M 1559-1899 (DCI)
Cop (Mf) 1599-1826 (BT) (SLC, SRO); C 1558-1888, M 1558-1883, Banns 1754-96, 1907-30, B 1558-1897 (SLC)

QUANTOXHEAD, WEST (Methodist)
OR C 1872-1923 (circuit) (SRO)

QUEEN CAMEL *see* **CAMEL, QUEEN**

QUEEN CHARLTON *see* **CHARLTON, QUEEN**

RADDINGTON St Michael (105) (Williton and Freemanors Hundred; Wellington Union)
  (united with Chipstable, 1971)
OR C 1814-93, M 1814-1961 (SRO) (CMB starting 1583 were extant 1914 but burned by 1935)
BT 1603, 1605-07, 1611-14, 1621-24, 1630-31, 1637, 1639-40, 1662-63, 1679-80, 1704-07,
  1725-29, 1731-33, 1749, 1751, 1753-55, 1757-59, 1762, 1764-65, 1767-69, 1771-73, 1775,
  1777, 1779, 1781, 1789-90, 1795-97, 1800-36 (SRO)
Cop 1603-1812 (BT) (Ptd, Dwelly 9, 15, 1922-26); 1814-36 (Ptd, Dwelly 8, 1921); M 1757-1837
  (SMI); C 1814-93, M 1837-99 (DCI)
Cop (Mf) 1603-1836 (BT) (SLC, SRO)

RADSTOCK St Nicholas (1,165) (Kilmersdon Hundred; Clutton Union)
OR C 1652-1986, M 1656-1966, Banns 1755-1913, B 1652-1950 (SRO) (registers from 1719 in
  1914 list)
BT 1597-1600, 1602-03, 1606-12, 1622-24, 1627-28, 1630-31, 1636-41, 1756, 1800-34 (SRO)
Cop 1719-1812 (Ms I SG); M 1754-1837 (NSMI); B 1789-1847 (SBDB); M 1750-1837 (SMI)
Cop (Mf) 1597-1834 (BT) (SLC, SRO); CB 1652-1901, M 1652-1900, Banns 1755-1901 (SLC)

RADSTOCK (Baptist) b 1844 (K 1931)

RADSTOCK Single Hill (Primitive Methodist later Methodist) b 1849
OR C 1900-48, 1958-89, M 1912-64 (Bristol RO)
Cop (Mf) C 1900-48, 1958-89, M 1912-64 (Bristol RO, SLC)

RADSTOCK Westfield (Primitive Methodist) b 1869, enlarged 1897 (K 1931)
OR C 1899-1959 (SRO)

RADSTOCK Ebenezer Chapel, Fortescue Road (Wesleyan) b 1902 (K 1931)
OR C 1843-1900 (circuit), C 1851-1958 (chapel) (Bristol RO); M 1900-55 (SRO)
Cop (Mf) C 1843-1958 (Bristol RO, SLC)

RADSTOCK St Hugh, Wells Hill (Roman Catholic) b 1913

RADSTOCK Frome Hill (Plymouth Brethren) (K 1931)

RADSTOCK (Reformed Methodist) (K 1931)

REDHILL Christ Church (chapelry of Wrington)
OR C 1844-96, M 1887-1984, Banns 1887-1976, B 1844-1975 (SRO)
Cop (Mf) C 1844-90, M 1887-1901, Banns 1887-1901, B 1844-1902 (SLC)

REDLYNCH St Peter (64) (chapelry in Bruton until 1733, united with Bruton, 1933, no separate
  registers) (Bruton Hundred; Wincanton Union)

RIMPTON St Mary (208) (Taunton and Taunton Dean Hundred; Sherborne Union 1835-96,
  Yeovil Union 1896-1930)
OR C 1537-64, 1653-1931 (gap 1659-61, 1690-1720), M 1654-93, 1721-1836 (defective 1654-1730
  with several gaps), Banns 1754-1813, B 1654-1812 (gap 1661-77) (SRO); B 1813+ (Inc)
BT 1598-99, 1601, 1603-09, one between 1604-25, 1611-12, 1622-24, 1629-30, 1634-39, 1662-64,
  1668, 1733, 1757, 1800-06, 1808-34, CB 1840-51 (SRO)
Cop M 1654-1837 (SMI)
Cop (Mf) 1598-1851 (BT) (SLC, SRO)

RIMPTON (Baptist) b 1870

RIMPTON (Wesleyan) b 1891 (K 1931)

ROAD alias RODE St Lawrence (954) (Frome Hundred; Frome Union)
OR C 1587-1995, M 1587-1988, Banns 1755-1911, B 1587-1995 (SRO)
BT 1597-1600, 1605-09, one between 1618-39, 1621-24, 1629-30, 1634-35, 1637-41, 1662-63,
   1667-68, 1676-77, 1728-29, 1750-51, 1802-32, 1834-37 (SRO)
Cop CB 1714-1840, M 1714-1837, Banns 1755-1837 (Ts I SG); CB 1733-1840, M 1733-1837
   (SRO); B 1776-1900 (SBDB); M 1754-1837 (SMI)
Cop (Mf) 1597-1837 (BT) (SLC, SRO); C 1587-1873, M 1587-1837, Banns 1755-1886,
   B 1587-1901 (SLC)

ROAD (Particular Baptist) f 1788 (K 1931)
OR Z 1783-1855, B 1787-1979 (SRO)
Cop (Mf) Z 1783-1855, B 1787-1979 (SLC, SRO)

ROAD (Wesleyan) b 1800 (K 1931)

ROAD HILL Christ Church (parish created from North Bradley in Wiltshire, united 1972 with
   Farleigh Hungerford, Tellisford, Road and Woolverton, all in Somerset, to form Road Major,
   q.v.) (Westbury and Whorwellsdown Union)
OR C 1824-1995, M 1853-1993, B 1827-1982 (SRO)
BT 1852-80 (Wilts RO)
Cop (Mf) 1852-80 (SLC, Wilts RO)

ROAD MAJOR (created 1972 from Road Hill, Wiltshire, and Farleigh Hungerford, Tellisford,
   Road and Woolverton, all in Somerset)
OR CMB 1972+ (Inc)

ROCKWELL GREEN see **WELLINGTON All Saints**

RODDEN (dedication unknown) (295) (chapelry in Boyton, Wiltshire, but in Somerset, until created
   a parish in 1802) (Frome Hundred; Frome Union)
OR C 1659-1964, M 1677-1837, Banns 1761-1818, 1824-1939, B 1693-1812 (SRO); B 1813+ (Inc)
   (1935 list gives C 1767+, M 1754+, B 1659+)
BT 1634-35, 1662-63, 1737-38, 1801-09, 1811-34, 1836-37, CB 1838, 1840-59 (SRO)
Cop C 1767-1812 (SCDB); B 1767-1837 (SBDB); M 1754-1837 (SMI)
Cop (Mf) 1634-1859 (BT) (SLC, SRO); C 1659-1901, M 1696-1700, 1754-1837, Banns 1761-1818,
   1824-1901, B 1696-1812 (SLC)

RODE see **ROAD**

RODNEY STOKE see **STOKE RODNEY**

ROWBARTON St Andrew (created from Taunton St James, 1879) (Taunton Union)
OR C 1880-1962, M 1880-1991, B 1880-1981 (SRO)
Cop (Mf) C 1880-1901, M 1881-1901, B 1880-1900 (SLC)

ROWBERROW St Michael (392) (Winterstoke Hundred; Axbridge Union)
OR C 1723-54, 1760-1979, M 1718, 1748-49, 1754-1989, Banns 1754-1812, B 1732-1980 (SRO)
BT 1599-1600, 1607-09, 1611-12, 1621-24, 1629-31, 1634-38, 1663-64, 1666-67, 1704, 1735,
   1805-19, 1821-29, 1831-32 (SRO)
Cop C 1723-1813 (incl. gap 1754-60), M 1718, 1748-49, 1732-1812 (SRO); C 1723-1812 (SCDB);
   B 1732-1812 (SBDB); M 1754-1837 (SMI)
Cop (Mf) 1599-1832 (BT) (SLC, SRO)

ROWBERROW (Baptist) f 1814
OR C 1816-37 (PRO: RG 4/1559)
Cop (Mf) C 1816-37 (SLC, SRO)

RUISHTON St George (400) (chapelry in Taunton St Mary Magdalene until 1744) (Taunton and
  Taunton Dean Hundred; Taunton Union)
OR C 1678-1969, M 1679-1985, Banns 1824-96, B 1678-1929 (register to 1747 in that of Creech
  St Michael) (gap CMB 1748-59) (SRO)
BT 1598-99, 1603-04, 1607-08, 1621-23, 1630-31, 1636-40, 1697-98, 1727-28, 1732-33, 1749-51,
  1759, 1763-64, 1766-76, 1782-84, 1801-30, 1836 (SRO)
Cop M 1679-1812 (Ptd, Phillimore 8, 1906); M 1679-1812 (Boyd); B 1813-1901 (SBDB);
  M 1679-87, 1754-1837 (SMI); C 1678-1899, M 1813-99 (DCI)
Cop (Mf) 1598-1836 (BT) (SLC, SRO); C 1678-1747, 1760-1901, M 1679-1901, Banns 1824-96,
  B 1678-1709, 1760-1902 (SLC)

RUNNINGTON St Peter (127) (Milverton Hundred; Wellington Union)
OR C 1585-1812, M 1590-1836, Banns 1761-1810, B 1590-1812 (SRO); CB 1813+ (Inc)
BT 1599-1600, 1602-08, 1611-13, 1621-24, 1629-31, 1634-39, 1662-63, 1666-67, 1677-80,
  1682-83, 1707, 1725-28, 1732, 1743, 1749, 1759, 1767, 1769-78, 1800-17 (SRO)
Cop M 1586-1812 (Ptd, Phillimore 11, 1908); M 1813-51 (Ts I SG); M 1586-1812 (Boyd);
  C 1726-1812 (SCDB); B 1726-1812 (SBDB); M 1586-1837 (SMI); C 1586-1812, M 1813-36
  (DCI)
Cop (Mf) 1599-1817 (BT) (SLC, SRO)

ST AUDRIES *see* **WEST QUANTOXHEAD**

ST CATHERINE (154) (chapelry in Batheaston) (Bath Forum Hundred; Bath Union)
OR CB 1752-1812, M 1756-1837 (SRO); CB 1813+ (Inc)
BT 1598-99, 1605-06, 1609, 1611, 1622-24, 1629-31, 1635-37, 1639-40, 1662-70, 1775-76,
  1785-88, 1790, 1793, 1796, 1798-1805, 1808-26, 1828-29, 1833, 1835-37, CB 1838-80 (SRO)
Cop 1598-1630 (Ptd, Dwelly 2, 1914); M 1756-1837 (NSMI); C 1752-1812 (SCDB);
  B 1752-1812 (SBDB); M 1598, 1605, 1629, 1754-1837 (SMI)
Cop (Mf) 1598-1880 (BT) (SLC, SRO); CB 1752-1812, M 1756-1837 (SLC)

ST DECUMANS St Decuman (2,120) (peculiar of the Prebendary of St Decuman's, Cathedral
  Church of Wells until 1845) (Williton and Freemanors Hundred; Williton Union)
OR C 1600-36, 1649-66, 1674-1984, M 1600-54, 1661-1989, Banns 1775-93, 1828-85,
  B 1602-70, 1679-1983 (SRO)
BT 1609-10, 1613, 1622-24, 1629-30, 1635-37, 1639-40, 1660, 1662-85, 1668-70, 1690-96,
  1813-24, 1828-30 (SRO); 1635, 1718-19, 1724-25, 1729-31, 1736-37, 1739-66, 1773-77,
  1779-84 (SRO: D/D/Ppb:84)
Cop 1600-65 (SRO); C 1739-60, M 1723-44, B 1740-44 (Bath Lib); B 1813-39 (SBDB);
  M 1603-53, 1750-1837 (SMI); C 1602-1879, M 1602-1899 (DCI)
Cop (Mf) 1609-1830 (BT) (SLC, SRO); C 1600-1886, M 1603-78, 1704-1885, Banns 1775-93,
  1809, 1828-50, 1884-85, B 1602-1886 (SLC)

ST DECUMANS Watchet (Strict Baptist) f 1808 b 1824 (K 1931)
OR M 1949-50 (SRO)

ST DECUMANS Swain Street (Wesleyan) b 1824 reb 1871 Station Road now Harbour Road

ST DECUMANS Watchet (Wesleyan) (Lewis 1831) b 1869 (K 1931)
OR C 1877-1901 (SRO)

ST DECUMANS The Temple, Watchet (United Methodist) f 1859 b 1860 cl 1962

ST DECUMANS Castle Hall, Swain Street, Watchet (Salvation Army) f 1882 reb 1928 South Road
  (K 1931)

ST MICHAELCHURCH St Michael (32) (chapelry in North Petherton until 1740)
  (North Petherton Hundred; Bridgwater Union)
OR C 1695-1812, M 1695-1812, 1837-1960, Banns 1779, 1818, B 1695-1783 (SRO);
  CB 1813+ (Inc)
BT 1598, 1605, 1607-12, 1623, 1630, 1636-37, 1639-41, 1730-32, 1736-37, 1741-48, 1752-53,
  1759-60, 1764-65, 1768, 1795-97, 1802-03, 1805-24 (SRO)
Cop 1695-1812 (Ptd, PRS 72, 1914); M 1695-1812 (Boyd); B 1695-1807 (SBDB);
  B 1813-1902 (SBDB); M 1639, 1695-1812 (SMI)
Cop (Mf) 1598-1824 (BT) (SLC, SRO); C 1695-1761, 1778-1801, M 1695-1754, 1781-83, 1792,
  1837, 1845-91, B 1695-1761, 1777-78, 1784-1807 (SLC)

ST THOMAS IN PENSFORD *see* **PENSFORD**

SALTFORD St Mary (360) (Keynsham Hundred; Keynsham Union)
OR C 1709, 1712-1956, M 1713-22, 1736-46, 1752-1971, Banns 1836-1928, B 1712-23, 1727,
  1736-1912 (SRO)
BT 1599-1600, 1605-08, 1621-22, one between 1616-40, 1622-24, 1630-31, 1635-41, 1660,
  1750-51, 1775-76, 1781-82, 1785-87, 1790-91, 1793-98, 1800-33, 1835-37, CB 1838-48 (SRO)
Cop C 1709-1837, M 1713-1837, B 1712-1837 (Ts I SG, SRO); CMB 1709-1812 (Bath Lib,
  British Lib); 1599-1661 (BT) (Ts SG, SRO); B 1813-58 (SBDB); M 1713-42, 1754-1837 (SMI)
Cop (Mf) 1599-1848 (BT) (SLC, SRO)

SALTFORD (Primitive Methodist) b 1866 (K 1931)

SALTFORD (Independent) (K 1931)

SAMPFORD ARUNDEL Holy Cross (427) (Milverton Hundred; Wellington Union)
OR C 1695-1994, M 1698-1979, Banns 1769-1812, 1824-1910, B 1699-1926 (SRO)
BT 1605-06, 1611, 1622-24, 1628-31, 1633-40, 1666-68, 1750-51, 1799-1825, 1827, 1831,
  1832-37, CB 1838, 1840-63 (SRO)
Cop M 1698-1812 (Ptd, Phillimore 11, 1908); M 1698-1812 (Boyd); C 1765-1812 (SCDB);
  B 1765-1885 (SBDB); M 1605-68 (BT), 1698-1837 (SMI); C 1695-1874, M 1813-36 (DCI)
Cop (Mf) 1605-1863 (BT) (SLC, SRO); C 1695-1874, M 1698-1837, Banns 1768-1812, 1824-89,
  B 1698-1886 (SLC)

SAMPFORD ARUNDEL Samford Moor (Baptist) b 1871 (K 1931)

SAMPFORD BRETT St George (197) (Williton and Freemanors Hundred; Williton Union)
OR C 1629-1965 (gap 1684-91), M 1629-1839 (gap 1683-91), Banns 1752-1810, B 1629-1812
  (gap 1677-91) (SRO); B 1813+ (Inc)
BT 1609-12, 1627-30, 1635-36, 1675, 1679-80, 1703-08, 1715, 1721-22, 1726-27, 1731-33, 1745,
  1751-54, 1757-60, 1762-65, 1767-80, 1782-1835, CB 1865-93 (SRO)
Cop 1609-79 (Ptd, Dwelly 2, 1914); CM 1629-99 (SRO); B 1738-1812 (SBDB); M 1609-12 (BT),
  1629-99, 1754-1837 (SMI); C 1629-1899, M 1629-1835 (DCI)
Cop (Mf) 1609-1893 (BT) (SLC, SRO)

SAMPFORD BRETT (Methodist)
OR C 1803-1923 (circuit) (SRO)

SANDFORD ORCAS St Nicholas (353) (Horethorne Hundred; Sherborne Union)
  (transferred to Dorset, 1895)
OR Z 1538-85, C 1585-1993, M 1540-1983 (1727-53 defective), Banns 1779-1812, 1823-33,
  D 1538-86, B 1586-1991 (Dorset RO)
BT 1598-99, 1601-04, 1607-09, 1611-12, one between 1616-40, 1617-22, 1630-31, 1637-38,
  1663-68, 1730-31, 1733-35, 1800-15, 1817-31, CB 1838, 1841-42, 1845-53, 1856 (SRO)
Cop M 1540-1837 (SG, Dorset RO); CB 1538-86 (SG, Dorset RO); B 1813-51 (SBDB);
  M 1754-1837 (SMI)
Cop (Mf) 1598-1856 (BT) (SLC, SRO)

SANDFORD ORCAS (Independent) f 1811 cl *c*1816

SANDFORD ORCAS (Methodist)
<u>Cop</u> B 1803-46 (SBDB)

SEABOROUGH (dedication unknown) (124) (Crewkerne Hundred; Beaminster Union)
(transferred to Dorset, 1895)
<u>OR</u> C 1562-1978, M 1562-1616, 1682-88, 1705-54, 1757-1811, 1813-36, 1838-1973, Banns
1757-88, 1824-1974, B 1654-58, 1673-76, 1688-1765, 1768-1811, 1813-1970 (Dorset RO)
<u>BT</u> 1594-98, 1608-13, 1622-24, 1627, 1629-30, 1636-40, 1662-67, 1707-09, 1732-35, 1742-43,
1747-53, 1755-56, 1758, 1762-65, 1767-73, 1775-88, 1807-13, 1837 (SRO)
<u>Cop</u> 1594-1623 (Ptd, Dwelly, 1914); M 1813-36 (SG); M 1562-1616, 1682-88, 1705-36
(Ts I SG); B 1813-51 (SBDB); M 1596, 1598, 1609, 1622-23 (BT), 1750-1837 (SMI)
<u>Cop</u> (Mf) 1594-1837 (BT) (SLC, SRO)

SEAVINGTON ST MARY (366) (South Petherton Hundred; Chard Union)
<u>OR</u> C 1716-1983, M 1754-1982, Banns 1754-1811, 1824, 1903, 1911, B 1741-1985 (SRO)
<u>BT</u> 1598-99, 1605-09, 1611-13, 1621-24, 1627-31, 1634-35, 1637-41, 1667-68, 1728-29, 1757,
1801-04, 1808-30, CB 1853-60, 1863, 1865 (SRO)
<u>Cop</u> 1621-23 (Ptd, Dwelly 8, 1921); B 1813-1901 (SBDB); M 1599, 1621, 1623 (BT), 1750-1837
(SMI); C 1716-1899, M 1754-1837 (DCI)
<u>Cop</u> (Mf) C 1716-1901, M 1754-1903, Banns 1754-1811, 1824, 1903, 1911, B 1741-1901
(SG, SRO); 1598-1865 (BT) (SLC, SRO)

SEAVINGTON ST MARY Hurcot (formerly in Ilton) (Wesleyan) f 1812 b 1885 (K 1931)

SEAVINGTON ST MARY - Beulah Chapel, Dark Lane (Bible Christian) f 1834 b 1859
cl before 1929

SEAVINGTON ST MICHAEL (397) (South Petherton Hundred; Chard Union)
<u>OR</u> C 1559-1944, M 1558-1983, Banns 1754-1811, 1824-1969, B 1578-1986 (SRO)
<u>BT</u> 1678, 1728, 1742-43, 1750-53, 1758-59, 1768-69, 1775, 1789-91, 1801-27, 1829-37,
CB 1839-43 (SRO)
<u>Cop</u> B 1813-1904 (SBDB); M 1754-1837 (SMI); C 1559-1899, M 1562-1899 (DCI)
<u>Cop</u> (Mf) C 1559-1901, M 1558-1810, 1817-1904, Banns 1754-1811, 1824-1911, B 1578-1905
(SG, SRO); 1678-1843 (BT) (SLC, SRO)

SELWOOD (chapelry in Frome, created Frome Selwood, 1873, q.v.)

SELWORTHY All Saints with TIVINGTON St Leonard (558) (Carhampton Hundred;
Williton Union)
<u>OR</u> C 1653, 1658, 1668, 1672-1963, M 1673-1994, Banns 1775-98, B 1571-79, 1673-1906 (SRO)
<u>BT</u> 1594-1602, 1607-12, 1616-17, 1623-24, 1636-40, 1663-64, 1668-69, 1675-76, 1678-80, 1701,
1703-09, 1721-22, 1726-27, 1732-33, 1750-51, 1756, 1764-65, 1767-69, 1771-73, 1775-80,
1789-91, 1793, 1802-37, CB 1838, 1840-55, 1857-58 (SRO)
<u>Cop</u> C 1594-1623, 1636-39, 1653-68, 1672-1840, M 1594-1623, 1636-39, 1663, 1668, 1673-1837,
B 1571-79, 1594-98, 1611-23, 1636-39, 1663-68, 1673-1838 (Ptd, T.L. Stoate, 1995);
B 1813-83 (SBDB); M 1754-1837 (SMI); C 1653-1899, M 1673-1836 (DCI)
<u>Cop</u> (Mf) 1594-1858 (BT) (SLC, SRO); C 1673-1902, M 1673-1839, Banns 1775-1800,
B 1571-79, 1673-1901 (SLC)

SHAPWICK St Mary (452) (Whitley Hundred; Bridgwater Union)
<u>OR</u> C 1591-1885, M 1591-1838, B 1590-1964 (SRO)
<u>BT</u> 1605-10, 1621-24, 1629-30, 1634-41, 1720-21, 1731-33, 1749, 1751-53, 1755-58, 1767-71,
1775, 1778, 1787-88, 1791, 1793, 1795-98, 1800-38, CB 1841-47 (SRO)
<u>Cop</u> 1605-40 (Ptd, Dwelly 2, 1914); B 1780-1900 (SBDB); M 1605-08, 1623, 1636-37, 1639-40
(BT), 1754-1837 (SMI)
<u>Cop</u> (Mf) 1605-1847 (BT) (SLC, SRO); C 1591-1885, M 1591-1838, B 1590-1901 (SLC)

SHAPWICK Meeting House, Polden Hill *see* **SUTTON MALLET**

SHEPTON BEAUCHAMP St Michael (648) (South Petherton Hundred; Chard Union)
OR C 1558-1913, M 1558-1975, B 1558-1984 (SRO)
BT two between 1576-1630, 1599-1602, 1606-14, 1616-18, 1621, 1623, 1827-30, 1635-40,
    1663-64, 1668-69, 1731-32, 1742-43, 1756, 1758, 1764-65, 1768-71, 1800-01, 1803-30,
    1832-33, 1836 (SRO)
Cop M 1558-1812 (Ptd, Phillimore 4, 1902); M 1558-1812 (Boyd); B 1789-1864 (SBDB);
    M 1558-1692, 1701-1837 (SMI); C 1558-1899, M 1813-99 (DCI)
Cop (Mf) 1599-1836 (BT) (SLC, SRO); CB 1558-1901, M 1558-1692, 1791-1900 (SLC)

SHEPTON BEAUCHAMP Buttle Lane & Church Street (Wesleyan) f *c*1812 b 1833 cl 1940

SHEPTON MALLET Board of Guardians
OR Z 1866-1930, D 1866-1930 (SRO)

SHEPTON MALLET Cemetery, Waterloo Road opened 1856 (7 acres) (K 1931)
OR B 1856-1973 (SRO)

SHEPTON MALLET St Peter and St Paul (5,330) (Whitstone Hundred; Shepton Mallet Union)
OR C 1635-1938, M 1635-1988, Banns 1723-31, 1754-1816, 1936-74, B 1635-1952 (SRO)
    (CMB from 1560 in 1914 list)
BT one between 1566-1609, one between 1597-1609, 1607-08, one between 1609-20, 1614-18,
    1621-24, 1629-31, 1634-38, ?1640, 1664-65, 1678-80, 1732-34, 1800-35 (SRO)
Cop 1566-1679 (Ptd, Dwelly 2, 1914); B 1791-1838 (SBDB); M 1566-1679 (BT), 1748-1837 (SMI)
Cop (Mf) 1607-1835 (BT) (SLC, SRO); C 1635-1901, M 1635-1900, Banns 1723-31, 1764-1816,
    B 1635-1901 (SLC)

SHEPTON MALLET Cowl Street (Presbyterian, later Unitarian) b 1697, reb 1785 (K 1931)
OR C 1757-1953, M 1837-1948, B 1802-1951 (SRO); C 1757-1837, B 1802-37 (PRO: RG 4/2058,
    2350, 2875)

SHEPTON MALLET Ebenezer Chapel (Methodist) f 1779 b 1819
OR ZC 1801-37 (PRO: RG 4/1560, 1561)
Cop (Mf) ZC 1801-37 (SLC, SRO)

SHEPTON MALLET Hephzibah Chapel, Commercial Road (Independent) f 1798, b 1801 (K 1931)
OR ZC 1801-36 (PRO: RG 4/2502); C 1838-90, M 1848-89, B 1802-1951 (SRO)
Cop (Mf) ZC 1801-36 (SLC, SRO)

SHEPTON MALLET St Nicholas later (1863) St Michael, West Shepton (Roman Catholic) b 1804
OR C 1765-1855, M 1767-86, 1810-25, 1841, 1849 (Bristol RO); C 1855+, M 1858+,
    DB 1856+ (Inc)
Cop (Mf) C 1765-1855, M 1767-86, 1810-25, 1841, 1849 (Bristol RO, SLC)

SHEPTON MALLET Paul Street (Independent) b 1819 (K 1931)
OR ZC 1830-37 (PRO: RG 4/2876); C 1857-1964, M 1924-30, B 1859-1948 (SRO)
Cop (Mf) ZC 1830-37 (SLC, SRO)

SHEPTON MALLET Commercial Road (Baptist) b 1875 (K 1931)

SHEPTON MALLET Downside (Wesleyan) b 1892 (K 1931)

SHEPTON MALLET Draycott (Salvation Army) (K 1931)

SHEPTON MALLET Board Cross (Plymouth Brethren) (K 1931)

SHEPTON MONTAGUE St Peter (452) (Norton Ferris Hundred; Wincanton Union)
OR C 1538-1964, M 1538-1754, 1779-1964, Banns 1889-92, ML 1908-40, B 1538-1964 (SRO)
  (registers badly damaged in church fire, 1964)
BT 1602-03, 1605-09, 1611-12, 1617-18, 1623-25, 1629-31, 1637-41, 1663-68, 1670-71, 1679-80,
  1704-05, 1734-35, 1749-52, 1754, 1800-30, 1832-36 (SRO)
Cop 1617-30 (Ptd, Dwelly 2, 1914); CMB 1538-1739 (SRO); B 1813-1905 (SBDB); M 1623, 1630,
  1779-1837 (SMI)
Cop (Mf) 1602-1836 (BT) (SLC, SRO); C 1813-1950, M 1779-1900, Banns 1889-92, B 1813-1907
  (SLC)

SHEPTON MONTAGUE (Independent) f 1662 b 1860, reb 1904 (K 1931)

SHIPHAM St Leonard (691) (Winterstoke Hundred; Axbridge Union)
OR C 1560-1620, 1642-53, 1659-1936, M 1560-1646, 1674-1961, Banns 1756-1812, B 1605-51,
  1665-74, 1686-1839 (SRO)
BT 1599, 1607-08, 1612, 1622-24, 1629-31, 1636-41, 1663-67, 1720, 1754, 1756-57, 1806,
  1808-13, 1815-18, 1824-27, 1829-37 (SRO)
Cop C 1639, 1674-1787, M 1560-1760, B 1606-1794 (Ts I SG); C 1558-1812, M 1560-1760,
  B 1615-1812 (SRO); B 1813-43 (SBDB); M 1560-1837 (SMI)
Cop (Mf) 1599-1837 (BT) (SLC, SRO)

SHIPHAM (Wesleyan) f 1825 b 1892 (K 1931)
OR C 1894-1972, M 1896-1938 (Bristol RO)
Cop (Mf) C 1894-1972, M 1896-1938 (Bristol RO, SLC)

SHOSCOMBE area in Wellow, joined to Foxcote, 1926

SKILGATE St John (227) (Williton and Freemanors Hundred; Dulverton Union)
OR C 1674-1860, M 1674-1960, Banns 1758-1815, 1825-1929, B 1674-1812 (SRO); B 1813+ (Inc)
BT one between 1595-1611, 1603-12, one between 1613-40, 1621-24, 1628-30, 1630, 1635-37,
  1639-40, 1662-67, 1671-73, 1679-80, 1697, 1704-08, 1710-12, 1714, 1731-33, 1749-53,
  1755-58, 1764-65, 1767-70, 1772-79, 1781-91, 1795-1837, CB 1838, 1840-48, 1850-55 (SRO)
Cop 1674-1722 (SRO); B 1803-12 (SBDB); M 1675-1721, 1754-1837 (SMI); C 1674-1861,
  M 1675-1899 (DCI)
Cop (Mf) 1603-1855 (BT) (SLC, SRO); C 1674-1812, 1838-61, M 1674-1903, Banns 1759-1815,
  1825-1905, B 1674-1812 (SLC)

SOCK DENNIS church demolished in late medieval times, and considered extra-parochial; in 1957
part was incorporated in Ilchester and the other part in Tintinhull (Tintinhull Hundred;
Yeovil Union)

SOMERTON Cemetery, Behind Berry opened 1875 (2 acres) (K 1931)

SOMERTON St Michael and All Angels (1,786) (part Pitney Hundred, part Somerton Hundred;
Langport Union)
OR C 1697-1970, M 1697-1968, Banns 1748-1817, 1823-1900, B 1697-1972 (SRO)
BT 1599-1600, one between 1600-40, 1606-07, 1611-14, 1623-24, 1627-30, 1631-38, 1640-41,
  1662-63, 1678-79, 1695-96, 1699-1702, 1705-09, 1724-27, 1745-46, 1750-52, 1755, 1760,
  1765-67, 1769-84, 1786-88, 1790-1824, 1826-37, CB 1838-41 (SRO)
Cop M 1697-1812 (Ptd, Phillimore 2, 1899); 1599-1699 (Ptd, Dwelly 2, 1914);
  M 1697-1812 (Boyd); B 1785-1812 (SBDB); M 1599-1837 (OR & BT) (SMI)
Cop (Mf) 1599-1841 (BT) (SLC, SRO); CM 1697-1886, Banns 1823-85, B 1697-1887 (SLC)

SOMERTON West Street (Independent) f 1785, b 1803 (K 1931)
OR C 1805-37, B 1807-37 (PRO: RG 4/1562)
Cop (Mf) C 1805-37, B 1807-37 (SLC, SRO)

SOMERTON (Bible Christian later United Methodist)
OR C 1837-84 (mission circuit) (SRO)

SOMERTON (Wesleyan) b 1846 (K 1931)

SOMERTON Meeting House (Society of Friends) b 1876 (K 1931)

SOMERTON (Salvation Army) b 1885 (K 1931)

SOMERTON St Dunstan (Roman Catholic) (Catholic Directory 1965)

SPARKFORD St Mary Magdalene (257) (Catsash Hundred; Wincanton Union)
OR C 1729-1812, M 1757-1993, Banns 1824-1910, B 1729-1994; C 1813+ (Inc)
BT 1602-09, 1611-14, 1619-24, 1627-30, 1636-373, 1639-40, 1663-64, 1669-70, 1675-76, 1678-79,
    1682-83, 1704-05, 1707-08, 1748-51, 1800-23, 1825-35 (SRO)
Cop C 1729-1812 (SCDB); B 1729-1812 (SBDB); M 1757-1837 (SMI)
Cop (Mf) 1602-1835 (BT) (SLC, SRO); CB 1729-1812, M 1757-1837, Banns 1824-1902 (SLC)

SPAXTON St Margaret (963) (Cannington Hundred; Bridgwater Union)
OR C 1558-1930, M 1559-1979, Banns 1769-72, B 1558-1862 (SRO)
BT 1598, one between 1604-21, 1607-08, 1629-30, one between 1630-36, 1636-41, 1662-63,
    1666-68, 1672-73, 1678-80, 1704-05, 1707-08, 1719-21, 1725-26, 1732-33, 1740-43, 1749-50,
    1755, 1759, 1765, 1767-71, 1774-75, 1777-83, 1787-90, 1794-1813, 1815-18, 1820-21,
    1823-29, 1833-34 (SRO)
Cop M 1558-1812 (Ptd, Phillimore 6, 1905); M 1558-1812 (Boyd); C 1688-1734 (SCDB);
    B 1688-1861 (SBDB); M 1558-1837 (SMI)
Cop (Mf) 1598-1834 (BT) (SLC, SRO)

SPAXTON (Wesleyan) f 1838 b 1858 (K 1931)

SPAXTON Merridge (Independent) b 1839 cl c1938

SPAXTON New Charlinch, Four Forks (Agapemonites) f 1845 cl 1957

STANDERWICK (dedication unknown) (97) (united with Beckington, 1660) (no separate registers)
    (Frome Hundred; Frome Union)

STANTON DREW St Mary (731) (Keynsham Hundred; Clutton Union)
OR C 1652-62, 1668-1983, M 1653-58, 1670-1983, B 1654-59, 1668-1948 (SRO)
BT 1599-1680, one between 1592-1680, one between 1600-40, 1602-03, 1605-08, 1611-12, 1614-18, 1621-24,
    1627-30, 1635-41, 1705-06, 1734-35, 1749-51, 1800-13, 1815-34 (SRO)
Cop 1599-1668 (Ptd, Dwelly 2, 1914); M 1754-1837 (NSMI); C 1653-1812 (SCDB);
    B 1654-1837 (SBDB); M 1599-1837 (OR & BT) (SMI)
Cop (Mf) 1602-1834 (BT) (SLC, SRO)

STANTON DREW (Wesleyan) (K 1931)

STANTON DREW Meeting House (Society of Friends) burial ground f 1669 (K 1931)

STANTON PRIOR St Lawrence (159) (Keynsham Hundred; Keynsham Union)
OR C 1572-1984, M 1572-1836 (gap 1707-35), B 1572-1753, 1777-1991 (SRO)
BT 1598-99, 1605, 1607-08, 1611-12, 1621-23, 1628-31, 1636-40, 1667-69, 1800-28, 1830-37,
    CB 1839, 1849, 1852-54, 1856-63 (SRO)
Cop 1571-1812 (Ts I SG, Bath Lib); C 1764-1812 (SCDB); B 1572-1812 (SBDB);
    M 1599, 1668 (BT), 1754-1837 (SMI)
Cop (Mf) 1598-1863 (BT) (SLC, SRO); C 1572-1812, M 1572-1642, 1653-97, 1706-07, 1735-1836,
    B 1572-1716, 1735-53, 1764-1812 (SLC)

STANTON PRIOR (Wesleyan) b 1863 (K 1931)
OR C 1912-64 (Bristol RO)
Cop (Mf) C 1912-64 (Bristol RO, SLC)

STAPLE FITZPAINE St Peter (415) (Abdick and Bulstone Hundred; Taunton Union)
OR C 1684-1925, M 1682-1984, Banns 1823-1950, B 1684-1991 (SRO)
BT 1599-1600, 1606-09, 1611, 1619-20, 1622-24, 1629-31, 1635-40, 1663-64, 1666, 1725-26,
    1742-43, 1749-51, 1756, 1759-60, 1762, 1764-65, 1767, 1770-73, 1775-76, 1778-82, 1784-88,
    1790-1814, 1816-38, CB 1839-55 (SRO)
Cop M 1682-1812 (Ptd, Phillimore 13, 1910); 1623 (Ptd, Dwelly 2, 1914); M 1682-1812 (Boyd);
    M 1682-1837 (SMI); C 1684-1899, M 1813-35 (DCI)
Cop (Mf) 1599-1855 (BT) (SLC, SRO); C 1684-1902, M 1684-1898; Banns 1823-1900,
    B 1684-1812 (SLC)

STAPLEGROVE St John (457) (Taunton and Taunton Dean Hundred; Taunton Union)
OR C 1559-1946, M 1559-1982, Banns 1824-1904, B 1558-1958 (SRO)
BT 1594-97, one between 1598-1642, 1599, 1603, 1605-08, 1611-12, 1617, 1619, 1621-24,
    1629-30, 1636-41, 1662-65, 1669-70, 1707-08, 1720-21, 1725-30, 1732-37, 1743, 1749-51,
    1769-71, 1796-97, 1800-13, 1816-25, C 1854-57 (SRO)
Cop CB 1558-1800, M 1559-1700 (SRO); C 1558-1945 (SCDB); B 1558-1958 (SBDB);
    M 1558-1700, 1751-1837 (SMI); CM 1558-1899 (DCI)
Cop (Mf) 1594-1857 (BT) (SLC, SRO); CB 1558-1901, M 1559-1901; Banns 1824-1901 (SLC)

STAWELL (dedication unknown) (214) (chapelry in Moorlinch) (Whitley Hundred; Bridgwater
    Union) (combined with those of Edington, Moorlinch, Sutton Mallet and Chilton Polden)
OR CB 1675-1812, M 1675-1758 (SRO) (Z 1653-66 in Moorlinch register); CB 1813+ (Inc)
BT 1598-99, 1606-11, 1621, 1623-24, 1627-31, 1636, 1637-40, 1664-67, 1720-21, 1813-24,
    1826-37 (CB 1839-40, 1846-51 with Moorlinch returns) (SRO)
Cop C 1675-1812 (SCDB); B 1675-1812 (SBDB); M 1675-1812 (SMI)
Cop (Mf) 1598-1851 (BT) (SLC, SRO); CB 1675-1812, M 1676-1737 (SLC)

STAWELL (Independent) b 1861 (K 1931)

STAWLEY St Michael (180) (Milverton Hundred; Wellington Union)
OR C 1653-1980, M 1654-1977, Banns 1755-1805, ML 1921, B 1653-1979 (SRO)
BT 1598-99, 1601-08, 1610-12, 1621-25, one between 1627-68, 1629-31, 1634-41, 1661-64,
    1668-69, 1672-73, 1678-80, 1707-08, 1727-28, 1743, 1749-54, 1759-60, 1764-65, 1767-74,
    1777-83, 1785-87, 1791, 1797-1816, 1818-23, 1825, 1827-36 (SRO)
Cop B 1813-1978 (SBDB); M 1754-1837 (SMI); C 1653-1880, M 1653-1899 (DCI)
Cop (Mf) 1598-1836 (BT) (SLC, SRO)

STAWLEY Union Chapel Appley (Baptist and Independent) (K 1931)

STEEP HOLME ISLAND (extra-parochial place, incorporated into Breane, 1966)
    (Bempstone Hundred; Axbridge Union)

STOCKLAND BRISTOL alias STOCKLAND GAUNTS St Mary Magdalen (202)
    (Cannington Hundred; Bridgwater Union)
OR CB 1538-1749, 1765-1812, M 1538-1837 (SRO); CB 1813+ (Inc)
BT 1597-1600, 1607-09, 1611-12, 1617-18, 1622-24, 1628-31, 1636-41, 1662-65, 1667-69,
    1672-73, 1679-80, 1703-07, 1709-10, 1719-21, 1737-38, 1742, 1748-49, 1768-69, 1775-76,
    1802-37, CB 1838, 1840-43 (SRO)
Cop M 1538-1807 (Ptd, Phillimore 6, 1905); CB 1538-1812 (SRO); C 1813-1990 (Ts I SG, SRO);
    M 1538-1812 (Boyd); C 1679-1812 (SCDB); B 1538-1812 (SBDB); M 1538-1837 (SMI)
Cop (Mf) 1597-1843 (BT) (SLC, SRO); CB 1538-1812, M 1538-1837 (SLC)

STOCKLAND BRISTOL Bethel Chapel, Steart (Independent) b 1847 cl c1938

STOCKLINCH MAGDALEN alias STOCKLYNCH MAGDALEN St Mary Magdalen (95)
  (Abdick and Bulstone Hundred; Chard Union) (united with Stocklinch Ottersey, 1931)
OR C 1712-1992, M 1712-1927, B 1712-1993 (SRO)
BT 1605-09, 1611, 1613-14, 1619-23, 1630, 1636-38, 1662-65, 1789-90, 1800-16, 1818-37,
  CB 1838-40, CMB 1841-42 (SRO)
Cop M 1712-76 (Ptd, Phillimore 4, 1902); 1712-55 (SG); M 1712-55 (Boyd); B 1712-1812 (SBDB);
  M 1712-1837 (SMI); C 1712-1812, M 1813-99 (DCI)
Cop (Mf) CB 1712-27, 1740-1812, M 1815-1927 (SG); 1605-1842 (BT) (SLC, SRO); CB 1712-27,
  1740-1812, M 1815-1901 (SLC)

STOCKLINCH OTTERSEY alias STOCKLYNCH OTTERSEY Blessed Virgin Mary (120)
  (Abdick and Bulstone Hundred; Chard Union)
OR C 1558-1954, M 1558-1971, Banns 1755-1812, 1823-85, B 1558-1976
  (gap CMB 1661-87) (SRO)
BT 1598-1600, 1602-03, 1605-10, 1612-14, 1619-25, 1629, 1634-36, 1639-41, 1662-65, 1690-91,
  1734-35, 1749, 1789-90, 1797-98, 1800-12, 1814, 1828-37 (SRO)
Cop M 1558-1812 (Ptd, Phillimore 4, 1902); 1609-62 (Ptd, Dwelly 2, 1914); 1558-1656 (SRO);
  M 1558-1812 (Boyd); C 1561-1650 (SCDB); B 1688-1906 (SBDB); M 1558-1837 (SMI);
  C 1563-1899, M 1813-99 (DCI)
Cop (Mf) C 1558-1660, 1688-1900, M 1558-1660, 1688-1812, Banns 1755-1812, 1823-85,
  B 1558-1660, 1688-1907 (SG, SLC); 1598-1837 (BT) (SLC, SRO)

STOGUMBER St Mary (1,294) (Williton and Freemanors Hundred; Williton Union)
OR C 1559-1984, M 1559-1969, Banns 1793-1887, B 1559-1981 (gaps CMB 1645-53, 1713-16,
  1743-47) (SRO)
BT 1605-14, 1621-24, 1630, 1634-35, 1637-40, 1662-63, 1669, 1699-1702, 1705-07, 1721-22,
  1726-27, 1731-32, 1749-51, 1753-60, 1762, 1764-66, 1769, 1771-73, 1775-78, 1782-90,
  1792-96, 1794-1819, 1829-30, 1833-39 (SRO)
Cop 1559-1644, 1653-1712 (Ts I SG); CB 1559-1795, M 1559-1837 (SRO); C 1754-1812 (SCDB);
  B 1717-1843 (SBDB); M 1717-1837 (SMI); CM 1559-1899 (DCI)
Cop (Mf) 1605-1839 (BT) (SLC, SRO); C 1559-1889, M 1559-1885, Banns 1793-1887, B 159-1886
  (SLC)

STOGUMBER (Baptist) f 1680 b c1726 reb 1869 (K 1931)
OR Z 1810-36 (PRO: RG 4/1565 & SRO T/PH/PRO 68)); M 1950-53 (SRO)
Cop (Mf) C 1810-36 (SLC, SRO)

STOGUMBER (Methodist) f 1840 cl c1916
OR C 1803-1923 (SRO)

STOGURSEY alias STOKE COURCY St Andrew (1,496) (part Cannington Hundred, part
  Williton and Freemanors Hundred; Williton Union)
OR C 1609-1953 (gap 1628-52), M 1595-1971 (gap 1630-52), B 1598-1878 (gap B 1624-52) (SRO)
BT 1599-1600, 1605-14, 1623-24, 1629-30, 1637-40, 1678-79, 1703-06, 1708-10, 1718-21,
  1732-33, 1742-44, 1748-52, 1755, 1758, 1765, 1767-72, 1775-76, 1787-90, 1796, 1802-19,
  1822-38, M 1839, CMB 1840-48, CB 1849-59, CMB 1860-66 (SRO)
Cop M 1595-1812 (Ptd, Phillimore 12, 1910); 1623 (Ptd, Dwelly 2, 1914); M 1595-1812 (Boyd);
  B 1729-1878 (SBDB); M 1595-1837 (SMI)
Cop (Mf) 1599-1866 (BT) (SLC, SRO)

STOGURSEY Castle Street (Independent) f 1786 b 1823 cl 1977

STOGURSEY Burton (Strict Baptist) b 1833 (K 1931)

STOGURSEY Stolford (Primitive Methodist) b 1846 bought by Baptists 1884 cl c1940

STOGURSEY Stolford (Independent) fl 1871-96

STOKE St Gregory (1,507) (peculiar of the Dean and Chapter of Wells until 1845) (North Curry Hundred; Taunton Union)
OR C 1561-1934, M 1561-1986, Banns 1754-87, 1849-1900, B 1561-1892 (SRO)
BT 1606-10 [with North Curry returns], 1610-11, 1613-14, 1639-40, 1664, 1695-98, 1760-63, 1807-08 [with North Curry returns], 1813-18, 1822, 1826-37, CB 1838, 1840-43, CMB 1846, CB 1850 (1818-24 in peculiar series) (SRO)
Cop C 1561-1744 (SCDB); B 1634-1841 (SBDB); M 1754-1837 (SMI)
Cop (Mf) 1606-1850 (BT) (SLC, SRO); CM 1561-1642, 1653-1901, B 1561-1642, 1653-1892 (published by SRO, 1996)

STOKE St Gregory Meeting House (Society of Friends)
Cop B 1791 (SBDB)

STOKE [St Gregory] (Baptist) b 1869 reb 1895 (K 1931)

STOKE [St Gregory] Stathe (Baptist) b 1887

STOKE St Mary (275) (Taunton and Taunton Dean Hundred; Taunton Union)
OR C 1676-1954, M 1679-1985 (gap 1749-54), B 1678-1988 (SRO)
BT 1602-03, 1606-10, 1619-20, 1622-24, 1627-30, 1634-40, 1663-64, 1669-70, 1672, 1679-80, 1743, 1750-51, 1753-54, 1759-60, 1764, 1767, 1770, 1774-84, 1789-90, 1801-19, 1821-32 (SRO)
Cop M 1679-1812 (Ptd, Phillimore 7, 1906); 1635 (Ptd, Dwelly 2, 1914); C 1677-1812, M 1679-1811, B 1679-1812 (SRO); M 1679-1812 (Boyd); C 1677-1812 (SCDB); B 1677-1812 (SBDB); M 1635 (BT), 1679-1748, 1754-1837 (SMI); C 1677-1899, M 1813-36 (DCI)
Cop (Mf) 1602-1832 (BT) (SLC, SRO); C 1677-1902, M 1677-1901, Banns 1755-1900, B 1677-1836 (SLC)

STOKE [St Mary] (Wesleyan) b 1825 (K 1931)

STOKE [St Mary] (Independent) f 1825 (Lewis 1831)

STOKE LANE alias STOKE ST MICHAEL (980) (chapelry in Doulting until 1826, renamed Stoke St Michael, 1972) (Whitstone Hundred; Shepton Mallet Union)
OR C 1644-1904, M 1644-1837 (gap 1696-1703), Banns 1754-1808, 1823-1900, B 1695-1941 (SRO)
BT 1607-08, 1621-24, 1629-30, 1636-40, 1663-64, 1678-79, 1803-35 (SRO)
Cop 1622 (Ptd, Dwelly 2, 1914); C 1644-97 (SCDB); B 1695-1848 (SBDB); M 1622 (BT), 1754-1837 (SMI)
Cop (Mf) 1607-1835 (BT) (SLC, SRO); C 1644-1901, M 1644-1837, Banns 1823-1900, B 1644-1901 (SLC)

STOKE LANE (Wesleyan) (Lewis 1831) b 1861 (K 1931)
OR C 1943-81 (Bristol RO)
Cop (Mf) C 1943-81 (Bristol RO, SLC)

STOKE LANE (Primitive Methodist) b 1881 (K 1931)

STOKE, NORTH St Martin (128) (Bath Forum Hundred; Keynsham Union)
OR C 1650-1813, M 1649-81, 1753-1973, Banns 1863-1926, B 1657-1975 (SRO); C 1813+ (Inc)
BT 1598, 1602-13, 1629-31, 1635-40, 1662-63, 1666-70, 1755-57, 1787-88, 1794-1801, 1805-19, 1822-25, 1827-38, CB 1839-40, 1842 (SRO)
Cop C 1559-1840, M 1605-38, 1649-1840, B 1603-63, 1678-1840 (Ts I SG); CMB 1655-1812 (Bath Lib, British Lib); 1598-1663 (BT), 1813-40 (SRO); M 1754-1837 (NSMI); B 1759-1903 (SBDB); M 1598, 1605 (BT), 1655-1837 (SMI)
Cop (Mf) 1598-1842 (BT) (SLC, SRO); C 1649-1812, M 1655-1899, Banns 1663-1902, B 1657-1904 (SLC)

STOKE PERO (dedication unknown) (61) (Carhampton Hundred; Williton Union)
OR C 1712-1813, M 1712-1838 (defective 1732-40, 1755-1812), B 1712-99 (SRO); CB 1813+ (Inc)
BT 1598-99, 1601, 1603-09, 1609, 1611-13, 1621-23, 1627, 1629-31, 1634-41, 1662, 1664,
 1667-70, 1672-73, 1678, 1704-09, 1712, 1731-33, 1746, 1751, 1757-60, 1762-63, 1765, 1767,
 1769, 1771-73, 1801-02, 1804-35 (SRO)
Cop 1613-30 (Ptd, Dwelly 2, 1914); C 1598-1640, 1662-1720, 1730-1835, M 1603-37, 1669-1720,
 1730-31, 1741-54, 1771-72, 1801-38, B 1598-1640, 1662-72, 1704-20, 1730-73, 1782-94,
 1801-36 (Ptd, T.L. Stoate, 1995); C 1712-1810 (SCDB); B 1712-94 (SBDB); M 1800-37 (SMI);
 C 1712-1813, M 1712-1836 (DCI)
Cop (Mf) 1598-1835 (BT) (SLC, SRO); C 1712-1810, M 1712-54, 1814-38, B 1712-99 (SRO)

STOKE, RODNEY alias STOKE GIFFORD St Leonard (333) (Winterstoke Hundred; Wells Union)
OR CM 1654-1984, Banns 1813-89, B 1654-1983 (SRO)
BT 1597-98, 1602-10, c1613, 1619-24, 1630, 1634-41, 1663-64, 1694-96, 1704-07, 1744-45,
 1748-51, 1755, 1776, 1799-1837, CB 1838, 1840-42, 1846-49 (SRO)
Cop 1602-1744 (Ptd, Dwelly 2, 1914); B 1788-1905 (SBDB); M 1602, 1607, 1609, 1621, 1635,
 1637, 1639-40, 1663 (BT), 1754-1837 (SMI)
Cop (Mf) C 1654-1867, M 1654-1901, B 1654-1906 (SG); 1597-1849 (BT) (SLC, SRO);
 C 1654-1904, M 1654-1901, B 1654-1906 (SLC)

STOKE, RODNEY (United Methodist) b 1876

STOKE, RODNEY (Baptist) (K 1931)

STOKE, SOUTH St James (266) (Bath Forum Hundred; Bath Union)
OR C 1704-1887, M 1704-1838, Banns 1823-1900, B 1704-76, 1783-1935 (SRO)
BT one between 1594-1618, 1598-1600, 1603, 1605-10, 1622-24, 1636-38, 1640, 1661-69,
 1738-39, 1800-13, 1815, 1817-19, 1821-31, CB 1838, C 1840, CB 1841, 1843-45, 1847-67
 (SRO)
Cop 1704-1812 (Ts I SG, Bath Lib, British Lib, SRO); M 1754-1837 (NSMI); B 1813-1900
 (SBDB); M 1754-1837 (SMI)
Cop (Mf) 1598-1867 (BT) (SLC, SRO); C 1704-1887, M 1704-1838, Banns 1770-81, 1823-1900,
 B 1704-76, 1783-1900 (SLC)

STOKE, SOUTH Midford (Wesleyan) b 1837 (K 1931)

STOKE SUB HAMDON St Mary the Virgin (1,365) (Tintinhull Hundred; Yeovil Union)
OR C 1558-1689, 1712-1965, M 1558-1676, 1753-1996, B 1558-1676, 1719-1992 (SRO)
BT 1593-98, 1602-03, 1605, 1607-08, 1613-14, 1621-24, 1629-30, 1636-37, 1639-40, 1666-70,
 1770-71, 1801-05, 1807-20, 1826-30, 1837, CB 1840-46, CMB 1847-49, 1851 (SRO)
Cop 1621-23 (Ptd, Dwelly 2, 1914); C 1558-1812 (SCDB); B 1558-1844 (SBDB);
 M 1621, 1623 (BT), 1754-1837 (SMI)
Cop (Mf) 1593-1851 (BT) (SLC, SRO)

STOKE SUB HAMDON (Wesleyan) b 1814

STOKE SUB HAMDON (Independent) f 1866
OR C 1866-1933, M 1899-1976 (SRO)

STOKE TRISTER St Andrew (428) (Norton Ferris Hundred; Wincanton Union)
OR C 1751-1886, M 1751-1985, Banns 1755-1848, B 1751-1954 (SRO)
BT one between 1591-1609, 1593-94, 1599-1600, 1602-03, 1606-07, 1611-14, 1617-24, 1629,
 1636-41, 1663-64, 1666-68, 1672-73, 1679-80, 1704-05, 1731-33, 1748-49, 1751-58, 1765-69,
 1773-74, 1777, 1800-20, 1822-28, 1830-37, CB 1838, 1840-47, 1849, CMB 1850, CB 1851-61
 (SRO)
Cop CMB 1751-1837 (SRO); M 1751-1837 (Boyd); C 1751-1812 (SCDB); B 1751-1865 (SBDB);
 M 1754-1837 (SMI)
Cop (Mf) 1593-1861 (BT) (SLC, SRO)

STON EASTON St Mary (386) (chapelry in Chewton Mendip until 1867) (Chewton Hundred; Clutton Union)
OR C 1813-1967, M 1813-1968, Banns 1879-1979, B 1813-1943 (SRO) (registers from 1572 listed in 1914; registers 1633-1812 listed in 1935, were destroyed by thieves in 1959)
BT 1594-99, 1602-03, 1606-12, 1621-24, 1627-30, 1636-37, 1639-40, 1663-64, 1667-69, 1691-92, 1695-96, 1704-06, 1734-35, 1756-57, 1802-36, CB 1850-52, 1854 (SRO)
Cop 1594-1669 (Ptd, Dwelly 2, 1914); B 1813-58 (SBDB); M 1594-1669 (BT), 1800-37 (SMI)
Cop (Mf) 1594-1854 (BT) (SLC, SRO)

STOURTON alias STOURTON with GASPER St Peter (653) (part Mere Hundred, Wiltshire, part Norton Ferris Hundred, Somerset; Mere Union. Somerset part transferred to Wiltshire, 1895; united with Bourton, Dorset and Zeals, Wiltshire, 1973)
OR C 1572-1687, 1691-1915, M 1578-1690, 1702-1987, B 1570-1684, 1691-1873 (Wilts RO)
BT 1623-37, 1660-63, 1672-79, 1691-1704, 1710-56, 1781-1880 (Wilts RO)
Cop CMB 1570-1800 (Ptd Harleian Society 12, 1887); M 1800-36 (SG); M 1578-1837 (Nimrod Index, *see* Wiltshire NIPR)
Cop (Mf) 1623-1880 (SLC, Wilts RO)

STOURTON St Benedict Bonham (Roman Catholic) transferred from Stourton to Bonham, Wiltshire, 1714

STOWELL St Mary Magdalene (123) (Horethorne Hundred; Wincanton Union)
OR CB 1574-1679, 1745-1812, M 1574-1677, 1745-55, 1761-69, 1805-1836, Banns 1806-10, 1823-32 (SRO); CB 1813+ (Inc) (registers began in 1745 in 1914)
BT one between 1600-30, 1602-13, 1616, 1621-24, 1634-37, 1639-40, 1662-65, 1673-74, 1733, 1735-36, 1775-81, 1783-84, 1802-37, CB 1844, 1849 (SRO)
Cop 1613-36 (Ptd, Dwelly 2, 1914); CB 1574-1807, M 1574-1768 (SRO); B 1574-1808 (SBDB); M 1621, 1636 (BT), 1750-1837 (SMI)
Cop (Mf) 1602-1849 (BT) (SLC, SRO); C 1574-1678, 1746-1812, M 1574-1678, 1746-47, 1762-63, 1806-36, Banns 1806-10, 1823-32, B 1574-1678, 1746-1807, 1812 (SLC)

STOWEY St Nicholas and St Mary the Virgin (234) (Chew Hundred; Clutton Union)
OR C 1570-1983, M 1570-1977, Banns 1754-1817, B 1656-1992 (SRO)
BT 1602, 1606-08, 1611, 1620-22, 1627, 1630-31, 1637-40, 1742, 1802-15, 1818-21, 1823 (SRO)
Cop 1602-30 (Ptd, Dwelly 2, 1914); CMB 1570-1812 (Index SRO); M 1754-1837 (NSMI); C 1570-1812 (SCDB); B 1645-1812 (SBDB); M 1570-1837 (SMI)
Cop (Mf) C 1570-1983, M 1570-1799, 1803-1977, Banns 1754-1817, B 1656-1812 (SG); 1602-1823 (BT) (SLC, SRO)

STOWEY, NETHER St Mary the Virgin (778) (peculiar of the Consistorial Decanal Court of Wells) (Williton and Freemanors Hundred; Bridgwater Union)
OR C 1640-1973, M 1645-1966, B 1640-1953 (SRO)
BT 1598-99, 1605-09, 1611, 1623-24, 1629-32, 1636-41, one between 1661-80, 1663-64, 1666-68, 1672-73, 1679, 1698-99, 1774, 1779-80, 1782, 1798, 1800-13, 1815-35, 1837 (SRO); 1729, 1731, 1741, 1745-46, 1748-58, 1761-63, 1765, 1768-71, 1773-75, 1779-80, 1782-97 (SRO: D/D/Pd:26/10)
Cop M 1645-1812 (Ptd, Phillimore 12, 1910); 1631-39 (Ptd, Dwelly 2, 1914); C 1640-1971, M 1640-1956, B 1640-1953 (and pre-1640 BTs) (SRO); M 1645-1812 (Boyd); B 1813-64 (SBDB); M 1631-1837 (OR & BT) (SMI)
Cop (Mf) 1598-1837 (BT) (SLC, SRO)

STOWEY, NETHER Lime Street (Independent) b 1807 cl *c*1974

STOWEY, OVER Cemetery opened 1882 (¼ acre, enlarged, 1909)

STOWEY, OVER St Peter and St Paul (592) (part Cannington Hundred, part Williton and Freemanors Hundred; Bridgwater Union)
OR C 1558-1940, M 1558-1992, Banns 1763-1812, B 1558-1932 (gap CMB 1654-86) (SRO)
BT one between 1568-1607, 1602-03, 1606-10, 1613-14, 1616-17, 1619-24, one between 1619-35, one between 1619-40, 1629-32, one between 1635-71, 1638-41, c.1660, 1666-68, 1670-71, 1673-74, 1678-79, 1704-05, 1709-10, 1719-21, 1725-26, 1732-33, 1742-43, 1752-53, 1768-71, 1773, 1775-79, 1801-37, CB 1838-45, 1856 (SRO)
Cop M 1558-1812 (Ptd, Phillimore 6, 1905); 1568-1813 (SG); C 1558-1940, M 1558-1974, B 1558-1932 (SRO); M 1558-1812 (Boyd); B 1727-1846 (SBDB); M 1558-1837 (SMI)
Cop (Mf) 1602-1856 (BT) (SLC, SRO)

STRATTON on the FOSSE St Vigor (407) (Kilmersdon Hundred; Shepton Mallet Union)
OR C 1641-1867, M 1641-1965, B 1641-1930 (SRO) (registers stated as starting 1698 in 1914)
BT 1599-1600, 1607-12, 1622-24, 1666-68, 1734-35, 1749-50, 1802-37, CB 1840-61, 1863 (SRO)
Cop 1599-1640 (Ptd, Dwelly 2, 1914); CMB 1641-1782 (Ms I SG); C 1738-1812 (SCDB); B 1710-1856 (SBDB); M 1607-09, 1623, 1666 (BT), 1754-1837 (SMI)
Cop (Mf) 1599-1863 (BT) (SLC, SRO)

STRATTON on the FOSSE St Benedict, Downside (Roman Catholic) f 1856
OR C 1877+, M 1943+, B 1900+ (Inc)

STREET Holy Trinity (899) (Whitley Hundred; Wells Union)
OR C 1600, 1636-1950 (gap 1679-84), M 1599-1600, 1636-1989 (gap 1679-1702), Banns 1823-91, B 1599-1600, 1636-1955 (SRO)
BT 1598-99, 1605-13, 1621-23, 1627-31, 1636-40, 1663-65, 1732-33, 1746-47, 1749-52, 1756-57, 1800-02, 1808-15, 1817-36 (SRO)
Cop C 1600-1755, M 1599-1755, B 1599-1762 (Ptd, A.J. Jewers, supplement to *The Genealogist* 11-13, 1898); B 1598-1852 (SBDB); M 1750-1837 (SMI)
Cop (Mf) 1598-1836 (BT) (SLC, SRO); C 1636-1901, M 1636-78, 1703-1901, Banns 1823-91, B 1681-1917 (SLC)

STREET Meeting House (Society of Friends) b 1836 (K 1931)
OR Z 1655-1783, M 1658-1765, 1777-83, B 1656-1782 (PRO: RG 6/83-84, 167, 1454)
BT B 1885-86, 1889-90, 1892, 1894-96, 1900 (SRO)
Cop (Mf) 1885-1900 (BT) (SLC, SRO)

STREET (Baptist) b 1814 (K 1931)
OR Z 1813-36 (PRO: RG 4/1422)
Cop (Mf) Z 1813-36 (SLC, SRO)

STREET Leigh Road later High Street (Wesleyan) f 1839 b 1893 (K 1931)
OR C 1948-58; M 1957 (SRO)

STREET (Independent) f 1853 (K 1931)

STREET (Primitive Methodist) b 1872 (K 1931)
OR C 1905-58 (SRO)

STREET (Salvation Army) b 1884 (K 1931)

STRINGSTON (dedication unknown) (128) (Cannington Hundred; Williton Union)
OR C 1633-1812, M 1634-1836, Banns 1754-89, B 1557-1811 (SRO); CB 1813+ (Inc)
BT 1602-03, 1605-09, 1611-12, 1621-23, 1628-31, 1636-39, 1661-64, 1666-67, 1672-73, 1678-80, 1718-21, 1730, 1732-3, 1749-52, 1755, 1759, 1764, 1767-71, 1775-7, 1801-18, 1820-33 (SRO)
Cop M 1634-1812 (Ptd, Phillimore 12, 1910); 1609-79 (Ptd, Dwelly 2, 1914); M 1634-1812 (Boyd); B 1557-1811 (SBDB); M 1609-1837 (OR & BT) (SMI)
Cop (Mf) 1602-1833 (BT) (SLC, SRO); C 1633-1812, M 1634-1722, 1734, 1742-1836, Banns 1754-89, B 1557-1723, 1742-1811 (SLC)

STRINGSTON (Independent) f 1786 b 1801 cl 1865-86

SUTTON BINGHAM All Saints (78) (Houndsborough, Barwick and Coker Hundred; Yeovil Union)
OR C 1742-1982, M 1824-1976, B 1755-1961 (SRO) (M 1766-1807 lost between 1914 and 1938)
BT 1605, 1609-10, 1621-22, 1627, 1629, 1639-40, 1662-63, 1724, 1802-16, 1819, 1821, 1823-26,
    1828, 1832-35 (SRO)
Cop 1605-21 (Ptd, Dwelly 2, 1914); C 1741-1812 (SCDB); B 1735-1901 (SBDB);
    M 1621 (BT), 1750-1837 (SMI)
Cop (Mf) 1605-1835 (BT) (SLC, SRO); C 1742-1904, M 1824-1901, B 1742-93, 1813-1901 (SLC)

SUTTON, BISHOPS Holy Trinity (created from Chew Magna, 1876) (Clutton Union)
OR CB 1848-58, 1863-1983, M 1877-1977, B 1849-57, 1877-1983 (SRO)

SUTTON, BISHOPS (Wesleyan) b 1778 (K 1931)

SUTTON, LONG Holy Trinity (957) (peculiar of the Dean and Chapter of Wells until 1845)
    (part Pitney Hundred, part Somerton Hundred; Langport Union)
OR C 1560-1899 (gaps 1563-76, 1586-99), M 1559-1989, Banns 1754-1812, 1823-1901,
    B 1560-1933 (gaps CMB 1653-60, 1666-1709) (SRO)
BT 1599-1600, 1602-03, 1606-13, 1616-18, 1621-24, 1629-331, 1635-37, 1639-41, 1678-79, 1756,
    1767-87, 1798-1808, 1819-22, 1826-28, 1830 (SRO)
Cop M 1559-1812 (Ptd, Phillimore 1, 1898); C 1560-1839, M 1813-40, B 1560-1840 (Ts I SG);
    CM 1560-1665, B 1560-1773 (SRO); M 1559-1812 (Boyd); C 1781-1812 (SCDB); B 1780-1854
    (SBDB); M 1559-1666, 1710-1837 (SMI); C 1559-1899, M 1813-99 (DCI)
Cop (Mf) 1599-1830 (BT) (SLC, SRO); C 1559-1665, 1710-1899, M 1559-1665, 1710-1900,
    Banns 1754-1812, 1823-1901, B 1559-1665, 1710-1901 (SLC)

SUTTON, LONG Meeting House (Society of Friends) b 1717 (K 1931)

SUTTON, LONG Knowle End (Independent) b 1865

SUTTON MALLET (dedication unknown) (153) (chapelry in Moorlinch) (Whitley Hundred;
    Bridgwater Union) (registers combined with Edington, Moorlinch, Stawell and Chilton Polden)
OR C 1781-1985, M 1968-74, B 1781-1989 (SRO) (Z 1653-66 in Moorlinch register)
BT 1598-99, 1603-10, 1621-24, 1627-31, 1636-38, 1664-65, 1668-69, 1720-21, 1800-O5, 1808-09,
    1813-15, 1817-27, 1829-37, CB 1839-40 (CB 1846-51 in Moorlinch returns) (SRO)
Cop B 1781-1812 (SBDB)
Cop (Mf) 1598-1851 (BT) (SLC, SRO); C 1781-1891, B 1781-1890 (SLC)

SUTTON MALLET Meeting House, Polden Hill (Society of Friends) (Monthly Meeting of Middle
    Division); f c.1657 moved to Shapwick 1690
OR Z 1657-1788, M 1661-1778, B 1657-1797 (PRO: RG 6/1412)

SUTTON MONTIS Holy Trinity (178) (Catsash Hundred; Wincanton Union)
OR C 1701-1993 (gap 1756-69), M 1701-1993, Banns 1758-1812, C 1701-1994 (SRO)
BT 1603-04, 1606-09, 1611-12, 1619-20, 1623-24, 1627, 1630-31, 1634-41, 1667, 1669, 1672-73,
    1747-50, 1752-54, 1756-57, 1760, 1765-67, 1769-70, 1780-86, 1800-17, 1819-28, 1830-32,
    1834-35, 1837, CB 1850-59 (SRO)
Cop C 1701-1812 (SCDB); B 1702-1812 (SBDB); M 1750-1837 (SMI)
Cop (Mf) 1603-1859 (BT) (SLC, SRO); C 1701-22, 1731-55, 1772-1812, M 1701-22, 1731-1840,
    Banns 1759-1808, B 1701-22, 1731-55, 1772-1812 (SLC)

SWAINSWICK St Mary (427) (Bath Forum Hundred; Bath Union)
OR C 1557-1948, M 1557-1945, B 1557-1889 (SRO)
BT 1602-14, 1622-24, 1629-30, 1635-40, 1664-67, 1732-33, 1735, 1745-46, 1800-24, 1827 (SRO)
Cop 1557-1840 (Ts I SG); CB 1557-1812, M 1754-1811 (Ts I Bath Lib); 1813-40 (SRO);
    M 1754-1837 (NSMI); B 1813-42 (SBDB); M 1754-1837 (SMI)
Cop (Mf) 1602-1827 (BT) (SLC, SRO)

SWELL St Catherine (87) (Abdick and Bulstone Hundred; Langport Union)
OR C 1559-1981, M 1559-1974, B 1559-1982 (SRO)
BT one between 1593-1621, 1598-1600, one between 1598-1622, 1607-10, 1611-12, 1619-22,
    1629-31, one between 1638-40, 1635-40, 1662-63, 1735-36, 1742-43, 1749-52, 1758-59,
    1762-72, 1774-82, 1789-90, 1801-14, 1816-17, 1820-22, 1824, 1826-29, 1831-37, C 1838-39,
    CM 1840, CMB 1841-44, CM 1845-49, CMB 1850-55, CB 1856, C 1857 (SRO)
Cop M 1559-1812 (Ptd, Phillimore 4, 1902); M 1713-54 (Ptd, Phillimore 5, 1904); 1592-1630
    (Ptd, Dwelly 2, 1914); M 1559-1812 (Boyd); B 1723-1982 (SBDB); M 1599-1837 (SMI);
    C 1560-1899, M 1813-99 (DCI)
Cop (Mf) 1598-1857 (BT) (SLC, SRO)

TATWORTH St John the Evangelist (created from Chard, 1866) (Taunton Union)
OR C 1866-1951, M 1852-1969, B 1866-1947 (SRO)
Cop C 1866-99, M 1852-99 (DCI)
Cop (Mf) CB 1866-86, M 1852-86 (SLC)

TATWORTH South Chard (Baptist) b 1909 (K 1931)

TAUNTON Board of Guardians
OR Z 1836-1932, C 1901-11, D 1836-1947 (SRO)

TAUNTON St Mary Magdalene and Bishops Hull Cemetery opened 1854 (14 acres) (K 1931)

TAUNTON St James Cemetery, Staplegrove Road opened 1877 (5 acres) (K 1931)

TAUNTON Borough (11,139)

TAUNTON St James (Taunton and Taunton Dean Hundred; Taunton Union)
OR C 1610-1980, M 1573-79, 1610-1988, Banns 1754-1823, B 1610-1891 (gaps CMB 1621-25,
    1639-46) (SRO)
BT 1606-07, 1611-12, 1621-24, 1636-38, 1663-64, 1667-68, 1734-40, 1800-31 (SRO)
Cop M 1610-1837 (Ptd, Phillimore 15, 1915); M 1610-1837 (Boyd); C 1628-95 (SCDB);
    B 1626-1837 (SBDB); M 1610-1837 (SMI)
Cop (Mf) 1606-1831 (BT) (SLC, SRO)

TAUNTON St Mary Magdalene (Taunton and Taunton Dean Hundred; Taunton Union)
OR C 1559-1991, M 1558-1990, Banns 1715-29, 1754-1824, 1898-1900, B 1558-1946 (SRO)
BT 1601-02, 1605-11, 1616, 1621-22, 1629-30, 1636-41, 1669-70, 1737-38, 1757-58, 1789-90,
    1800-O5, 1807-38 (SRO)
Cop M 1558-1728 (Ptd, Phillimore 9, 1907); M 1728-1812 (Ptd, Phillimore 10, 1907);
    C 1558-1601, 1777-86 (Index SRO); M 1558-1812 (Boyd); B 1813-41 (SBDB); M 1558-1837
    (SMI)
Cop (Mf) 1601-1838 (BT) (SLC, SRO); CB 1558-1901, M 1558-1900, Banns 1754-1824,
    1898-1901 (SLC)

TAUNTON Holy Trinity, Trinity Street (created from Taunton St Mary Magdalene, 1842)
    (Taunton Union)
OR C 1842-1944, M 1852-1968, B 1842-96 and a few 1906-57 (SRO)
Cop (Mf) C 1842-84, M 1852-86, B 1846-84 (SLC)

TAUNTON All Saints (created 1967 from Taunton Holy Trinity, West Monkton, Taunton St James
    and Cheddon Fitzpaine as Halcon All Saints, renamed 1972)
OR M 1953-83, Banns 1953-89 (SRO); C 1967+ (Inc)

TAUNTON St Andrew (until 1972 Rowbarton St Andrew, q.v.)

TAUNTON St John (until 1972 Bishops Hull St John the Evangelist, q.v.)

TAUNTON St Peter, Lyngford (until 1972 Lyngford St Peter, q.v.)

TAUNTON Mary Street (Unitarian, formerly Presbyterian) f 1646 b 1721 (K 1931)
OR ZC 1762-1837, B 1797-1837 (PRO: RG 4/2937, 3324)
Cop (Mf) ZC 1762-1837, B 1797-1837 (SLC, SRO)

TAUNTON Paul's Meeting House, Paul Street (Independent) f 1662, b 1672, reb 1797 (K 1931)
OR ZC 1699-1837, B 1785-1837 (PRO: RG 4/1567); C 1837-1983, M 1844-59, B 1837-60 (SRO)
Cop (Mf) ZC 1699-1837, B 1785-1837 (SLC, SRO)

TAUNTON Meeting House, Bath Place (Society of Friends) b 1693 (K 1931)
OR C 1910-58 (SRO)
Cop B 1794-1837 (SBDB)

TAUNTON Octagon Chapel and the Temple, Upper High Street (Wesleyan) f 1778 b 1811
    (K 1931)
OR ZC 1785-1837, B 1824-37 (PRO: RG 4/1144, 1734, 4045); C 1840-1959, M 1905-79,
    B 1841-59 (SRO)
Cop (Mf) ZC 1785-1837, B 1824-37 (SLC, SRO)

TAUNTON Silver Street (Baptist) f 1782, b 1814 (K 1931)
OR Z 1782-1837, B 1823-36 (PRO: RG 4/3219)
Cop (Mf) Z 1782-1837, B 1823-36 (SLC, SRO)

TAUNTON St George, Billet Street (Roman Catholic) f 1790 b 1845 (K 1931)
OR C 1806-1900, M 1841-1933, D 1841-53, B 1856-1927 (SRO)

TAUNTON Our Lady of Delours (convent from 1807) (Roman Catholic)
OR Z 1860-1934, DB 1855-1945; Graves 1810-1953 (SRO)

TAUNTON Octagon Chapel, Middle Street (Baptist, who left 1826, then Plymouth Brethren
    b 1816 (K 1931)
OR Z 1816-26 (PRO: RG 4/1566)
Cop (Mf) Z 1816-26 (SLC, SRO)

TAUNTON Victoria Street (Wesleyan) b 1840 (K 1931)

TAUNTON North Street (Independent) b 1843 (K 1931)
OR C 1878-92 (SRO)

TAUNTON Ebenezer Chapel, Magdalene Street (United Methodist) b 1864 (K 1931)
OR C 1905-35 (SRO)

TAUNTON Albemarle Chapel (Baptist) b 1875 (K 1931)

TAUNTON Rowbarton (Independent) b 1878 (K 1931)

TAUNTON Blue Ribbon Gospel Association Chapel b 1882

TAUNTON Duke Street (Salvation Army) b 1885 (K 1931)

TAUNTON St Teresa of Lisieux, Eastwick Road (Roman Catholic) b 1959

TELLISFORD All Saints (162) (Wellow Hundred; Frome Union)
OR C 1538-1995 (gaps 1678-1700, 1734-41), M 1593-1988 (gaps 1661-71, 1686-1700, 1734-41),
    B 1553-1995 (gaps 1684-1700, 1734-41) (SRO)
BT 1602-03, 1606-09, 1611-12, 1621-24, 1627-30, 1636-40, 1663, 1675-76, 1728-29, 1733-34,
    1745-46, 1756, 1803-36 (SRO)
Cop 1538-1934 (Index SRO); B 1742-1812 (SBDB); M 1754-1837 (SMI)
Cop (Mf) 1602-1836 (BT) (SLC, SRO); C 1538-1731, 1742-1807, M 1593-1733, 1743-1800,
    1813-36, Banns 1754-1810, B 1553-1807 (SLC)

TEMPLECOMBE *see* **COMBE, ABBAS**

THEALE Christ Church (created from Wedmore, 1828, refounded 1844)
OR C 1828-1912, M 1844-1958, Banns 1844-1900, B 1828-1989 (SRO)
Cop (Mf) C 1828-1901, M 1844-1901, Banns 1844-99, B 1828-1900 (SLC)

THEALE Newtown (Bible Christian) 19th century

THORN COFFIN St Andrew (101) (Tintinhull Hundred; Yeovil Union)
OR C 1695-1978, M 1695-1832, B 1695-1974 (SRO)
BT 1597-1600, 1607-14, 1619, 1622-23, 1629-30, 1634-37, 1639-41, 1663, 1666-70, 1678, 1681,
    1704-05, 1731, 1739-41, 1747, 1749-50, 1769-71, 1773, 1775-76, 1802-13, 1815-35 (SRO)
Cop 1609-23 (Ptd, Dwelly 2, 1914); M 1754-1851 (Ts I SG); C 1695-1812 (SCDB);
    B 1695-1972 (SBDB); M 1609, 1755-1837 (SMI)
Cop (Mf) 1597-1835 (BT) (SLC, SRO)

THORN FALCON Holy Cross (273) (North Curry Hundred; Taunton Union)
OR C 1725-1942, M 1726-1991, Banns 1824+, B 1726-1991 (SRO)
BT 1598-1600, 1602-08, 1611-14, 1616-18, 1621-23, 1629-30, 1636-41, 1662-63, 1701-08,
    1727-29, 1732-43, 1749-51, 1754-55, 1764-69, 1775-76, 1780-87, 1801-27, 1829-31, 1834-35
    (SRO)
Cop M 1726-1812 (Ptd, Phillimore 8, 1906); B 1813-62 (SRO); M 1726-1812 (Boyd);
    B 1726-1812 (SBDB); M 1726-1837 (SMI); C 1725-1899, M 1813-41 (DCI)
Cop (Mf) 1598-1835 (BT) (SLC, SRO); C 1725-1903, M 1726-1841, B 1726-1812 (SLC)

THORN ST MARGARET (165) (originally a chantry, but parochial since the dissolution)
    (peculiar of the Dean and Chapter of Wells until 1845) (Milverton Hundred; Wellington Union)
OR C 1813-1992, M 1761-1971, Banns 1761-1809, B 1813-1989 (SRO)
BT 1605-07, 1611-12, 1621-24, 1627-28, 1630, 1636-40, 1813-17, CB 1842-48 (SRO)
Cop M 1721-1812 (Ptd, Phillimore 11, 1908); 1623 (Ptd, Dwelly 2, 1914); M 1721-1812 (Boyd);
    M 1721-48, 1761-1837 (SMI); M 1813-99 (DCI)
Cop (Mf) 1605-1848 (BT) (SLC, SRO); M 1761-1810, 1817-85, Banns 1761-1809, 1823 (SLC)

THURLBEAR alias THURLBERE St Thomas (202) (chapelry in Taunton St Mary Magdalene until
    1858) (North Curry Hundred; Taunton Union)
OR C 1700-1988, M 1700-1986, Banns 1754-1902, B 1700-1991 (SRO)
BT 1601, 1613-14, 1617-18, 1621-24, 1629-31, 1635-41, 1663-64, 1666-67, 1676-77, 1728,
    1734-37, 1740-41, 1744-45, 1749, 1756-57, 1759, 1764, 1767, 1770-71, 1774-75, 1777-83,
    1785-86, 1789-90, 1798, 1801-32 (SRO)
Cop M 1700-1812 (Ptd, Phillimore 7, 1906); 1613-76 (Ptd, Dwelly 2, 1914); CB 1700-1800,
    M 1700-1812 (SRO); M 1700-1812 (Boyd); B 1700-1810 (SBDB); M 1613-76 (BT), 1700-1837
    (SMI); C 1700-1899, M 1813-36 (DCI)
Cop (Mf) 1601-1832 (BT) (SLC, SRO); C 1700-1905, M 1700-1901, Banns 1754-1902,
    B 1700-1810 (SLC)

THURLOXTON St Giles (229) (North Petherton Hundred; Bridgwater Union)
OR C 1559-1918, M 1559-1961, Banns 1755-1810, B 1559-1813 (SRO); B 1813+ (Inc)
BT 1594-97, 1599, one between 1600-40, 1603, 1605-09, 1611-12, 1622-23, one between 1624-40,
    1628-30, 1636-40, 1664-67, 1672-73, 1678-79, 1704-05, 1707-10, 1718-21, 1732, 1734-37,
    1740-46, 1748-50, 1760, 1764, 1766, 1775, 1799-1814, 1824 (SRO)
Cop M 1559-1812 (Ptd, Phillimore 12, 1910); CB 1558-1812 (Ms SG); CMB 1813-79 (SRO);
    1558-1879 (SRO); M 1559-1812 (Boyd); C 1559-1695 (SCDB); B 1559-1693 (SBDB);
    M 1559-1837 (SMI); C 1559-1899, M 1813-99 (DCI)
Cop (Mf) 1594-1824 (BT) (SLC, SRO); C 1558-1901, M 1558-1900, Banns 1755-1810,
    B 1558-1813 (SLC)

TICKENHAM St Quiricus and St Julietta (427) (Portbury Hundred; Bedminster Union 1836-99,
    Long Ashton Union 1899-1930)
OR C 1538-1985, M 1649-1993, Banns 1824-1900, B 1538-1946 (SRO)
BT 1594-97, 1605-13, 1617-18, 1621-22, 1629-30, 1638-41, 1664-65, 1732-33, 1747-48, 1753-54,
    1757-58, 1768, 1774-75, 1801-14, 1816-19, 1823-26, 1828-29, 1832-36 (SRO)
Cop CB 1538-1812, M 1649-1752 (SRO); CB 1538-1800 (Index SRO); M 1754-1837 (NSMI);
    B 1813-1903 (SBDB); M 1649-1837 (SMI)
Cop (Mf) 1594-1836 (BT) (SLC, SRO); C 1538-1901, M 1649-1900, Banns 1824-1900,
    B 1538-1903 (SLC)

TICKENHAM (Plymouth Brethren) b 1865 (K 1931)

TIMBERSCOMBE St Petrock (453) (peculiar of the Prebendary of Timberscombe until 1845)
    (Carhampton Hundred; Williton Union)
OR C 1656-1876, M 1656-1994, B 1656-1924 (SRO)
BT 1598-99, 1602-03, 1605, 1607-12, 1621-24, 1629-30, 1636-41, 1662-64, 1666-69, 1678-79,
    1691, 1813-14, 1816-25, CB 1847-50 (SRO); 1725-26, 1729-34, 1736-37, 1757-63, 1765-69,
    1775-83 (SRO: D/D/Ppb:92)
Cop 1598-1678 (Ptd, Dwelly 2, 1914); CB 1598-1611, 1621-40, 1656-1837, M 1598-1611,
    1621-40, 1656-1748, 1754-1837 (Ptd, T.L. Stoate, 1995); B 1656-1901 (SBDB); M 1598-1837
    (SMI); CM 1656-1837 (DCI)
Cop (Mf) 1598-1850 (BT) (SLC, SRO)

TIMBERSCOMBE (United Methodist) b 1837 (K 1931)

TIMSBURY St Mary (1,367) (Chew Hundred; Clutton Union)
OR C 1561-1908 (gaps 1639-44, 1666-70), M 1561-1918 (gaps 1645-53, 1659-74),
    Banns 1805-1903, B 1561-1904 (gap B 1663-73) (SRO)
BT 1603, 1605-14, 1621-24, 1627, 1629-30, 1637-38, 1640-41, 1662-64, one between 1677-86,
    1679-80, 1732-34, 1742-43, 1746-49, 1751-54, 1800-24 (SRO)
Cop 1561-1812 (Ts I SG, SLC, Bath Lib); 1561-1678 (SRO); M 1754-1837 (NSMI);
    C 1798-1812 (SCDB); B 1741-1846 (SBDB); M 1561-1678, 1754-1837 (SMI)
Cop (Mf) 1603-1824 (BT) (SLC, SRO); C 1561-1901, M 1561-1644, 1654-58, 1675-1901.
    Banns 1805-1903, B 1561-1662, 1674-1900 (SLC)

TIMSBURY (Wesleyan) b 1805 (K 1931)
OR C 1803-37 (PRO: RG 4/1735); C 1843-1900 (circuit) (Bristol RO)
Cop (Mf) C 1803-37 (SRO, SLC); C 1843-1900 (Bristol RO, SLC)

TIMSBURY (Independent) b 1820 (K 1931)

TIMSBURY (Primitive Methodist) b 1848

TIMSBURY (United Methodist) b 1865 (K 1931)

TINTINHULL St Margaret (473) (Tintinhull Hundred; Yeovil Union)
OR C 1561-1608, 1653-1949 (defective 1573-99), M 1561-1620, 1630-1986, B 1561-1608,
1672-1910 (SRO)
BT 1593-1600, 1607-14, 1617, 1619-24, 1629-31, 1636-37, 1639-40, 1662, 1666-67, 1704-05,
1731-32, 1735-38, 1746-51, 1769-74, 1801-04, 1806-24 (SRO)
Cop 1598-1623 (Ptd, Dwelly 2, 1914); M 1561-1753 (SRO); C 1561-1812 (SCDB);
B 1561-1852 (SBDB); M 1561-1837 (SMI)
Cop (Mf) 1593-1824 (BT) (SLC, SRO)

TINTINHULL (Baptist) b 1869

TINTINHULL (Independent) (K 1931)

TOLLAND St John the Baptist (121) (Taunton and Taunton Dean Hundred; Taunton Union)
OR C 1708-1971, M 1706-1835, B 1706-1814 (SRO); B 1814+ (Inc)
BT 1598-1600, 1603, 1605-14, 1622-24, 1627-29, 1638-41, 1662-63, 1703-07, 1716, 1732-34,
1736, 1800-14, 1816, 1820-36, CB 1840, 1842-46 (SRO)
Cop C 1708-1812 (SCDB); B 1706-50 (SBDB); M 1757-1837 (SMI); C 1708-1899, M 1708-1835
(DCI)
Cop (Mf) 1598-1846 (SLC, SRO); C 1708-1900, M 1706-1835, Banns 1757-1812, B 1706-50 (SLC)

TREBOROUGH St Peter (105) (Carhampton Hundred; Williton Union)
OR C 1693-1977, M 1694-1759, 1773-93, 1804-15, 1842-1933, B 1693-1976 (SRO) (registers listed
as starting in 1813 in 1914)
BT 1593-95, 1597-1600, 1605-08, 1611-12, 1615, 1621-23, 1627-31, 1636-40, 1662-70, one
between 1664-80, 1674-75, 1678-80, 1703-08, 1721-22, 1724-25, 1729-30, 1732-35, 1739-43,
1745-47, 1749-51, 1754, 1756-57, 1765-66, 1769, 1801-14, 1830-31, 1836 (SRO)
Cop B 1693-1975 (SBDB); M 1694-1837 (SMI); C 1693-1869, M 1694-1899 (DCI)
Cop (Mf) 1593-1836 (BT) (SLC, SRO)

TRENT St Andrew (449) (Horethorne Hundred; Sherborne Union) (transferred to Dorset, 1895)
OR C 1560-1976, M 1558-1837, Banns 1754-1812, 1823-83, B 1558-1907 (Dorset RO)
BT 1598-99, 1601-04, 1606-09, 1613-14, 1617, 1619-20, 1623-24, 1629-30, 1636-37, 1640-41,
1662-63, 1675-77, 1733-35, 1747, 1800-02, 1806-13, 1815-18, 1820, 1822-24, 1827-28,
1830-37, CB 1838, CMB 1840 (SRO)
Cop 1598-1675 (Ptd, Dwelly 2, 1914); C 1560-1701, MB 1558-1837 (Dorset RO); M 1558-1837
(Ts I SG); B 1813-51 (SBDB); M 1601, 1607, 1623, 1675 (BT), 1754-1837 (SMI)
Cop (Mf) 1598-1840 (BT) (SLC, SRO)

TRENT Adber (Primitive Methodist) b 1865

TRULL All Saints (506) (Taunton and Taunton Dean Hundred; Taunton Union)
OR C 1538-74, 1656, 1669-1954, M 1539-74, 1671-1972, B 1538-74, 1670-1961 (SRO)
BT 1598-99, 1607-08, 1617, 1623-24, 1627-30, 1636-41, 1663-64, 1666-67, 1706-08, 1734,
1754-55, 1759-60, 1802-35 (SRO)
Cop M 1671-1744 (Ptd, Phillimore 7, 1906); 1598-1666 (Ptd, Dwelly 2, 1914); M 1744-1812 (SG);
CMB 1538-74 (SRO); M 1671-1812 (Boyd); C 1669-1924 (SCDB); B 1678-1846 (SBDB);
M 1671-1744, 1755-1837 (SMI); C 1538-1899, M 1755-1899 (DCI)
Cop (Mf) 1598-1835 (BT) (SLC, SRO)

TRULL (Baptist) b 1895 (K 1931)

TWERTON on AVON alias TWIVERTON St Michael with St Peter (2,478)
(Wellow Hundred; Bath Union)
OR C 1582-1970, M 1587-1976, Banns 1754-1815, 1825-1906, B 1538-1659, 1668-1920 (SRO)
BT 1599-1600, 1605-13, 1617, 1622-24, 1627-30, 1636-38, 1640-41, 1666-69, 1745-47, 1800-33, 1835-37, CB 1838, 1840-50 (SRO)
Cop C 1582-1840, M 1587-1840, B 1538-1840 (Ts I SG); CMB 1538-1812 (Bath Lib, British Lib); 1813-40 (SRO); B 1813-41 (SBDB); M 1587-1837 (SMI)
Cop (Mf) 1599-1850 (BT) (SLC, SRO); C 1582-1901, M 1587-1900, Banns 1754-1815, 1825-1901, B 1538-1659, 1668-1895 (SLC)

TWERTON on AVON St Peter (chapelry to Twerton Avon St Michael)
OR C 1880-1981, M 1880-1983, Banns 1880-1983 (SRO)

(For nonconformist chapels in Twerton see under **BATH**)

TWERTON, SOUTH Church of the Ascension (created from Twerton on Avon, 1912) (Bath Union)
OR CMB 1912+ (Inc)

TWERTON HILL St Barnabas (created from Twerton on Avon, 1957)
OR CMB 1957+ (Inc)

UBLEY St Bartholomew (340) (Chewton Hundred; Clutton Union)
OR C 1671-1917, M 1671-1972, Banns 1797-1809, 1831, 1874-95, B 1671-1975 (SRO)
BT 1598, 1607-13, 1616-17, 1622-24, 1629-31, 1636-41, 1664-65, 1678-80, 1705, 1775-76 (in West Harptree), 1800-15, 1817, 1819, 1821-23 (SRO)
Cop 1609-23 (Ptd, Dwelly 2, 1914); M 1754-1837 (NSMI); C 1671-1794 (SCDB); B 1671-1889 (SBDB); M 1609, 1616 (BT), 1754-1837 (SMI)
Cop (Mf) 1598-1823 (BT) (SLC, SRO); C 1671-1886, M 1671-1885, Banns 1797-1809, 1831, 1874-95, B 1671-1890 (SLC)

UBLEY (Wesleyan) (Lewis 1831) b 1863 (K 1931)

UPHILL St Nicholas (306) (Winterstoke Hundred; Axbridge Union)
OR Z 1696-1701, C 1704-1926, M 1705-1959, B 1701-1958 (SRO)
BT 1598-99, 1605-10, 1621-24, 1629-31, 1638-41, 1663, 1748-51, 1754-56, 1768-69, 1798-1834 (SRO)
Cop 1598-1623 (Ptd, Dwelly 2, 1914); B 1701-1871 (SBDB); M 1609, 1623 (BT), 1754-1837 (SMI)
Cop (Mf) 1598-1834 (BT) (SLC, SRO)

UPHILL (Baptist) (Lewis 1831)

UPHILL (Wesleyan) b 1840 (K 1931)

UPTON St James (344) (Williton and Freemanors Hundred; Dulverton Union)
OR C 1708-1936, M 1708-1940, Banns 1783-1812, 1825-1900, B 1708-1812 (gap CMB 1768-71) (SRO); B 1813+ (Inc)
BT 1597-99, 1602-06, 1609, 1611-12, 1621-24, 1629-31, 1634, 1636-38, 1662-64, 1669-70, 1703-11, 1721-22, 1727-29, 1731-33, 1744-45, 1749-52, 1754-60, 1762, 1764-65, 1767-68, 1773-75, 1779-93, 1795-1832, CB 1844-48 (SRO)
Cop 1623 (Ptd, Dwelly 2, 1914); C 1708-68 (SCDB); B 1708-1812 (SBDB); M 1623 (BT), 1710-1837 (SMI); CM 1708-1899 (DCI)
Cop (Mf) 1597-1848 (BT) (SLC, SRO); C 1708-1901, M 1708-40, 1756-1900, Banns 1800-14, 1825-1903, B 1708-1812 (SLC)

UPTON (United Methodist) reb 1878 (K 1931)

UPTON NOBLE St Mary Magdalen (282) (Bruton Hundred; Shepton Mallet Union)
OR C 1677-1718, 1730-43, 1813-1982, M 1680-88, 1703-05, 1708, 1735-37, 1848-1981,
 B 1677-89, 1695-1712, 1717-19, 1730-43, 1826-54 (SRO) (some registrations at Batcombe)
BT 1754-59, 1802, 1805-11, 1814-18, 1823, 1825-35, CB 1838-39 (SRO)
Cop C 1677-1743 (SCDB); B 1677-1862 (SBDB)
Cop (Mf) 1754-1839 (BT) (SLC, SRO); C 1677-1718, 1730-43, 1813-87, M 1680-88, 1703-05,
 1708, 1735-37, 1848-85, B 1677-89, 1695-1712, 1717-19, 1730-43, 1826-54 (SLC)

UPTON NOBLE (Wesleyan) b 1818 (K 1931)

VOBSTER St Edmund (created from Mells, 1852) (Wells Union)
OR CM 1848-1983, Banns 1848-1903, B 1848-1900 (SRO)
Cop (Mf) C 1848-1900, M 1848-99, Banns 1848-1903 (SLC)

VOBSTER (Wesleyan) b 1898 (K 1931)

WALCOT St Swithin (26,023) (Bath Forum Hundred; Bath Union) (renamed Bath Walcot, 1972)
OR C 1691-1913, M 1728-1971, Banns 1754-88, B 1691-1948 (SRO)
BT 1599-1601, 1605-12, 1619-20, 1623-24, 1629-31, 1636-41, 1662-64, 1668-70, 1699-1700,
 1732-33, 1745-52, one between 1729-50, 1755-61, 1765-69, 1774-76, 1784-94, 1796-1837,
 CB 1838, CMB 1839, CB 1840-75 (SRO)
Cop 1699 (Ptd, Dwelly 2, 1914); 1691-1901 (Index SRO); C 1694-1792 (SCDB);
 B 1711-1838 (SBDB); M 1699 (BT), 1728-1837 (SMI)
Cop (Mf) 1599-1875 (BT) (SLC, SRO); C 1691-97, 1706-29, 1732-1838, M 1728-1837,
 Banns 1754-71, B 1711-17, 1721-1837 (Ptd, SRO, 1996)

WALCOT Holy Trinity (created from Walcot St Swithin, 1839, renamed Bath Holy Trinity, 1952)
 (Bath Union)
OR C 1840-1925, M 1840-1952 (SRO)

WALCOT St Saviour (created from Walcot St Swithin, 1839, renamed Bath St Saviour, 1967)
OR CM 1840-1955, B 1840-1901 (SRO)

WALCOT St Andrew (Bath Union)
OR M 1873-1942 (SRO)
Cop CM 1873-1979 (Index SRO)

(For nonconformist chapelries within Walcot see **BATH**)

WALTON Holy Trinity (635) (chapelry in Street until 1886) (Whitley Hundred; Wells Union)
OR C 1671, 1678, 1680-1970, M 1696-1992 (gap 1742-54), Banns 1755-1812, 1824-79,
 B 1678-1992 (SRO)
BT 1607-13, 1617-18, 1621-23, 1629-31, 1636-41, 1663, 1732-33, 1747-48, 1800-18, 1821-25,
 1827-37, CB 1838, 1840-51 (SRO)
Cop 1617-63 (Ptd, Dwelly 2, 1914); B 1678-1860 (SBDB); M 1617-63 (BT), 1754-1837 (SMI)
Cop (Mf) 1607-1851 (SLC, SRO); C 1671-1902, M 1696-1900, Banns 1824-79, B 1678-1901 (SLC)

WALTON (Wesleyan) (Lewis 1831)

WALTON (Primitive Methodist) (K 1931)

WALTON in GORDANO St Paul, Walton by Clevedon (297) (Portbury Hundred;
 Bedminster Union 1836-99, Long Ashton Union 1899-1930)
OR CB 1667-1813, M 1667-1837 (SRO); CB 1813+ (Inc)
BT 1598-1600, 1603, 1605-07, 1609-12, 1618, 1623-24, 1629-31, 1634-41, 1662-68, 1749-50,
 1752-53, 1800-02, 1804-15, 1817-18, 1824-25, 1848-53 (SRO)
Cop 1599-1662 (Ptd, Dwelly 2, 1914); M 1754-1837 (NSMI); M 1609-39 (BT), 1750-1837 (SMI)
Cop (Mf) 1598-1853 (BT) (SLC, SRO)

WALTON in GORDANO (Independent) b 1871 (K 1931)

WAMBROOK St Mary (217) (created from Chardstock, Dorset, transferred to Somerset, 1895) (peculiar of the Prebendary of Chadstock, Salisbury Cathedral until 1847) (Beaminster Hundred; Chard Union)
OR C 1653-1909, M 1653-1971, Banns 1754-1811, 1824-1900, B 1653-1812 (SRO); B 1813+ (Inc)
BT 1597-1699, 1734-1880 (Wilts RO)
Cop M 1655-1837 (SG, Dorset RO); 1653-1812 (SRO); M 1655-1837 (SMI); C 1625-1909, M 1655-1970, B 1645-1891 (DCI)
Cop (Mf) 1597-1880 (BT) (Dorset RO)

WAMBROOK Chard Road (Wesleyan) b 1908 cl by 1961

WANSTROW St Mary (410) (Frome Hundred; Frome Union) (united with Nunney, 1974)
OR C 1570-1875, M 1571-1987, Banns 1755-1876, 1908-87, B 1571-1939 (SRO) (registers start 1653 in 1914 list)
BT 1593, 1605-O7, 1616, 1619-24, 1629-30, 1636-41, 1666-67, 1678-79, 1800-17, 1819-31 (SRO)
Cop 1605-78 (Ptd, Dwelly 2, 1914); B 1783-1851 (SBDB); M 1605, 1623, 1636, 1678 (BT), 1754-1837 (SMI)
Cop (Mf) 1593-1831 (BT) (SLC, SRO); C 1570-1875, M 1571-1901, Banns 1755-1812, B 1571-1902 (SLC)

WANSTROW (Wesleyan) b 1835

WANSTROW (Primitive Methodist) b 1877 (K 1931)

WATCHET *see* **ST DECUMANS**

WAYFORD St Michael (219) (early entries in Crewkerne) (Crewkerne Hundred; Chard Union)
OR C 1704-1896, M 1709-1981, B 1704-1980 (until 1812 defective) (SRO)
BT 1594-1600, 1605-09, 1613-14, 1622-23, 1629-31, 1636-37, 1639-41, 1662-64, 1667-68, 1672, 1704-05, 1707-09, 1728, 1736-37, 1743-44, 1749-52, 1756-58, 1762-64, 1767-75, 1777-92, 1794-95, 1797-1814, 1816-22, 1824, 1828-33, 1835-37, CB 1838, 1842-44 (SRO)
Cop 1613-39 (Ptd, Dwelly 2, 1914); C 1704-1896, M 1709-1837 (Ms I SG); B 1704-1883 (SBDB); M 1613, 1639, 1709-1837 (SMI); C 1704-1896, M 1709-1899 (DCI)
Cop (Mf) 1594-1844 (BT) (SLC, SRO); C 1704-1896, M 1709-1900, B 1704-1901 (SLC)

WEARE St Gregory (764) (Bempstone Hundred; Axbridge Union)
OR CM 1637-1985, Banns 1755-90, 1798-1808, B 1637-1889 (SRO)
BT 1598-99, 1603-04, 1607-11, 1613-14, 1621-24, 1629-30, 1636-41, 1644-45, 1663, 1669-70, 1704-05, 1710, 1740-41, 1747-51, 1754-56, 1758-59, 1765-68, 1770-71, 1775-78, 1780-84, 1786, 1800-14, 1816, 1818-19, 1821-24, 1828-37 (SRO)
Cop 1598-1639 (Ptd, Dwelly 2, 1914); C 1789-1812 (SCDB); B 1789-1846 (SBDB); M 1598-1629 (BT), 1750-1837 (SMI)
Cop (Mf) 1598-1837 (BT) (SLC, SRO)

WEARE (United Methodist) b 1846 (K 1931)
OR C 1872-1962 (Bristol RO)
Cop (Mf) C 1872-1962 (Bristol RO, SLC)

WEARE (Baptist) (K 1931)

WEDMORE St Mary the Virgin (3,557) (peculiar of the Dean of Wells until 1845)
(part Bempstone Hundred, part Glastonbury Twelve Hides Hundred; Axbridge Union)
OR C 1561-1941, M 1561-1941, Banns 1787-1814, 1823-1949, B 1561-1939 (SRO)
BT 1598, 1606-12, 1616-17, 1621-24, 1629-30, 1636-37, 1639-41, 1683-84, 1805-37, CB 1838-65
(SRO); 1741, 1747-48, 1750-51, 1753, 1759, 1761-62, 1766-68, 1770-85, 1792-1802 (SRO:
D/D/Pd:26/11)
Cop C 1561-1812, M 1561-1839, B 1561-1860 (Ptd, Suffolk Green Books 22, E. Jackson, 1886-90);
M 1561-1837 (Boyd); B 1728-1843 (SBDB); M 1561-1837 (SMI)
Cop (Mf) M 1845-1901, B 1826-1900 (SG); 1598-1865 (BT) (SLC, SRO); CM 1561-1900,
Banns 1754-1902, B 1561-1902 (SLC)

WEDMORE (Baptist) f 1600 (K 1931)

WEDMORE (Wesleyan) b 1817 (K 1931)

WEDMORE Crickham (Baptist) b 1840 (K 1931)

WEDMORE Clewer (Baptist) b 1840 (K 1931)

WEDMORE Heath House (Wesleyan) (K 1931)

WELLINGTON Board of Guardians
OR Z 1867-1929, 1943, D 1867-1914 (SRO)

WELLINGTON Cemetery opened 1875 (4 acres) (K 1931)

WELLINGTON St John the Baptist, High Street (4,762) (West Kingsbury Hundred;
Wellington Union)
OR C 1683-1976, M 1683-1982, B 1683-1944 (SRO)
BT 1612, 1616-19, 1621-23, one between 1635-40, 1637-38, 1672-73, 1679-80, 1682, 1729-30,
1736-37, 1747-48, 1750-53, 1759, 1762-63, 1766-89, 1801-02, 1809-23, 1825-37, 1840-41
(SRO)
Cop M 1683-1812 (Ptd, Phillimore 11, 1908); C 1616-1782, M 1616-82, B 1616-82, 1744-60
(Ts I SG); 1683-1837 (SRO, SLC); M 1683-1812 (Boyd); C 1683-1812 (SCDB); B 1683-1841
(SBDB); M 1616-1837 (OR & BT) (SMI)
Cop (Mf) 1612-1841 (BT) (SLC, SRO)

WELLINGTON alias ROCKWELL GREEN All Saints (created from Wellington
St John the Baptist, 1890) (Wellington Union)
OR C 1890-1982, M 1890-1987 (SRO)

WELLINGTON School Chapel
OR C 1932-38 (SRO)

WELLINGTON Meeting House, High Street (Society of Friends) (K 1931)
OR C 1690-1955, M 1676-1835, B 1695-1908 (SRO)
Cop B 1791-1837 (SBDB)

WELLINGTON Lower Meeting, Fore Street (Presbyterian, then Congregational) f 1689, became
Independent 1730 b 1861 (K 1931)
OR ZC 1786-1837, B 1812-37 (PRO: RG 4/4046); C 1786-1865, M 1847-78, B 1812-48 (SRO)
Cop (Mf) ZC 1786-1837, B 1812-37 (SLC, SRO)

WELLINGTON South Street (Baptist) f 1739 b 1833, reb 1877 (K 1931)
OR Z 1714-1837, B 1784-1911 (SRO); Z 1784-1837, B 1785-93, 1809-30 (PRO: RG 4/1736, 1750)
Cop (Mf) Z 1784-1837, B 1785-93, 1809-30 (SLC, SRO)

WELLINGTON Mantle Street (Wesleyan) f 1787 (K 1931)
OR ZC 1813-37 (PRO: RG 4/2936); C 1813-1910, M 1959-71 (SRO)

WELLINGTON Waterloo Road (United Methodist) (Taunton Circuit) f 1848 b 1899 (K 1931)

WELLINGTON Millway Chapel, North Street b 1862

WELLINGTON Wrangway (Independent) b 1882 (K 1931)

WELLINGTON (Plymouth Brethren) f 19th century

WELLINGTON Rockwell Green (Baptist) (K 1931)

WELLINGTON Holywell Lake (Baptist) (K 1931)

WELLINGTON Scott's Lane (Salvation Army) (K 1931)

WELLINGTON St John Fisher, Mantle Street (Roman Catholic) b 1937

WELLOW Cemetery opened 1900 (1¼ acres) (K 1931)

WELLOW St Julian (960) (Wellow Hundred; Bath Union)
OR C 1561-1959, M 1562-1967, B 1561-1959 (SRO)
BT 1599-1600, 1609-12, 1623-24, 1629-31, 1636-38, 1662-68, 1676-77, 1732, 1747-53, 1755-56,
    1760-61, 1765-67, 1798-1804, 1806-10, 1812-19, 1822-37, CB 1854-55 (SRO)
Cop 1599-1623 (Ptd, Dwelly 2, 1914); M 1754-1837 (NSMI); B 1813-53 (SBDB); M 1599, 1610,
    1623 (BT), 1754-1837 (SMI)
Cop (Mf) 1599-1855 (BT) (SLC, SRO)

WELLOW (Wesleyan) b 1808
OR C 1838-1912 (chapel), C 1843-1900 (circuit) (Bristol RO)
Cop (Mf) C 1838-1912 (Bristol RO, SLC)

WELLOW Ebenezer Chapel (United Methodist) b 1854 (K 1931)
OR C 1864-1987 (Bristol RO)
Cop (Mf) C 1864-1987 (Bristol RO, SLC)

WELLOW Shoscombe (Independent)
OR M 1901-63 (Bristol RO)
Cop (Mf) M 1901-63 (Bristol RO, SLC)

WELLOW by the roadside (Methodist)
OR M 1949-86 (SRO)

WELLOW Shoscombe (Methodist)
OR C 1976-83 (SRO)

WELLS Board of Guardians
OR Z 1838-1918, D 1879-1914 (SRO)

WELLS Cemetery, Portway opened 1855 (8 acres) (K 1931)

WELLS City of (6,649)

WELLS St Andrew (Wells Cathedral) (Wells Forum Hundred; Wells Union)
OR C 1661+, M 1668-1754, 1861+, B 1665+ (Inc)
BT none
Cop C 1661-1982, M 1668-1754, 1861-1981, B 1665-1980 (Ts I SG, SRO)

WELLS St Cuthbert (Wells Forum Hundred; Wells Union)
OR C 1608-1951, M 1608-1956, Banns 1754-1869, 1910-33, B 1608-1919 (SRO)
BT 1607, 1627-30, 1636-37, 1802, 1805-31 (1813-21 includes Liberty of St Andrew), CB 1838,
    1840-50, 1852-85 (SRO)
Cop C 1666-1838 (Index SRO); B 1727-1839 (SBDB); M 1609-1837 (SMI)
Cop (Mf) 1607-1885 (BT) (SLC, SRO); C 1609-1901, MB 1609-1900, Banns 1754-1869 (SLC)

WELLS St Thomas, East Wells (created from Wells St Cuthbert, 1858) (Wells Union)
OR C 1858-1959, M 1858-1972, Banns 1858-1900, B 1858-1971 (SRO)
Cop (Mf) CMB 1858-1901, Banns 1858-1901 (SLC)

WELLS Grove Lane Chapel or Union Street (Independent) b 1750 (united with Baptist chapel,
    Union Street, 1916) (K 1931)
OR ZC 1790-1836, B 1790-94 (PRO: RG 4/2122)
Cop (Mf) ZC 1790-1836, B 1790-94 (SLC, SRO)

WELLS Ebenezer Chapel, Union Street (Baptist) f 1814 (united 1916 with old Congregational
    chapel in Union Street)
OR Z 1814-35 (PRO: RG 4/2935)
Cop (Mf) Z 1814-35 (SRO, SLC)

WELLS Southover (Wesleyan) (Shepton Mallet Circuit) (Lewis 1831) b 1865 (K 1931)

WELLS St Joseph and St Theresa, Chamberlain Street (Roman Catholic) f 1875 b 1890
OR C 1876+, M 1875+, D 1875+ (Inc)

WEMBDON St George (289) (North Petherton Hundred; Bridgwater Union)
OR C 1665-1965, M 1676-1993, Banns 1757-1803, B 1665-1958 (SRO)
BT two between 1590-1620, 1603, 1605-09, 1621-22, one between 1625-40, 1636-37, 1640-41,
    1666, 1670, 1679-80, 1704-07, 1718-21, 1725-26, 1730-33, 11735-37, 1742-43, 1746-50,
    1752-53, 1759, 1764-65, 1767-70, 1773-84, 1786-89, 1800-08, 1810-37, CB 1838 (SRO)
Cop C 1665-1812, M 1671-1754, B 1673-1758 (SRO); B 1813-51 (SBDB); M 1746-1837 (SMI)
Cop (Mf) 1603-1838 (BT) (SLC, SRO)

WEST BUCKLAND *see* **BUCKLAND, WEST**

WESTBURY St Lawrence (681) (peculiar of the Dean of Wells until 1845) (Wells Forum Hundred;
    Wells Union)
OR C 1654-1911, M 1654-1837 (gap 1713-33), Banns 1755-1812, B 1654-1882 (SRO)
    (registers started 1713 in 1914)
BT 1607-09, 1611-12, 1622-24, 1627-31, 1636-41, 1664-65, 1678-79, 1705-06, 1802-05, 1809-37
    (SRO); 1749, 1753, 1800-02 (SRO: D/D/Pd:26/12)
Cop 1623-39 (Ptd, Dwelly 2, 1914); B 1654-1843 (SBDB); M 1636-37, 1639 (BT), 1750-1837
    (SMI)
Cop (Mf) 1607-1837 (BT) (SLC, SRO)

WESTBURY (United Methodist) f 1858 b 1872 (K 1931)

WESTBURY (Wesleyan) b 1864 (K 1931)

WESTFIELD St Peter (created from Midsomer Norton, Radstock, Kilmersdon,
    Stratton on the Fosse and Holcombe, 1953)
OR CMB 1953+ (Inc)

WESTON All Saints (2,560) (Bath Forum Hundred; Bath Union) (renamed Bath Weston All Saints, 1967)
OR C 1538-1951 (gaps 1554-56, 1676-79), M 1538-1969 (gaps 1643-56 and 1659-64),
  Banns 1754-1821, 1836-64, B 1538-1955 (gap 1654-64) (SRO)
BT 1598-99, 1602-03, 1605-09, 1611-14, 1623-26, 1629-31, 1634-41, 1662, 1666-69, 1748-51,
  1755-58, 1765, 1768-69, 1784-88, 1790-94, 1796-1815, 1817-37, CB 1838, 1840-80 (SRO)
Cop 1538-1840 (Ts I SG, SRO, Bath Lib, British Lib); M 1539-1837 (SMI)
Cop (Mf) 1598-1880 (BT) (SLC, SRO); C 1538-1901, M 1538-1642, 1656-59, 1665-1900,
  Banns 1754-1821, 1835-64, B 1538-1642, 1653-1901 (SLC)

WESTON St John the Evangelist (created from from Weston All Saints, 1841, refounded 1879)
  (Bath Union)
OR C 1878-1950, M 1879-1930 (SRO)

WESTON (Wesleyan) (Lewis 1831)

WESTON (Independent) (K 1931)

WESTON BAMPFYLDE Holy Cross (123) (Catsash Hundred; Wincanton Union)
OR C 1728-1993, M 1747, 1752, 1755-1990, B 1741-1993 (SRO)
BT 1598-99, 1606-07, 1621-31, 1636-41, 1662-65, 1667-69, 1672-73, 1683-84, 1704-05, 1707-08,
  1733-34, 1751, 1757, 1800-22, 1824-37, CB 1838, 1840-47, 1850, CMB 1856, CB 1857-69,
  CMB 1870-71, CB 1872-73, CMB 1874 (SRO)
Cop 1623-83 (Ptd, Dwelly 2, 1914); 1813-35 (Ts SG); M 1625, 1639, 1672 (BT), 1754-1837 (SMI)
Cop (Mf) 1598-1874 (BT) (SLC, SRO); C 1728-1812, M 1747, 1752, 1755-1835, B 1741-1812
  (SLC)

WESTON in GORDANO St Peter and St Paul (124) (Portbury Hundred; Bedminster Union
  1836-99, Long Ashton Union 1899-1930)
OR C 1685-1920 (gaps 1729-33, 1736-40), M 1694-1837 (gaps 1701-09, 1720-32, 1743-47),
  Banns 1754-1800, B 1684-1812 (SRO); B 1813+ (Inc)
BT 1593-97, 1599-1600, 1605-06, 1609-12, 1622-24, 1630-31, 1634-37, 1639-40, 1662-65,
  1748-49, 1800-15, 1817-20, 1822-37, CB 1838-50, CMB 1851-53 (SRO)
Cop 1593-1639 (Ptd, Dwelly 2, 1914); M 1754-1837 (NSMI); M 1605, 1622, 1754-1837 (SMI)
Cop (Mf) 1593-1853 (BT) (SLC, SRO)

WESTON in GORDANO (Independent) b 1850

WESTON super MARE Cemetery, Bristol Road opened 1856 (20 acres)

WESTON super MARE St John the Baptist (1,310) (Winterstoke Hundred; Axbridge Union)
OR C 1668-1904, M 1682-1933, B 1668-1885 (SRO)
BT 1599-1600, 1613-14, 1621-24, 1636-38, 1747-51, 1754, 1756-57, 1759, 1761, 1767-70,
  1777-78, 1800-04, 1808-14, 1822-33, 1835-36 (SRO)
Cop M 1682-1837 (Ptd, Phillimore 14, 1913); 1668-1850 (Ts I SG, SRO); 1668-1812 (SLC);
  M 1754-1837 (NSMI); M 1682-1837 (Boyd); B 1813-51 (SBDB); M 1682-1703, 1710-1837
  (SMI)
Cop (Mf) 1599-1836 (BT) (SLC, SRO); C 1668-1886, MB 1668-1885 (SLC)

WESTON super MARE Emmanuel, Oxford Street (created from Weston super Mare St John, 1847)
  (Axbridge Union)
OR C 1847-1914, M 1847-1927, B 1847-56 (SRO)

WESTON super MARE Christ Church (created from Weston super Mare St John, 1855)
  (Axbridge Union)
OR C 1855-1944, M 1856-1963 (SRO)

WESTON super MARE Holy Trinity, South Road (created from Weston super Mare St John, 1862) (Axbridge Union)
OR C 1861-1958, M 1862-1969 (SRO)
Cop (Mf) C 1861-1902, M 1862-1900 (SLC)

WESTON super MARE St Paul, Clarence Park (created from Weston super Mare Emmanuel and Uphill, 1912) (Axbridge Union)
OR C 1897-1948, M 1897-1949 (SRO)

WESTON super MARE All Saints, All Saints Road (created from Weston super Mare St John, 1902) (Axbridge Union)
OR CMB 1902+ (Inc)

WESTON super MARE St Saviour, Locking Road (created from Weston super Mare Emmanuel and Weston super Mare Christ Church, 1903) (Axbridge Union)
OR CMB 1903+ (Inc)

WESTON super MARE Good Shepherd (chapel to St Paul) cl 11964
OR C 1930-64, M 1956-62 (SRO)

WESTON super MARE St Andrew, Bournville (created from Bleadon, Uphill, Weston super Mare St Paul and Weston super Mare St Saviour, 1960)
OR CMB 1960+ (Inc)

WESTON super MARE Boulevard (Independent) b 1827 (K 1931)
OR C 1829-36 (PRO: RG 4/4047)
Cop (Mf) C 1829-36 (SLC, SRO)

WESTON super MARE Meeting House, Oxford Street (Society of Friends) b 1846 (K 1931)

WESTON super MARE Wadham Street (Baptist) b 1847 (K 1931)

WESTON super MARE Station Road (Wesleyan) f 1847 b 1900 (K 1931)

WESTON super MARE Victoria Chapel, Regent Street (Wesleyan)
OR C 1849-1923, M 1886-99 (Bristol RO)
Cop (Mf) C 1849-1923, M 1886-99 (Bristol RO, SLC)

WESTON super MARE St Joseph, Camp Road (Roman Catholic) f 1851 b 1865
OR C 1859+, M 1909+, DB 1916+ (Inc)

WESTON super MARE Boulevard (United Methodist) b 1853 (K 1931)
OR C 1863-1917, 1950 (Bristol RO)
Cop (Mf) C 1863-1917, 1950 (Bristol RO, SLC)

WESTON super MARE Bristol Road (Baptist) b 1866 (K 1931)

WESTON super MARE Locking Road (United Methodist Free) b 1877 (K 1931)
OR C 1877-1942 (Bristol RO)
Cop (Mf) C 1877-1942 (Bristol RO, SLC)

WESTON super MARE Upper Church Road (Wesleyan) b 1881 (K 1931)

WESTON super MARE Meadow Street (Primitive Methodist)
OR M 1905-69 (Bristol RO)
Cop (Mf) M 1905-69 (Bristol RO, SLC)

WESTON super MARE Brighton Road (Primitive Methodist) b 1908 (K 1931)
OR M 1909-69 (Bristol RO)
Cop (Mf) M 1909-69 (Bristol RO, SLC)

WESTON super MARE Moorland Road (Independent) b 1926 (K 1931)

WESTON super MARE Corpus Christi, Ellenborough Park South (Roman Catholic)
    b 1929 (K 1931)

WESTON super MARE Walliscote Road (Baptist) (K 1931)

WESTON super MARE Wadham Street (Christian Spiritualist) (K 1931)

WESTON super MARE West Street (National Spiritualist) (K 1931)

WESTON super MARE First Church of Christ Scientist, Graham Road (Christian Science) (K 1931)

WESTON super MARE Carleton Street (Salvation Army) (K 1931)

WESTON super MARE Our Lady of Lourdes, Baytree Road, Milton (Roman Catholic) b 1938

WESTONZOYLAND St Mary (937) (Whitley Hundred; Bridgwater Union)
OR C 1558-1955, M 1558-1970, Banns 1754-1803, 1807-20, B 1558-1933 (SRO)
BT 1597-1600, 1602-03, 1607-08, 1610-12, 1621-24, 1627-30, 1636-37, 1640-41, 1663-64,
    1731-35, 1747-52, 1755-57, 1768-70, c1775-76, 1778-79, 1782, 1784-85, 1791, 1800-38,
    1840-46 (SRO)
Cop M 1558-1812 (SRO); B 1813-57 (SBDB); M 1558-1837 (SMI)
Cop (Mf) 1597-1846 (BT) (SLC, SRO)

WESTONZOYLAND (Wesleyan) b 1873 (K 1931)

WHATLEY St Edmund (386) (Frome Hundred; Frome Union)
OR C 1672-1924, M 1672-1949, Banns 1764-1818, B 1672-1812 (SRO); B 1813+ (Inc)
BT 1598-1600, 1602-03, 1605-12, 1616-17, 1621-24, 1629-31, 1636-37, 1639-41, 1665, 1675,
    1732-35, 1737-38, 1750-51, 1753-56, 1802-30, 1832, 1834-37, M 1838, CMB 1839 (SRO)
Cop M 1754-1837 (SMI)
Cop (Mf) 1598-1839 (BT) (SLC, SRO); C 1673-1903, M 1673-1902, Banns 1764-1818,
    B 1672-1812 (SLC)

WHEATHILL St John the Baptist (56) (Whitley Hundred; Wincanton Union) (united with
    East Lydford, 1965)
OR C 1813-98, M 1838-1939, B 1813-1932 (SRO) (registers from 1779 survived in 1914)
BT one between 1589-1629, 1605-08, 1611-12, 1621-23, 1627-30, 1636-40, 1663-65, 1669-70,
    1704, 1755, 1789-90, 1799-1800, 1804-06, 1808-14, 1816-17, 1819-29, 1831-34, 1836, B 1864
    (SRO)
Cop 1623 (Ptd, Dwelly 2, 1914); B 1813-1906 (SBDB); M 1623 (BT), 1800-37 (SMI)
Cop (Mf) 1605-1864 (BT) (SLC, SRO); C 1813-98, M 1838-95, B 1813-1906 (SLC)

WHITCHURCH St Nicholas (423) (chapelry in Long Ashton until 1720) (Keynsham Hundred;
    Keynsham Union)
OR C 1565-1966, M 1567-1961, Banns 1754-1918, B 1569-1915 (Bristol RO)
BT 1607-08, 1622-24, 1630, 1635-37, 1639-41, 1662-63, 1753, 1755-58, 1800, 1802-03, 1805-19
    (SRO)
Cop M 1754-1837 (NSMI); B 1752-1839 (SBDB); M 1754-1837 (SMI)
Cop (Mf) 1607-1819 (BT) (SLC, SRO); C 1565-1966, M 1567-1961, Banns 1754-1918,
    B 1569-1915 (Bristol RO, SLC)

WHITCHURCH (Independent) b 1872 (K 1931)

WHITELACKINGTON St Mary (254) (peculiar of the Dean of Wells until 1845)
(Abdick and Bulstone Hundred; Chard Union)
OR C 1687-1949, M 1695-1988, Banns 1755-1812, 1825-53, B 1678-1992 (SRO)
BT 1607-10, 1612-13, 1616, 1619, 1621-24, 1630-31, 1638-41, 1662-65, 1667, 1669-70, 1816,
1818-37, CB 1838, 1840-65 (SRO)
Cop M 1695-1837 (Ptd, Phillimore 13, 1910); 1609-23 (Ptd, Dwelly 2, 1914); M 1695-1837 (Boyd);
M 1609-23 (BT), 1695-1837 (SMI); C 1687-1899 (DCI)
Cop (Mf) C 1678-1900, M 1678-1837, Banns 1755-1812, 1825-53, B 1678-1812 (SG, SLC);
1607-1865 (BT) (SLC, SRO)

WHITESTAUNTON St Andrew (318) (South Petherton Hundred; Chard Union)
OR C 1659-1883, M 1692-1983, Banns 1755-1818, 1824-1916, B 1692-1985 (SRO)
BT 1606-12, c1615, 1621-24, c1627, 1629-31, 1635-40, 1669-70, 1731-32, 1736-37, 1742-44,
1749-52, 1755-56, 1758-85, 1767-69, 1771-74, 1776-89, 1791-93, 1795-1836, CB 1909 (SRO)
Cop M 1606-1811 (Ptd, Phillimore 4, 1902); M 1606-1811 (Boyd); B 1813-1900 (SBDB);
M 1606-08, 1692-1837 (SMI); C 1659-1883, M 1606-1966, B 1692-1968 (DCI)
Cop (Mf) 1606-1836, 1909 (BT) (SLC, SRO); C 1659-66, 1692-1883, M 1659-66, 1692-1902,
Banns 1755-1818, 1824-1902, B 1659-66, 1692-1901 (SLC)

WICK St Lawrence (281) (chapelry in Congresbury until 1954, when severed)
(Winterstoke Hundred; Axbridge Union) (tranferred to Avon, 1974)
OR C 1625-1910, M 1615-1834, B 1813+ (Inc)
BT 1598-99, 1607-10, 1619-23, 1627-31, 1636-38, 1640-41, 1663-64, 1679-80, 1720-21, 1747-48,
1752-59, 1799-1817, 1819, 1821, 1823-25, 1830-36 (SRO)
Cop M 1754-1837 (NSMI); M 1754-1837 (SMI)
Cop (Mf) 1598-1836 (BT) (SLC, SRO); C 1625-1885, M 1615-1837, B 1635-1813 (SLC)

WICK (Wesleyan) b 1862 (K 1931)
OR C 1862-1936 (Bristol RO)
Cop (Mf) C 1862-1936 (Bristol RO, SLC)

WIDCOMBE St Thomas a Becket (8,704) (chapelry in Bath St Mary de Stalls until late medieval
times, renamed Bath Widcombe, 1967) (Bath Forum Hundred; Bath Union)
OR C 1574-1967, M 1612-1937 (M 1755-1812 at Bath St James), B 1592-1773, 1812-1977 (SRO)
BT 1813-37 (SRO)
Cop CB 1813-40, M 1612-1754, 1813-40 (Ts I SG, SRO); CB 1574-1812, M 1612-1754 (Bath Lib)
Cop (Mf) 1813-37 (BT) (SLC, SRO)

WIDCOMBE (Methodist)
OR B 1834-37 (PRO: RG 4/1755)
Cop (Mf) B 1834-37 (SLC, SRO)

WILLITON Board of Guardians
OR Z 1838-1943, D 1838-1956 (SRO)

WILLITON St Peter (chapelry in St Decumans until 1784) (Williton and Freemanors Hundred;
Williton Union)
OR C 1792-1967, M 1829-1973, B 1831-1838 (SRO)
BT 1750-60 (SRO: D/D/Ppb:84)
Cop C 1792-1899, M 1829-79 (DCI)
Cop M 1829-37 (SMI)

WILLITON (Strict Baptist) f 1813 b 1844 cl 1919

WILLITON Fore Street (Wesleyan) b 1820 reb 1883 Tower Hill (K 1931)
OR C 1872-1923 (circuit) (SRO)

WILTON St George (795) (chapelry in Taunton St Mary Magdalene until 1739)
(Taunton and Taunton Dean Hundred; Taunton Union)
OR C 1558-1969, M 1559-1987, Banns 1755-1812, 1842-1901, B 1558-1874 (SRO)
BT 1598-99, 1605-10, 1613-14, 1616, 1621-24, 1629-30, 1636-38, 1640-41, 1661-64, 1666-67,
1707-08, ?1720-21, 1726, 1728-29, 1737-38, 1747-50, 1800-29, 1831 (SRO)
Cop 1558-1837 (Ptd, J.H. Spencer, 1890); M 1558-1837 (Boyd); B 1558-1850 (SBDB);
M 1598, 1609, 1613, 1615, 1623, 1663 (BT), 1754-1837 (SMI)
Cop (Mf) 1598-1831 (BT) (SLC, SRO); C 1558-1901, M 1569-1900, Banns 1755-1814, 1842-1901,
B 1558-1874 (SLC)

WILTON St Michael, Galmington (chapelry to Wilton St George)
OR M 1971-91, B 1967-88 (SRO)

WINCANTON Board of Guardians
OR Z 1893-1930, D 1866-1907 (SRO)

WINCANTON Cemetery, Glyns opened 1887 (K 1931)

WINCANTON St Peter and St Paul (2,123) (Norton Ferris Hundred; Wincanton Union)
OR C 1636-37, 1640-84, 1686-1969, M 1636-76, 1683-1978, Banns 1754-1812, 1823-1900,
B 1636-87, 1692-1926 (SRO)
BT 1593-96, c.1600, 1603-04, 1607-08, 1621-22, 1627-30, 1637-41, 1672-73, 1678-79, 1683-84,
1704-05, 1732-34, 1749-53, 1755-57, 1760, 1800-28, 1830-35, CB 1838, 1847, CMB 1851,
CB 1852, 1855-59, 1869, 1871 (SRO)
Cop 1629-72 (Ptd, Dwelly 2, 1914); M 1775-1829 (Ts SLC); C 1636-1812, M 1636-1837,
B 1636-1812, 1863-71 (SRO); B 1813-43 (SBDB); M 1629, 1636-37, 1672 (BT), 1754-1837
(SMI)
Cop (Mf) C 1636-1887, M 1640-1722, 1731-1889, Banns 1754-1812, 1823-1901, B 1636-1885
(SG, SLC); 1593-1871 (BT) (SLC, SRO)

WINCANTON Mill Street (Independent) b 1770 (K 1931)
OR C 1798-1837, B 1815-25 (PRO: RG 4/2123, 2352, 2581)
Cop (Mf) C 1798-1837, B 1815-25 (SLC, SRO)

WINCANTON (Baptist) b 1833 (K 1931)

WINCANTON Meeting House, High Street (Society of Friends) b 1867 (K 1931)

WINCANTON High Street (Wesleyan) (Sherborne Circuit) f 1876 b 1916 (K 1931)

WINCANTON St Luke and St Teresa, South Street (Roman Catholic) f 1881 b 1908

WINCANTON (Primitive Methodist) b 1885

WINCANTON Station Road (Plymouth Brethren) (K 1931)

WINDMILL HILL St Michael and All Angels (created from Bedminster, 1902)
(Bedminster Union 1836-99, Long Ashton Union 1899-1930)
OR CMB 1902+ (Inc)

WINFORD St Mary and St Peter (865) (Hartcliffe with Bedminster Hundred; Bedminster Union
1836-99, Long Ashton Union 1899-1930)
OR C 1655-1917, M 1656-1983, B 1655-1935 (SRO)
BT one between 1582-1621, 1598-99, 1607-13, 1621-23, 1626-27, 1629-31, 1635-41, 1662-64,
1669-70, 1684-85, 1732-33, 1748-49, 1776, 1800-35, CB 1838, 1840-49 (SRO)
Cop 1609-39 (Ptd, Dwelly 2, 1914); M 1754-1837 (NSMI); B 1813-48 (SBDB); M 1609, 1630,
1639 (BT), 1754-1837 (SMI)
Cop (Mf) 1598-1849 (BT) (SLC, SRO)

WINFORD (Baptist) b 1824 (K 1931)

WINFORD Felton (Independent) b 1835

WINFORD Ridghill (Baptist) b 1858

WINSCOMBE St James (1,526) (Winterstoke Hundred; Axbridge Union)
OR C 1662-1900 (gap 1725-31), M 1658-1944, Banns 1754-1811, 1823-1958, B 1662-1903 (SRO)
BT 1591-92, 1598-99, 1605-06, 1611-12, 1619-24, 1629-31, 1634-38, 1640-41, 1668-69, 1736-37,
    1798-99, 1805, 1808-12, 1814-18, 1820-37, CB 1838-59 (SRO)
Cop 1598-1623 (Ptd, Dwelly 2, 1914); M 1754-1837 (NSMI); M 1598, 1623, 1754-1837 (SMI)
Cop (Mf) 1591-1859 (BT) (SLC, SRO); CB 1662-1900, M 1658-1754, 1768-1900, Banns
    1754-1812, 1823-1901 (SLC)

WINSCOMBE Sandford (Wesleyan) f 1791 b 1898 (K 1931)
OR B 1803-1907 (Bristol RO)
Cop (Mf) B 1803-1907 (Bristol RO, SLC)

WINSCOMBE (Baptist) b 1833 (K 1931)

WINSCOMBE Meeting House, Sidcot (Society of Friends) (K 1931)
BT B 1865-72 (SRO)
Cop (Mf) 1865-72 (BT) (SLC, SRO)

WINSFORD St Mary Magdalen (524) (Williton and Freemanors Hundred; Dulverton Union)
OR C 1660-1965, M 1660-1978, Banns 1754-1881, B 1660-1915 (SRO)
BT 1594-97, 1607-14, 1621-24, 1629-30, 1639-40, 1662-63, 1679-80, 1698-99, 1703-10, 1712-13,
    1721-27, 1729-34, 1743-44, 1748-49, 1751-57, 1762, 1764-65, 1767-69, 1771-74, 1777-79,
    1797-98, 1800-12, 1811-27, 1829-38, 1841 (SRO)
Cop 1621-39 (Ptd, Dwelly 2, 1914); C 1608-1751, M 1607-1751 (SRO); B 1813-86 (SBDB);
    M 1621-23, 1639 (BT), 1754-1837 (SMI); C 1753-1899, M 1754-1899 (DCI)
Cop (Mf) 1594-1841 (BT) (SLC, SRO); C 1660-1902, M 1660-1901, Banns 1754-1881,
    B 1660-1903 (SLC)

WINSFORD (Wesleyan) (Lewis 1831) b 1835 reb 1889 (K 1931)
OR C 1803-72 (circuit) (SRO)

WINSHAM St Stephen (932) (peculiar of the Consistorial Court of the Dean and Chapter of Wells
    until 1845) (part East Kingsbury Hundred, part South Petherton Hundred; Chard Union)
OR CB 1559-1925, M 1559-1982, Banns 1754-1810, 1899 (SRO)
BT 1599-1600, 1606-07, 1609-10, one between 1621-39, one between 1621-40, 1621-24, 1629-31,
    1636-38, 1640-41, 1695-96, 1770-71, 1773-78, 1781, 1785-87, 1790-91, 1793-98, 1800-18,
    1820-26, 1829-30 (1772 in peculiar series) (SRO)
Cop M 1754-1837 (SMI); CM 1559-1899 (DCI)
Cop (Mf) 1599-1830 (BT) (SLC, SRO); CMB 1559-1886, Banns 1754-1810, 1899 (SLC)

WINSHAM (Independent) f 1687 b 1811 (K 1931)
OR C 1810-37, B 1811-37 (PRO: RG 4/2934); CM 1969-73 (SRO)
Cop (Mf) C 1810-37, B 1811-37 (SLC, SRO)

WINSHAM (Plymouth Brethren) (K 1931)

WITHAM FRIARY St Mary the Virgin (574) (peculiar of the Dean of Wells until 1845)
    (Witham Friary Liberty, Frome Hundred; Frome Union)
OR C 1695-1925, M 1696-1974, Banns 1823-76, B 1684-1910 (SRO)
BT 1621-22, 1813-37, CB 1838, 1840-48, 1852-53 (SRO)
Cop C 1695-1837, M 1696-1837, B 1684-1836 (Ms I SG); B 1813-82 (SBDB); M 1750-1837 (SMI)
Cop (Mf) 1621-1853 (BT) (SLC, SRO); CM 1695-1900, Banns 1823-77, B 1684-1901 (SLC)

WITHAM FRIARY (United Methodist Free) b 1863

WITHIEL FLOREY St Mary (89) (Taunton and Taunton Dean Hundred; Williton Union 1836-96, Dulverton Union 1896-1930) (united with Brompton Regis, 1958)
OR C 1697-1966, M 1697-1956, Banns 1764-1808, 1870-1900, B 1697-1970 (SRO)
BT 1598-99, 1603-14, 1621-23, 1629-30, 1634-37, 1640-41, 1662-69, 1672, 1703-04, 1706-09, 1725-26, 1728-29, 1731-33, 1735-36, 1748-51, 1753-57, 1759, 1762-65, 1769-81, 1785-95, 1797, 1800-02, 1804-21, 1823-28, 1830, 1832-36, CB 1846-48 (SRO)
Cop 1609-29 (Ptd, Dwelly 2, 1914); B 1813-1900 (SBDB); M 1609, 1613, 1623 (BT), 1755-1837 (SMI); CM 1697-1899 (DCI)
Cop (Mf) 1598-1848 (BT) (SLC, SRO); C 1697-1909, M 1697-1901, Banns 1764-1813, 1870-1901, B 1697-1768, 1779-1900 (SLC)

WITHYCOMBE St Nicholas (332) (Carhampton Hundred; Williton Union)
OR C 1669-1897, M 1672-1841, Banns 1754-1813, 1824-40, B 1669-1812 (gap 1714-44) (SRO); B 1813+ (Inc)
BT 1605-08, 1611-12, 1621-24, 1629-31, 1636-38, 1663-64, 1667-70, 1701-02, 1704-O5, 1711-13, 1728, 1731-33, 1750-51, 1775, 1800-18, 1820, 1822 (SRO)
Cop M 1670-1745, 1750-1837 (SMI); C 1669-1897, M 1670-1837 (DCI)
Cop (Mf) 1605-1822 (BT) (SLC, SRO); C 1669-1897, M 1670-1841, Banns 1754-1813, 1824-1903, B 1669-1812 (SLC)

WITHYCOMBE (United Methodist) b 1845 (K 1931)

WITHYPOOL St Andrew (212) (chapelry in Hawkridge) (Williton and Freemanors Hundred; Dulverton Union)
OR C 1771-1985, M 1771-1970, B 1771-1812 (SRO); B 1813+ (Inc) (registers from 1653 survived in 1914 and apparently in 1935)
BT 1598-1600, 1605-08, 1611, 1622-24, 1629-31, 1636-41, 1662-63, 1666-69, 1679-80, 1700, 1702-07, 1709-12, 1721, 1726-29, 1731-33, 1743-44, 1746-48, 1751, 1754, 1759, 1762-63, 1765, 1767-69, 1772-76, 1778-80, 1789-90, 1799-1821, 1823-28, 1830, 1832-36 (SRO)
Cop M 1754-1837 (SMI); C 1771-1899, M 1813-99 (DCI)
Cop (Mf) 1598-1836 (BT) (SLC, SRO); C 1771-1907, M 1813-1902, B 1771-1812 (SLC)

WITHYPOOL (Wesleyan) b 1881 (K 1931)

WIVELISCOMBE St Andrew (3,047) (peculiar of the Prebendary of Wiveliscombe until 1845) (West Kingsbury Hundred; Wellington Union)
OR C 1558-1885, M 1558-1872, Banns 1754-1812, 1823-1935, B 1558-1893 (gaps B 1625-34, CMB 1688-95) (SRO)
BT 1598-99, 1606-10, 1622-24, one between 1617-45, one between 1618-40, 1630-31, 1639-40, 1662-63, one between 1663-80, 1666-67, 1696-97, 1742-44, 1813-31, 1833-37 (1709-10, 1779-83 in peculiar series) (SRO)
Cop 1598-1637 (Ptd, Dwelly 2, 1914); B 1704-1838 (SBDB); M 1598-1637 (BT), 1754-1837 (SMI); CM 1558-1872 (DCI)
Cop (Mf) 1598-1837 (BT) (SLC, SRO); CM 1558-1872, Banns 1754-1816, 1823-85, B 1558-1875 (SLC)

WIVELISCOMBE Golden Hill (Independent) f 1662 b 1708, reb 1825 (K 1931)
OR ZC 1709-1837, B 1812-37 (PRO: RG 4/4048)
Cop (Mf) ZC 1709-1837, B 1812-37 (SLC, SRO)

WIVELISCOMBE Lambrooke (Wesleyan) (Wellington Circuit) b 1845 (K 1931)
OR C 1876-1920 (SRO)

WIVELISCOMBE St Richard, Silver Street (Roman Catholic) b 1942

WOODLANDS St Katharine (created from Frome Selwood, 1872) (Frome Union)
OR CMB 1872+ (Inc)
Cop B 1813-36 (SBDB)

WOOKEY St Matthew (1,100) (peculiar of the Subdean of Wells) (Wells Forum Hundred;
Wells Union)
OR C 1565-1925, M 1565-1964, Banns 1754-1833, 1946-68, B 1558, 1565-1949 (SRO)
BT 1607-08, 1611-14, 1621-24, 1630-31, 1635-37, 1639-41, 1801-09, 1813-36, CB 1838-47 (SRO);
1729-30, 1733-44, 1750-54 (SRO: D/D/Psd:5)
Cop B 1813-42 (SBDB); M 1754-1837 (SMI)
Cop (Mf) 1607-1847 (BT) (SLC, SRO); C 1565-1902, M 1565-1900, Banns 1754-1833,
B 1558, 1565-1901 (SLC)

WOOKEY (Baptist) b 1884

WOOKEY HOLE St Mary Magdalen b 1874 (created from Easton, 1973) (Wells Union)
OR CMB 1874+ (Inc)

WOOKEY HOLE (Wesleyan) b 1871 (K 1931)
OR M 1936-67 (SRO)

WOOLAVINGTON St Mary (412) (Whitley Hundred; Bridgwater Union)
OR C 1694-1970, M 1694-1985, Banns 1793-1900, B 1694-1934 (SRO)
BT 1605-09, 1611-12, 1621-24, 1627-30, 1636-37, 1639-40, 1643-62, 1666-67, 1741-42, 1748-51,
1754-56, 1767, 1800-31, 1833-37, 1839-42, CB 1848 (SRO)
Cop B 1813-96 (SBDB); M 1754-1837 (SMI)
Cop (Mf) 1605-1848 (BT) (SLC, SRO); C 1694-1902, M 1695-1714, 1730-1901, Banns 1793-1900,
B 1696-1902 (SLC)

WOOLAVINGTON (Wesleyan) b 1838 (K 1931)
OR C 1842-1925 (SRO)

WOOLLEY All Saints (104) (united with Bathwick before 1535) (Bath Forum Hundred;
Bath Union)
OR CB 1560-1812, M 1560-1835 (gap 1744-54) (SRO); CB 1813+ (Inc)
BT 1606-10, 1619, 1623, 1627, 1629, 1636-39, 1662-63, 1666-67, 1677, 1732-33, 1744, 1748-54,
1754-59, 1765-68, 1776-77, 1785-88, 1790-94, 1796-1837, CB 1838, 1840, 1842-53, C 1854,
CB 1855-60, 1862-68 (SRO)
Cop C 1563-1840, M 1564-1840, B 1560-1840 (Ts I SG); CB 1668-1812, M 1668-1835 (Bath Lib,
British Lib); CMB 1813-40 (SRO); M 1754-1837 (SMI)
Cop (Mf) 1606-1868 (BT) (SLC, SRO)

WOOLVERTON St Lawrence (207) (Frome Hundred; Frome Union) (abolished and incorporated
into Rode Major, 1972)
OR C 1813-1995, M 1839-1992 (SRO); B 1813+ (Inc Rode Major) (C 1761-1812, M 1754-1837,
Banns 1754-1812, B 1774-1812 stolen from church, c1965)
BT 1598-1600, 1607-09, 1611-14, 1621-23, 1630-31, 1634-40, 1663-65, 1747-48, 1750-52,
1757-58, 1802-32, 1834-35 (SRO)
Cop M 1754-1837 (SMI)
Cop (Mf) 1598-1835 (BT) (SLC, SRO)

WOOTTON COURTENAY All Saints (426) (Carhampton Hundred; Williton Union)
OR C 1558-1871, M 1560-1642, 1650-63, 1672-1994, Banns 1754-1815, 1824-98, B 1562-1949
(SRO)
BT 1594-96, c.1600, 1606-08, 1611-12, 1621-24, c.1630, 1637-41, 1662-70, 1678-79, 1699-1702,
1704-09, 1721-22, 1725-29, 1731-33, 1737, 1740-41, 1743-44, 1746-51, 1754-56, 1759,
1761-62, 1764-73, 1775, 1777-84, 1786-1837, CB 1838, 1840-56, 1858 (SRO)
Cop C 1558-98, 1603-43, 1650-64, 1667-92, 1694-1837, M 1560-96, 1603-42, 1650-64, 1672-87,
1695-1836, Banns 1754-1837, B 1558-98, 1603-43, 1650-80, 1687-89, 1694-1837
(Ptd, T.L. Stoate, 1995); B 1813-1900 (SBDB); M 1560-1837 (SMI); C 1558-1871,
M 1560-1836 (DCI)
Cop (Mf) 1594-1858 (BT) (SLC, SRO); C 1558-1871, M 1558-1836, Banns 1754-1814, 1824-98,
B 1558-1902 (SLC)

WOOTTON, NORTH St Peter (307) (chapelry in Pilton until 1845) (peculiar of the Precentor of
Wells) (Glastonbury Twelve Hides Hundred; Wells Union)
OR C 1566-1886, M 1565-1987, Banns 1784-1812, B 1566-1966 (SRO)
BT 1608-09, 1611-14, 1621-24, 1629-30, 1635-37, 1639-41, 1668-70, 1814-16, 1818-25, 1827-28,
1830-34, CB 1838 (SRO); 1687, 1699, 1701, one between 1710-15, 1712, 1715, 1803-07
(SRO: D/D/Ppr:8)
Cop 1608-39 (Ptd, Dwelly 2, 1914); C 1783-1813 (SCDB); B 1813-1902 (SBDB); M 1613,
1621-22, 1636 (BT), 1750-1837 (SMI)
Cop (Mf) 1608-1838 (BT) (SLC, SRO); C 1565-1887, M 1565-1641, 1654-1837, Banns 1758-1807,
B 1565-1783, 1813-1903 (SLC)

WOOTTON, NORTH (Baptist) b 1830 (K 1931)

WORLE St Martin (770) (Winterstoke Hundred; Axbridge Union)
OR C 1598-1958, M 1598-1990, Banns 1755-81, 1823-96, B 1598-1964 (CMB 1598-1712
very defective) (SRO)
BT 1607-08, 1622-24, one between 1629-40, 1636-37, 1640-41, 1720-21, 1742-45, 1747-51,
1754-56, 1800-29 (SRO)
Cop B 1813-52 (SBDB); M 1754-1837 (SMI)
Cop (Mf) 1607-1829 (BT) (SLC, SRO); CM 1598-1901, Banns 1755-81, 1823-96,
B 1598-1900 (SLC)

WORLE (Wesleyan) (Lewis 1831)

WORLE Lawrence Street (United Methodist Free) b 1837 (K 1931)
OR C 1879-1912, M 1965-77 (Bristol RO)
Cop (Mf) C 1879-1912, M 1965-77 (Bristol RO, SLC)

WORLE (Baptist) b 1880

WRAXALL All Saints (802) (Portbury Hundred; Bedminster Union 1836-99, Long Ashton Union
1899-1930)
OR C 1563-1965, M 1562-1972 (gap 1718-53), B 1562-1912 (SRO)
BT 1598, 1609-12, 1614, 1616, 1621-22, 1626-31, 1636-41, 1678, 1732-33, 1801-17, 1820-22,
1824-37, CB 1838, 1840, CMB 1841-68 (SRO)
Cop M 1562-1812 (Ptd, Phillimore 4, 1902); 1614-78 (Ptd, Dwelly 2, 1914); M 1562-1812 (Boyd);
B 1813-38 (SBDB); M 1562-1717, 1754-1837 (SMI)
Cop (Mf) 1598-1868 (BT) (SLC, SRO)

WRAXALL Failand (Wesleyan) (K 1931)

WRINGTON All Saints (1,540) (Brent with Wrington Hundred; Axbridge Union)
OR C 1538-1951, M 1538-1986, Banns 1754-1812, B 1538-1980 (SRO)
BT 1604-05, 1607-08, 1613-14, 1621-24, 1629-30, 1636-37, 1639-41, 1662-65, 1667-69, 1672-73,
    1748-51, 1761-62, 1769-75, 1783-86, 1801-18, 1820-22, 1824-33, CB 1844-47 (SRO)
Cop 1806-07 (Ptd, Dwelly 5, 1917); M 1754-1837 (NSMI); B 1813-36 (SBDB); M 1754-1837 (SMI)
Cop (Mf) 1604-1847 (SLC, SRO); C 1538-1901, M 1538-1900, Banns 1754-93, B 1538-1880 (SLC)

WRINGTON (Independent) f 1662 (K 1931)

WRINGTON (Wesleyan) (Lewis 1831) b 1878 (K 1931)
OR C 1868-1968 (Bristol RO)
Cop (Mf) C 1868-1968 (Bristol RO, SLC)

WRITHLINGTON St Mary Magdalen (245) (Kilmersdon Hundred; Frome Union)
    (united with Radstock, 1971)
OR C 1663, 1665, 1673, 1675-1971, M 1708, 1729-1975, B 1691-1978 (SRO)
BT 1598-99, 1603-04, 1606-11, 1621-22, 1629-31, 1636-41, 1732-33, 1747, 1756, 1800, 1802-09,
    1811-33, CB 1838 (SRO)
Cop M 1754-1837 (NSMI); B 1813-1900 (SBDB); M 1754-1837 (SMI)
Cop (Mf) 1598-1838 (BT) (SLC, SRO); C 1675-1900, M 1744, 1754-1902, B 1691-1900 (SLC)

WRITHLINGTON (Wesleyan)
OR C 1843-1900 (circuit) (Bristol RO)
Cop (Mf) C 1843-1900 (Bristol RO, SLC)

WRITHLINGTON (Primitive Methodist) f 1872 b 1913 (K 1931)

WYKE CHAMPFLOWER Holy Trinity (St Peter until 1623) (93) (chapelry in Bruton until 1748)
    (Bruton Hundred; Wincanton Union)
OR C 1677-1993, M 1840-1969, B 1625-1992 (SRO)
BT 1746, 1802-03, 1805-14, 1816, 1822-28, C 1841, CB 1842-44 (SRO)
Cop (Mf) 1746-1844 (BT) (SLC, SRO); C 1677-1812, M 1840-81, B 1625-1810 (SLC)

YARLEY St Thomas (ancient chapel demolished in 1550, there are no registers)

YARLINGTON St Mary (283) (Bruton Hundred; Wincanton Union)
OR C 1655-1964, M 1655-1993, Banns 1759-1819, B 1655-1993 (gap CMB 1714-17) (SRO)
BT 1599-1608, 1611-12, 1619, 1621-25, 1637-41, 1662-64, 1667-70, 1672-73, 1676, 1733-34,
    1750-53, 1755-57, 1760, 1765-69, 1800-17, 1819-37, CB 1838-63 (SRO)
Cop C 1599-1673, M 1599-1673, 1700-1851, B 1599-1673 (Ts I SG); M 1750-1837 (SMI)
Cop (Mf) 1599-1863 (BT) (SLC, SRO); C 1655-1902, M 1655-1837, Banns 1759-1819,
    B 1655-1813 (SLC)

YATTON St Mary (1,865) (peculiar of the Prebendary of Yatton in the Cathedral Church of Wells)
    (Winterstoke Hundred; Bedminster Union 1836-99, Long Ashton Union 1899-1930)
OR C 1675-1965, M 1676-1979 (gap 1804-12), Banns 1870-1969, B 1675-1970 (SRO)
BT 1605-12, 1622-24, 1636-39, 1662-64, 1677-80, 1695-98, 1749-51, 1753-54, 1813-44,
    CB 1845-70 (SRO); 1690, 1692-93, 1699-1701, 1703-11, 1713-15, 1717-24, 1726-27, 1735-36,
    1739, 1742-43, 1788-92, 1804-12 (SRO: D/D/Ppb:113)
Cop 1623-79 (Ptd, Dwelly 2, 1914); CB 1675-1761, M 1754-1837 (SRO); M 1754-1837 (NSMI);
    B 1813-39 (SBDB); M 1623-79 (BT), 1750-1837 (SMI)
Cop (Mf) 1605-1870 (SLC, SRO); CB 1675-1886, M 1676-1886, Banns 1754-1809, 1870-85 (SLC)

YATTON Meeting House, Claverham (Society of Friends) (Monthly Meeting of N.Division) b 1866
OR Z 1649-1707, 1756-66, M 1658-97, B 1655-1707 (PRO: RG 6/1023)
BT B 1865-68 (SRO)
Cop B 1826 (SBDB)
Cop (Mf) 1865-68 (BT) (SLC, SRO)

YATTON Claverham (United Methodist) b 1867 (K 1931)

YATTON (United Methodist) f 1840 b 1888 (K 1931)

YATTON Horsecastle (Plymouth Brethren) b 1857 (K 1931)

YATTON St Dunstan and St Antony (Roman Catholic) (Catholic Directory 1965)

YEOVIL Board of Guardians
OR Z 1836-1914, D 1836-1914 (SRO)

YEOVIL Cemetery, Preston Road opened 1860 (13 acres) (K 1931)

YEOVIL St John the Baptist (5,921) (Stone Hundred; Yeovil Union)
OR C 1563-1952, M 1563-1960, Banns 1754-99, B 1563-1944 (SRO)
BT 1607-08, 1611-13, 1616, 1621-22, 1629-30, 1640-41, 1662-63, 1728-31, 1733-34, 1740,
    1797-1837, CB 1838, 1840-61 (SRO)
Cop C 1671-78, M 1654-98 (SRO); M 1750-1837 (SMI)
Cop (Mf) 1607-1861 (BT) (SLC, SRO); C 1563-1812, M 1563-1889, Banns 1653-57, 1764-79,
    B 1565-1812, 1857-1944 (Ptd, SRO, 1996)

YEOVIL Holy Trinity, Peter Street (known as Hendford until 1972, q.v.)

YEOVIL St Michael and all Angels, Pen Mill (created from Yeovil, 1897) (Yeovil Union)
OR CMB 1897+ (Inc)

YEOVIL St Andrew (chapelry to Yeovil St John the Baptist)
OR C 1907-80, M 1935-89 (SRO)

YEOVIL South Street (Baptist) b 1688, reb 1829 (K 1931)
OR Z 1810-36 (PRO: RG 4/1737)
Cop (Mf) Z 1810-36 (SLC, SRO)

YEOVIL Vicarage Street Chapel (Presbyterian) f 1704
OR ZC 1751-59 (PRO: RG 4/2937); ZC 1833-37, D 1833-36 (PRO: RG 4/2933)
Cop (Mf) ZC 1833-37, D 1833-36 (SLC, SRO)

YEOVIL Princes Street (Independent) b 1792 reb 1878 (K 1931)
OR C 1793-1836, B 1815-36 (PRO: RG 4/1793); C 1836-1911, M 1909-79, B 1843-60 (SRO)
Cop (Mf) C 1793-1836, B 1815-36 (SLC, SRO)

YEOVIL Vicarage Street (Plymouth Brethren) f 1857 (K 1931)

YEOVIL Vicarage Street (Wesleyan) (Lewis 1831) b 1864 (K 1931)
OR C 1846-1960, M 1945-70 (SRO)

YEOVIL South Street (Primitive Methodist) b 1865 (K 1931)

YEOVIL Pen Mill (Wesleyan) b 1870 (K 1931)

YEOVIL Newtown (Primitive Methodist) b 1872, reb 1891 (K 1931)
OR M 1914-34 (SRO)

YEOVIL (Reformed Episcopalian) b 1880

YEOVIL Holy Ghost, The Avenue (Roman Catholic) f 1887 b 1899

YEOVIL Huish (Baptist) b 1895 (K 1931)

YEOVIL Tabernacle, Tabernacle Lane (Calvinist) (K 1931)

YEOVIL Middle Street (Salvation Army) (K 1931)

YEOVIL MARSH All Saints (created from Yeovil, 1872) (Yeovil Union)
OR C 1872-1979 (SRO); MB 1872+ (Inc)

YEOVILTON St Bartholomew (275) (Somerton Hundred; Yeovil Union)
OR C 1710-1948, M 1710-1976, Banns 1755-98, 1940-62, B 1710-1979 (SRO) (registers from
    CB 1653 and M 1655 listed in 1914 and 1935; in 1914 list shown as being in the same volume
    as 1710-1812 but this appears to be a mistake)
BT 1599, 1606-14, 1621-24, 1630-31, 1636-41, 1662-69, 1730-32, 1749-50, 1775-76, 1800-03,
    1805-21 (SRO)
Cop M 1655-1802 (Ptd, Phillimore 2, 1899); CMB 1594-1666 (Ptd, Ilchester & District LHS
    Occ Papers 67, 1986); 1599-1623 (Ptd, Dwelly 2, 1914); M 1803-51 (Ts I SG);
    M 1655-1812 (Boyd); B 1813-37 (SBDB); M 1599-1623 (BT), 1655-1837 (SMI)
Cop (Mf) 1599-1821 (BT) (SLC, SRO); CB 1710-1903, M 1710-1900, Banns 1755-1805 (SLC)

143